Empire of the Superheroes

WORLD COMICS AND GRAPHIC NONFICTION SERIES

Frederick Luis Aldama and Christopher González, editors

The World Comics and Graphic Nonfiction series includes monographs and edited volumes that focus on the analysis and interpretation of comic books and graphic nonfiction from around the world. The books published in the series use analytical approaches from literature, art history, cultural studies, communication studies, media studies, and film studies, among other fields, to help define the comic book studies field at a time of great vitality and growth.

OTHER BOOKS IN THE SERIES

ANNA PEPPARD, ED.
*Supersex: Sexuality, Fantasy,
and the Superhero*

MATT YOCKEY, ED.
*Make Ours Marvel: Media
Convergence and a Comics Universe*

ALLAN W. AUSTIN AND
PATRICK L. HAMILTON
*All New, All Different? A History of
Race and the American Superhero*

MARK HEIMERMANN AND
BRITTANY TULLIS, EDS.
*Picturing Childhood: Youth in
Transnational Comics*

JORGE SANTOS
*Graphic Memories of the
Civil Rights Movement: Reframing
History in Comics*

DAVID WILLIAM FOSTER
*El Eternauta, Daytripper,
and Beyond: Graphic Narrative
in Argentina and Brazil*

BENJAMIN FRASER
*The Art of Pere Joan: Space,
Landscape, and Comics Form*

CHRISTOPHER PIZZINO
*Arresting Development: Comics at the
Boundaries of Literature*

JAN BAETENS
*The Film Photonovel: A Cultural
History of Forgotten Adaptations*

FREDERICK LUIS ALDAMA
*Graphic Borders: Latino Comic Books
Past, Present, and Future*

MARC SINGER
*Breaking the Frames: Populism and
Prestige in Comics Studies*

EMPIRE
OF THE SUPER-HEROES

America's Comic Book Creators and the Making of a Billion-Dollar Industry

MARK COTTA VAZ

Concept and Initial Research
in Collaboration with Mark Zaid, Esq.

University of Texas Press ◆ Austin

Requests for permission to reproduce material from this work should be sent to:
    Permissions
    University of Texas Press
    P.O. Box 7819
    Austin, TX 78713–7819
    utpress.utexas.edu/rp-form

♾ The paper used in this book meets the minimum requirements of ANSI/NISO Z39.48–1992 (R1997) (Permanence of Paper).

LIBRARY OF CONGRESS CATALOGING-IN-PUBLICATION DATA

Names: Vaz, Mark Cotta, author. | Zaid, Mark S.
Title: Empire of the superheroes : America's comic book creators and the making of a billion-dollar industry / Mark Cotta Vaz ; concept and initial research in collaboration with Mark Zaid, Esq.
Other titles: World comics and graphic nonfiction series.
Description: First edition. | Austin: University of Texas Press, 2021. | Series: World comics and graphic nonfiction series | Includes bibliographical references and index.
Identifiers: LCCN 2020032961
    ISBN 978-1-4773-1647-4 (cloth)
    ISBN 978-1-4773-2181-2 (library ebook)
    ISBN 978-1-4773-2182-9 (non-library ebook)
Subjects: LCSH: Superheroes—United States—Comic books, strips, etc.—History. | Comic books, strips, etc.—Publishing—United States—History. | Authors and publishers—United States. | License agreements—United States.
Classification: LCC PN6725 .V39 2020 | DDC 741.5/352—dc23
LC record available at https://lccn.loc.gov/2020032961

doi:10.7560/316474

To the Amazing Comic Book Creators . . .
and with love to my parents, August and Bettylu Vaz, who never
threw out my comic books.

CONTENTS

COMIC BOOK BABYLON

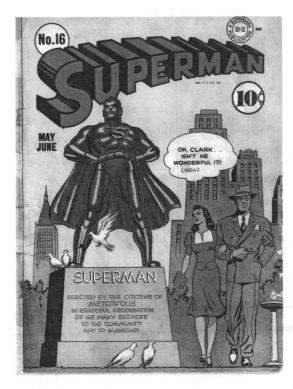

Under the *Superman* title the fine print reads: REG US PAT OFF (Registered, United States Patent Office). The ownership is made clear inside: "Entire contents copyrighted 1942 by Superman, Inc."

SUPERMAN #16 (MAY/JUNE 1942), COVER ART BY FRED RAY.

When the Grand Central Hotel opened at Broadway and Third in New York City in 1870, it was a palace worthy of the Gilded Age, excesses included. Two years later, in a violent encounter on the grand stairway, shady financier Ned Stokes, lover of voluptuous showgirl Josie Mansfield, shot and mortally wounded his former business associate and Mansfield's previous paramour, flamboyant robber baron James Fisk. By 1965 the hotel, renamed the Broadway Central and a shadow of its former glory, hosted one of the first comic book conventions. Joseph and Lillian Uslan, who drove their preteen son Michael and his friend Bobby Klein to the convention, were aghast, but game, at the sight of the old building. It didn't get better inside: its lobby walls crawled with cockroaches and drunks crowded the bar they passed on the way to the elevator. But when the elevator door opened onto the showroom floor, Michael and Bobby discovered a tribal gathering of several hundred true believers. "At that convention, we realized there were other comics geeks like us," Uslan recalled. "It was one of life's great revelations."[1]

The ramshackle hotel partially collapsed in 1973, killing four and injuring a dozen, and it was demolished soon after. In retrospect, the tawdry venue seemed appropriate for a pulp medium that barely survived the previous decade's comic book burnings and censorship crackdowns. Michael's parents were supportive, but most adults didn't understand "comics geeks" and their obsessions, particularly the magnetic attraction of costumed superheroes. "Reading comic books then was *really* subversive," Uslan recalls. "When I think back, most of my friends were forbidden to bring comic books into the house. Some were forbidden to read them."

Other contemporary horrors requiring parental vigilance included that bane of propriety, *Mad* magazine. (Many a copy smuggled into a classroom, if discovered by an adult, was instant wastebasket fodder.) There were provocative trading cards like *Mars Attacks!*, by Len Brown and Woody Gelman, featuring atrocities committed by ghoulish Martian invaders with skeletal faces and gigantic exposed brains. It was a time when comics, pulp magazines, science-fiction novels, genre films, and trading cards were in the shadows and under the radar of mainstream culture. Len Brown recalls Gelman calling fans of such fare "Third Eyes"—a term of endearment—in the mystical tradition of the "inner eye" that sees beyond surface illusion to higher realms of consciousness. "Back in the sixties, when Woody coined the term," Brown says, "it was unusual to find people who collected comics or were obsessed with genre films. Third Eyes were a subculture."

Uslan was of the post–World War II generations who grew up with comics as an established form of entertainment. There were no comic book shops—kids got comics from newsstands or off the racks at general stores. Fans knew comics had a history; besides the sequentially numbered periodicals themselves, occasional reprints provided an intoxicating glimpse into a storied past. In the distant future fans would get answers and network with fellow obsessives at the touch of a handheld electronic device, but in the era of the Third Eyes it required shoe-leather detective work to find rare back issues or track down forgotten creators. Knowledge was shared through fanzines, letters, and tribal gatherings.

Behind the glorious façade of the "Golden Age of Comics" were certain truths: most creators never owned their creations, they worked without a steady salary or share in merchandising deals, and many were worn down by financial hardships, alcoholism, and health problems.[2]

"The so-called Golden Age didn't seem so golden at the time," recalls comic book pioneer Will Eisner. "A lot of strange and seedy characters were starting comics. I remember one guy who had no teeth, and he'd chew little bits of old newspaper while he talked to you. It's hard to convey the gritty look of those days—it was a dangerous time."[3]

THE SUPERMAN DEAL

The strangest legend concerned Superman, the omnipotent superhero that started the superhero myth and launched the nascent comic book business. The young creators, writer Jerry Siegel and artist Joe Shuster, were living in Cleveland and still in high school when they began shopping their creation to tabloid publishers and newspaper syndicates, suffering years of rejection before Detective Comics, Inc. (DC), in New York City, decided to publish Superman as the cover feature for the debut of one of the earliest comic books—*Action Comics*. But publisher Harry Donenfeld, a notorious purveyor of erotic pulp magazines, wasn't sold on the future of comics and was appalled at the *Action* cover art—a muscular man, costumed like an acrobat or circus strongman, *lifting a car over his head*. This wasn't the two-fisted cowboy, dapper sleuth, or globetrotting adventurer of normal pulp fiction.

Despite Donenfeld's doubts, the wheels began turning. On March 1, 1938, Siegel and Shuster got a one-page boilerplate contract:

> I, the undersigned, am an artist or author and have performed work for [the] strip entitled SUPERMAN.
>
> In consideration of $130.00 agreed to be paid by you, I hereby sell and transfer such work and strip, all good will attached thereto and exclusive right to the use of the characters and story, continuity and title of strip contained therein, to you.

To cash the check, Siegel and Shuster had to sign the contract, granting DC all rights to Superman. Secretary/treasurer Jacob "Jack" Liebowitz, who conducted the "negotiations," claimed this was the "businesslike way of doing things."

The check *misspelled* their names: "Pay to the Order of: Seigel & Schuster." "Well, at least this way we'll see him in print," Jerry said to Joe, and they signed on the back *twice*, using both incorrect and correct name spellings. The check that purchased Superman was stamped "PAID" on March 5, 1938, in care of the Cleveland Trust Company.[4] The decision to sign would define and consume their lives.

There was nothing sinister about the deal—it was business as usual. Siegel and Shuster had already signed the same one-page contract accepting payment and transferring rights for other DC work. "The standard trade practice in the comic book industry was that you sold an idea . . . [the publisher] owned it," Will Eisner explains. "Siegel and Shuster brought Superman to DC—they owned it."

In fact, the $130 for Superman was only part of paycheck #649, issued for $412 on March 1. The balance included $210 for thirteen pages of *Slam Bradley* and eight pages of *Spy* for *Detective Comics* #1 ($10 per page); $36 for a four-page *Federal Men* in *New Adventure Comics* ($9 per page); and $36 for four pages of *Doctor Occult* and a two-page *Radio Squad* ($4 and $10 per page, respectively).[5]

No one except the optimistic duo from Cleveland believed Superman, much less the fledgling ten-cent comic book medium, had a future. But Superman was an overnight phenomenon, and within a year a comic book industry took root in New York as other publishers tried to cash in with their own costumed heroes.

The pioneering creators of the comic book superheroes, not that much older than the dazzled kids who were the medium's chief customers, lacked business savvy that would have assured them that exclusive title of ownership—copyright. The corporate owners controlled the creations and cut the business deals that, to their giddy shock, spun pulp-paper adventures into gold.

But even with that first flush of success, no one thought it would last. Michael Uslan, who from boyhood began exploring comics history, recalls the bare-knuckle world of pulp publishing, the shady deals and rumors of organized crime involvement, the disposable, ephemeral nature of it all: "This was still the Depression and then World War II. They did not have in mind they were creating a permanent art form or characters that would live in contemporary folklore—they were trying to pay the rent, put food on the table, trying to keep their kids afloat if they had a family. No one thought they were creating anything that would survive beyond the following months. It was a medium akin to yesterday's newspaper. No one thought there was a pot of gold at the end of the rainbow."[6]

MILTON AND THE PIRATES

Comic books were considered the vulgar offspring of newspaper comic strips. They largely began as tabloid vehicles for selling

The comics have always marketed characters through ancillary merchandising, such as newspaper comics strip star Dick Tracy's crime-smashing appearance in his own "pop-up" picture book.

THE "POP-UP" DICK TRACY: CAPTURE OF BORIS ARSON (CHICAGO: PLEASURE BOOKS, INC., 1935), COVER ART BY CHESTER GOULD.

reprinted strips, while newspaper adventure strips—*Tarzan, Dick Tracy, Buck Rogers* and *Flash Gordon, The Phantom, Mandrake the Magician*—influenced many of the early comic book superheroes. So exalted was the newspaper strip that comic books were often referred to as "strips."

A big city might boast three or more independent newspapers with several daily editions, and reading the black-and-white daily strips and all-in-color Sunday comics pages was an American ritual. Strips telling ongoing stories—a creative challenge, given built-in restrictions of no more than four daily panels—were often the reason readers plunked down their three cents (the price of a *New York Times* in 1938). The most popular creators were well paid and celebrated, but creative rights and ownership troubled the most successful: case in point, Milton Caniff.

Caniff began his career in New York in the early thirties with various syndicated strip assignments, notably *Dickie Dare*, an adventure series featuring the young title character and his adult mentor, Dan Flynn. Caniff got his big break in 1934 when Capt. Joseph Patterson, head of the powerful Chicago Tribune–New York News Syndicate, called Caniff and asked if he was interested in doing a strip for him, one brimming with "real blood and thunder adventure," Caniff recalled. "That's why I got the nod, because that's what I was doing in *Dickie Dare*. This is what he wanted: a kid, an older guy with muscles, pretty girls."

Patterson, knowing comics sold papers, took a personal interest in the strips his publishing empire ran. In 1931, when the adventure strip was new, Patterson met an ambitious cartoonist named Chester Gould who came calling with a detective strip called *Plainclothes Tracy*. Patterson proposed the enduring title—*Dick Tracy*—and his violent origin in which civilian Tracy witnesses the murder of his sweetheart Tess Trueheart's father, swears to avenge the crime, and enlists with the plainclothes police squad.

Patterson had the broad strokes of the new strip ready when he met Caniff. "Ever do anything on the Orient?" Patterson asked. "You know, adventure can still happen out there. There could be a beautiful lady pirate, the kind men fall for."[7] The result, *Terry and the Pirates*, begins with the young title character, Terry Lee, and his adult pal and mentor, Pat Ryan, sailing China's coast to Shanghai when the seductive Dragon Lady and her pirates hijack their vessel—Milton and *Terry* were off and running.

Caniff had a spacious studio, an assistant, and a secretary. To provide realistic references he directed and photographed scenes of models in costume. *Terry and the Pirates* was an Air Force favorite, and when Caniff attended the Air Force Association Convention of 1947, he was seen in conversation between future president Gen. Dwight D. Eisenhower and war hero Gen. James Doolittle. That year a *Time* cover feature celebrated Caniff and the launch of his new adventure strip, *Steve Canyon*. The popular strip earned the cartoonist endorsement deals for everything from Rheingold Lager Beer and Walker's DeLuxe Whiskey to Thom McAn shoes and "the world's finest writing instrument," the Sheaffer Snorkel fountain pen.

But the breakthrough of 1947 was preceded by what Caniff called "the worst two years I've spent, ever." In the decade since he began *Terry*, Caniff was increasingly troubled that he didn't own the strip, although at the outset he echoed Siegel and Shuster's enthusiasm when they found a home for Superman. "I was just glad to be published," Caniff recalled. "I hadn't thought about the ownership of *Terry* at the beginning, but somewhere along the line, I began to think, 'I'm working my tail off here, and at the end of it, I'm still just a well-paid slave. If I fell over with a stroke tomorrow, the syndicate would own this thing.' That's when I began to think about some way of getting out from under this ownership problem. I was lying awake nights thinking about it."

Caniff's contract was set to expire in 1946, and he began looking elsewhere. "The creator should own the property and lease it to the syndicate during its lifetime," Caniff concluded. "But *he* should own it. . . . Switching syndicates was a big change to attempt, and I was personally willing to do it as long as I was assured that after it was done I wouldn't be sitting at home with an empty bag."[8]

In 1944 Caniff made a secret handshake deal with Marshall Field III to create a comic strip for the wealthy entrepreneur's new Field Enterprises Syndicate. It was classic win-win—Field would add a superstar creator to his syndicate, and Caniff was guaranteed ownership of whatever feature he created, a 33 percent raise in base salary, and a share in licensing deals. But early in 1945 news of the agreement was leaked in mighty Walter Winchell's popular newspaper column. Caniff was suddenly in an acrimonious relationship with Patterson and his syndicate during the final contractual years on *Terry*. Caniff hadn't even dreamed up a title for his new strip, and until his contract was fulfilled conceptual development had to be conducted solely within his imagination.

"Long before the phrase 'intellectual property' had become common currency among creators, Milton Caniff understood the concept and its ramifications under the law," writes comics historian Bruce Canwell. "If he doodled or jotted down ideas—and there is no known evidence he did—they were quickly burned or otherwise destroyed, since even items languishing in the studio waste basket or home garbage cans might be fodder for a legal claim against him." Patterson's enmity with Caniff did not end with the publisher's death, which coincided with the expiration of Caniff's contract in 1946: for several decades Patterson's *New York Daily News* blacklisted him.[9] Caniff left, but *Terry* kept rolling—the syndicate selected cartoonist George Wunder to take over the strip.

Caniff had his new *Steve Canyon* strip to call his own, but if a superstar suffered sleepless nights over creative rights, what of his unsung brethren toiling for low page rates in the backwaters of comic book publishing?

The pulp magazines, which also influenced comics, were another rough and tumble corner of the publishing world. During the Depression painter Walter M. Baumhofer, down to his last month's rent, gambled the rent money to hire a model and paint a "spec" cover for publisher Street & Smith. As in the comic books to come, a great pulp cover was key to an impulse buy, and Baumhofer's arresting image of a masked highwayman in a yellow slicker holding a Winchester rifle not only made the September 3, 1932, cover of *Western Story*, but the publisher also offered a contract for fifty covers a year, work that included depicting the first "super" hero of the pulps, Doc Savage. That contract pretty much ended the Depression for him, Baumhofer recalled. "The idea of a long-term contract . . . seems to have been instigated by this deal," adds popular illustration historian Fred Taraba.[10]

Superman was the Big Bang of comic books, and in its aftermath there were fortunes to be made—and fought over. Joe Simon, who with Jack Kirby created Captain America, recalled Golden Age get-togethers where comic book publishers casually dispensed threats of lawsuits and restraining orders with the next round of cocktails and cards.[11] But legal efforts by artists to claim ownership or other creative rights, if they happened at all, were lonely, quixotic crusades. "We thought of it vaguely," Jack Kirby recalled of the business side. "But we weren't oriented to business. . . . We never had accountants. We never had lawyers. The publisher did. At that time, I wasn't intent on looking ahead. I was young. We were all young."[12]

Licensing and litigation shaped pulp mythology and the emerging comics publishing industry: there was a fine line between inspiration and theft of "intellectual property," with many a fictional character prospering or perishing upon the parsing of copyright law.

In *Fleischer Studios, Inc., v. Ralph A. Freundlich, Inc.*, Fleischer's control of its popular Betty Boop animated cartoon was threatened because "Inc." (Incorporated) was omitted in the copyright notice. The mistake was judged trivial, and the Fleischers continued producing their Jazz Age flapper's cartoons and merchandising. But Helen Kane, the singer who inspired Betty Boop, filed a $250,000 lawsuit against Fleischer Studios and partner Paramount Pictures, charging them with stealing her singing style. "The testimony in this curious trial seems to have centered on who had coined the phrase 'boop-oop-a-doop,'" writes animation historian Charles Solomon. "The Fleischers won the case by proving that a black entertainer named Baby Esther had used 'boop-oop-a-doop' before either Helen Kane or Betty Boop."[13]

Copyright law is enshrined in the US Constitution, Article I, Section 8, as among the powers mandated to Congress "to promote the progress of Science and useful Arts, by securing for limited Times to Authors and Inventors the exclusive Right to their respective Writings and Discoveries." The Copyright Act of 1790 stipulated an initial copyright period of fourteen years, renewable for another fourteen—a maximum of twenty-eight years—after which the property belonged to the public. But Congress kept lengthening the "limited Times." In 1831 copyrights were renewable up to forty-two years; the act of 1909 made it fifty-six.

"Copyright springs into existence once an idea is fixed in a tangible form of expression," says John Mason, a literary agent and entertainment attorney based in Bethesda, Maryland, with over twenty years' experience doing transactional and litigation work. "You have people who believe there is a vast public benefit to having works go into the public domain to be exploited by everyone, and I believe that. On the other hand, and this is true also, is [the idea of] incentivizing to create original works by allowing a monopoly to exploit that. The roots of copyright go back to the Gutenberg Bible and who got to control the first printing presses, and the Statute of Anne in England [also known as the Copyright Act of 1710, the first copyright regulation by the government and courts]. The Founding Fathers were ahead of their times, putting that idea in the body of the Constitution."

Mason recalls that in the aftermath of director Guillermo del Toro's 2018 Oscar-winning Best Picture, *The Shape of Water*, about four prospective clients approached him, each alleging the critically acclaimed movie stole his or her idea. Mason had to break the news to them: "No one can own an idea, or a broad concept. Most people don't understand the high bar of originality that has to be crossed. But, guess what? It is *real* subjective. . . . In the comics industry there was a lot of exploitation and a lack of clarity as to who was an employee, who was an independent contractor." Given that copyright protection invests in the creation of a work, ownership claims lay in establishing the terms under which a work was created.[14]

The Copyright Act of 1909 was in force during the dramatic expansion of mass media in the first half of the twentieth century. The fifty-six-year renewal term provided an initial twenty-eight-year protection period, and, upon its expiration, authors could apply for a renewal for the remaining years. In 1966, the year after the early comics fans gathered at the broken-down Broadway Central, the initial copyright term for superheroes began expiring, with Superman first up for renewal.

Supreme Court precedent under the 1909 act interpreted the renewal term to "permit the author, originally in a poor bargaining position, to renegotiate the terms of the grant once the value of the work has been tested. . . . Congress attempted to alleviate the problem of the inability of authors to know the monetary value of their works prior to commercial exploitation."[15] It seemed made to order for that first generation of young, inexperienced comics creators, but the devil was in the details.

Mark Zaid, a Washington, DC, attorney specializing in national security law and an acclaimed "superlawyer" on behalf of national security whistleblowers, observes that the law is inextricably bound up in the business of comics. He bought his first comic book in 1974 when he was seven and by high school was collecting and selling comics, a hobby that faded in law school.

That changed after Zaid's legal career took off when he represented forty family members of victims of the December 21, 1988, terrorist bomb that blew up Pan American Airways flight #103, a case that concluded with a settlement from the Libyan government in 2001. Fast forward to 2019, when Zaid got national attention as one of the lawyers representing the whistleblower in the Ukraine scandal that led to the impeachment of President Donald Trump. In between, with a successful career underway, he returned to comic books as a hobby, collecting vintage titles and lecturing on the legal battles over superheroes.

"When people become solidified in their careers and have disposable income, they tend to turn to things they fondly remember from childhood days," Zaid says. "I bought a lot of stuff, including a high-grade *Superman* #2 and *Detective Comics* #31. As I got really involved in the hobby, I also got involved in its politics and history, the court cases, how the law impacted comic books and shaped the development of characters—essentially the hobby merged with my day job as a 'spy' lawyer."[16]

Comic book controversies feature some of the biggest names in comics history. Will Eisner was at the center of the first superhero lawsuit, while Joe Simon and Jack Kirby were cheated out of a handshake deal share in their cocreation, Captain America. The cocreation of Batman by cartoonist Bob Kane and writer Bill Finger was solely credited to Kane. There was conflict between the "Silver Age" team of writer/editor Stan Lee and artist Jack Kirby, both claiming authorship of Marvel characters that would eventually generate *billions* on global movie screens.

But the most contentious creation was the superhero that started it all, as Siegel and Shuster were relegated to the sidelines while Superman literally became his own corporation. DC protected its star property with legal threats and, in its case against the publisher of rival superhero Captain Marvel, legal warfare.

Legal action involving Superman began barely a year after his *Action* debut, sporadically continuing into the new millennium, making Superman one of the most litigated figures in fiction. Along the way Superman led the expansion of superhero mythology into other mass media: newspaper strips, radio, motion pictures, television, and video games, not counting manifold merchandising tie-ins. And down the timeline, comic book's original sin—Siegel and Shuster's creative martyrdom—inspired creators' rights for the industry.

The epic story begins in the early 1930s, on a hot summer's night in Cleveland, in a house on Kimberley Avenue . . .

CHAPTER 1

IN THE BEGINNING

What led me into conceiving Superman in the early thirties? Listening to President Roosevelt's "fireside chats" . . . being unemployed and worried during the depression and knowing hopelessness and fear. Hearing and reading of the oppression and slaughter of helpless, oppressed Jews in Nazi Germany . . . seeing movies depicting the horrors of privation suffered by the downtrodden . . . reading of gallant, crusading heroes in the pulps, and seeing equally crusading heroes on the screen in feature films and movie serials (often pitted against malevolent, grasping, ruthless madmen). I had the great urge to help . . . help the despairing masses, somehow.

How could I help them, when I could barely help myself? Superman was the answer.

JERRY SIEGEL
concluding comments from a 1975 press release,
"A Curse on the Superman Movie!"

DREAMING

Teenager Jerry Siegel was tossing and turning in bed, unable to sleep through a long, hot summer night, "when all of a sudden it hits me. I conceive a character like Samson, Hercules and all the strong men I ever heard tell of rolled into one. Only more so." Siegel remained in a state of creative agitation, hopping out of bed to write down thoughts, back to bed to try and sleep, up again to dash off another idea. At dawn he ran to the Shuster house a few blocks away to rouse his pal Joe, the artist who would give form to a hero unlike any in legend or literature.[1]

Siegel loved recounting that hot summer night when the gestating Superman idea burst forth from his imagination. Comics historian Gerard Jones notes, "The existing recordings of the young Siegel's voice do not suggest a commanding figure: His voice is thin and adenoidal, shyness chokes him high in the throat, his tones are flat, and he rushes impatiently past small talk. But when he speaks of an idea that excites him, there's a sudden quaver. You hear his belief in what he has."[2]

Siegel and Shuster were both born in 1914 and met as students at Glenville High School in Cleveland. They were kindred spirits—unathletic and shy, they shared a Jewish heritage, a passion for science fiction, and the ambition to break into the glamorous world of syndicated strips. Among their earliest collaborations was *Futurities*, a potential feature imagining everything from space stations to futuristic fashions. They submitted *Interplanetary Police* to United Features Syndicate and when they got a letter back, tore open the envelope in excitement—and froze at the word "Congratulations!" It was a deflating disappointment. The syndicate deemed their submission an "interesting strip," but couldn't use it.[3]

Superman was the pinnacle of Siegel and Shuster's love of science fiction. The origin story that ultimately appeared in *Action Comics* #1 was summed up in a single sentence: "As a distant planet was destroyed by old age, a scientist placed his infant son within a hastily devised space-ship, launching it toward earth!" The mythical premise would be expanded upon in the years ahead.

Superman's first incarnation was as an evildoer with telepathic super powers in "The Reign of the Super-Man," in the third issue, January 1933, of Siegel and Shuster's self-published fanzine, *Science Fiction: The Advance Guard of Future Civilization* (reportedly run off the mimeograph machine at Glenville High). "A couple of months after I published this story, it occurred to me that a Superman as a hero rather than a villain might make a great comic strip character in the vein of Tarzan, only more super and sensational than that great character," Siegel recounted.[4]

That same year Siegel and Shuster saw the first issue of a black-and-white tabloid comic book, *Detective Dan: Secret Operative No. 48*, starring a dead ringer for Dick Tracy. Unlike most early comic books filled with newspaper strip reprints, *Detective Dan* had original material. An editorial notice mentioned prospects for a second issue, and Siegel and Shuster submitted *The Superman: A Science Fiction Story in Cartoons* to the publisher, Consolidated Book Publishers of Chicago. The company accepted the strip but quickly rescinded the offer, deciding to get out of the risky new comic book business.

Bitterly disappointed, Shuster reportedly threw the only copy into a roaring fireplace. A startled Siegel snatched from the flames the cover proclaiming "The Most Astounding Fiction Character of All Time" and featuring a shirtless hero diving towards a crook holding a gun on a gagged and trussed man. The cover had the requisite pulp magazine ten-cent cover price and an indication they wanted to own their creation—a © 1933 copyright notice in their names.[5]

TARZAN, FLASH, AND THE GLADIATOR

The idea of a "super" being goes back to mythological figures and, closer to modern times, to German philosopher Friedrich Nietzsche's ideal of an *Ubermensch*, or Superman, in his 1883 book *Also sprach Zarathustra*. But Siegel and Shuster had plenty of inspiration in the emerging mass-media dream worlds of comic strips, motion pictures, radio broadcasts, and pulp novels. "Pulps," so-called for their cheap, untrimmed paper flecked with wood fiber, had heroes like Doc Savage, the embodiment of mental and physical perfection hailed as "Superman" by Street & Smith in a 1934 house ad. Siegel was even inspired by the Popeye the Sailor animated cartoons, imagining that a hero with Popeye's super strength (after downing a fortifying can of spinach) would make "a very dynamic adventure strip."[6]

Tarzan was a major influence. Edgar Rice Burroughs's "Tarzan of the Apes" first appeared in the October 1912 issue of *The All-Story* magazine. In the story an aristocratic couple die after being shipwrecked in Africa, and their orphaned baby boy is raised to manhood by jungle apes. Burroughs admitted owing inspiration to Mowgli, the jungle boy of Rudyard Kipling's *The Jungle Book*, and even to Rome's founding myth of Romulus and Remus, twin babies fathered and abandoned by the god Mars but rescued and raised by a she-wolf.[7]

Tarzan's global popularity generated an industry of licensed products. Burroughs, who owned the copyright, earned a fortune. "Long before movies came with merchandising rights and a battery of lawyers, Burroughs turned Tarzan into the first mass-market action hero," writer Bruce Watson observes, adding that Burroughs "fiercely defended his plots and royalties." Burroughs become so wealthy that on March 26, 1923, he formed Edgar Rice Burroughs, Inc., basing his corporation in a town he created— Tarzana, California.[8]

The licensing of a *Tarzan* newspaper strip dramatically impacted strips *and* comic books. "The adventure comic strip characteristic of the 1930s was something new, suddenly appearing, for all practical purposes, in 1929," writes William H. Young, pinpointing the debut of artist Hal Foster's *Tarzan* in January 1929. Previously, comic strips had a flat, "proscenium presentation," with panels rendered from a fixed vantage point, as an audience would watch a play. "With the advent of *Tarzan*, the aesthetic standards of the comic strip came in for an abrupt change. . . . Just as the movie camera was finding increased freedom to move virtually anywhere, Foster never relied on the static proscenium approach to illustrate Tarzan's adventures. Reader acceptance of this new style of comic strip was immediate."[9]

In 1932 a weekly *Tarzan* radio adventure began, and *Tarzan the Ape Man*, the first "talkie" Tarzan movie starring Johnny Weissmuller, was released. An article about Burroughs's successful merchandising of his creation inspired Siegel: "I thought: Wow!

Superman is even more super than Tarzan; the same thing could happen with Superman. And I mentioned it to Joe, he got real enthused, and I walked in a day to two later, and he had made a big drawing of Superman showing how the character could be merchandised on box-tops, T-shirts, and everything."[10]

Burroughs's other popular character—John Carter, a Virginian transported to Mars during the Civil War—inspired a scientific rationale to explain how Superman, conceived as a refugee from the doomed planet, Krypton, became super-powered. "The John Carter stories did influence me," Siegel admitted. "Carter was able to leap great distances because the planet Mars was smaller than the planet Earth; and he had great strength. I visualized the planet Krypton as a huge planet, much larger than Earth; so whoever came to Earth from that planet would be able to leap great distances and lift great weights."[11]

Another influence was *Flash Gordon*, by artist Alex Raymond and writer Don Moore, which began in 1934 as King Features' answer to the science-fiction strip *Buck Rogers*. In the first installment, a seemingly deranged scientist, Dr. Hans Zarkov, orders Flash and the beautiful Dale Arden, at gunpoint, into a rocket ship that flies to the mysterious planet Mongo, where racist stereotypes prevail—the athletic and virile Anglo-Saxon Flash, Yale graduate and "world renowned polo player," stands in contrast to Ming the Merciless, despotic ruler and another of the inscrutable Orientals menacing pulp fiction in that era. But Raymond created a compelling world, his realistic and dynamic art exuding cinematic energy. By 1936 *Flash Gordon* was syndicated in more than five thousand newspapers and licensing included that year's *Flash Gordon* movie serial, released by Universal Pictures and starring Olympic athlete Buster Crabbe.[12]

Modern comics artist Alex Ross observes that Raymond's "graphic realism" is evident in the early superhero comics: "In the rush to create new characters to fit this mold, many artists took inspiration directly from the *Flash Gordon* strip, primarily in its many inventive costumes and fantastic concepts. Artists also imitated exact poses from Raymond's amazing figure drawing, adding his hard work to a 'swipe file' which they used to draw their comics." Planet Mongo even resembled Superman's home world of Krypton, Ross adds: "It might be said, for metaphorical purposes, that Superman was the son of Flash Gordon."[13]

Joe Shuster's depiction of Superman captured not only a distinctive muscleman look (and details such as his jaunty cowlick of hair) but also a dramatic persona and spirit of derring-do inspired by one of the era's renowned silver screen stars. "In the silent films, my hero was Douglas Fairbanks Senior, who was very agile and athletic," Shuster explained. "He had a stance which I often used in drawing Superman. You'll see in many of his roles—including Robin Hood—that he always stood with his hands on his hips and his feet spread apart, laughing—taking nothing seriously. . . . Fairbanks would swing on ropes very much like Superman flying—or like Tarzan on a vine. . . . [Jerry and I] agreed the feeling of action as he was flying or jumping or leaping—a flowing cape would give it movement. . . . I also had classical heroes and [circus] strongmen in mind." [14]

There was another, and controversial, influence—writer Philip Wylie's novel *Gladiator* (1930). James Steranko, himself a celebrated comics creator, writes, "Superman was a variation of pulp heavyweight Doc Savage," but *Gladiator* was "a blueprint" informing "the essence of Superman and his development."[15]

Gladiator tells the story of a scientist whose experiment allows his son, Hugo Danner, to be born with superhuman powers—the boy outruns trains and leaps over treetops (flying was, perhaps, too much like a Peter Pan fairy tale). In a scientific rationale, Hugo's father describes his son's super strength as equivalent to ants proportionately carrying many times their weight, his leaping ability comparable to grasshoppers able to jump fifty times their length.

Keeping their heroic identities separate and secret from their civilian selves would be a paramount concern for most superheroes, and Wylie's story even established a rationale for that premise. "You're not an ordinary human being," his father warns

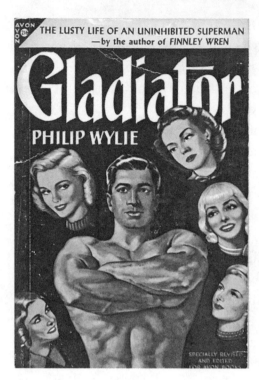

THE LUSTY LIFE OF AN UNINHIBITED SUPERMAN
—by the author of FINNLEY WREN

Gladiator

PHILIP WYLIE

This Avon paperback edition of Philip Wylie's *Gladiator* (originally published in 1930) presents super-powered Hugo Danner as a "lusty . . . uninhibited superman." Even if Siegel and Shuster had been inspired by Wylie's character, DC's editorial dictates for Superman did *not* duplicate Danner's dalliances.

GLADIATOR COVER, AVON EDITION, 1949.

Hugo. "When people find that out, they'll . . . fear you. So you see, you've got to be good and kind and considerate—to justify all that strength."[16]

Writer C. A. Brandt reviewed *Gladiator* in the June 1930 issue of *Amazing Stories*, and Siegel and Shuster were probably among the legion of science-fiction fans alerted to Hugo's exploits. Sam Moskowitz, another contemporary critic, hailed *Gladiator* as "probably the greatest tale of a physical superman since the Biblical story of Samson."

Wylie biographer Robert Howard Barshay later wrote that although Hugo was a "prototype of the comic book hero Superman," the emotional and conflicted Hugo, burdened by his powers, "presaged the modern superhero who recognizes the limits of his power, develops a social consciousness, experiences deep anxiety, makes painful decisions and is responsible for their often ambiguous consequences. . . . Wylie's *Gladiator* embodies a very contemporary outlook before it was fashionable."

Also in the early thirties, Wylie and coauthor Edwin Balmer arguably provided another key inspiration in *When Worlds Collide* (1933) and its sequel, *After Worlds Collide* (1934). In the first book scientists discover two planets careening through the solar system, one a larger sphere that will obliterate Earth, the other a smaller, Earth-like world that could be habitable. The scientists form the League of the Last Days; its members include Anthony Drake, a young New York socialite, and Cole Hendron, a great astrophysicist and engineer. Drake is in love with Eve, Hendron's daughter. Hendron leads the building of two "Arks," rocket ships to escape their doomed world and colonize the smaller sphere. Of course, the idea of escaping a doomed world for a habitable one would make Superman more than another muscle-bound pulp hero.[17]

THE COMING OF SUPERMAN

In 1933, the year Siegel and Shuster decided to transform their fanzine character Super-Man from villain to hero, Franklin Roosevelt was sworn in as president of the United States and Nazi Party leader Adolf Hitler, new chancellor of Germany, began taking dictatorial control of his country. For two Jewish kids, Hitler's anti-Semitic policies and Aryan super-race theories were terrifying. Stir in the economic inequalities of the Great Depression, add a shattering personal tragedy—Jerry Siegel's father, Michael, died in 1932 under mysterious circumstances during an apparent robbery—and Superman was transformed into a champion of the oppressed.

When Superman rose phoenix-like from the flames into which Shuster had tossed their inaugural effort, it was in the costumed form that influenced the look of super beings to come. Superman wore a red cape, blue colored tights with red trunks, red midcalf boots, and he bore a red "S" emblem on his broad chest. He was in good company: the character called *The Phantom*, conceived by writer Lee Falk (creator of *Mandrake the Magician*) and artist Ray Moore, debuted as a King Features strip on February 12, 1936. He wore a skintight purple outfit and a mask with inscrutable white spaces for eyes, suiting the mysterious ruler of an African kingdom.

Superman was hardwired with innate qualities that would define the superhero, including his secret alter ego, newspaper reporter Clark Kent. Most superheroes favored the secret identity gambit of hiding behind a mask, but not Superman—the last son of Krypton was the public person, Kent the disguise. Shuster drew up announcements for Superman confirming their sky-high ambitions: "The Greatest Single Event Since the Birth of Comic Strips"; "The Strip Destined to Sweep the Nation"; and "The Greatest Super-Hero of All Time!"[18]

THE COMIC BOOK

What is popularly considered the first modern American comic book was the inspiration of Harry L. Wildenberg, sales manager for Eastern Color Printing Company of Connecticut, and Eastern salesman Max Charles "M. C." Gaines, who decided to collect newspaper strips into a tabloid periodical. The result, published in 1934, was *Famous Funnies*, the first comic book on the newsstands, distributed by the mighty American News Company, founded in 1864. It was reprinted material, but it set the standard four-color format priced at a dime.[19]

Each issue of *Famous Funnies* required editor/production manager Stephen A. Douglas to take syndicate proofs of a licensed strip and prepare them for the new format. "This involved, unfortunately, relettering, enlarging, and sometimes cutting the copy in the balloons and captions so it wouldn't reproduce too teeny-weeny," comics historian Ron Goulart notes. "Small lettering was a real concern and source of criticism for the early reprint comic books, where Sunday pages usually ran at one-fourth of

Comic books initially drew on newspaper comic strips for material and inspiration. This back cover of a 1938 *Terry and the Pirates* giveaway celebrates the syndicated stars that were only a Popped Wheat purchase away.

TERRY AND THE PIRATES, PUBLISHED BY SIG. FEUCHTWANGER, NEW YORK, 1938, BY ARRANGEMENT WITH FAMOUS ARTISTS SYNDICATE, CHICAGO.

their intended newspaper size. . . . Douglas also had to extend a panel here and there to make it fit the pages just right, and he would white out any dot patterns that might interfere with the laying on of color."[20]

A few entrepreneurs, like Harry "A" Chesler (the middle initial was for show), were convinced comics would be a big industry based on original material. In 1936 Chesler opened a studio in Manhattan at 276 Fifth Avenue, reportedly the first to produce original story and art for the new medium. It was an industry built by Jewish creators, editors, and publishers who were often restricted from high-end advertising and other mainstream fields. "A lot of Jews got into lower-end magazines, like Harry Donenfled, who got into 'girlie' type magazines," notes attorney Mark Zaid.[21]

Malcolm Wheeler-Nicholson, the man who really got the comic book business rolling, was a former US Cavalry officer whose autobiography is vivid enough to be real—chasing bandits along the US-Mexican border, leading an infantry battalion against Bolsheviks in Siberia, commanding headquarters cavalry of American forces in the Rhine. He left the army "a major equipped with a select assortment of racing and polo cups, a sabre, and a battered typewriter," he attested.[22]

Creig Flessel, an early comic book artist, colorfully recalled Wheeler-Nicholson as "a smiling, blue-eyed dapper little man who carried the ubiquitous writer's briefcase and cane, wore a beaver hat and spats, a camel's hair coat was on his arm and he smoked cigarettes using a long holder. He was married to the lady-in-waiting to the Queen of Sweden."[23]

Wheeler-Nicholson, who insisted on being addressed as "Major," began his post-military career writing pulp adventures. In 1934, the year Siegel and Shuster began shopping Superman around, the Major founded National Allied Publications, Inc., in New York, a comic book company devoted to original material, an idea more practical than revolutionary: original material was cheaper than a newspaper syndicate's licensing fee of $15 a page. In February 1935 the Major launched *New Fun*, a tabloid-sized black-and-white comic book.[24]

Siegel and Shuster, still looking for a Superman newspaper syndication deal, got a foothold in comic books at National Allied with two single-page features in *New Fun* #6—*Henri Duval of France, Famed Soldier of Fortune*, and *Doctor Occult, the Ghost Detective* (both under the pseudonyms Leger and Reuths). They offered Superman to National—and the Major was interested. But National's finances were shaky, and it was an ordeal getting a paycheck. The poorly run company saw editors moving on, leaving Vincent "Vin" Sullivan and Frederick Whitney "Whit" Ellsworth, both in their twenties, to shoulder the work. Siegel and Shuster decided to keep working on their National features while continuing to offer their prized creation to the syndicates.[25]

By 1937 Wheeler-Nicholson was getting glossy covers off the presses of Donny Press, a printing company owned by Harry

Donenfeld, who also owned Independent News (IND), the company distributing National's titles. As a publisher, Donenfeld favored salacious magazines that lured customers with painted covers featuring scantily clad women in peril.

FROM SMUT TO SUPERMAN

Harry Donenfeld was born in 1893 in Romania, arrived in America with his family in 1900, and settled in the Jewish slums of New York's Lower East Side.[26] Short and scrappy, he got his start in his uncle's printing business. During Prohibition he reputedly smuggled liquor into the United States in the hollowed cores of paper shipments from Canada. The printing and distribution business was mobbed-up, as was Harry, whose friends included gangster Frank Costello. Donenfeld often joined Costello when he got a shave from his favorite barber, John Szokoli, at New York's Waldorf Astoria hotel. When the barber died, Frank asked Harry to see what he could do for the man's son. Joe Szokoli, who had artistic talent, began contributing to Donenfeld's "Spicy" line of pulp magazines.[27]

In the tangled web of pulp publishing, one strand links Donenfeld to Max and Moses Annenberg, Russian immigrants of Prussian Jewish ancestry who came of age in Chicago's underworld. In 1923 Moses Annenberg had to organize six million promotional brochure inserts for Hearst publications and gave the lucrative contract to Donenfeld, who with his wife, Gussie, founded Elmo Press, Inc. The company was chartered for "magazines and newspapers," capitalized at $25,000, and located at 32 West 22nd Street in New York—the address of Tab Printing Corporation, owned by Harry's friend Theodore Epstein, who printed the *Daily Racing Tabloid* for Moses Annenberg.[28]

In 1931 Donenfeld hired Jacob "Jack" Liebowitz as his accountant and business manager. Liebowitz, born in 1900 and a Jewish immigrant from present-day Ukraine, was an accountant for the

Ladies' Garment Workers' Union in New York until the 1929 stock-market crash. As with Costello and his barber's son, Jack's father Julius Liebowitz approached Harry about a job for Jack. Donenfeld and Liebowitz complemented each other—Harry's street smarts and boozy sociability; Jack's business instincts and tenacious drive.

That year Donenfeld formed Donny Press at 143 West 20th Street, the same address as his Elmo Press. He also started Donenfeld Magazines Publishing Corporation, leasing office space on the ninth floor of 480 Lexington, a skyscraper occupying a midtown block near the art deco city-within-a-city of Rockefeller Center, then under construction. The main lobby was at 480 Lexington, the south side entrance and address were at 46th Street, the west side faced Park Avenue, and on the north was 47th Street—a puzzle box of addresses, entrances, and exits.[29]

Donenfeld had thriving publishing and printing enterprises—the distribution piece fell into place when he partnered with Paul Sampliner, who cofounded Eastern Distributing Corporation with Warren Angel in 1924. Eastern specialized in distributing bawdy material and the magazines of pioneering publisher Hugo Gernsback. To maximize profits Sampliner and Angel provided credit to new publishers in exchange for partial ownership and use of affiliated printers, including Donenfeld's Donny Press.

When Angel left to form rival distributor Kable News Company, Sampliner became president and majority owner of Eastern Distributing. But Kable attracted Eastern's clients, and Eastern piled up debt. Sampliner declared bankruptcy in September 1932 in the Southern District of New York, with the receivership of the Irving Trust Company appointed by Judge Alfred C. Coxe (who would oversee the tumultuous copyright infringement trial between Superman and Captain Marvel). On a busy September 15 Donenfeld declared bankruptcy for Elmo Press and joined Sampliner in forming Independent News, the distribution company they headquartered at 245 Park

Avenue—the west side entrance to the 480 Lexington Avenue building.[30]

The Barreaux Art Agency, run by Adolphe Barreaux, became part of Donenfeld's growing pulp empire. Barreaux reportedly got Donenfeld interested in comics by contributing *Flossie Flip*, his sexy chorus girl strip, to *Police Gazette*, the venerable tabloid Harry and his brother Irving bought through their company Merwil Publishing. The venture got too high a profile, underscored by *Time* magazine's reporting: "Merwil Publishing Co. issues five of the smuttiest magazines on the newsstands—*Snappy*, *Spicy*, *Gay Parisienne*, *La Paree*, *Pep*. They consist of sleazy stories, drawings and 'art study' photographs of undressed females. Mrs. Hersey edits them." *Time* couldn't resist spotlighting gray-haired Merle Hersey, the divorced daughter of a Methodist minister and member of the Daughters of the American Revolution, who revealed the *Police Gazette*'s editorial strategy: "Lots of sex, underworld stuff with a sex angle, and plenty of pictures of semi-nude night-club girls."[31]

In 1934 Fiorello La Guardia was elected New York's mayor and declared war on the underworld and vice, adding political weight to guardians of public decency outraged at Donenfeld's publications. That year a judge declared *Pep* obscene, but it is now comics lore that Donenfeld employee Herbie Siegel took the rap, serving a brief prison stint in exchange for lifetime employment.[32]

Donenfeld kept publishing smut, but he now used front companies and avoided paper trails. "If there were censorship problems, or if the magazines sold poorly, he could fold up his tent and escape in the fog," reports pulp historian David Saunders (son of artist Norman Saunders). "But despite his many false fronts there are still a few unbroken threads that run continuously throughout his entire shady business. Everything was printed by Donny Press, distributed by Independent News, and illustrated by the Barreaux Art Agency." Donenfeld was running a "clandestine organization," Saunders concludes.[33]

Major Wheeler-Nicholson was a client of Donenfeld and Liebowitz, who took an interest when his National Allied Publications began sinking in a rising tide of red ink and proposed they go into business. Their new company was incorporated as Detective Comics around December 28, 1936, and headquartered at 480 Lexington Avenue.[34] DC absorbed National's properties, including Siegel and Shuster's features. Editor Whit Ellsworth left for Hollywood (he would return at a critical juncture when litigation threatened a promising new character), leaving Vin Sullivan editor of the line that kicked off with a new title named after the company.

Sullivan even drew the first cover of *Detective Comics*, the visage of a stereotypical Oriental villain. The Major and artist Tom Hickey supplied "The Claws of the Red Dragon," an exotic thriller set in San Francisco's Chinatown. Siegel and Shuster contributed *Bart Regan, Spy*, and were asked to prepare a second feature: "We want a detective hero called Slam Bradley," the Major wrote them. "He is to be an amateur, called in by police to help unravel difficult cases."

"We rarely knew what Slam might do next," Siegel recalled. "We made up the cliff-hanging suspense and hair-breadth escapes as we went along. The really greatest suspense of all, though, was wondering when and if we would get paid for producing these extravagant cartoon fantasies. Payment checks, it seemed to us, were painfully slow and far-between in coming. . . . To temporarily escape from our worries and woes, Joe and I would redeem empty milk bottles, scavenging a few cents to pay for our admissions into B-movies where we would thrill to the kind of feverish stuff we were pouring into our comics pages."

Shuster recalled the Cleveland winter he spent working on *Slam Bradley* and *Spy* for *Detective* #1: "I worked in my apartment, cold and shivering because my family could not afford coal to heat the rooms. I could barely draw because my hands were so frozen. So I wore cotton gloves and several layers of sweaters. I used my mother's breadboard as a drawing board and on Friday nights, the night my mother baked the bread for the weekend meals, she would say, 'Joe, I need the breadboard now.' My artwork went into limbo until she had finished baking."[35]

Detective Comics was released in the winter of 1937. The issuing of this and other titles followed the publishing practice of providing copies to distributors usually two months *before* the cover date. The cover date of each issue thus appeared current throughout its shelf life, providing an end date for dealers to pull unsold copies and return them to the publisher.

The young Cleveland-based creators were now prolific, proven content providers, assets to a new company—their suspense over paychecks was about to become a bad memory. On December 4, 1937, Siegel and Shuster signed a two-year contract to continue furnishing features that "shall be and become the sole and exclusive property of [Detective Comics] and [Detective Comics] shall be deemed the sole creator thereof." In legal language, this meant buying the rights was as good as being the creator of the property. The contract also gave DC right of first refusal for new features, allowing sixty days to exercise an option.[36]

Vin Sullivan continued editing, Donenfeld was on the road distributing for Independent News, and secretary/treasurer Liebowitz oversaw editorial and production as DC's second in command. The lineup was *Detective Comics*, *More Fun*, and *New Comics*, the latter retitled *New Adventure Comics* and, finally, by issue #32, *Adventure Comics*. A fourth title, proposed by Liebowitz, would be a sixty-four-page anthology of original material called *Action Comics*.[37]

The new title was being discussed during the transition between the Wheeler-Nicholson regime and formation of DC. On December 6 Siegel wrote Mr. J. S. Liebowitz—Siegel's correspondence would soon carry the familiar "Jack"—to report that the signed two-year contract had been mailed the day before, with pages for the Major heading out the next day. This letter, written on the letterhead of "Publication Enterprises Co., 10622 Kimberley Avenue" (Siegel's Cleveland home address), reported: "Since we do 10 pages per month for Nicholson magazines, we are to receive $90 for them—Herewith find enclosed suggested characters for ACTION COMICS."

Siegel proposed a thirteen-page color feature, *Bob Hazard*, a "world-wide adventurer . . . a la *Slam Bradley.*" *The Crimson Horseman* was a six-page black-and-white series starring "a masked, cloaked rider of mystery who metes out justice in a law-less cattle country." Another six-page black-and-white proposal was *Chesty Crane*, a goodhearted athlete whose "big talk" gets him into "tight situations."

A fourth idea would have been a precedent-setting twenty-six-page color feature, what Siegel called a "novel cartoon." *The Wraith* would introduce "a most unusual detective," whose "abnormal glands" heightened his senses: he could see through walls, "follow scents like a bloodhound. . . . [He] possesses the strength of a dozen men . . . tracks down criminals like a prowling beast . . . [and] comes and goes as mysteriously as a ghost." Siegel argued there was the mystical precedent of popular pulp crime fighters like the Shadow, adding, "The length of the complete novel cartoon can be played up as a feature that no other comic magazine possesses." The proposed characters never came to life, although Siegel would create a spectral crime fighter for DC, the Spectre. In the far-off future the "novel cartoon" would be called a "graphic novel."

Siegel and Shuster were still making syndicate rounds with four weeks of *Superman* strip samples, one week completely written, drawn, inked, and ready for publication, the other three needing inking. One publisher was intrigued but felt the character would work best as a color comic book, not a black-and-white daily strip. The creators twice brought *Superman* to McClure Syndicate at 75th West Street, the syndicate passing each time. But they made a third submission in late 1937, thanks to the interest of M. C. Gaines, of *Famous Funnies* fame.[38]

Meanwhile, an *Action Comics* "ashcan," a dummy edition establishing copyright and trademark, was approved, its place-holder cover art strangely picturing a ghoulish figure in monkish robes holding a bloody dagger and glaring over its shoulder at the reader. *Action* features included Zatara, a top-hatted magician hero inspired by *Mandrake the Magician*. Harried editor Vin Sullivan needed more magic—and it would be coming with Siegel and Shuster's Superman.

The Major enjoyed none of DC's imminent success. Wheeler-Nicholson mismanaged his company and did not treat his creators well—Siegel later lamented to Liebowitz the drama of awaiting a paycheck—but the former adventurer also had the bad timing of pioneering a new frontier. "Distributors were still reluctant to handle comic books, newsstands even more reluctant to give them rack space," writes Ron Goulart.[39]

But although Major Wheeler-Nicholson might have been a bad businessman, that was not the reason he lost the company he created. He was forced out by Donenfeld and Liebowitz, attests Michael Uslan, whose "deep dive" into comics history includes a stint in the 1970s trying to put order to the "DC Closet," a disorganized space full of company paperwork and corporate records—including the correspondence and signed agreements by which the Major's company went "bankrupt" and was transferred over to Donenfeld and Liebowitz.

It was clear in the bankruptcy that the trustee appointed by the judge was not an impartial guy, but close to Donenfeld and, I believe, at times was on his payroll. It was a pretty obvious setup. This was pretty common in the pulp era, a way certain people, and companies, or printers would take over the actual properties themselves. And in the context of the Depression, publishers were setting up operations on shoe-string budgets. It was week-to-week, if not day-to-day, how to get revenue in and your staff paid and freelancers paid, trying to keep your head above water. It's not that National Allied was the only one not keeping up with payments for artists, writers, and staff.

Liebowitz and Donenfeld had set up to give [the Major] money, but in a quasi-legal way so they could drive the costs up and control the flow of money, making him vulnerable to [them] taking over the entire thing. It solidified their position of strength to push him over the side. Coincidence or not, all this concluded moments before *Action* #1 came out.[40]

CHAPTER 2

WORLD OF TOMORROW

And so begins the startling adventures of the most sensational strip character of all time—SUPERMAN! A Physical Marvel, a Mental Wonder, Superman Is Destined to Reshape the Destiny of a World! Only in Action Comics Can You Thrill at the Daring Deeds of This Superb Creation! Don't Miss an Issue!

Action Comics #1, copy ending the first Superman story

BIG BREAK

By the winter of 1937 Siegel and Shuster were signed to provide new features for the next two years and were pitching feature ideas for the proposed *Action Comics*—it seemed destined Superman would end up at DC. It is even possible that *Superman* samples came full circle to Donenfeld. In 1934, when Siegel began trying to sell *Superman*, he sent query letters on June 20 and October 4 to Super Magazines, Inc., editor Frank Armer—whose partner was Donenfeld. (Other than the "Super" name, the company was another salacious Donenfeld pulp enterprise.)[1]

M. C. Gaines first saw *Superman* in January 1936, while producing and printing the first issue of *Popular Comics: America's Favorite Funnies* for Dell Publishing Company. He couldn't use the character, but by December of that year he was at McClure Syndicate, where his responsibilities included supervising the printing of *Detective Comics*. Gaines was considering a possible newspaper strip tabloid weekly and asked Siegel for another look at *Superman*.

Gaines's young assistant at McClure, Sheldon Mayer, was excited to see *Superman* again, having first seen the samples while working with Gaines on *Popular Comics*. Gaines decided a tabloid newspaper strip wasn't feasible but still had *Superman* when DC called to discuss the new title. He recalled: "The Detective Comics people . . . told me they want to come out with another book called Action Comics, they have already had the title registered; did I have any material available? I said, 'Yes, I have got some here from Siegel which I think is very good and which should be a natural for that type of book, depicting action according to the title.'"

Gaines later explained, "I was so impressed with this strip when I first got it. . . . I made an effort at the time to have it used for newspaper syndication but my organization, McClure Syndicate . . . did not feel they were ready to go into any additional promotion for a daily feature."[2] That soon changed, but in the hope that McClure might win the printing contract for the new title, Gaines forwarded *Superman* to 480 Lexington.

In January 1938 DC decided to buy *Superman*. Editor Vin Sullivan liked the character, envisioning it as a big thirteen-page feature. The only problem was the samples were in the daily panel newspaper format. On February 1, 1938, the strips were returned to Siegel and Shuster with the request that they resubmit in comic book form, 8 panels per page, 104 total.[3]

"It was a rush job, and one of the things I like least to do is rush my artwork," Shuster recalled. "The only solution Jerry and I could come up with was to cut up the strip into panels and paste the panels on a sheet [of cardboard] the size of the [comic book] page. If some panels were too long, we would shorten them—cut them off—if they were too short, we would extend them."[4]

Siegel, the team leader, recalled Joe's work—"under [his] supervision"—included inking the three weeks of penciled strips. The trimming and resizing issues were similar to what Stephen

Douglas faced on *Famous Funnies*. To attain the number of requested panels, Shuster added new artwork, including an opening page offering "A Scientific Explanation of Clark Kent's Amazing Strength." A final panel at the bottom of page 13 filled its width, depicting Superman swelling his chest and snapping binding chains, with the copy of Siegel and Shuster's dreams: "And so begins the startling adventures of the most sensational strip character of all time—SUPERMAN!"[5]

With *Superman* came the realization that comic books were a more expansive medium than daily strips, presenting new creative possibilities. When all sample panels and new art were added and the panel quota still was not met, the creators decided against arbitrarily cramming in more. "Jerry told me that Detective preferred having eight panels per page but in our judgment this would hurt the property," Shuster explained. "I specifically refer to the very large panel appearing on what would be page 9 of the thirteen-page release. We did not want to alter this because of its dramatic effect. Accordingly, on this page but six panels appeared."

That large panel showed Superman lifting a car and smashing its hood, sending the left tire spinning off as two frightened men flee. When the reformatted story was resubmitted around February 16, 1938, Siegel was told this image would be "the template" for the cover.[6] Shuster embellished it, placing the dramatic viewpoint closer on Superman and showing a third man cowering in the background. The cover would become one of the most iconic in comic book history, a visual herald of a new kind of hero and, in the pulp tradition, impulse-buy material. But publisher Donenfeld didn't think the image all that iconic. "When Harry Donenfeld first saw that cover of Superman holding that car in the air, he really got worried," Sheldon Mayer recalled. "He felt that nobody would believe it, that it was ridiculous . . . crazy."

"Donenfeld had little or nothing to do with the selection of features and things of that nature," Sullivan told historian Ron

Goulart. "When [Siegel and Shuster] showed this thing to me that they'd been trying to sell, it looked good to me, and I started it. And that's how Superman got going."[7]

In the coming Golden Age of Comics, writers were usually responsible for directing the artist's work, as Siegel did for *Action*. Siegel proclaimed a partnership but considered himself Superman's creator. "When the strip was started I deliberately decided to pay [Joe] on a 50% partnership basis instead of paying him a flat salary out of the gross earnings, because I was just as anxious to see him make out well, as well as do well myself," Siegel explained to Jack Liebowitz in 1942. "I think I gave him as decent a break as any artist-collaborator could expect, and I don't begrudge him a cent of the hundreds of dollars a week he's now earning for having so associated himself with me."[8]

On March 1, before *Action* went to press, Jerry and Joe got the check that included their Superman work, along with the one-page release. In addition to *Superman* and *Zatara*, the anthology included a cowboy hero strip called *"Chuck" Dawson*, cartoony *Sticky-Mitt Stimson*, *The Adventures of Marco Polo*, the exploits of light heavyweight boxer *"Pep" Morgan*, intrepid reporter *Scoop Scanlon*, and *Tex Thomson*, an oil-rich Texan traveling the world in search of adventure.

House ads in *Detective Comics* #15 and *More Fun Comics* #31 announced *Action Comics* #1: "Brand New! And Just What You've Been Waiting For . . . Look for this dandy new magazine filled with original adventure features and pictures in Color!" There was no Superman copy on the cover itself, nor any Superman announcement in the black-and-white house ads—the image spoke for itself.

Action Comics #1, cover-dated June 1938, was officially published on April 18. (Unless otherwise noted, issues listed will include the cover-dated information.) A one-page introduction explained an infant was launched to Earth in a rocket ship from a doomed and nameless planet, a child with extraordinary powers based on a "physical structure . . . millions of years advanced."

Superman is a whirlwind, stopping a husband from beating his wife ("You're not fighting a woman, now"), and grabbing a treasonous political lobbyist by an ankle and leaping high into the air to get the terrified man to confess.

The central drama was the strange love triangle between Superman, his alter ego, bespectacled *Daily Star* newspaper reporter Clark Kent—a hapless contrast to his superhero self—and Lois, Kent's attractive young colleague at the newspaper who thinks he's spineless and swoons for Superman. (She isn't identified as Lois "Lane" until *Action* #2.)

In that first story Clark asks Lois for a date and she grudgingly agrees. "Why is it you always avoid me at the office?" Clark asks as they dance at a nightclub. "Please Clark! I've been scribbling 'sob stories' all day long. Don't ask me to dish out another" (introducing the famously fearless reporter as an advice-for-the-lovelorn columnist). Burly Butch Matson sees them dancing, and when he tries to cut in, Kent plays "his role of a weakling," pleading with Lois to dance with the fellow.

"You can stay and dance with him if you wish but I'm leaving now!" no-nonsense Lois declares, slapping Butch on her way out. Butch and his gang kidnap Lois and are driving away when Superman, leaping "like a released rocket," overtakes their car and shakes and breaks it—giving Butch and his gang a measure of immortality as the frightened men on the cover. He rescues Lois, leaping into the night sky with the captivated woman in his arms.

Independent News distributed *Action* in the United States and Canada through a network of seven hundred distributors capable of placing comics and magazines into an estimated 85,000 outlets, including newsstands and magazine racks at stationery stores, drug stores, and department stores. *Action* #1 "net page sales," as Liebowitz termed it, numbered approximately 130,000 copies.[9]

Superman's first appearance caught the attention of author Philip Wylie, whose *Gladiator* hero, Hugo Danner, outran trains and leapt over treetops; Superman was introduced as able to out-run trains and leap "1/8 of a mile; hurdle a twenty-story building." Hugo's father, a scientist like Superman's dad, described his son's powers as equivalent to ants proportionately carrying many times their weight and grasshoppers jumping fifty times their length, the analogies used in the "scientific explanation" of Superman's powers. The similarities were such that Wylie considered legal action in 1940.[10]

Superman's debut didn't seem to cause a stir in the executive suites at 480 Lexington. The *Action* #2 cover by Leo E. O'Mealia pictured a man parachuting from a downed plane with a gun in one hand, his free arm wrapped around a woman (possibly swiped from the first *Flash Gordon* Sunday strip of January 7, 1934). Superman stories appeared in all successive issues, but without a mention on covers featuring O'Mealia's pulp adventure art. *Action* sales kept rising, but it took four issues, fan feedback, and DC newsstand surveys to pinpoint *why*—kids wanted the comic with Superman in it!

The untitled Superman story in *Action* #5, later referred to as "Superman and the Dam," marks the third time Superman sweeps Lois off her feet and provides a good example of the breakneck thrills and super-Herculean feats that got kids excited. When a dam begins cracking, threatening to flood Valleyho Town, the unnamed *Daily Star* editor asks Lois Lane to get him Clark Kent. Lois volunteers for the dam assignment, but the harried editor responds in the sexist spirit of the times: "Can't. It's too important! This is no job for a girl!"

"No job for a woman, eh?" Lois muses as she grabs a taxi to get the story. When Clark learns Lois is "pulling a double-cross" he suits up as Superman and speeds by leaps and bounds—he still can't fly—to the impending disaster. He can't stop the dam from bursting but leaps ahead of the rushing waters. He looks back—floodwaters have buried an abandoned taxi, with Lois trapped inside. He bounds back, dives underwater to scoop her up, blasts to the surface, and is off like a shot, racing past the rushing waters,

The breathless pacing of early *Superman* stories is on display here as he dives, sprints, and soars into the air to rescue Lois Lane from floodwaters caused by a breaking dam. No wonder the kids said, "Give me the comic with Superman in it!"

"SUPERMAN AND THE DAM" (TITLE ADDED LATER), *ACTION COMICS* #5 (OCTOBER 1938), PAGE 8, ARTIST JOE SHUSTER. THE STORY WAS LATER REPRINTED IN *SUPERMAN* #3 (WINTER 1940).

leaping ahead to a mountaintop to topple a pinnacle of rock, diverting the flood from the town.

Lois kisses her hero.

"*Wow*! What a kiss!" Superman exclaims.

"A super-kiss for a Super-man!"

Superman takes her into his arms, soaring above the mighty river he created. "Enough of that! I've got to bring you back to safety—where I'll be safe from you!"

"The first time you carried me like this I was frightened—just as I was frightened of you. But now I love it—just as I love you."

Superman touches down, safely, leaving Lois in Valleyho Town. "Don't go!" she implores. "Stay with me . . . always."

"Perhaps we'll meet again," Superman says, as he turns to leap away.

By *Action* #7 Superman was on the cover in midleap hundreds of feet above the city, holding a frightened man by his foot. The image, inspired by the incident in the first issue, was not duplicated inside—it was impulse-buy imagery. For the first time, a cover notice announced: "SUPERMAN: Appearing in This Issue and in Every Issue" and "Reg. U.S. Pat. Off" (Registered United States Patent Office).

THE WORLD TOMORROW

Superman was dreamed up and gestated in Cleveland, but it was in New York City—media capital, home to publishing and commercial radio networks, corporate headquarters of movie companies, where merchandising deals were made—that Superman and the superhero mythology were truly born. The soaring skyline was ambition and success made concrete. In 1931 the new Empire State Building was the world's tallest; two years later it served as monument to civilization in *King Kong* when the film's gigantic ape scaled it only to be shot down by fighter planes. Aviation itself was the stuff of miracles: Pan American Airways, headquartered in New York, made the first scheduled commercial airmail flight across the Pacific Ocean in 1935, a feat likened to a Jules Verne fantasy, and began trans-Atlantic service only a year after Superman appeared. The Depression continued, but the crisis stirred a creative ferment, with federal arts programs of the Works Progress Administration energizing New York's theater scene and public art celebrating the power of science harnessing nature's forces.

"Come Tour the Future!" Visitors to General Motors' "Futurama" exhibit look down on a diorama of 1960 from their "traveling sound-chair."

FUTURAMA BOOKLET, NEW YORK WORLD'S FAIR, 1939–1940, P. 7.

A passing generation recalled the closing of the frontier; a new generation marveled at a fantastic future taking form. The year Superman appeared, a vision of that future was rising from the ash heaps of Flushing Meadows in Queens. The New York World's Fair, open from 1939 through 1940, presented dazzling glimpses of the visual broadcast medium of television, of super-highways, and of other wonders summed up in the theme "The World of Tomorrow." "Futurama," General Motors' contribution, staged a time-traveling look at America in 1960, where visitors in moving conveyor "sound-chairs" looked down, godlike, on a scaled miniature motorway crossing verdant valleys and mountain passes, heading towards a mighty metropolis, "This magic city of progress."[11]

A DC-licensed tie-in appeared as the *New York World's Fair*

The Underwood Elliott Fisher Exhibit at the World's Fair boasted this gigantic four-teen-ton typewriter capable of typing on stationery 9 by 12 feet long. (Note the City of Tomorrow in the background, along with the Fair's iconic Trylon and Perisphere.)

"THE GIANT UNDERWOOD MASTER TYPEWRITER," NEW YORK WORLD'S FAIR, 1939–1940, POSTCARD.

Comics (a big, ninety-six pages priced at a hefty twenty-five cents), which included a Superman story that, following the theme, nick-named Superman the "Man of Tomorrow," a moniker that stuck (along with "Man of Steel" and others). Superman personified the Super Future.

Meanwhile, even before confirmation of Superman's success, McClure was reconsidering a *Superman* strip. Siegel and Shuster, emerging as major players, were already making arrangements with the syndicate on behalf of DC. The day *Action* #1 was released, Siegel mailed Liebowitz their latest signed releases for *Radio Squad*, *Doctor Occult*, *Federal Men*, *Spy*, and *Slam Bradley* (the cover letter on stationery for the "American Artists League," headquartered at Siegel's home address). "In their latest letter, McClure has instructed us to draw up the two weeks' releases of SUPERMAN and get them submitted on July 1st," Siegel reported. "This, Joe and I will do. When we submit the drawn up strip to them, I'll inform you at once. I've no doubt but that if you drop

Writer Bill Finger, inspired by the giant typewriter of the World's Fair, used it as a dramatic prop in this 1949 *Batman* story.

"THE MAN WITH THE AUTOMATIC BRAIN!," *BATMAN* #52 (APRIL/MAY 1949), P. 11, ART BY BOB KANE AND LEW SAYRE SCHWARTZ.

in on the McClure Newspaper Syndicate at that time to discuss matters, that your presence will aid materially in the selling of the strip."[12]

The future looked bright for the "boys," as Donenfeld and Liebowitz called them. Siegel and Shuster dreamed Superman would be big—it was heady stuff, having dreams come true.

CHAPTER 3

MORE SUPER THAN TARZAN

We visualized Superman toys, games, and a radio show—
that was before TV—and Superman movies. We even visualized Superman billboards. And it's all come true.

JOE SHUSTER
"Of Supermen and Kids with Dreams," *Nemo*, 1983

BIG TIME

Jerry celebrated Superman's sale by buying a Royal Portable
Quiet Deluxe typewriter to keep tapping out stories during train
rides and hotel stays when he had business in New York. DC
allowed them to set up their own studio in Cleveland and hire
artists—a must, given the problems Joe was having with his
eyesight.

The boys celebrated the phenomenon with a knowing wink
in *Action* #6. After only six appearances the superhero was still
a "mystery man" who was viewed with suspicion by police and
other authorities. A caption in the *Action* #6 story reminds readers, "Clark Kent *is* Superman!" The story begins with news that
newspapers are chronicling Superman's exploits. Trying to cash
in is con artist Nick Williams, who poses as Superman's manager and meets with the *Daily Star* editor and his ace reporter
on the Superman story, a *very* intrigued Clark Kent. "The more
Superman news you print, the better it is for both of us," Williams
argues. "Well, I'll guarantee to give you news of his exploits before
he pulls them, if you'll print it."

In Siegel and Shuster's tongue-in-cheek nod to their character's licensing potential, a grifter claims Superman has allowed his name to be used for commercial endorsements; a startled Clark Kent views this blimp ad for "Superman gasoline." By coincidence the story was published around the time of the first Superman licensing deal.

"SUPERMAN'S PHONY MANAGER" (TITLE ADDED LATER), *ACTION COMICS* #6 (NOVEMBER 1938), P. 2, PANEL 8, ART BY JOE SHUSTER. THE STORY WAS LATER REPRINTED IN *SUPERMAN* #3.

Williams turns on the office radio in time to catch an announcer introducing "a new, astounding radio adventure program series entitled *Superman*." Outside the office window a passing zeppelin trails a banner reading, "Use 'Superman Gasoline' for Super Power!" Also in view is a billboard image of Superman pacing a speeding car, the "Superman Streamline Special, America's Favorite Automobile."

"I've also licensed Superman bathing-suits, costumes, physical development exercisers, and movie rights, to name a few," the smirking Williams explains, ready to close the deal. "Why, I've even made provisions for him to appear in the comics!"

Of course, the Man of Tomorrow knows it's a con and foils the scheme.

Satirizing Superman's media and merchandising potential revealed the chutzpah of Siegel and Shuster. They had done the math—if Tarzan was a mighty merchandising machine, and if Superman was more super than Tarzan, that equaled even mightier licensing opportunities. By coincidence or fate, *Action* #6, cover-dated November 1938 and on sale around September, coincided with Superman's first licensing success.

THE MCCLURE DEAL

The McClure Newspaper Syndicate won the *Action* printing contract, as M. C. Gaines hoped, and that September McClure proposed a license for a syndicated *Superman* strip. Siegel and Shuster asked Donenfeld for return of syndication rights. The publisher declined but assured them something would be worked out, and Liebowitz invited them to join the negotiations with McClure. Siegel caught a train to New York, arriving stiff and sleepy from an uncomfortable night spent in coach for lack of fare for a sleeper berth.[1]

McClure outlined terms in a three-page letter, dated September 22, 1938, to DC and Siegel and Shuster. "This letter, when signed by each of you, will serve as our agreement," wrote McClure president Richard H. Waldo. "In line with our discussions, we are prepared to go ahead with newspaper syndication of a daily strip, six days a week, entitled 'Superman' and owned by Detective." The syndicate proposed giving Detective Comics notice in writing by registered mail before June 1, 1939, the date at which a five-year agreement would begin "to permit the Artists to supply 'Superman' strip exclusively to us for syndication in newspapers in the United States, Canada and all other parts of the world."[2]

The agreement included compensation and royalty percentages for the creators, but they were incidental—terms were addressed to Superman's *owners*: "The material contained in the feature which we syndicate will be copyrighted in our name, but copyright reverts to Detective at the termination of this contract. The title 'Superman' shall always remain the property of Detective and the feature may be used by Detective for any other purpose except daily or weekly newspaper publication. Our agreement covers newspaper rights only. Radio, motion pictures, silent and talkie, book and all other rights are retained and owned by Detective. . . . In the event the Artists shall at any time fail to furnish the feature, and so breach this agreement, . . . Detective may appoint other artists to do the feature and strip."

In a key clause McClure agreed to return the original art "so that said drawings may be used by Detective in the publication 'Action Comics,' six months after newspaper release, without charge or for any substituted magazine."[3]

The contract required DC to pay the artists, reserved rights for a Sunday *Superman* strip, and included a six-week option period of first refusal for new syndicate features from DC. The agreement concluded with a note emblematic of the times and imperiled foreign markets: "It is understood that in the event of an outbreak of a European war, in which Great Britain should become involved during the period of October 1, 1938, to February 1, 1939, the McClure Syndicate has the right to cancel this agreement."[4] While in New York, Siegel proposed the option period be raised from four to eight months. (Great Britain and France declared war on Germany on September 3, 1939, and the option clause never came into play.)

McClure's five-year deal was matched by DC's own five-year employment contract to Siegel and Shuster, also dated September 22. "Your signature to this agreement is one of the inducements [for] us to execute the . . . McClure contract," explained Donenfeld's two-page agreement letter, implying the syndication deal wouldn't happen unless the boys agreed to terms. They were to continue providing forty-six monthly pages at the page rate of $10 for *Superman, Slam Bradley,* and *Spy*; and $9 for *Radio Squad* and *Federal Men.* They would also receive 30–40 percent of the strip's "net proceeds," based on the McClure contract.

"All material, art and copy shall be owned by us and at our option, copyrighted or registered in our name or in the names of the parties designated by us," the publisher added, emphasizing DC was "exclusive owner" of Superman and all properties Siegel and Shuster created for Wheeler-Nicholson. DC had the "right to reasonably supervise the editorial matter" and a first refusal option for any proposed features. And, by the way, their contract could be terminated at any time and other artists substituted.[5]

Siegel returned to Cleveland, flushed with success. Having heard rumors of creators getting $15 a page, he impulsively dashed off a "Dear Jack" letter on September 26 asking for a raise, citing Superman's first-place ranking in a reader's poll of *Action* features and its being "resold in Latin America and Mexico."

It was, perhaps, the impertinent tone of Siegel's letter that would make Liebowitz's blood boil: *"It is our desire that commencing with the SUPERMAN release we next submit, we receive $15 per page* [italic text here is underlined in the original letter]," Siegel demanded. "But the strongest reason we want $15 per page on SUPERMAN at once is because we believe it deserves it inasmuch as the strip is instrumental in the satisfactory sale of ACTION COMICS. . . . We are certain that you will find this rate for the SUPERMAN pages upon which we insist, completely reasonable when you consider SUPERMAN's worth. Awaiting your prompt reply."

Liebowitz received the letter while working with Gaines on final details of Siegel's option-period proposal. Two days later Siegel got a "prompt reply," which included three copies each of the McClure and DC contracts for Jerry's and Joe's signatures. By the third paragraph of his cover letter, Jack got down to the pay raise.

"Frankly, when I got through reading [your letter], it took my breath away. I did not anticipate that when I asked you to come to New York to discuss this matter of newspaper syndication, that you would want to take advantage of this visit and try to boost your price on 'Superman.' . . . Where you got the idea that anyone was receiving $15 a page I'd like to know." Artists usually got $6 a page, so they were already getting more than anyone, Liebowitz explained. Publishing *Action Comics* #1 was "a tremendous gamble involving many thousands of dollars. . . . You took no such gamble. . . . When 'Superman' reaches the same popularity as Dick Tracy, Orphan Annie, Skippy, Mutt & Jeff and dozens of other topnotch [newspaper strip] features, you will be in a position to ask for more money—and we will be more than happy to compensate you accordingly."

Liebowitz downplayed the *Action* poll cited by Siegel:

Don't forget that there are 64 pages in the magazine and that there isn't any magazine being published today that can sell on the basis of any one feature. . . . As a matter of fact, we have today opened the other mail on the poll. . . . 25% indicated "Zatara" to be their favorite feature, 20% like "Pep Morgan," 15% like "Tex Thomson" and only 30% have designated "Superman" as their favorite, the balance being scattered among the other features in the magazine, so come off your high horse.

Is it possible that because we treated you like a human being you suddenly got a swell head? . . . We were trying to give you, an inexperienced young man, the benefit of our experience and good will, in order that you get ahead in your ambition to become somebody in the comic field.

Liebowitz *again* warned, "Also bear in mind, that we own the feature 'Superman' and that we can at any time replace you in the drawing of that feature and that without our consent this feature would not be in syndication and therefore you would be the loser in the entire transaction."[6]

It was a chastened Siegel that mailed back signed contracts, along with a "Dear Jack" cover letter on another of his personal letterheads, "The Siegel-Shuster School of Humor . . . How to Be Funny . . . Laugh as You Learn."

"Thanks for your long detailed letter in which you explained many things to our complete satisfaction," Siegel began. "My previous letter was evidently written under a misunderstanding. You see, we had absolutely no idea what you were paying for other features. . . . Your information that we are already receiving $4.00 and $3.00 more per page than other contributors gives us the proper perspective. As I've mentioned before, Joe and I appreciate (especially after having worked for Nicholson) that we are getting a good deal from Detective Comics, Inc. Your payments are prompt, your handling friendly and courteous—and who could ask for anything more! . . . Joe and I are anxious and ready to do our best on SUPERMAN so that all parties concerned will profit. And we still wear the same size hats."[7]

But even in the poll Liebowitz cited, Superman placed first in a crowded field—and it wasn't Zatara or Pep Morgan that was the first comic book character to cross into the rarefied medium of newspaper syndication. Liebowitz's comment that publishing *Action Comics* #1 was "a tremendous gamble involving many thousands of dollars," and that Siegel and Shuster had taken "no such gamble," foreshadowed legal precedent by which publishers would claim ownership over "works for hire."

The unflappable Siegel remained in go-getter mode. Taking advantage of the DC contract option clause, he served up *Superboy* on November 30, 1938. His synopsis explained the feature "would relate the adventures of Superman as a youth. . . . I'd like the strip to have a large number of pages, such as thirteen so that I could develop it as well as Superman. . . . There'd be lots of humor, action, and the characters would be mainly children of about 12-years rather than adults." There was eagerness and pride in handing Donenfeld and Liebowitz another sure-fire hit, exclusive rights included: "Also, inasmuch as this strip will probably be used as a newspaper feature, I should think that you would want to own all rights to it by having it first appear in your magazine." Detective Comics officially passed on December 2, 1938. But *Superboy* was Siegel's passion project and he submitted it again in December 1940, this time with a complete script. DC again declined.[8]

"COMICS WERE BEGINNING TO LOOK LIKE A WINNER"

By the time *Action* #11 appeared, 472,000 copies were distributed, with projected sales of over 350,000.[9] In a last nod to its anthology format, the cover of *Action* #12 featured *Zatara*, with the notice, "This month and every month: Superman." The cover included a

Superman had only been published for four years when Lois Lane took readers down memory lane. Building on her romantic infatuation with Superman, writer Jerry Siegel has her reportorial instincts wondering if newspaper colleague Clark Kent and Superman are one and the same.

"MAN OR SUPERMAN?," *SUPERMAN* #17 (JULY/AUGUST 1942), P. 5, PENCIL ART BY JOE SHUSTER, INKS BY JOHN SIKELA.

logo of the *Action* #1 image of the hero expanding his chest and busting his chains. By *Action* #16, the chain-busting emblem was a fixture on the cover's upper left corner, the better to spot the title when overlaid by magazines on crowded newsstands. By *Action* #19, Superman became the title's sole cover subject.

Superman's mythology began expanding with the first newspaper strip on January 16, 1939, in the *Houston Chronicle*. Superman's home planet was identified as Krypton, a world of "beings which represent the human race at its ultimate peak of human development!" In Superman's *Action* #1 origin, his father was "a scientist" and his mother wasn't mentioned; the inaugural strip introduced Jor-L, Krypton's greatest scientist, sprinting faster than an express train, leaping to the balcony of his home where his wife, Lora, lay in bed with their newborn son—Kal-L.

Across nine daily strips Jor-L realizes Krypton's end is near, but the ruling council rejects his proposal for "an ark of space." Jor-L builds a small prototype spacecraft, but planet-cracking tremors begin before his test launch to the optimum world, Earth. By the tenth strip, moments before Krypton explodes, Kal-L's brave parents launch their child in the rocket ship. The spacecraft safely lands on Earth and a "passing motorist" delivers the child to an orphanage. As in *Action* #1, the astounding discovery of a child in an alien spacecraft apparently goes unreported.[10]

M. C. Gaines and Sheldon Mayer, with their insider view of the Superman phenomenon, decided to organize their own comics publishing company—and Donenfeld wanted in. "Comics were beginning to look like a winner to Harry Donenfeld," writes Paul Levitz, future DC editor, president, and publisher, in his seventy-fifth-anniversary history of the company. "But rather than increase his risks with unproven titles, he made a deal just to distribute a new line that Gaines and Mayer were launching from downtown offices at 225 Lafayette Street. He would market these with his titles, help with contracts and printing, and in return he convinced Gaines to take in Liebowitz as a partner. Liebowitz's eye for business detail would balance Gaines's entrepreneurial energy, and the still very young Mayer was there to provide a singular editorial viewpoint."[11]

Gaines named his line All-American Comics, after its first magazine, *All-American Comics*, an anthology whose first issue, cover-dated April 1939, did not feature superheroes but included *Scribbly*, Mayer's feature about a young cartoonist, daring young aviator *Hop Harrigan*, and *Mutt & Jeff* strip reprints. Liebowitz retained his position at DC and stewardship of Superman. Donenfeld, with his penchant for shadow companies, maintained All-American was a separate company, an illusion helped by DC's offices being in bustling midtown, while All-American was downtown, near Little Italy and Chinatown.

LOOKING FOR A HERO

In early 1939 the only arguably "super" characters other than Superman were the Arrow, first appearing in Centaur Publications' *Funny Pages* #21 (September 1938), and DC's Crimson Avenger, which debuted in *Detective Comics* #20 (October 1938). Editor Vin Sullivan wanted a new superhero that could do for *Detective* what Superman had done for *Action* and looked to the Crimson Avenger, a crime fighter in the pulp magazine tradition: he had no super powers, carried a gas gun, and wore a cape, eye mask, and floppy hat. Crimson Avenger got a cover shot on *Detective* #22 but failed to stir the kids.

Sullivan turned to other creators, including Robert Kahn, an ambitious young man from the Bronx, who, like many Golden Age creators growing up in New York, graduated from DeWitt Clinton High School. Kahn changed his Jewish last name to Kane when he began submitting cartoon fillers to DC in 1936. He since teamed with Bill Finger, fellow DeWitt grad and aspiring writer, who at twenty-four was a few years older.

In 1938 Kane and Finger sold *Rusty and His Pals* and *Clip Carson* to DC, but this was no second coming of Siegel and

Shuster—Kane's byline alone adorned *Rusty* and *Clip*. "Kane was not by nature a collaborator," writes DC historian Martin Pasko. "He dreamed of being considered an auteur, but one who employed anonymous assistants—called 'ghosts'—with whom no glory need be shared, just as his heroes Caniff and Al Capp, did."

Kane signed his comics "Rob't Kane," but by the third appearance of the new character he created with Finger, he began using "B◯B," swiping the artfully designed signature style that Milton Caniff applied to *Terry and the Pirates*—a box enclosing "MILTON CANIFF"—with a box around his own name and the same exaggerated "◯" in "B◯B."[12]

Thankfully, Kane showed Finger his initial sketches for "Bird-Man"—a hero with mechanical wings suited in red, orange, and yellow. Bird-Man "just didn't feel right," Finger recalled.

The writer suggested something menacing—how about a bat?[13]

CHAPTER 4

SHADOW REALM

The "Bat-Man," a mysterious and adventurous figure, fighting for righteousness and apprehending the wrong doer, in his lone battle against the evil forces of society. . . . His identity remains unknown.

Opening caption, *Batman*'s debut, "The Case of the Chemical Syndicate," *Detective Comics* #27 (May 1939)

DARK AVENGERS

Bob Kane's artwork for the cover of *Detective* #27 was an acrobatic contrast to Superman's car-lifting cover feat: two criminals on a rooftop watch a figure costumed in black, wearing a mask and a bat-eared cowl, swoop in, his black cape spreading like wings as his right arm grips a silken cord impossibly tethered in space, his left arm curled around the neck of his criminal prey.

Mystery surrounded Batman. In the first story, it is not until the last panel that the masked crime fighter is revealed as wealthy young Bruce Wayne, whose earlier appearance as a bored socialite conceals the grim vigilante within. There was a crystalline duality between Superman and Batman, starting with the latter having no super powers. If Superman didn't need a mask and worked normal daylight hours, "The Bat-Man," as first called, was an "eerie figure of the night" that stuck to the shadows and played as rough as the underworld evildoers he hunted. Superman was the true identity and Clark Kent the disguise; Batman was the masked persona that allowed wealthy Bruce Wayne the freedom to wage his war on crime.

Batman's Gotham City was darker than Superman's sunlit

Metropolis, as DC writer and editor Denny O'Neil once described: "My standard definition of Gotham City is, it's New York below Fourteenth Street after eleven o'clock at night. Recognizably New York, but with emphasis on the grimmer aspects of the city."[1] As writer and cartoonist Jules Feiffer cinematically put it, Batman's world "managed to get that Warner Brothers' fog-infested look."[2]

DC historian Martin Pasko credits Finger with keeping Kane on track "design element by design element, with Finger repeatedly resisting Kane's initial ideas and suggesting alternatives, until they arrived at Batman with his bat-eared cowl and mask, scalloped bat-wing cape, and finned gauntlets. From Superman . . . they borrowed the chest emblem conceit, and from Doc Savage they took the Utility Belt gimmick."[3] Finger even suggested a *Phantom* touch—leave the eyes behind the mask an eerie, inscrutable blank.[4]

Of Batman's manifold influences, the greatest was the Shadow, the first pulp "superhero," a mysterious crime fighter with mystical powers and physical prowess who dispensed justice with his twin automatics. By the time of Batman's creation, the Shadow was a multimedia star. Bill Finger acknowledged, "I patterned my style of writing after The Shadow."[5]

The Shadow began as the narrator introducing Street & Smith's radio drama *Detective Story Hour*, which was first broadcast on July 31, 1930. Many listeners felt a chill hearing the voice utter, with maniacal laughter, "Who knows what evil lurks in the hearts of men? The Shadow knows!" Series writer Harry Charlot christened the mysterious host "The Shadow," played for five years by Frank Readick Jr.[6] "The voice caught on, and Street & Smith decided to protect their property from being 'borrowed' by copywriting the character in a magazine," James Steranko writes.[7]

In 1931 the ten-cent Street & Smith *Shadow* magazine gave form to the spectral voice thanks to painted covers and black-and-white interior art from Graves Gladney, George Rozen, Edd Cartier, Tom Lovell, Creig Flessel, and others. They conjured the Shadow as a tall, lean figure with piercing eyes and aquiline nose; he was cloaked in black and wore a black slouch hat. The strip's atmosphere was steeped in mystery and death, the pantheon of evil including exotic arch villain Shiwan Khan.

The pulp *Shadow* came to life through the imagination of main writer Walter Gibson, a former reporter who wrote books on true crime and magic, including one revealing the secrets of Houdini's greatest illusions. Gibson wrote under an alias, each issue's contents page noting: "From the Shadow's Private Annals as Told to Maxwell Grant." Gibson was a writing machine—ten years into the *Shadow*, he calculated having produced over ten million words across two hundred novels.[8]

The Shadow did for pulps what Superman would do for comic books, and the impact was as unexpected. *The Shadow* magazine was so successful Street & Smith took it from monthly to biweekly release. "The Shadow was going so good, it fooled hell out of everybody," recalled Gibson. Managing editor "[Henry William] Ralston wanted to start another adventure magazine, but for a long time he didn't even have a title." The follow-up was Street & Smith's own Superman, Doc Savage.[9] (At DC the "Superman" came first, followed by the dark, mysterious crime fighter.)

By 1937 the Shadow returned to his native medium a fully realized character, first played by stage and radio actor-director-producer Orson Welles.[10] With Shadow adventures in the pulps and radio, the persona evolved. In the radio dramas it was revealed the Shadow had the power "to cloud men's minds, so they could not see him," the perfect figment of the imagination for the aural medium.

"Batman inherited The Shadow's world of dark alleys, rooftop skylights, secret passages, death traps and chiaroscuro, as superbly visualized by Tom Lovell and Edd Cartier in *The Shadow Magazine*," Batman artist Jerry Robinson recalled. "It's understandable that Bob and Bill looked toward The Shadow when called upon to create a new hero after the runaway success of Siegel and Shuster's *Superman*. . . . The Shadow had revitalized the publishing world in 1931 by reviving the long-dormant single-hero format that mushroomed with the arrival of

The Shadow, star of radio and pulp magazines in the early 1930s, influenced the comic book superheroes to come, particularly Batman. The "Face of Doom" shown here has even been credited with inspiring Batman's nemesis, Two-Face.

THE SHADOW (MARCH 15, 1938), STREET & SMITH PUBLICATIONS.

comic books. . . . Walter Gibson's Shadow novels had laid much of the groundwork for comic book superheroes."[11]

BLACK BAT

"The Bat-Man" launched in *Detective* #27 (May 1939) in "The Case of the Chemical Syndicate." The six-page tale of murders connected with Apex Chemical Corporation opened with Bat-Man atop a rooftop, silhouetted against a bright harvest moon. The tale, set in an unnamed city, introduced Police Commissioner Gordon and his friend, socialite Bruce Wayne. At the conclusion a Bat-Man punch knocks the villain, screaming, into an acid tank. "A fitting end for his kind," the crime fighter observes. *Shadow* experts Anthony Tollin and Will Murray argue Finger's story was inspired—Tollin says "lifted"—from "Partners of Peril," a 1936 *Shadow* magazine adventure written by Gibson pinch-hitter Theodore Tinsley. "Finger did not simply draw inspiration from this thunderous tale, he adapted it outright!" Murray writes. "It's the same story, same death trap [the acid tank]."

"'Partners of Peril' is the smoking gun that proves the Shadow/Batman connection," Tollin adds. "It also raises questions about Bob Kane's actual contribution to Batman's creation." Tollin notes that Finger provided most of the creative touches informing Batman, arguing that even Kane's contention that Douglas Fairbanks's adventure film *The Mark of Zorro* (1920) influenced him might actually have been spurred by Finger, who kept an extensive archive of images, often attaching the appropriate visual reference to one of his scripts for an artist, and had possibly done so with images of Fairbanks—the swashbuckling actor that also inspired Joe Shuster—as the daring, masked Zorro.

"Writing for comics is a difficult job," Bill Finger once explained. "You have to describe a scene so completely that the artist knows exactly or as nearly as possible what to draw." Did "Partners of Peril" also inspire Finger's creation of Commissioner Gordon and his friendship with "his young socialite friend"? Early in that *Shadow* story, a wealthy idler named Lamont Cranston visits Police Commissioner Ralph Weston. "The two were excellent friends," the story explains, "although never for a moment had Weston ever suspected that this tall, well-groomed clubman with the pleasant smile and rather piercing eyes was, in fact, the grim avenger of crime that police and crooks alike knew only by the grim pseudonym of The Shadow."

As the two attackers rushed again, the Black Bat sent one of them reeling backward (CHAP. VI)
19

Only a few weeks separated *Batman*'s debut from that of the pulps' Black Bat—the characters were so similar that if the timeline were reversed, Bob Kane admits he probably would have abandoned his Gotham crimefighter. In this interior illustration, the Black Bat takes on two attackers.

"THE WHITE WITCH," *BLACK BOOK DETECTIVE* #2, VOL. 18 (SPRING 1944), P. 19.

"I'm astounded to learn how much Bill's first Batman script borrowed from that novel," adds Jerry Robinson. "Bob and Bill had no idea of Batman's future popularity when they rushed out that first story. Given the ephemeral nature of pulp fiction, I'm sure they never expected their first Batman story to be traced back to a two-and-a-half-year-old pulp thriller."

Street & Smith apparently raised no objections about the lifting of the *Shadow* story line, but a legal threat did emerge with the appearance of Black Bat, a crime fighter that first appeared in the July 1939 issue of *Black Book Detective*, a pulp magazine from Better Publications (also called a "Thrilling Publication"). The Black Bat wore a black guise with a cloak that unfurled like wings, striking fear in criminals, just like Batman, and he fought crime by any means necessary, as did Batman. Both were loners, each was hailed as a "Nemesis of Crime," and each even appeared in a "Detective" magazine.[12]

Kane claimed he never knew of Batman's pulp doppelganger, but if the Black Bat had been published first, "I would have been forced to scrap my new creation and literally go back to the drawing board for an entirely different concept," he wrote. "A scant sixty days made the difference between Batman's becoming a new superstar in comics and being consigned to oblivion."[13]

Both publishers were preparing to sue, but Whit Ellsworth, a former writer for Better Publications, returned to DC in time to help avert a lawsuit (and eventually establish moral guidelines that Batman never kill or even carry a gun). The agreement included respecting each other's turf—Black Bat would stay out of comic books; Batman would steer clear of the pulps.[14]

THE LEGEND OF THE BATMAN

When Kane met with Donenfeld about the usual boilerplate contract, he enlisted his father's help to actually negotiate terms. Will Eisner, a DeWitt Clinton classmate, recalled his ambitious colleague seizing his main chance. "I was at [Kane's] house in the Bronx the day he went down with his father to sign the first contract for Batman," Eisner said. "We both dreamed of careers. Bob dreamed of theatrical-type success. I wasn't so sure comics wasn't a stopover. It was very surprising when Bob did Batman. We had talked about doing this mysterious thing. My judgment was he was responding to a market, a need, and he turned his hand to it—we had both grown up with the Saturday adventure serials."[15]

Batman was a hit, and DC wasn't shy about featuring him. After *Detective* #27 every succeeding cover featured either Batman, an iconic "The Batman" head-shot logo, or a notice: "Another thrilling episode of The Batman in this issue." It wasn't until *Detective* #33 (November 1939), the issue in which Batman became the permanent cover subject, that Bill Finger's origin story appeared without credit, a tight, two-page, twelve-panel noir masterpiece, "Legend: The Batman and How He Came to Be!" Finger's story innocently but ominously opens: "Some fifteen years ago. Thomas Wayne, his wife, and son, were walking home from a movie."

A gun-toting crook appears, demands Mrs. Wayne's necklace, and as Thomas Wayne tries to protect her, fires twice. The murderer vanishes into the night, leaving Bruce alone with his dead parents sprawled on the sidewalk. The boy swears an oath to avenge their deaths by dedicating his life to a war on criminals. His father's estate leaves him wealthy, allowing Bruce to grow into adulthood training his mind in order to become a "master scientist" and developing his body "to physical perfection." He is ready but needs a disguise. One night in his lonely mansion, pondering his destiny in front of a crackling fireplace, Wayne mutters, "Criminals are a superstitious, cowardly lot. So my disguise must be able to strike terror into their hearts. I must be a creature of the night, black, terrible, a . . . a . . ." And a black bat flew in through an open window.

The secret of Bruce Wayne's motivation to become Batman was Finger's final piece of a creative puzzle that, once in place, made the masked crime fighter an enduring figure of popular fiction. Bruce's loss spoke to the deepest fears of readers who were about the same age as Bruce himself. Superman and the costumed do-gooders yet to come happily served justice, often for no discernable reason. In contrast, Bruce's motivation to fight crime was intensely personal and psychologically complex. But with returning editor Ellsworth ordering that Batman be disarmed, the grim vigilante became a wisecracking crime fighter, particularly when he began sharing adventures with Robin, the Boy Wonder (secretly Bruce's young ward, Dick Grayson). The psychological damage of his parent's murder—the compulsion to dress like a bat to execute endless vengeance—was kept in the shadows, like a terrible family secret. It would be up to future creators to fathom the tortured character's emotional depths.

But Kane gave the brush to his talented collaborator, who settled for anonymity and the page rate. Michael Uslan reflected on *why* Bill Finger seemed to accept his anonymity: "In my teens I met so many comic book writers and artists, and what I absorbed was that most of them were very quiet people. They spent their lives isolated, working at easels, cubicles, at their homes. The point is, it would have been an anomaly for a writer or artist from the pulps or comics to make demands, or even concern themselves with getting a credit."[16]

There were rumors about Kane's big contract, but Will Eisner maintained that Kane only got a promise of work and a hefty page rate—Kane's killer Batman deal came later.[17] Eisner had no illusions about comics.

> Publishers could start a comic easy if they could get a distributor who would then sell to the newsstands. . . . Distributing has always been a rough game. It was real gangster stuff. I remember once when I was selling newspapers on Wall Street during the mid-1930s. . . . At three in the afternoon a truck would roll by, and packages of papers would be kicked off to all of us who were waiting for our quota. Out of the truck would also come a route man. On his finger was a ring that had a half-moon-shaped claw or hook on it so you could cut the rope that tied the papers together. Occasionally two distributors would show up at the same corner at the same time, and there'd be a fight. I once saw one guy cut another pretty good with this hook.[18]

Will Eisner was a native New Yorker whose Jewish immigrant father, a backdrop painter for the thriving Yiddish theaters, encouraged his son's talent for drawing and storytelling. In 1937 Eisner was twenty years old and contributing cartoons to *Wow! What a Magazine*. When it folded Eisner and the magazine's editor, Jerry Iger, formed one of the early comic book packaging companies, renting studio space in a building on 40th Street catering

Bill Finger's taut tale of how Batman came to be provided a psychological reason for Bruce Wayne's war on crime. The origin story first appeared in *Detective Comics* #33 but was re-presented with the "Legend of the Batman" background in the debut of the crimefighter's solo title.

"THE LEGEND OF THE BATMAN," *BATMAN* #1 (SPRING 1940), ART BY BOB KANE.

THE BOY'S EYES ARE WIDE WITH TERROR AND SHOCK AS THE HORRIBLE SCENE IS SPREAD BEFORE HIM.

FATHER.. MOTHER!

...DEAD! THEY'RE D..DEAD

DAYS LATER A CURIOUS AND STRANGE SCENE TAKES PLACE.

AND I SWEAR BY THE SPIRITS OF MY PARENTS TO AVENGE THEIR DEATHS BY SPENDING THE REST OF MY LIFE WARRING ON ALL CRIMINALS

AS THE YEARS PASS BRUCE WAYNE PREPARES HIMSELF FOR HIS CAREER. HE BECOMES A MASTER SCIENTIST.

TRAINS HIS BODY TO PHYSICAL PERFECTION UNTIL HE IS ABLE TO PERFORM AMAZING ATHLETIC FEATS.

DAD'S ESTATE LEFT ME WEALTHY. I AM READY.. BUT FIRST I MUST HAVE A DISGUISE.

CRIMINALS ARE A SUPERSTITIOUS COWARDLY LOT, SO MY DISGUISE MUST BE ABLE TO STRIKE TERROR INTO THEIR HEARTS. I MUST BE A CREATURE OF THE NIGHT, BLACK, TERRIBLE.. A A.

.. AS IF IN ANSWER, A HUGE BAT FLIES IN THE OPEN WINDOW!

A BAT! THAT'S IT! IT'S AN OMEN.. I SHALL BECOME A BAT!

AND THUS IS BORN THIS WEIRD FIGURE OF THE DARK.. THIS AVENGER OF EVIL. 'THE BATMAN

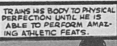

to bookies and "fly-by-night operators," Eisner said. He put up the money and got top billing: Eisner & Iger.[19]

WILL EISNER MEETS VICTOR FOX

Late in 1938 a short, bald, cigar-chomping figure with outsized ambitions visited Eisner & Iger. Victor S. Fox, head of Bruns Publications, had dreamed up a Superman clone called Wonder Man and asked Will Eisner to do it. Eisner was dubious. Wonder Man seemed too close to Superman—how would DC react? Iger wasn't worried, and Fox was paying them well.

The legend of Victor Fox says he was a DC bookkeeper who saw the *Action* #1 sales figures, went to lunch, and never came back, leaving to be first to cash in on the phenomenon with his own superhero line. The first part of the story certainly wasn't true, as Gerard Jones writes: "Fox never worked for Detective Comics. He was probably never a bookkeeper. He was an English-born Jew who had come to America at the end of the [first] world war and for twenty years hustled from one financial scam, racket, and dubious investment to another."[20]

Fox's Superman steal *was* a betrayal, but one more complicated and incestuous than that of a scheming employee. Fox had been welcome in Detective Comics' offices ever since Bruns began business in 1937, the same year as DC and at the same address, 480 Lexington Avenue—DC on the ninth floor, Bruns on the seventh. Donenfeld once had a 50 percent partnership interest in Bruns, and Fox was a client of Independent News, regularly visiting the distributor's office at 480 Lexington to check daily sales numbers for his periodical, *World Astrology Magazine*. There he took a keen interest in *Action* and Superman's role in its success. Liebowitz later testified that Fox "has had full and complete knowledge of the existence of *Action Comics* . . . [and] its principal feature 'Superman.'"

Around early March 1939, Victor Fox showed up at Liebowitz's office at about five P.M., sharing news that Bruns was ready to release a new comics magazine. "He said his magazine was going to contain the best features of comic magazines on the stands; it would have detective, adventure, action, fun," Liebowitz recalled. "I had no idea at the time, of course, that he was contemplating any [copyright infringement]."[21]

CHAPTER 5

SUPERMAN VERSUS WONDER MAN

The comic strip feature SUPERMAN is wholly original, displaying the fantastic and imaginative exploits of one Clark Kent, a man endowed with supernatural attributes. . . . While at times SUPERMAN is pictured as a person wearing ordinary clothes, his superhuman feats commence only with his shedding such normal clothes and his assuming the costume of a tight-fitting, acrobatic-appearing uniform with the letter "S" emblazoned on his chest.

JACK LIEBOWITZ
testifying to the mythical construct of
the first superhero, sworn deposition, in *DC v. Bruns*

WONDER COMICS #1

Jack Liebowitz didn't suspect what Victor Fox was up to until an advance copy of *Wonder Comics* #1 was brought to him on Wednesday, March 15, 1939. Liebowitz's informants reported "substantial quantities" had been printed, with Fox bypassing DC's Independent News and contracting with Kable News Company, Inc., and Interborough News Company to begin distribution that Friday, around the same release date as *Detective Comics* #27.

On the cover a blonde muscleman in a red leotard strode across the sky to a rooftop, his outstretched hand crushing the nose of a bomber flown by a Japanese pilot. (Japan had invaded China in 1937, and war rumors circulated in the Pacific.) The cover blurb read: "Every Month Featuring 14 Pages of the Daring, Superhuman Exploits of the Wonder Man: 64 pages of thrills in full color." Fox copied DC's sixty-four-page format, and if Superman's adventures featured an industry-leading thirteen pages, Wonder Man would go one page better. The visual language of Superman was so new—no one had seen a character lifting automobiles overhead, outrunning trains, having bullets harmlessly bounce off his body—that Liebowitz judged the cover a composite of covers from *Action* #7, featuring Superman suspended in space, and *Action* #10, showing an airborne Superman punching a fighter plane.

Wonder Man did not wear a cape or mask and was of earthly origin—a ring empowered him—but he was otherwise engineered from the Superman blueprint. Newspaper reporter Clark Kent was "meek"; Wonder Man's alter ego, radio engineer and inventor Fred Carson, was "timid." Like Superman, Carson went into action after stripping off his outer garments for a costume that included a "W" chest emblem. As with Superman, bullets harmlessly bounced off his body, and he didn't fly but could leap incredible distances. Superman was introduced as "Champion of the Oppressed" and the "Strongest Man on Earth"; Wonder Man was "Champion of the Oppressed" and the "Mightiest Human on Earth." The story itself seemed swiped from *Action* #2, wherein Superman intervenes to stop a foreign war.

The next day, March 16, Liebowitz gave a sworn deposition at the US District Court for the Southern District of New York requesting a temporary injunction halting the next day's scheduled distribution and sale of *Wonder Comics* #1, naming as defendants Bruns and distributors Kable and Interborough. Liebowitz declared that plaintiff DC "will be irreparably injured and it is impossible to estimate the amount of damage which plaintiff will suffer unless such restraint and injunction be immediately granted."

Liebowitz's deposition summed up the unique qualities of DC's star property: "The SUPERMAN is portrayed in feats of remarkable superhuman strength and speed. He is depicted as leaping from building to building, as running faster than trains, piercing the brick walls of buildings; SUPERMAN is impervious to bullets; crushes guns as if they were so much paper; SUPERMAN is presented as the 'Champion of the oppressed, the physical marvel who had sworn his existence to helping those in need.'"[1] Liebowitz accused Bruns of stealing these unique characteristics, even citing *Wonder Comics'* "superficial similarities" to *Action*—same trim size, page number, and features.

Liebowitz had rebuked Siegel's request for a raise because Superman had yet to prove more popular than comic strips like *Dick Tracy*. Now he claimed DC would be "irreparably injured" by this copycat character, asserting that Superman was a prized asset and star of *Action Comics*:

> Since the inception of the publication of said magazine the amount of copies printed and the sales thereof have steadily risen in volume. . . . [Superman] is by far the most popular and hence the most important comic strip feature in said magazine. In fact, the magazine while entitled "ACTION COMICS" has become known to its reading public as "SUPERMAN,". . . further concrete evidence of the importance of the "SUPERMAN" feature is the fact that under license from the plaintiff, the McClure Newspaper Syndicate . . . has for some time and is presently distributing for use in daily newspapers throughout the United States a "SUPERMAN" comic strip in serialized form. . . .
>
> It is clearly evident that defendant BRUNS PUBLICATIONS, INC., through Mr. Fox, has attempted and is attempting to make improper use of the knowledge it has obtained of plaintiff's magazine "ACTION COMICS" and of the copyrighted material in each issue thereof including of course the principal feature "SUPERMAN."[2]

Will Eisner's graphic novel became a thinly disguised account of how "Vince Reynard" (a.k.a. Victor Fox) directed Eisner to lie in court about their deal to create Wonder Man, a direct steal of Superman. In his foreword to *The Dreamer*, Eisner explained that his book "intended as a work of fiction, ultimately took on the shape of a historical account."

THE DREAMER, A GRAPHIC NOVELLA SET DURING THE DAWN OF COMIC BOOKS, BY WILL EISNER (KITCHEN SINK PRESS), P. 39.

The temporary injunction was *not* granted, and Wonder Man burst upon an unsuspecting world as scheduled. The distribution of 300,000 copies of *Wonder Comics* began on March 15–16, with final copies shipped on March 22.[3]

But DC swiftly got its day in court. Judge John M. Woolsey would hear the case, *Detective Comics, Inc., v. Bruns Publications*, in a nonjury trial on April 6. With the comic book industry centered in New York City, the US District Court for the Southern District of New York had jurisdiction and would arbitrate this and many superhero cases to come.

For Victor Fox to triumph, attorneys for Bruns and codefendants Kable News and Interborough News had to convince the judge that Wonder Man was Will Eisner's unique creation. The defendants would claim Wonder Man was created in January 1938, months before Superman's first appearance in *Action* #1, but in a super-stretching of credulity they would add they had *never heard* of Superman until DC's lawsuit. By the time the trial began, about thirteen issues of *Action* had been released, the "Superman at the World's Fair" story had appeared in *New York World's Fair Comics* #1, and *Superman* was in newspaper syndication.

Fox owed $3,000 in commissions to Eisner & Iger and used that as leverage. "[Fox] was a little Edward G. Robinson [gangster] type of a guy," Eisner recalled. "He looked me straight in the eye and said, 'Kid, you go into court and you tell them it was your idea. Try anything else and you will never see the money I owe you.'"[4]

SUPERHEROES ON TRIAL

The trial included the testimony of Jack Liebowitz, Jerry Siegel, Kable executive Warren Angel, Max Gaines, Sheldon Mayer, Harry Donenfeld, Victor Fox, and, of course, Iger and Eisner. In opening remarks DC attorney Horace S. Manges declared a potential licensing empire was at stake: "I wanted to get into the record the fact that there is a very serious license question that we are trying to protect and must protect. If these people plagiarize, of course we cannot keep up the license which is of immense value."

Bruns Publications' attorney Asher Blum countered that Will Eisner created and developed Wonder Man without knowledge of Superman and "induced the defendant Bruns Company to publish his material."[5] DC established that in January 1938 it decided to publish *Superman*, and as proof of ownership Manges offered into evidence the March 1, 1938, agreement granting Superman rights to DC and the check that included payment for that first story.

Siegel took the stand, explaining his job was to write the scripts, which included directing the artwork. In less than a year Superman was so popular they needed additional artists, with the "apprentice" making rough sketches that Shuster completed. When Bruns attorney Blum accused Superman creators of copying King Features' costumed hero the Phantom, Siegel replied that he submitted *Superman* to King Features long before he saw *The Phantom*—in other words, *Phantom* might have been swiped from *Superman*.[6]

DC's attorney methodically established Fox's access from March 4, 1937, when Fox opened his office at 480 Lexington. Under friendly questioning, Liebowitz testified Fox saw *Action* sales numbers as a client of Independent News. Judge Woolsey jumped in: "Were they things that anybody could look at in the Independent News Company?" Liebowitz replied that Fox was anxious to know how his *World Astrology Magazine* was selling and described how every day sales figure cards for IND distributed magazines came in from across the county. "I might say that the *World Astrology Magazine* . . . sold around 33 percent of the total copies distributed and *Action Comics* enjoyed sales of 80 or 85 percent," he pointedly added.[7]

Max Gaines testified for the plaintiff as managing editor and co-owner of All-American Comics. He contradicted the defendants' contention they had no knowledge of Superman prior to the lawsuit, testifying that Iger came to his office in April 1938 and Gaines gave him copies of five comics he was working on, including *Action* #1. Sheldon Mayer, who personally pulled the titles from their files, corroborated Gaines' testimony. Jerry Iger stuck to the story that Wonder Man was created in January 1938. "We talked about a superhuman type of thing, a modern Samson idea," he testified.

Victor Fox went on the offensive, declaring that in January 1938 he shared a dummy copy of Bruns's *Kid Comics* with Donenfeld, which included Wonder Man. Not only had Superman been inspired by Wonder Man, Fox contended, but DC also stole other *Kid Comics* features for *Detective*, *More Fun*, and *Adventure Comics*.

When Donenfeld took the stand, Manges asked if Fox had submitted to him a dummy for *Kid Comics*. "No, sir," he replied. Did he submit a dummy with the Wonder Man concept? "No, sir." Donenfeld further testified he couldn't have met Fox in January— after a New Year's Day cruise to Havana, he'd stayed in Miami through early February.

All the while Wonder Man's "creator" agonized over whether to commit perjury or reveal that Fox instructed him to copy Superman.[8] The incident became part of comic book history: how Eisner testified their client *ordered* him to copy Superman, and a vengeful Fox refused to pay what he owed the shop. Eisner celebrated his courageous stand in *The Dreamer*, his 1986 autobiographical "graphic novella" of "The Dawn of Comic Books." But in 2010 the long-forgotten trial transcripts surfaced, revealing the truth—Eisner had *lied* under oath, testifying that Wonder Man *was* his creation and that he had presented concept sketches to Victor Fox in January 1938.

"And until you heard of this lawsuit, you, the creator of 'Wonder Man,' never read the strip 'Superman,' is that right?" DC attorney Manges pressed.

"That is true," Eisner answered.

"At any time did Mr. Fox suggest to you calling the figure 'Wonderman'?"

"No. It was my thought."[9]

Eisner's complicity didn't even swing the outcome. On April 13, 1939, almost a year after *Action* #1 hit the stands, and less than five days after testimony and plaintiff exhibits that included comparison panels showing Wonder Man swipes of Superman feats, Judge Woolsey ruled "infringement has been shown both texturally and pictorially. . . . The defendant could hardly have gone further than it has done." Woolsey declared a permanent injunction, forbidding Bruns from publishing Wonder Man and allowing DC to recover all court costs and $1,500 in damages from the defendant. Codefendants Kable and Interborough were ruled "secondarily liable" in case Bruns couldn't pay.[10]

Fox immediately appealed.

After the trial Eisner & Iger continued contributing to Fox publications—circumstantial evidence that Eisner went along with Fox's duplicity. With Wonder Man in limbo pending appeal, the third issue of *Wonder Comics* became *Wonderworld Comics*, for which Eisner and artist Lou Fine created the Flame, a superhero with the mystical ability to control fire and temperature. And, decades later, Eisner loved recounting how Eisner & Iger passed on offerings from two young guys from Cleveland—one was *Spy*, the other *Superman*.

"The one inarguable truth . . . is that nearly every name on the witness list had a lasting effect on the history of the industry," historian Ken Quattro notes in a retrospective article on the trial. "All were present in the nascent years of a new medium, and chances are that none of them knew at the time that it would evolve into an art form. This was a business—the lowest end of the publishing industry. . . . From our perspective, it's hard to separate the legends that surround these men and the fact that they were only men—susceptible to pressure, to telling half-truths, to blatant lying. No better, nor worse, nor different than anyone else. Just men. Not a Superman among them."[11]

Eisner wasn't around to respond to the resurfaced trial transcripts, having passed away five years before they came to light. In his foreword to *The Dreamer*, Eisner explains that his account of the Golden Age "comes out of the cluttered closet where I store ghosts of the past, and from the yellowing memories of my experience."[12] Perhaps he was haunted by the moral compromise of his youth and erased his memory of it. Decades later he had become a giant in the industry—the comic industry's annual honors for excellence are called the Eisner Awards—so he might have been spinning revisionist history. Eisner might even have embraced the old adage about printing the legend, not the facts—*The Dreamer* presented the legend of the unscrupulous bookkeeper's betrayal.

One consequence of the trial was that Siegel absorbed details of his character's "immense value," which didn't allay his growing anxiety over having signed him away. Still, he remained eager to please. In 1941 science-fiction publishing pioneer Hugo Gernsback wrote him regarding his proposed character Superboy. Siegel reported to Liebowitz: "As far as the title, SUPERBOY, is concerned if our strip is ever released it could be called SUPERKID. But it wouldn't hurt for you to caution Mr. Gernsback what he can expect if his SUPERBOY ever infringes on SUPERMAN in any way."[13] (Gernsback's idea appears to have gone no further.)

On May 18, 1939, perhaps as a reward to Siegel for his testimony, DC copyrighted the bylines running on every Superman story since *Action* #1: "by Jerome Siegel and Joe Shuster." ("Jerome" soon become "Jerry.")[14] It was not largesse—the September 22, 1938, contract gave DC the right to copyright their property "in our name or in the names of the parties designated by us."

Fox continued his comics line and, like many publishers, began hiring in-house artists and writers instead of farming out work. One young artist at Fox Comics was Jacob Kurtzberg, a fearless, two-fisted scrapper from the Lower East Side. The artist, who became famous as Jack Kirby, described how Fox would lean back in his office chair, a big cigar in his mouth, exulting, "I'm the king of comics!"

"Victor Fox was a character," Kirby reflected. "We would watch him, and of course we would smile because he was a genuine type. . . . I don't think Fox sharked any of the people who worked with me. We were small fish to Fox. He was a man with big ambitions. . . . We turned out the amount of pages he wanted, and he'd publish them. Like most of the fellows we got along fine. I couldn't picture myself liking a guy like Fox, but I did. I genuinely liked Victor Fox."[15]

WONDER MAN DECISION

The year 1940 brought a precedent-setting ruling on the Wonder Man appeal to the Court of Appeals, 2nd Circuit, in New York. Fox's lawyers argued Superman was based on public-domain characters from myth and literature, such as Hercules, and did not enjoy copyright protection. Circuit Judge Augustus N. Hand, in his April 29 decision, wrote, "Complainant [DC] is not entitled to a monopoly of the mere character of a 'Superman' who is a blessing to mankind." However, Superman was not "a mere delineation of a benevolent Hercules" but "an arrangement of incidents and literary expressions original with the author" making them "proper subjects of copyright and susceptible of infringement."

Judge Hand ruled that infringement "is amply substantiated." Hand, clearly amused, added:

> But if the author of "Superman" has portrayed a comic Hercules, yet if his production involves more than the presentation of a general type he may copyright it and say of it: "A poor thing but mine own." Perhaps the periodicals of the complainant are foolish rather than comic, but they embody an original arrangement of incidents and a pictorial and literary form which preclude the contention that Bruns was not copying the antics of "Superman" portrayed in "Action Comics." We think it plain that the defendants have used more than general

types and ideas and have appropriated the pictorial and literary details embodied in the complainant's copyrights.[16]

An emboldened Liebowitz surveyed the industry for Superman infringement. "In several instances we had our attorneys proceed, and in one instance I know we had a consent decree and in other instances the attorneys for these people we complained of agreed to desist," he recalled.[17]

Rival publishers were now aware there was big money to be made with a Superman-like hero, but they had to enter the field with more grace and ingenuity than shown by Fox's brazen swipe, particularly as many were clients of DC's Independent News. But the backwater pulp enterprise was ready to go big time. The superhero gold rush of 1939 included Fawcett Publications, Inc., a Minnesota company that published *Mechanix Illustrated*, *Popular Mechanics*, and other periodicals. Fawcett relocated to New York to begin its comics line, setting up editorial offices in the Paramount Building at Broadway and 43rd.

"The immediate and enormous success of Superman called for the creation of a tribe of successors—but where were they to come from?" writes cartoonist Jules Feiffer, who got his start with his mentor, Will Eisner. "Not from other planets; Superman had all other planets tied up legally. . . . The answer, then, rested with science. . . . Science had run amuck—setting loose a menagerie of flying men, webbed men, robot men, ghost men, minuscule men, flexible-sized men, men of all shapes and costumes blackening the comic book skies like locusts in drag."

"Understandably," Feiffer added, "this Pandora's box of men-of-steel was viewed gravely by the Superman people."[18]

CHAPTER 6

THE FIRST GENERATION

We live in a world of fantasy.

LLOYD JACQUET

comics packager, in 1939 conversation with Joe Simon

PILGRIMAGE

Joe Simon grew up in Rochester, New York, the son of Harry Simon, a tailor and Jewish immigrant from England. Joe broke into the newspaper business as a teenager and was a daily deadline renaissance man: sports writing and cartooning, courtroom drawing, fiction and spot illustrating, photography, and photographic retouching. Despite the Depression, the growth of commercial radio broadcasting began draining newspapers of advertising revenue. Although corporations would build synergistic multimedia companies, at the outset print media was so afraid of broadcast media it mounted a brief "War on Radio."[1] Simon became collateral damage—the *Syracuse Journal-Telegram*, where he worked, lost so much ad revenue to radio the newspaper folded in 1937.

Joe Simon was out of a job, but he was only twenty-three years old and eager for adventure. Beguiled by the legend of New York City, he decided to follow the Hudson River to

the land of Damon Runyon and his rogue band of characters residing along Broadway's Great White Way. . . . When I neared the end of my pilgrimage, Manhattan came into sight with the

Empire State Building and the Chrysler Building, both of them new, shining in the distance. As far as I was concerned it was a dream come true.... New York was my Mecca. I wasn't going to give up until they *carried* me out.[2]

FUNNIES, INC.

Simon's first stop was the *New York Journal-American*, flagship paper for William Randolph Hearst's media empire. Simon was recommended to Paramount Pictures and got a job retouching publicity stills at the Paramount Building. After a year he moved to the art department of MacFadden Publications, a line that went back to the first science-fiction magazine, Hugo Gernsback's *Amazing Stories*, and that now included *True Story*, *True Detective*, *True Romances*, and *Photoplay*.[3]

One day in 1939 MacFadden art director Harlan Crandall called Simon into his office. "There's a new business that's starting to use a lot of artists," said Crandall, adding that it seemed tailor-made for Joe. "It's called comic books."[4] Crandall's friend, Lloyd Jacquet, a veteran of Malcolm Wheeler-Nicholson's National Allied Publications ran Funnies, Inc., a packager of comic book features. Simon made an appointment to meet Jacquet.

It was after five in the evening when Simon, samples in hand, arrived at the Funnies address at a rundown building on 45th, off Times Square. He walked up a worn flight of stairs, down a dimly lit hallway, and entered a large room with a big table crowded with artists and covered with artwork and art supplies. In one corner a tough-looking young guy was pounding the keys of a battered Underwood. He introduced himself as Mickey Spillane.

Joe noticed an artist at the big table using a brush to ink pencil art for something called "The Human Torch." The guy looked about Joe's age, and, as he inked, his glasses kept sliding down his nose and he kept pushing them up.

"Where did you get the idea for the Human Torch?" Simon

asked. Slightly irritated, the artist ignored him. Simon repeated his question.

"Where did you get that suit?" snapped Carl Burgos, the Torch's creator.

"You Simon?" asked a man who strode in with an air of command. It was Lloyd Jacquet, a fortyish World War I veteran dressed in English tweeds, a gray-checkered vest, and black shoes polished to gleaming.

Jacquet ran his company while holding a "day job" at the McClure Syndicate. He had been art director at Centaur Publications where he worked with young artist Bill Everett on a character called Amazing-Man. Before setting up his studio, Jacquet published Everett's creation, *Namor the Sub-Mariner*, a sea-dwelling super being, for *Motion Picture Funnies Weekly*, a movie theater giveaway. Funnies, Inc., was now producing *Sub-Mariner*, *Human Torch*, and other superhero series for the first comics title from a new outfit getting into the comics superhero business—pulp publisher Martin Goodman's Timely Comics. Jacquet assigned Simon a story at what he learned was "the universal price" of $7 a page, payable upon publication.

As Simon left Jacquet's office and passed though the outer room, he heard someone at the table call out: "Nice suit." It was Carl Burgos.[5]

Simon recalled his first comic book job was penciling and inking a six-page *Ranch Dude* story for *Amazing-Man Comics*. He was used to being a salaried newspaper employee with a daily deadline turnaround and had not realized his "completed" pages next went to a colorist, photo engraver, and printer, followed by shipping and distribution. It took *months* to get a freelance check.[6] But Simon's fortunes in 1939 held more than freelance assignments. Martin Goodman, who wanted to bypass packagers and develop titles in-house, would hire Joe as Timely's first editor.

Before that, Simon had a stint at Fox Comics. The roguish charm of the "King of Comics" was lost on him, but there he met Jack Kirby, the creative partner who would work alongside him at

Timely. They were a perfect team and a study in contrasts: Joe was tall, lean, broad-shouldered, already a newspaper veteran; Jack was short, husky, had run with a street gang in his youth, and had experience as an "in-betweener" animator at the Max Fleischer Studio near Times Square, a factory-like grind he was happy to be rid of.

"Jack was just a bullpen guy at Fox Comics," explains Steve Saffel, a New York book editor and close friend of Simon in his later years. "It was Joe who recognized Jack's innate talent. After the Wonder Man lawsuit, Eisner & Iger kept packaging and selling stuff to Fox Comics. But Eisner had also been acting as the in-house editor at Fox, and he left that position, and that's what opened up the slot Joe moved into. So, the first big legal battle in the comic book industry led to the creation of the Simon and Kirby team. I think Joe was the one Martin Goodman wanted, but Joe's attitude was, 'We come as a team.' I think Kirby was a little reluctant because he was worried about losing his salaried job at Fox." (Simon later said that he and Jack, children of the Depression, knew the value of a job.)[7]

TIMELY HEROES

Martin Goodman, a Brooklyn native and child of Lithuanian Jewish immigrants, had many companies—shades of Donenfeld!—including Western Fiction Publishing Co., Inc., with editorial offices in the RKO Building at Radio City. Western's titles included the science-fiction pulp *Marvel Science Stories*, which was later shortened to *Marvel Stories*. Goodman used the "Marvel" appellation, even duplicated the graphic lettering, for the first title from Timely Comics, headquartered at the McGraw Hill Building at 330 West 42nd Street.

Marvel Comics #1 (October 1939), on newsstands by late summer, featured *The Angel, Masked Raider, Ka-Zar the Great*, and *Sub-Mariner. The Human Torch* was the cover feature, with cover

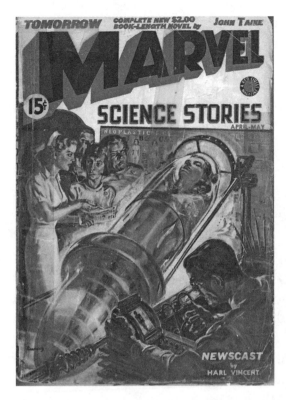

This dramatic *Marvel Science Stories* cover portrays "a beauty parlor of the future—A Mechanical Fountain of Youth." This 1939 pulp magazine appeared the same year publisher Martin Goodman began Timely Comics with *Marvel Comics* #1.

MARVEL SCIENCE STORIES, VOL. 1, #4 (APRIL/MAY 1939), COVER ART BY NORMAN SAUNDERS.

art by science-fiction pulp illustrator Frank R. Paul, sole honored guest at that year's first World Science Fiction Convention in New York. Paul was paid $25 for the fantastical image of a flaming man burning through a vault-like structure, reaching for a frightened man firing a gun in self-defense.[8]

The Human Torch and Sub-Mariner defined Timely's raw, rock 'em, sock 'em style. The super powers of Timely characters were often freakish, more burden than blessing, a twist on the emerging superhero myth that would be expanded upon decades in the future when Timely became Marvel Comics. The Torch and Sub-Mariner had their adventures in New York, unlike the mythical cities inspired by New York where Superman and Batman worked.

The "Human" Torch was a misnomer: the character was an android, a botched experiment that burst into flame when it came in contact with oxygen, thus compelling its imprisonment in an airtight glass container lowered into wet cement. But a slow leak causes oxygen to enter the container, and the Torch ignites, blowing open the burial pit, unleashing the anguished android: "I'm burning alive! Why must everything I touch turn to flame!"

Carl Burgos wrote, penciled, inked, and lettered Torch stories. "[Burgos] was young and full of fire," comics historian Les Daniels writes, tongue-in-cheek. "Like most of his colleagues, he was a gifted amateur—at the dawn of comic books and superheroes there were no comic book professionals. Seasoned artists worked on newspaper strips; the young comic book artists were inventing a new form and they relied on energy rather than experience."[9]

Bill Everett later denied that while creating Sub-Mariner he was concerned about avoiding a copyright suit. "I don't recall ever being afraid of anything like that. My point, in particular, was to be different! Not because we were afraid of plagiarism or infringing on anyone else's copyright. . . . We tried to outdo Superman, but, because Superman had come from another planet and therefore was not an Earth person, and my character was, I had to dream up some reasons for this character to have [the powers] that he has."[10]

Sub-Mariner is an "Ultra-Man of the deep," a sea-and-land dweller with "the strength of a thousand men" who is "a youth of dynamic personality," as described in *Marvel Comics* #1. He is royalty—Prince Namor. Everett's eclectic inspirations included Coleridge's poem "The Rime of the Ancient Mariner" and the blended notions of "Submarine" and "Mariner"; Namor was "Roman" spelled backwards. Unlike costumed superheroes, Sub-Mariner was virtually naked except for swimming trunks. Ankle wings allowed him to fly—a classy swipe from Giovanni Bologna's statue of fleet-footed Mercury.[11]

Namor did not use his powers to serve humanity; he *hated* humans, though half human himself. With angular facial features accentuated by arching eyebrows and pointed ears, Namor is the child of an undersea princess and an American sea captain waging a genocidal bombing campaign against the underwater kingdom— the amphibian race versus the "white monsters," a sea-dwelling elder notes. Namor's mother, identified as "resembling the female of the white race" (probably to avoid miscegenation charges), is ordered by the elders to spy and "work your feminine wiles to our racial advantage." But she falls in love with the sea captain and they marry. After fleeing, she gives birth to Namor, and the undersea survivors spend the next twenty years preparing to attack the hated surface-dwellers.

By issue #3 of the retitled *Marvel Mystery Comics*, Namor's mission is summarized: "The Sub-Mariner, amphibious demon of the Earth[, is] bent on an inspired campaign against the white man[,] mainly American[,] who has all but obliterated his South Antarctic race—revenge is his motive and evil is his intent."

Burgos and Everett saw possibilities in their respective creation's elemental mediums of fire and water. During a clash in *Marvel Mystery Comics* #9, the foes move at breakneck speed across New York. Leading up to the fight (in issue #7), Sub-Mariner sees the Empire State Building and sneers, "So—they're proud of this, are they?" Flying to the pinnacle, he detaches the mooring mast for dirigibles and sends it crashing to the streets below, causing more damage to the skyscraper than Kong. Fittingly, by 1942 Timely had moved to the fourteenth floor of the Empire State Building.

SUMMER OF '39

Seven major publishers were challenging DC in the summer and latter half of 1939, unleashing the first wave of superheroes and comics titles. In addition to Timely's *Marvel* anthology, there were Victor Fox's Flame in *Wonderworld Comics* #3 and Blue Beetle and Green Mask in *Mystery Men Comics* #1. Centaur Publications rolled out Amazing-Man in *Amazing-Man Comics* #5. Quality Comics unleashed Eisner's miniature-sized hero, Doll Man, in *Feature Comics* #27. Harvey Comics started the adventure anthology titles *Speed Comics* and *Champion Comics*. MLJ Comics, which would become Archie Comics, began *Blue Ribbon Comics* and *Top-Notch Comics*, the latter featuring the Wizard. Better

The superhero gold rush of '39 introduced such titles as Victor Fox's *Mystery Men Comics*, featuring the Blue Beetle, a character that didn't get the coveted cover spot until issue #7.

MYSTERY MEN COMIC #7 (FEBRUARY 1940), COVER, FOX PUBLICATIONS, INC.

Publications, pulp publisher of *Black Bat*, began its comics line with *Best Comics*. (None of its comics starred Black Bat, respecting the agreement with DC.) By the end of 1939 there were some fifty new titles, nearly double the previous year.[12]

Another contender, Fawcett Publications, Inc., was still settling in at the Paramount Building. By September 1939 Executive Director Ralph Daigh promoted William "Bill" Lee Parker from coordinating editor of Fawcett's movie magazines to heading its new comic book line and creating the lead superhero. Parker had no comics experience—not unusual, given the medium was no more than seven years old.

A dynamic industry was rising on the work of raw young talent. "Swiping" was a negative consequence of inexperienced creators writing and drawing stories on tight deadlines. Celebrated magazine illustrators and syndicated strip artists could pose live models and design lighting and atmospheric effects and use the final photographic references to inspire their artwork. Young comic book artists had no such resources. But why did you need professional models when the likes of Alex Raymond or Milton Caniff were putting it out there daily?

"My school was Alex Raymond and Milton Caniff," Jack Kirby admitted. "[Raymond] was just a wonderful illustrator. His bodies had a flexibility and he had a beautiful line to his drawing. I guess I wasn't the only admirer of Raymond, and I'm proud to say I copied him unmercifully."[13]

Artist Wallace "Wally" Wood, who came to prominence a decade later, had a similar affection for the creator of Flash Gordon: "I had a dream when I was about six, that I found a magic pencil. It could draw just like Alex Raymond. You know, I've been looking for that pencil ever since"[14]

"Good swiping is an art in itself," Jules Feiffer explained. "One can, for example, scan the first 15 years of any National Publication [DC Comics] and catch an album of favorite *Terry and the Pirates*, *Prince Valiant* or *Flash Gordon* poses signed by dozens of different artists. . . . Swipes, if noticed, were accepted as part of comic-book folklore."[15] But examples of alleged imitations of imagery within the comics medium had already been used as exhibits in the Wonder Man trial.

It wasn't all swiping, of course. One early creative realization was that copying the newspaper strip's structured rows of panels boxed in everything; the grid inhibited action. "So we soon began to break out of that with *Batman*," Golden Age artist Jerry Robinson recalled. "We needed space for him to move, the upshots, downshots, dramatic sequences that we couldn't do otherwise. We met some resistance there because the publishers were not artists. They thought the more [panels] they had in the page, the more they were getting for their money."[16]

Despite working in a lowly realm of publishing—or perhaps because of it—there was an esprit de corps among first-generation comics creators. "There was, and is, a brotherhood and love between artists," artist Don Rico recalled. "We created a brand-new art form and were raw as hell, raw in what we were supposed to do. [The biggest concern] was meeting the deadlines. I recall one day I got a call from an editor to bat out three complete ten-page stories in a weekend. I called up the fastest people I knew, the fastest penciller and inker. I put on a huge pot of coffee, cooked up a lot of spaghetti, and by Monday we had thirty pages of—well, I won't necessarily call it art, but that's as good a term as any."[17]

There were exceptions—it's hard to dispute Bill Finger's raw deal from ostensible partner Kane—but there was no denying a universal commitment to the work. Jack Kirby recalled a "code of integrity which nobody ever broke. . . . Everybody was dead serious in doing the best they could."[18]

"We were a *generation*," Jules Feiffer declared. "We thought of ourselves the way the men who began movies must have. . . . Business was booming. New titles coming out by the day, too many of them drawn over a two-day weekend. . . . This was the birth of a new art form! A lot of talk about that: how to design better, draw better, animate a figure better—so that it would jump, magically off the page. Movies on paper—the final dream!"[19]

Jack Kirby's kinetic and muscular imagery always seemed close to bursting off the page—it certainly broke through panel borders. "Jack came out of a tough neighborhood," notes Mark Evanier, a comics writer, historian, and Kirby friend and biographer. "He was a short guy but a tough guy. In a fight with someone a foot taller, I'd bet on Jack. Jack was never afraid of a fight. And that showed in his drawings. . . . When his characters threw a punch, I think he felt it in his own body."[20]

Dick Sprang was a freelance pulp magazine artist who started as a packager in a studio loft at 42nd between Fifth Avenue and Grand Central terminal. In 1941, when Sprang was twenty-seven, Whit Ellsworth hired him as a *Batman* ghost artist. Sprang, who became one of the great *Batman* artists, was influenced by movies, a business and artform barely a decade into its own Golden Age as a talking and color medium.

"Tricky perspectives, aerial shots, worm's eye views,

compositional variation from panel to panel, the knack for drama, are primary to interpreting the script of an action story," Sprang once explained.

> You have to be able to draw anything from any angle, dramatically. To do this, you probe, as a movie camera probes, searching for the best way to shoot a scene. Unlike a movie, you're working in a static medium; your panels, in movie terms, are frozen frames. Into them you strive for the peak action, mood, and suspense which promises carrying interest to the next panel. The style of your work is the essence of the adventure comic. There's a complexity of unique secondary characters which you must create, a rhythm, a pace, a tempo, and hopefully, a striking imagery that tells the story. If these are achieved, the result is style, which is to say, richness within the medium.[21]

That dream of "movies on paper" led creators to haunt movie theaters. The year 1939, when comics switched into high gear, has been called Hollywood's greatest year, delivering such enduring classics as *The Wizard of Oz*, *Stagecoach*, and *Gone with the Wind*. By 1941 comics creators were drawn to Orson Welles's *Citizen Kane*, absorbing the dynamic imagery Welles crafted with cinematographer Greg Toland: deep-focus and tracking shots, tilted angles, moody atmosphere. "I reasoned at the time that during the early '40s the readership was all influenced by the movies," Eisner recalled. "Consequently, I had to write in a 'moving' language. I see pictures, sequential art, as I call it, as a language."[22]

Will Eisner was a rare combination of writer, artist, and businessman. Eisner & Iger even formed its own comics syndicate, Universal Phoenix Features.[23] Eisner dreamed of creating comics for a more adult market in the promised land of newspaper syndication—and of *owning* his creations. "The reason at the time I wanted to retain the ownership is that I wanted to maintain the integrity of the content," he explained. "The only way to do that is to own the copyright. . . . To simply own a copyright doesn't mean you're going to make a lot of money. It depends on how much exploitation you're able to do with it."[24]

During the industry expansion of '39, Eisner made his big move for a syndicated newspaper comic book feature, selling his share of the studio to Iger for $20,000, including interest in characters he created. Iger bragged he got the better of the deal, but Eisner had a shrewd eye for talent, and stellar artists like Lou Fine and Bob Powell joined him.[25]

Eisner's dream aligned with that of Everett "Busy" Arnold, publisher of Quality Comics, who started his career with Greater Buffalo Press, which printed Sunday color comics. Arnold had joined forces with a colleague from printing days, Henry Martin, who envisioned a sixteen-page color comic book supplement for Sunday newspapers. Arnold reckoned Eisner, who created Doll Man for him, was the perfect content provider.[26]

Eisner insisted on owning the copyright for his creations, and Arnold and Martin objected. There were concerns that the United States would be drawn into the war in Europe, and if Eisner went to war and something happened to him, what about the fate of his characters? Eisner deftly proposed a partnership providing reversion of rights. "We agreed that the stories would carry [Arnold's] copyright and that at any time I returned [from war], I would get the copyright back," Eisner recalled.[27]

Eisner set up his studio at 5 Tudor City, near the *New York Daily News* building on 42nd Street, on a hill where goats once grazed. A former slum area transformed in the twenties by the Tudor City development, the address retained a gritty atmosphere overlooking "Blood Alley," a stretch of slaughterhouses along the East River. Tudor City would become a popular venue for cartoonists' studios, including Milton Caniff's.

Arnold and Martin wanted their lead hero to follow the craze for costumed heroes. Eisner didn't care for the genre, and not because of the Wonder Man debacle. He was a story guy and felt heroes with secret identities emphasized character over story. One account has Eisner at his Tudor City studio when his telephone rang—it was "Busy," anxious to discuss the hero-in-progress. Eisner heard a jukebox in the background and Arnold sounded tipsy. On the spot, sketching as he talked, Eisner said he was thinking of a detective, tall and sophisticated, like movie star Cary Grant. "What about his costume, the newspapers want a costumed hero," Arnold interjected. Eisner explained his detective would wear gloves and a domino mask, like the Lone Ranger. It sounded good to Arnold.[28]

The resulting hero—the Spirit—debuted in the "Comic Book Section" syndicated supplement on June 2, 1940. In a seven-page origin story, criminologist and private detective Denny Colt is presumed dead after being splashed with chemicals during a fight with the evil Dr. Cobra. Such accidents transformed other mortals into super beings, but Denny fell into a death-like coma. Buried alive, he awakens and rises from his grave to track down Cobra, who is shot dead by Denny's friend, Police Commissioner Dolan.

Eisner once explained that "all the good gimmicks had been taken." His character had no super powers, nor the deep pockets of a millionaire Bruce Wayne to finance his crimefighting. "Denny Colt had to do it the hard way. . . . He had to fight crime uninsulated. He always ran the risk of getting the stuffings kicked out of him." *The Spirit* became a vehicle for Eisner's fables and twist-ending thrillers. It was all about story—sometimes the Spirit only made a brief appearance.[29]

SUPERMAN #1

DC forged ahead in the busy summer of '39 with a groundbreaking sixty-four-page magazine devoted to a solo character—Superman. Liebowitz once argued no magazine could be sold on a single feature, but he embraced the reality that kids wanted the comic with Superman in it!

As with Bill Finger's tight Batman origin, Superman's story

A year after his first appearance in *Action Comics*, Superman became the first superhero to carry his own solo title. Batman, Wonder Woman, Green Lantern, and others would soon follow with their own solo titles.

SUPERMAN #1, FACSIMILE EDITION OF 1939 ISSUE (CHRONICLE BOOKS, 1999), COVER ART BY JOE SHUSTER.

was briskly retold in two pages and twelve picture panels, opening with a splash panel of the spacecraft bearing the "infant son" of a Krypton "scientist" hurtling into outer space as the planet explodes. The story introduces the Kents, an elderly couple who discover the infant in his ship. In one panel the boy is taken to an orphanage; in the next the Kents reappear to adopt him. By the next panel years have passed, and Mr. Kent is counseling the husky lad (as Hugo's father did in *Gladiator*): "Now listen to me, Clark! This great strength of yours—you've got to hide it from people or they'll be scared of you." His foster mother quickly adds, "But when the proper time comes you must use it to assist humanity."

Other than the origin, *Superman* #1 largely reprinted stories from *Action* #1–4. New material included a one-page "Scientific Explanation of Superman's Amazing Strength," reprising the proportionate abilities of ants and grasshoppers, noting the gravitational differences between Krypton and Earth, and picturing inhabitants leaping across a skyscraper skyline as examples of "millions of years" of evolution producing "physical perfection." There were four new story pages in which Superman stops a lynch mob, using the incident to land his Clark Kent alter ego a job at the *Daily Star*, and he apprehends a murderess, twisting her arm to get a signed confession. The story then picks up as a reprint of the *Action* #1 story.

There were special features. A double-page ad announced charter membership in the "Supermen of America" fan club: for a dime, members received a certificate of membership, full-color membership button, and Superman's Secret Code to decipher Superman's Secret Message in each issue of *Action Comics* (presumably so fans would not abandon the anthology title). The *Action* #1 image of Superman bursting his chains filled the back cover, while a feature inside introduced the creators of "America's Greatest Adventure Strip!" Jerry and Joe were stars.

There was synergy between *Superman*, *Action*, and McClure Syndicate, as contractually arranged, but Liebowitz later professed surprise that the first three issues of *Superman* largely reprinted stories from *Action* #1–4 and color versions of the syndicated 1939 black-and-white strips. For instance, *Superman* #2 (Fall 1939) reprinted three colorized stories from the daily strip. *Superman* #3 (Winter 1939) reprinted two strip continuities, with stories reprinted from *Action* #5 and #6 rounding out that issue. An untitled *Superman* #3 story reprinted from the strips, about a sadistic orphanage superintendent (later titled "Superman and the Runaway"), dropped a sequence of strip panels contrasting massive Krypton and a much smaller Earth, with text: "A Scientific Explanation of Superman's Super Strength[:] Superman was born on a planet whose gravitational pull was much greater than that of our Earth's—thus his incredible feats of strength!"[30]

The solo title began as a quarterly, with net sales for the first issue of 434,965 copies. The second issue nearly doubled that with 800,994. *Superman* #3 soared past a million at 1,055,784. Sales stayed in the stratosphere: *Superman* #4: 1,333,822 and

#5: 1,187,023. By issue #6 the title went bimonthly, with sales of 1,254,332. The sales figures held:

#7: 1,262,893
#8: 1,301,785
#9: 1,399,208
#10: 1,278,668
#11: 1,121,961
#12: 1,270,212

Action, with a single Superman story, stayed close to a million. The month before Fawcett's competing *Captain Marvel Adventures* appeared, *Action* had net sales of 912,159 copies.[31]

Siegel and Shuster won monetary recognition on December 19, 1939, when DC initiated a "supplemental employment agreement" increasing their compensation and royalties from newspaper syndication and other licensing. As with every contractual opportunity, they were reminded that DC was Superman's "sole and exclusive owner."[32]

In Siegel's opinion, the sudden onslaught of superheroes in the summer and fall of '39, including DC's growing roster, were *all* infringing on his Superman idea. In fact, DC had just made Superman its own corporation. Siegel singled out DC's Hour-Man, whose "miracle" pill endows him with an hour of Superman-like strength, speed, and stamina. (Ironically, late in 1939 Siegel created *The Spectre* with Hour-Man artist Bernard Bailey.) Siegel complained in a letter addressed to Liebowitz in care of Superman, Inc.; Liebowitz wrote back on March 1, 1940, cautioning Siegel to address editorial concerns to Detective Comics, Inc., as the Superman Corporation was handling outside licensing only, not editorial matters related to the comics. Of Siegel's complaint, he wrote, "It would definitely be against our better interest to have an imitation of Superman in our own books, in spite of the fact that all competing magazines carry an imitation of Superman."[33]

DC was about to be challenged by the superhero gestating at rival Fawcett whose powers matched Superman's own.

CAPTAIN THUNDER

Fawcett executive director Ralph Daigh was looking forward to the result of editor Bill Parker's assignment to create a superhero—the successful launch of Fawcett's entire comics line depended upon it. When the big day arrived, Parker walked into Daigh's office with his synopsis for a character drawn from his personal experiences in the National Guard and horse cavalry. The hero's name conjured military prowess and elemental power: Captain Thunder.

"The Thunder represented my interpretation of what the character was going to be," Parker recalled. "One of the important elements of it was the phenomenon of lightning bolt, thunder and black cloud, and Captain Thunder fitted in with that and also gave a feeling, to my mind, of the omniscience that the character was supposed to possess."

Parker proposed a modern updating of King Arthur and his Knights of the Round Table, with Captain Thunder leading an elite squad of six or seven hand-picked men, each endowed with a special ability. The King Arthur legend had beguiled Parker as a boy, and he felt young readers would be similarly inspired.[34] Parker wrote a note that Thunder would be the "captain of [a] company of Super-Men who end wars by pitting their strength against aggressors."[35]

But Daigh felt a supporting cast would detract from the main character, arguing that instead of spreading powers among an elite squad, they should be embodied in the main hero. "Bill left that decisive meeting very enthused," Daigh recalled, "after proposing that the lone 'Captain Thunder's' alter-ego be a small, young boy . . . a newsboy with the enviable power to turn himself into an adult manifesting the diverse super qualities of Greek gods."[36]

Parker conceived an orphan newsboy in a city he imagined as

New York. "[The orphan] was selected by an old man who all his life for a good many hundreds of years had had the mission of protecting the poor and the weak and defenseless, and this old man knew that he was coming to the end of his life and wanted to pass on the torch to somebody else, and selected this newsboy," Parker later explained.

> I wanted a dramatic way of having the meeting between the newsboy and the old man and it occurred to me that it was a fanciful but perhaps dramatic way to have the old man living actually underneath the city; and the boy . . . got on a subway train at Times Square and wound up in an underground cavern where this old man dwelt, and there he received from the old man the qualities and characteristics and the mission of carrying on the life's work of the old man. . . . This boy who I named Billy Batson . . . was given at that time the power of transforming himself at will into Captain Thunder by using a magic word.

The "old man" was the wizard Shazam, and his name was the magic word, an acronym for attributes Billy Batson received when he said "Shazam" and became Captain Thunder: Solomon (wisdom), Hercules (strength), Atlas (stamina), Zeus (power), Achilles (courage), and Mercury (speed).

Captain Thunder's visual design, and that of his supporting cast, began in September 1939 when Al Allard, Fawcett's art director, paired Parker with Charles Clarence "C. C." Beck, a cartoonist who believed comics should be drawn with simplicity and humor and who drew inspiration from Fawcett's morgue of motion-picture stills. Hollywood star Fred MacMurray was a main model for the hero, while other references included Cary Grant, Buster Crabbe, Basil Rathbone, and Douglas Fairbanks Jr., son of the silent screen star that inspired the creators of Superman and Batman.[37]

"We spent weeks working out the characters for our stories," Beck later explained. "Bill typed descriptions of various characters on yellow copy paper for me to draw. I drew whatever he specified. Many, many characters were born and died during those weeks."[38]

The publisher insisted Captain Thunder suit up with a cape and tight-fitting costume. Beck worked up a quasi-military outfit similar to his recent drawing of the title character in the operetta *The Student Prince*. "Well, I wanted the character to wear a military cape, a Hessian cape or one of that kind," Parker recalled, emphasizing the military theme. "I wanted him to wear little gold lightning bolts as spurs, and I wanted him to wear high boots, military boots. . . . The only one that was adopted was the cape." Mercury's "lightning spurs," as Parker called them, instead inspired a lightning bolt chest emblem.[39]

The design process went back and forth between Parker and Beck and "the penthouse where the big bosses work," Beck explained. Parker would head upstairs with Beck's sketches, usually descending with discouraging news to keep drawing.

At one point Daigh brought in about twenty comics for reference, including a few *Superman* magazines. Beck picked up one, glanced at the first page—a spaceship streaking away from an exploding planet, the opening panel from *Superman* #1. By the end of 1939 the syndicated strip was going strong, twenty issues of *Action* had been published, and the quarterly *Superman* had seen summer, fall, and winter issues.

By November '39 Parker circulated a memo about a hero combining "the best aspects of Mandrake the Magician and Superman."[40] Thunder was emerging not as a magician but a magical being. Beck later claimed he and Parker did *not* want to imitate Superman—any such references were a sop to the penthouse bosses. "Well, we both knew you can only sneak things past people, you can't hit them in the face with it," Beck explained. "So we proceeded to give them a character that looked somewhat like Superman, but in character was entirely different." Beck claimed "any time we tried to do something good, or better than Superman, it was nixed. Finally Bill Parker said, 'Dammit, all they want is a carbon copy of Superman, and I'm not going to give it to them.'"[41]

Beck insisted he and Parker wanted to outshine the first wave of superhero comics, which they felt were badly written and illustrated. "We decided to give our readers a real comic book, drawn in comic strip style and telling an imaginative story, based not on the hackneyed formulas of the pulp magazine, but going back to the old folk-tales and myths of classic times. . . . Fawcett was not very happy with the new character Parker came up with, but they decided to publish it anyway."[42]

Captain Thunder was to be the cover feature of an anthology, *Flash Comics*. Fawcett submitted an ashcan, but All-American beat them to the Patents and Trademark Office with its own *Flash Comics*. Fawcett's follow-up was a *Thrill Comics* ashcan, but Better Publications was registering *Thrilling Comics*. The publisher settled on *Whiz Comics*, probably inspired by founder Wilford Hamilton "Captain Billy" Fawcett's flagship magazine, *Capt. Billy's Whiz Bang*. Three title changes, but the ashcan covers remained the same—Thunder breaking chains shackling him to a wall as a hoodlum raises a knife and another fires a gun.

Mark Zaid explains that as comic books and superheroes demonstrated financial value, publishers rushed to register every conceivable title. DC, not content with *Action*, registered *Double Action Comics* with the patent office, for example. "As far as the law's impact on comics, who got to the trademark office first made all the difference," Zaid concludes. Then Fawcett learned that *Flash Comics* would include a character named John L. Thunder. It was a blessing—Daigh never liked "Captain Thunder." Fawcett artist Pete Costanza claims he suggested "Captain Marvelous," mercifully shortened to "Marvel." Daigh characterized the name change "as more befitting a hero of marvelous capabilities."[4]

CHAPTER 7

SUPERMAN, INC.

Get behind your work with zest and ambition to improve and forget about book rights, movie rights and all other dreams. I'll let you know as soon as things happen. After all, you must realize that we have a bigger stake in [Superman] than you have and we will take care of things in the proper manner.

JACK LIEBOWITZ
in a letter to Jerry Siegel, 1940

WONDER WOMAN

All-American launched its line of superheroes with *Flash Comics*. The first issue was on the stands by late 1939 and introduced the Flash, Hawkman, and Johnny Thunder. All-American maintained its symbiotic relationship with DC but took care that its superheroes not muscle in on Superman's all-around skill set of super strength, speed, and invulnerability. The Green Lantern was Alan Scott, another costumed ring-bearer who came into possession of a mystical green lantern that charged his power ring. The Flash was university student Jay Garrick, who, during a late-night science experiment, clumsily knocked over beakers of chemicals, breathed the fumes, and was miraculously imbued with super speed. An All-American innovation was the Justice Society of America, the first superhero team-up. The roll call included Flash, Green Lantern, Hawkman, Hour Man, Johnny Thunder, and Siegel's creation the Spectre—who assembled for their first meeting on the cover of *All-Star Comics* #3 (Winter 1940–1941).

All-American introduced Wonder Woman in *All-Star* #8. The character's creators, Dr. William Moulton Marston, inventor of the lie detector, and artist Harry Peter, were older than most laboring in the field. Marston envisioned Wonder Woman as an Amazon princess as "lovely as Aphrodite—as wise as Athena—with the speed of Mercury and the strength of Hercules" who lived with powerful females on uncharted Paradise Island. She wore a yellow tiara, and her bare shoulders and arms were offset by a red bustier adorned with a yellow eagle design. A star-spangled blue skirt became tights, and her long, lithe legs were fitted with near-knee-high red boots.

In Wonder Woman's first appearance, a plane crashes on Paradise Island, and the pilot, American serviceman Captain Steve Trevor, survives thanks to the ministrations of Wonder Woman. She falls in love and follows Trevor to America, where she takes the civilian guise of Diana Prince and as Wonder Woman joins the home-front fight against the Axis Powers of World War II. Her saga truly began in *Sensation Comics* #1 (January 1942) and expanded with a solo title that summer.

Marston, who wrote under the pseudonym Charles Moulton, had taken a strange path to All-American. An article on the comics phenomenon in the October 25, 1940, issue of the *Family Circle* featured Marston noting the implications of Orson Welles's 1938 radio adaptation of H. G. Wells's novel, *War of the Worlds*, a broadcast that terrified thousands into believing an actual Martian invasion was underway. "There are millions of normal men and women today who have no mental resistance at all to tales of the weirdly impossible," Marston concluded. "Orson Welles' fascinating radio experiment proved that Americans today are living an imaginary mental life in a comics-created world!"

According to Sheldon Mayer, publisher M. C. Gaines was concerned Marston might become a powerful anticomics voice, so he co-opted the threat by hiring him. What Gaines got was a man living with two women and having children with both, "unusual now and extraordinary in Marston's day," Les Daniels notes.

It gets better. Marston conceived Wonder Woman as "psychological propaganda for the new type of woman who should, I believe, rule the world." He wrote:

What woman lacks is the dominance or self assertive power to put over and enforce her love desires. I have given Wonder Woman this dominant force but have kept her loving, tender, maternal and feminine in every other way. Her bracelets, with which she repels bullets and other murderous weapons, represent the Amazon Princess' submission to Aphrodite, Goddess of Love and Beauty. Her magic lasso, which compels anyone bound by it to obey Wonder Woman and which was given to her by Aphrodite herself, represents woman's love charm and allure by which she compels men and women to do her bidding.

Marston's stories indulged submission and bondage fantasies, with Wonder Woman herself regularly tied up, chained, spanked, and occasionally ensnared by her own lasso. Taking note, Josette Frank of the Child Study Association of America, a member of DC's editorial advisory board, wrote Gaines on February 17, 1943: "I know also that your circulation figures prove that a lot of other people *are* enthusiastic [about Wonder Woman]. Nevertheless, this feature does lay you open to considerable criticism from any such group as ours, partly on the basis of sadistic bits showing men chained, tortured, etc." The following January, Frank asked that her name be removed from the advisory group for *Sensation Comics* and *Wonder Woman* because of "sex antagonisms and perversions."

In a long reply letter to Gaines, Marston argued, "The only hope for peace is to teach people who are full of pep and unbound force to *enjoy* being bound. . . . It is the secret of women's allure—women *enjoy* submission, being bound. This I bring out in the Paradise Island sequences where the girls beg for chains and enjoy wearing them."

This issue of *Sensation* included a house ad announcing the debut of Wonder Woman's solo title, noting her swift ascent as "one of the leading comic book characters of America." In the companion ad, the amazing Amazon is front and center as a member of the Justice Society.

Marston's argument would seem of nil appeal to guardians of decency, but Marston had his supporters, including DC advisory board member Dr. Lauretta Bender, who argued that the super heroine did not revel in sadism and that Marston was handling his "experiment" very well, indeed. The idea of professionals lending their approval to such "perversions" would outrage future anticomics crusader Dr. Fredric Wertham.[1] Marston's fascination with bondage continued to the delight of certain fans and derision from critics, including those declaring the Amazon a lesbian—Diana Prince evoked a certain Greek poet from the isle of Lesbos with her stock exclamation, "Suffering

Sappho!" Regardless, All-American had a big hit in Dr. Marston's experiment.

SUPERMAN, INC.

Superman kept evolving. In *Action* #13 (June 1939), the Man of Tomorrow is up in the clouds, apparently starting to fly. Red-haired evil scientist Lex Luthor first appears in *Action* #23 and is seemingly killed in the flaming crash of his floating dirigible headquarters. Luthor survives but loses his hair—Siegel and Shuster seemingly equated baldness with villainy—and Superman has his nemesis.

The year 1940 proved pivotal. That January Whitney Ellsworth was named editorial director of the entire line. DC and All-American dropped the pretense of being separate companies, as All-American titles began carrying the cover notice, "A DC Publication," with *All-American Comics* and *Flash Comics* promoted alongside *Detective*, *Action*, *Adventure*, and *More Fun* as the industry-leading "Big Six Comic Magazines." DC was in negotiations with Republic Pictures for a live-action Superman movie, a radio adventure series was in the works, and a full-color Sunday strip was introduced with a major publicity push on November 5, 1939.[2] The moves into multimedia storytelling paralleled merchandising deals that included "Supermen of America" fan club items, puzzles and games, ties and handkerchief sets, belts and suspenders, dolls, toys, and bubblegum cards adorned on the back with the now-familiar chain-busting Superman.

Donenfeld and Liebowitz had also organized a separate corporation to "promote the sale of licenses on games and toys and exploit the Superman character on radio and the movies," Liebowitz explained. "Later on we also decided that the copyright should be taken in the name of Superman, Inc. so as to avoid confusion when we have a licensee of Superman using the figure

"Facing the Firing Squad": Lois inexplicably faces a firing squad as Superman arrives in the nick of time, all of it explained on the back of the card. Superman Gum was one of many products licensed by Superman, Inc.

SUPERMAN GUM CARD #36, SUPERMAN, INC., 1940.

and name; it would be a little confusing to have it copyrighted by Detective Comics, Inc."[3]

In the beginning the Superman Corporation was the licensing arm only. A two-page letter from Detective Comics, Inc., dated January 18, 1940, and addressed to Superman, Inc., constituted the agreement: "The Superman Corporation, through license received all Detective Comics rights outside of publication rights and proceeded to do all the things that were done by Detective Comics in those particular fields." Robert Maxwell was installed as head of the licensing division.

Although properly incorporated under the laws of the State of New York, the relationship between DC and Superman, Inc., was incestuous. Donenfeld and Liebowitz did not have an attorney present when they came to terms. Both corporations shared the same officers and board of directors: Donenfeld as president, Paul Sampliner vice president, and Liebowitz managing finances for both as secretary-treasurer. The initial agreement established Superman, Inc., as DC's "exclusive agent to exploit Superman,

By 1942 Superman's media exposure included a backlog of Paramount animated films and a coast-to-coast radio show broadcast over the Mutual Broadcasting System.

SUPERMAN HOUSE ADS, BOTH FROM *SUPERMAN* #19 (NOVEMBER/DECEMBER 1942).

the trademarks and copyrights and/or other rights therein in any manner whatsoever," for a period ending March 31, 1945.

Superman comics retained the Detective Comics, Inc., copyright. In the near future a mistake in assigning copyright would put DC's star in legal jeopardy.[4]

THIS IS A JOB FOR SUPERMAN!

The Superman licensing push in 1940 included promotions ("Get on the Superman Band Wagon: Superman Is Ready to Work for You in 1941"), a proposal for a "Clark Kent" journalism scholarship, and a "Superman cave" to open the holiday season at Macy's Toyland on November 16, 1940. Macy's display department prepared papier-mâché figures of Superman performing feats of strength, although Maxwell disapproved a number of them, which were not used. The visual representation of the star property by ancillary partners was becoming a concern. For example, Maxwell objected to the ad agency Kenyon & Eckhardt for their "unauthorized use of Superman figure."

Maxwell was involved in the radio show as director and supervisor; his duties ranged from hiring writers to arranging commercial sponsors. The *Superman* radio show was underway by February 1940, gaining listeners as it was broadcast up to five times a week across the United States, the territory of Hawaii, and Canada.[5] During casting it had been debated whether to hire one actor to play meek Clark Kent, another for mighty Superman. Law student Clayton "Bud" Collyer, putting himself through college doing radio, played both, going tenor for the alter ego, baritone for the superhero.

The radio show announced the appearance of Superman with a chorus: "Look! Up in the sky! It's a bird! It's a plane!" Narrator Jackson Beck intoned: "*It's Superman!* Yes, it's Superman—strange visitor from the planet Krypton who came to earth with amazing physical powers far beyond those of mortal men, and who, disguised as Clark Kent, mild-mannered reporter for a great metropolitan newspaper, wages a never-ending battle for truth and justice." The radio program added to the mythos and popularized such phrases as "Up, up, and away!" and "This is a job for Superman!"[6] The radio show named Clark and Lois's boss Perry White, who took his place behind the editor's desk in 1940 in *Superman* #7. (He was initially called "White" and didn't get his full name until *Superman* #10.) That year, the newspaper became the *Daily Planet*.[7]

CREATIVE PRESSURE

Siegel and Shuster were "no longer sole arbiters of their brain-child's destiny," comics creator Grant Morrison writes. "Superman needed the power of ten men, and more, to supply the demand for his incredible feats. . . . Superman now had a metamorphic, elastic quality that would allow him to survive."[8]

The Superman Corporation required the boys to subsume themselves to DC's corporate strategy. A vivid example appears in Liebowitz's angry letter on January 25, 1940, responding to an innocent Siegel letter that included a clipping of an unauthorized interview he and Joe gave the *Cleveland Plain Dealer*. Liebowitz took issue with their assumptions, explaining DC was going after a number of licenses and setting up a Superman publicity department that would hereafter speak for the character.

"You might have mentioned in your interview that the first ones who saw something in the Superman strip was Detective Comics, Inc., who bought all rights to it. You might have said that you have a very satisfactory arrangement with Detective Comics, Inc., as compensation for the transfer of all your rights, so hereafter *we forbid you* [author's emphasis] to grant any interviews relating to Superman and his development. Please refer all inquiries to our office. You can readily see the harm that will be done if things are not handled from a central source and if statements are issued which . . . conflict with one another."

Superheroes evolved as their creators added narrative flourishes. Here, Superman completes his mountain-top "Secret Citadel," later known as the Fortress of Solitude and located in the icy wasteland of the Arctic. The "World Premiere of Superman" poster in the background of the bottom panel is probably a reference to the ongoing series of animated short films that premiered in 1941.

"MUSCLES FOR SALE," *SUPERMAN* #17 (JULY/AUGUST 1942), P. 5, ART BY JOHN SIKELA.

Liebowitz's letter chronicled numerous "misstatements" in the *Plain Dealer* clipping regarding Superman licensing, downplaying the potential upside:

> On the radio proposition, we expect to sign any day with Becker Flour Co.—we to pay the cost of producing the program and they pay so much per station. The net result of this transaction will show us a loss of $800, every week, so at the present time this is nothing to gloat over. Our job, in order to get out of this hole, will be to sell other radio stations from record transcriptions which we make from the original broadcast. This will not come for a long time, depending of course whether the present program is successful.

He mentioned "the many shortcomings" of Wayne Boring, an artist at the Cleveland shop Siegel was enthusiastic about, and reminded Jerry that editorial director Whit Ellsworth had mailed him an approved cover design that had to be at 480 Lexington by week's end. Jerry needed to tell Joe that his cover sketches should *always* show Superman as the biggest and most prominent figure, and where were the releases for the May *Action*? And McClure called: they were up to deadline and had yet to receive dailies and Sundays. "I have not received a copy of the detailed Superman continuity which has been recently okayed by us," he concluded. "We are going over this script with a fine tooth comb. Please type your synopsis double spaced and on one side of the paper . . . and forget about book rights, movie rights and all other dreams. I'll let you know as soon as things happen. After all, you must realize that *we have a bigger stake in it than you have* [author's emphasis] and we will take care of things in the proper manner." The bottom line: "You've got to give us plenty of time for okaying, so get busy."[9]

The character's foundational mediums of comic books and syndicated strips remained the responsibility of Siegel, Shuster, and their studio. But there were growing concerns about the quality of art coming from Cleveland. The pressure was telling, especially on an increasingly fragile Shuster. "As usual, Joe is feeling ill," Siegel reported to Liebowitz in the summer of 1940. "He is in such a run-down condition that his doctor advised him to take a week off. As a result he is spending this week at a Cedar Point summer resort." Joe tried to attain a Superman-like physique, at one point bulking up from 112 to 128 pounds on a regimen of weight lifting and a diet of steak and milk. He increased his height of five feet, two inches (the same as Donenfeld) by wearing "built-up" shoes.[10]

THE LETTER

A six-page letter from Siegel and Shuster, doubtlessly written by Siegel and dated May 8, 1940, was sent to Liebowitz regarding "increased rates for SUPERMAN material . . . we believe we merit and need." They currently divided $60 a week—Siegel got $30 as writer, Joe around $20, Joe's assistant got $10. But circulation had rocketed from 130,000 for *Action* #1, with *Superman* "hitting 1,500,000." That translated into *$110 per page.* As a compromise, they asked for higher royalty participation, while increased page rates would address DC's quality concerns.

"Of late, editorial reaction has been that more polish and care is needed in the presentation of SUPERMAN magazine material." To this end, Siegel reported that Paul Cassidy, a promising assistant hired in January for a trial period set to expire in June, was contributing fifty-two pages a month, but without "a substantial" page-rate increase they would have to cut Cassidy's pages to thirty-nine, although he would then likely return to a previous post as an art instructor in Milwaukee. With a rate increase they could also bring in Paul Lauretta, a "splendid artist" who worked on the early Sunday strip and the solo title. They could then produce up to sixty-five pages of "highly polished" Superman material a month and perhaps even allow the now bimonthly *Superman* to go monthly. Siegel settled on "at least" $500 for each thirteen-page *Superman* story, relying on DC's "sense of fair play."

Siegel resented other super characters but used that point to advantage: "In general, we think we merit your best consideration because of how our character has helped build up your organization. . . . The success of SUPERMAN has led you into producing other features such as BATMAN, FLASH, etc. upon which you will no doubt profit greatly. All this stemmed directly from our character and we hope you will keep in mind our value to the organization when considering rate increases."

They also demanded a financial share in the radio program and the anticipated movie serial, concluding: "Almost any syndicate would be pleased to have us work for them now (though not so long ago it was a very different story) but personally we like working for DETECTIVE COMICS and hope the association continues until eternity. . . . We completely realize DETECTIVE COMICS gave us our big opportunity, and that much of SUPERMAN's success and rapid development has been due to your live-wire activity."[11] The creators were not ushered into partnership with Superman, Inc.

By 1942 Siegel would look to the upcoming five-year contract renewal, lamenting even having a renewal unless by mutual agreement and feeling anguished at not being "smart enough to ask for better terms in the first place."[12]

Still, quality problems continued. In November 1940 Ellsworth wrote Siegel that the latest dailies and Sundays were "again quite bad." Ellsworth personally had "to shorten a number of ape-like arms, and to remove extremely curly forelocks from Superman's forehead, and to *de-sex* Lois. . . . The magazine releases are even worse than anything I have to say about the syndicate stuff." Whit was sending back two *Action* covers as unacceptable in "idea or execution," *again* requesting that concept sketches be sent in for approval *before* submitting finished art. "All in all, Jack Liebowitz and I are both very disappointed with the artwork, and we both feel that something drastic is soon going to have to be done."[13]

BATMAN #1

Bill Finger remained the main writer of Batman stories for *Detective Comics*, while working with ghost artists, including Jerry Robinson, a student at Columbia University who began by inking *Detective* #36, #37, and #38, the latter issue introducing Robin the Boy Wonder. Robinson later claimed to have contributed the sidekick's name, inspired by a renowned edition of *Robin Hood* illustrated by N. C. Wyeth, and he also sketched a quasi-medieval Robin costume based on his memory of Wyeth's artwork. Bob Kane would assert *he* named Robin after Robin Hood.[14]

Following up on Robin's introduction was a solo *Batman* title, scheduled for a Spring 1940 cover date. In addition to *Detective*, Kane now had to come up with four new feature-length stories. Batman's origin was reprinted, with textual tweaks and a more dramatic layout, and "Dr. Hugo and the Monsters," a completed story planned for *Detective*, was moved to the solo title. Robinson was taking a creative writing class at Columbia and volunteered to write another needed story.[15]

Robinson wanted to create a villain worthy of Batman, the serious and focused crime fighter, and found it in the sinister visage of a joker playing card. Robinson's concept was so compelling he was persuaded to let Finger write the story that Kane would illustrate. "I reluctantly agreed," Robinson recalled, "though I must admit I had tears in my eyes. I was eighteen at the time. If it had been at a later point I might have had second thoughts. . . . Bill was such a sweet guy, and I knew he would do a great job with it."[16]

The character they called the Joker appeared fresh out of a nightmare, although no explanation was given for his shocking appearance: chalk-white skin, green hair, beady black eyes, red lips drawn in a fiendish smile. Tall, lean, dressed in a long-tailed purple suit and black string tie, the Joker was the first psychopath of the comics. His inaugural crime spree involved secretly injecting victims with venom that killed within twenty-four hours and prophesying the death that came at the appointed hour and left victim's faces contorted into ghastly grins.

The Joker outclasses Batman in pure ferocity. In a face-off on a bridge over a river, Batman can't get off a punch as the Joker explodes a left off his jaw, follows with a "wicked kick" to the head, and pushes the unconscious hero into the river, where the shock of cold water awakens him. In the first of innumerable encounters to come, the Joker wins by a knockout.

The final story in *Batman* #1 is a second Joker story, which ends with the "grim jester" dying from a knife wound. But Ellsworth knew the character was too good a bad guy to lose, and before going to press told Kane to redraw the final panel. In the scene a startled doctor, examining the Joker in an ambulance, exclaims, "This man—he isn't dead! He's still alive—and he's going to *live!*"[17]

The Joker's creation is one of many cautionary tales of the mysteries and intrigues of collaboration. Kane claimed *he* was inspired by a joker playing card—Robinson's sketch came *after* he created the villain with Finger. Kane noted that Finger, with his exhaustive

Death was in the cards when the Joker dealt the hand. Adding to the mystery of the maniacal character was the absence of any explanation for his nightmarish appearance.

JOKER STORY, *BATMAN* #1 (SPRING 1941), P. 1, ART BY BOB KANE.

archives, contributed production stills from the German film *The Man Who Laughs* (1928), picturing actor Conrad Veidt in facial makeup disfigured into a grotesque grin. If Robinson had come to him first with the joker playing card, he would not have drawn the character like Conrad Veidt in the movie, Kane argued.[18]

Too much time has passed to marshal the undeniable proof a judge or jury might accept, and the participants have gone where no earthly summons can reach them. Years later, a writer conducting a phone interview with Kane asked about the mystery of the Joker's creation: there was Robinson's joker card sketch, the swipe of Veidt's gruesome character, Finger's script, Kane's artwork. Would it be accurate to say the Joker's creation was collaborative?

Kane, his voice rising, replied, "Who are you going to believe, him [Robinson] or the horse's mouth!? I should have *sued* the son of a bitch years ago!" He threatened to take this outrage to DC's publisher and slammed down the phone.[19]

SUPERMAN DAY

The Superman Corporation guided Superman's fortunes with an emphasis on mainstream appeal. Robert Maxwell and publicist Allen "Duke" Ducovny, with Macy's Toyland as sponsor, arranged for "Superman Day" at the New York World's Fair on July 3, 1940. VIPs wore red, white, and blue ribbons with buttons affixed with the iconic image of Superman swelling his chest and busting his chains. Siegel and Liebowitz posed together, all smiles for the camera. A wary Donenfeld inexplicably rode the back of an elephant. Stage actor Ray Middleton appeared in Superman cape and costume. An estimated 36,000 kids showed up, some competing in athletic contests for the title of "America's Super-Boy and Super-Girl."[20]

To mark the fair's second year, the licensed 1940 edition of *New York World's Fair Comics* featured Clark and Lois heading to New York and the fair, this time reporting for the *Daily Planet*, while Bruce Wayne and Dick Grayson visited the fair in a separate adventure. Superman, Batman, and Robin did appear together for the first time on the cover, artist Jack Burnley posing them against a backdrop of the fair's signature 610-foot-tall Trylon spire and 80-foot-diameter Perisphere.

That autumn there was an even bigger public Superman event: a gigantic Superman float, four-and-a-half-stories high and costing about $15,000, bobbed high above the crowds lining the streets for Macy's Thanksgiving Day Parade.[21]

In the spring of 1940, in a fitting tribute to the inaugural year of Superman, Inc., Donenfeld commissioned his prized pulp cover artist, H. J. Ward, to paint a Superman portrait, reportedly paying him $150 for the job, more than it cost to own the character. The painting became a fixture at 480 Lexington—the grinning, boyish superhero standing on a rocky bluff overlooking the golden skyline of Metropolis, arms akimbo and fists on hips, cape rustling in the breeze.[22]

The corporate strategy of taking on copyright infringers put newcomer Fawcett Publications in the sights of Superman, Inc. The cover of Fawcett's *Master Comics* #1 (March 1940), introduced Master Man, "World's Greatest Hero," leaping over skyscrapers with a damsel in his arms, thanks to a magical vitamin capsule.[23] DC threatened legal action and Fawcett terminated the character after six appearances.

But Fawcett wasn't going to stand down over Captain Marvel, who had already been unveiled in the first issue of *Whiz Comics* (February 1940). The cover copy announced a new superhero in town: "Gangway for Captain Marvel!" The cover art probably gave Donenfeld and Liebowitz pause. Superman lifted a car overhead in his inaugural cover, but here "The World's Mightiest Man" was not breaking a sweat as he effortlessly flicked a car against a brick wall, sending a telltale gangster's machine gun flying and the right tire spinning off.

CHAPTER 8

PATENTS AND PATRIOTS

Smashing thru, CAPTAIN AMERICA came face to face with Hitler.

Captain America #1, cover text

WAR FEARS

The war in Europe was officially underway when Nazi Germany invaded Poland on September 1, 1939. The United States was neutral, and a strong isolationist movement pushed for the country to remain so. Siegel and Shuster did dispatch Superman to Germany's supposedly impregnable Siegfried Line, where he twists a cannon into a pretzel shape, knocks down fortifications, and grabs Hitler, declaring, "I'd like to land a strictly non-Aryan sock on your jaw, but there's no time for that!" Superman also takes to the air "at a clip that would outdistance the fastest plane"—he's clearly flying now—and stops in Moscow to collar Joseph Stalin. With a dictator under each arm, he flies to Geneva and a meeting of the League of Nations. With Superman as witness, a judge pronounces Hitler and Stalin guilty of "unprovoked aggression against defenseless countries."[1]

Superman's intervention in international affairs was unusual, particularly as the two-page comics feature appeared in mainstream *Look* magazine. In response the Nazi weekly *Das Schwarze Korps* assailed the "physically circumcised" Siegel for serving "poison" for America's youth to swallow, declaring, "Superman ist ein Jude!" (Superman is a Jew!)[2]

Jerry Robinson responded to the Luftwaffe's Blitzkrieg of London by creating a masked, non-super-powered character named London for publisher Lev Gleason. Robinson described his creation as a cross between a suave Englishman and an American comic book hero, the name inspired by a phrase from British prime minister Winston Churchill: "London can take it." *London* allowed Kane's ghost to step out of the shadows with a "Jerry Robinson" byline. "I took great delight in writing the script and I must say it was overloaded with lavish prose," added Robinson, who finally put his Columbia writing classes to use.

London was created in March 1941 during a working weekend with other artists on the top floor of a midtown brownstone. The United States was not at war, but a paper shortage limited publishers to publishing only when they had a paper allotment, Robinson recalled.

> I was working with Charlie Biro and Bob Wood when we suddenly heard Gleason Publications got an unexpected paper allotment. They notified us that if we could come up with the contents for a magazine over the weekend, they could use the paper. If they didn't use it by a certain date, they'd lose that allotment. . . . It was mostly Bob and Dick Wood, my close friend Bernie Klein, George Roussos and myself. We worked day and night. . . . We each created a feature for ourselves that we wrote and drew. We discussed the ideas so that we would get a balance of a variety of characters.[3]

That whirlwind weekend would be celebrated for its Golden Age grit—the intrepid creators worked through a blizzard that shut down New York City. Bernie Klein got the short straw to venture into the storm in search of food. He found a downtown bar open and returned with a dozen fresh eggs and a can of beans. Their makeshift studio didn't have a stove or hot plate, so they pried up ceramic bathroom tiles to make a square, burning newspapers to heat the tiles upon which they fried the eggs and heated the beans.[4]

By 1941 it seemed inevitable that America would get in the fight overseas. The Selective Training and Service Act, passed by Congress the previous year, authorized the first peacetime conscription in US history. Businesses girded for an unprecedented workforce drain if war was declared. But short of a declaration of war, a powerful neutral sentiment remained, along with concerns for the European market—don't even criticize Hitler. But a couple of Jewish guys at Timely Comics had other ideas.

THE COMING OF CAPTAIN AMERICA

The emphasis of rival publishers on avoiding Superman's likeness produced an evolutionary strain of fantastical characters—DC's legal department couldn't touch Timely's surly, near-naked Sub-Mariner or its flaming android Torch. But new and marketable archetypes might inspire their own infringers. On the first page of the Human Torch story in *Marvel Mystery Comics* #20, below "Reg. U.S. Pat. Off." and other copyright notices, appeared a red-lettered "WARNING!" The text that followed probably befuddled youngsters attracted to the cover depicting Sub-Mariner attacking a Nazi torpedo boat:

> Marvel Comics well-known characters, The Human Torch, Sub-Mariner, The Angel, and Ka-Zar have been registered in the United States Patent Office, and are further protected by United States Copyright with every issue, as are the full contents of this magazine.
>
> This is notice that infringers of the characters, in whatever form or manner, will be prosecuted by the publisher to the full extent of the law.
>
> Publisher Marvel Comics.

The issue included a full-page ad crowded with patent and copyright notices, depicting the Torch exclaiming, "I Lead! While others try to imitate me!" The text added, "The Human Torch doesn't copy anybody! He was first—and stays first with new ideas all the time!" Accompanying illustrations showed such firsts as melting through steel and writing with fire. The Torch demonstrated the latter by skywriting a fiery message to potential infringers: "BEWARE."[5]

The Torch and Sub-Mariner were about to become part of a triumvirate of Timely superstars. Joe Simon, dreaming up a new hero, considered *Batman*'s strong sales and concluded its basic appeal consisted of stories built around "weird archfiends" like the Joker. But the all-time archfiend was in the daily headlines: Hitler, along with his "goose-stepping minions." Simon concluded, "All that was left to do was to devise a long-underwear hero to stand up to him." He needed a name and considered "Super American," but there were enough "super" characters. "Captain America" had a nice ring. He named Cap's kid partner, Bucky Barnes, after a high school pal, Bucky Pierson.

Simon pitched the star-spangled costumed hero, complete with a red, white, and blue triangular-shaped shield, to Martin Goodman. The publisher wanted to launch the character as a solo title and made a verbal agreement with Simon for 25 percent profit participation: 15 percent for Simon, and 10 for the artist. As Simon ruefully recalled, "We shook hands on the deal. Artists are notoriously poor businessmen."[6]

Simon and Kirby made a team as Timely editorial directors and storytellers. Their own creative process was an unusual collaborative flow that began by brainstorming story and plot together, with Simon usually doing the rough layouts and Kirby the tight penciling. "I did most of the writing, but Jack could write, too," Simon explained. "We'd script the story right on the board, and make notes in the margins. Jack was excellent at following the story, adding to it, or reinventing it if that was what it needed. By the time we got done laying it out on paper, though . . . it was an entirely different script. . . . I was doing most of the inking. Jack was too exceptional a penciler to waste him on inking, in my opinion. I was a brush man, and didn't use much pen at all. . . . Whenever we worked together, we tried to make it mesh."[7]

The first issue of *Captain America* (March 1941) didn't bother to take Hitler before a tribunal—Captain America rocks the Fuehrer's face with a roundhouse punch on the cover. Simon and Kirby were sending a message; the issue hit the newsstands around January, almost a year before Germany's Axis partner, Japan, made the surprise attack on Pearl Harbor that brought America into the war.

In the story Axis spies and saboteurs endanger the home front. In response, the Federal Bureau of Investigation tests a serum to build up body and brain tissue to superhuman levels. (There wasn't time to replicate Bruce Wayne's years of study and physical training.) The test subject, a physically unfit but patriotic kid named Steve Rogers, is injected and instantly bulks up to heroic proportions. A planned "corps of super-agents" is not to be, though, as an Axis spy—they *are* everywhere—shoots and kills the scientist who'd developed the serum, of which there was only the test dose. America's lone super soldier retains the guise of Steve Rogers, Army private, while his regiment's young mascot, Bucky Barnes, becomes his masked partner, as the patriotic hero stands as "sentinel of our shores." Readers were invited to send their dimes to become members of Captain America's "Sentinels of Liberty."

The first issue introduced Cap's nemesis, the Red Skull, a crazed Nazi with a hideous red death-skull countenance, whose criminal hypocrisy is revealed. "Of course you realize," he tells his underworld minions, "the main item in overthrowing a government is money!" The action was nonstop, violent, and horrific—and a hit with kids. The second issue print run was over a million copies.[8]

Homegrown US Nazis didn't like two Jews insulting Hitler and picturing Nazis as money-grubbing fiends. Simon and Kirby laughed off death-threat letters and threatening phone calls, with street fighter Jack ready to take on all comers. But when menacing groups of men began loitering in front of Timely's 42nd Street offices, New York police officers began manning shifts around the building. During this tense period, a phone call came in to Timely from a man who said he was Mayor La Guardia and asked for the editor of *Captain America*. Simon took the call. "You boys over there are doing a good job," came the unmistakable voice, Simon recalled. "The City of New York will see that no harm comes to you."[9]

There was a legal problem with Captain America—MLJ Magazines' own star-spangled super patriot, the Shield, wore a shield-patterned costume and had been published first, in *Pep Comics* #1 (January 1940). Simon, Kirby, and Goodman were called to a meeting with MLJ editor John Goldwater to listen to a litany of potential legal actions. But an understanding was reached that included Simon's suggestion that Cap's shield be rounded, like the garbage can lids he used during boyhood snowball fights. A brilliant idea, the aerodynamic new shield was in Cap's hands by issue #2. As the meeting ended, Goldwater boldly pulled Simon and Kirby aside, chuckling as he offered them a deal while Goodman seethed. Simon later learned both had worked for Hugo Gernsback, been publishing partners, and involved with Donenfeld's Independent News. "It was then that I began to understand how incestuous the business could be," Simon recalled.[10]

Cap had been threatened with legal action for alleged infringing, yet a few months later Timely house ads carried the notice: "Imitators Beware! Now that Captain America has attained such a vast following, many comic books are attempting to copy his costume and deeds. The Publishers of Captain America hereby serve notice that they will prosecute to the full extent of the law any and all such acts of infringement—There is only One Captain America."[11]

Meanwhile, Joe and Jack suspected they were being cheated out of their royalty agreement, suspicions confirmed when Timely's accountant, Morris Coyne, told them their promised royalties were being eaten up. Goodman was charging company expenses to *Captain America*. "These days they call that 'Hollywood accounting,'" Simon lamented. "It's why blockbuster movies never turn a profit."

Liebowitz was happy to meet with the disgruntled team. Simon recalled Liebowitz as "an astute businessman who wanted to make a deal. His thin mustache was secured on a chiseled face that appeared to be in its late thirties, capping a slim frame that seemed even younger." Simon and Kirby should be at DC, Liebowitz agreed, approving a one-year contract at $250 a week.

Simon recalled rumors of Harry Donenfeld's mob connections as the "short, brusque middle-aged man" came in and out of the spacious executive offices during the meeting with Liebowitz, "followed by a huge, rough looking aide in a chauffeur's uniform." Happy Harry toasted the new contract with a round from a giant bottle of scotch on a swivel stand, the ominous man in the chauffer's uniform doing the pouring. "Donenfeld was still toasting when we left," Simon recalled.

Simon and Kirby's impending departure from Timely somehow became known, the suspected tattler a seventeen-year-old employee and relative of Goodman's named Stanley Lieber. The kid later recalled Simon and Kirby "were producing the comics at that time for this company" and in that capacity hired him. "And my job was to really be an assistant. . . . I got them their lunch sandwiches, and I filled their [ink bottles]—in those days they dipped the brushes in ink and used pencil sharpeners. And I sharpened the pencils. I erased the pages after they were finished."[12]

Simon and Kirby had given the kid a break, having Lieber write a Captain America "text piece" story in issue #3. He used his first name to form his pen name of Stan Lee. The name stuck, and Lee would next work with Kirby twenty years later. In the meantime, Simon and Kirby left Timely after *Captain America* #10. Goodman had new writers and artists take over *Captain America* and promoted his young relative to interim editor until he could find someone "mature." Stan Lee, the new editorial head of Timely, never left.

In 1941, while still busy on *Captain America*, Simon and Kirby moonlighted for Fawcett. Their work at Timely did not prohibit outside projects, but they were discreet about this one, renting a hotel room to secretly labor on the inaugural issue of *Captain Marvel Adventures*. They had two weeks to deliver a sixty-four-page magazine, with stories scripted by Fawcett writer Manly Wade Wellman. Joe and Jack knew it was a rush job, and it showed. Still, *Captain Marvel Adventures* was a blockbuster success, sending Captain Marvel further into the stratosphere after the character's already successful launch in *Whiz Comics*.[13]

WHIZ

The first issue of *Whiz* told Bill Parker's story of orphan Billy Batson hawking newspapers outside a subway station when a mysterious stranger leads him to a magical subway that whisks the boy to a subterranean cave where he meets the wizard Shazam. The issue introduced media mogul Sterling Morris, who gives Batson a job as a reporter on WHIZ radio, and Marvel's nemesis, a diminutive, bald evil scientist named Sivana, the name a fusion of "Shiva" and "nirvana." Beck based Sivana's likeness on a druggist that ran a drugstore near his home.[14]

Whiz features included breakout star Spy Smasher. "If Captain Marvel was the Superman of the Fawcett universe, then Alan Armstrong, a.k.a. Spy Smasher, was its Batman," writes author and graphics designer Chip Kidd. "Having no actual superpowers other than his cunning intellect, physical fitness, and knack for brilliant invention, Armstrong assumed the pose of bored Virginia socialite by day and the Axis-thwarting Spy Smasher by night. Though his costume appears to be that of an aviator, his chief means of transportation was the Gyrosub, a

Star superheroes often had fan clubs, but DC charged unfair competition when Superman's rival Captain Marvel did it. This image of Captain Marvel posing with Billy Batson shows an impossible pairing—when Billy says "Shazam," he is replaced in time and space by Captain Marvel.

WHIZ COMICS #24 (NOVEMBER 28, 1941), HOUSE AD.

combination airplane, autogyro, speedboat, and submarine of his own devising."[15]

With Fawcett's approval, C. C. Beck set up his own studio with assistant Pete Costanza. Parker wrote scripts for less than a year before returning to active military service on October 15, 1940. The main writer thereafter was Otto Binder, a science-fiction pulp specialist who claimed to have encouraged the careers of two fans named Siegel and Shuster.[16] A Captain Marvel fan club was launched, and the hero began doing cross-promotional ads for Fawcett magazines like *Mechanix Illustrated*.

"Whimsy" is the word often used to describe Captain Marvel tales. There was fun at the hero's expense—Sivana gleefully derided his enemy's bright red uniform, calling him "The Big Red Cheese," a term of endearment to fans. A growing "Marvel Family" included Captain Marvel Jr. and Mary Marvel. The supporting cast included Binder and Beck's inspired creation Tawny, a talking tiger with a penchant for wearing tweed suits and living peacefully among humans.

Villainy was abundant in Captain Marvel's world, what Jules Feiffer called "a Disneyland of happy violence."[17] There was Captain Nazi, nemesis of Captain Marvel Jr., and the sinister Mr. Mind, a talking, bespectacled worm that led the Monster Society of Evil in an epic serialized story in *Captain Marvel Adventures* from 1942–1945. Black Adam, Marvel's evil counterpart, was introduced after having flown five thousand years from the star system to which Shazam had banished him. (The villain bears an uncanny resemblance to Hollywood style-reference Basil Rathbone.)

Sivana was the epitome of villainy. In one story he and his equally evil lookalike son and daughter are tired of being persecuted in the press. "Nobody ever hears *our* side of the story," Sivana exclaims. They plot a hostile takeover of a newspaper called *World's Greatest*, ordering publisher Colonel McWatters to sign over control. When McWatters indignantly refuses, Sivana's daughter puts a gun to his head and, with a giggle, pulls the trigger.[18]

Captain Marvel ends up on the psychiatrist's couch when a comely gal calls him a "big, red cheese," the insult he always ignored when it was uttered by arch foe Sivana. Golden Age Captain Marvel tales were known for their whimsy and never hesitated to have good-natured sport with Shazam's chosen one.

"CAPTAIN MARVEL'S INFERIORITY COMPLEX," *CAPTAIN MARVEL ADVENTURES* #80 (JANUARY 1948), P. 5, ART BY C. C. BECK.

With Captain Marvel muscling in on the marketplace, it was clear he was on a collision course with Superman.

"Sadly, the most savage reprisals in comic books were saved, just as in revolutions, not for one's enemies but for one's own kind," Feiffer writes. "If, for a moment, Superman may be described as the Lenin of superheroes, Captain Marvel must be his Trotsky. Ideologically of the same bent, who could have predicted that within months the two would be at each other's throats—or that, in time, Captain Marvel would present the only serious threat to the power of the man without whom he could not have existed?"[19]

CHAPTER 9

UP, UP AND AWA-A-Y!

Donenfeld remains free at any time to discharge them. . . . Siegel and Shuster sometimes fall to brooding about how nice it would have been had they held out for a fat percentage of all future profits. But in the end they always reach the same Pollyannaism: "Even if we were making three or four times as much, we wouldn't be doing anything very different than we're doing now. As it is, we have to keep pinching ourselves."

JOHN KOBLER
"Up, Up And Awa-a-y!" *Saturday Evening Post*, 1941

REPUBLIC SUPERHEROES

Superman was ready to break into movies with a live-action serial at Republic Pictures, a Hollywood "B" studio. A young company boasting experience and resources, Republic was established in 1935 by Herbert J. Yates (founder and president of Consolidated Film Industries, a film-processing lab), after he saw a chance to leverage six "Poverty Row" studios struggling to pay their bills at his lab: Monogram Pictures, Mascot Pictures, Liberty Pictures, Majestic Pictures, Chesterfield Pictures, and Invincible Pictures. Yates gave them the choice to foreclose or merge into a studio under his control. They merged.

Republic was the sum of its parts. Liberty Pictures provided its Liberty Bell as an interim logo before the new studio worked up its own symbol of an eagle poised at a mountain peak above the clouds. Mascot Pictures specialized in serials and contributed a first-rate production facility and singing cowboy Gene Autry, who joined Roy Rogers and John Wayne as Republic stars. The consolidation collectively pooled resources—production staff, industry contacts, and a stock company of veteran character actors.[1] As with Universal and Columbia, Republic excelled in low-budget but high-quality matinee serials with cliffhanger endings.

In May 1940 a potential live-action Superman serial was discussed by Republic executive producer Sol Siegel and producer Hiram S. Brown Jr. But Brown had creative concerns and shared them with Siegel:

> Superman was invulnerable to any kind of danger that we could create for him. . . . I believed the appeal of the strip was based on the fantastic exploits of Superman, and that to do justice to the serial we would have to duplicate those feats that we saw in the comic strip, and possibly go farther and make them more fantastic, and that to do that it would make the serial very, very costly, and over all my objection was that the character was not sympathetic because you couldn't get yourself into a frenzy worrying about a character that has no weakness.

Nonetheless, the following month Brown got the go-ahead to develop a thirteen-episode Superman story with Norman S. Hall, story editor of Republic's serial department, and the writing team of Sol Shor, Peter Adreon, Joe Poland, and Barney Sarecky. But after only two months, executive producer Siegel halted production. "His explanation to me was . . . [that] negotiations with the owners of Superman were unsatisfactory," Brown said. "What the particulars were he did not discuss with me. He did say we were not going to make the picture, and to abandon it."[2]

Republic contemplated legal action for breach of contract, even while seamlessly transitioning to a rival property that would claim bragging rights as the first live-action superhero movie.[3]

Adventures of Captain Marvel was planned as a twelve-episode, black-and-white live-action series directed by William Witney and John English, with Republic's core *Superman* team assigned the new project, including producer Hiram Brown, story editor Norman Hall, and writers Shor and Poland, with Ronald Davidson, who did some work on *Superman*.[4]

Brown's objection to Superman was his invulnerability, so what was the difference with Captain Marvel, who was as super as Superman?

"Superman could not be in trouble in any relations with human beings, unless they had some power commensurate with the powers that were inherent in Superman," Brown explained. "Not having that problem in the Captain Marvel serial, we could get back to human beings . . . because we had the Billy Batson character to fall back on. Billy Batson is just as vulnerable as you or I. We wrote a different picture entirely." As with the plan for *Superman*, Captain Marvel's character did not usually figure in the cliffhanger endings, which instead put Batson and other vulnerable characters in peril.[5]

Captain Marvel's magical nature was another distinction the filmmakers noted and incorporated, the opposite of Superman's science-fiction origin and pseudo-scientific rationale for his powers. "I suggested that we supply an atmosphere or mood that would make the magic more believable," Brown added. "I wanted the opening of the picture laid in a romantic spot, a far off country, where mysticism or magic would be more believable than in a city atmosphere."[6]

As with *Superman*, Brown cautioned Hall and his writers against scripting feats too difficult and expensive to create. For the illusion of flight, Republic turned to its award-winning special effects and miniature effects team of Howard and Theodore Lydecker. The brothers utilized a system they had prepared for *Superman*. A seven-foot papier-mâché figure in a silk-and-cotton costume, both arms outstretched in a flying pose, was connected to pulleys by two sets of wires, one wire attached to each shoulder and calf; gravity propelled it forward, simulating a figure in flight.[7]

The production was advertised as "Based on the character in WHIZ COMICS magazine," but it was *loosely* based. Billy Batson was not a boy but a young man, a radio broadcaster on an archeological expedition to the "Valley of the Tombs" in Siam (present-day Thailand). There is no magical subway ride—Shazam secretly appears to Batson during the expedition to bestow the magic word.

Frank Coghlan Jr. played Billy Batson, and Tom Tyler suited up as Captain Marvel. Tyler, a prizefighter and record-setting amateur weight lifter in his youth, had an innate toughness. After high school he worked as a seaman in the merchant marines, a coal miner in Pennsylvania, and a lumberjack in the Pacific Northwest. His muscular physique and rugged good looks made him a star of low-budget Westerns and serials. By the time Tyler was offered $250 a week to play Captain Marvel, he had been in over one hundred pictures, from playing a charioteer in the silent-screen *Ben-Hur* (1925) to Luke Plummer, the gunslinger who faces off against John Wayne's Ringo Kid in the climactic shoot-out of *Stagecoach* (1939).[8]

The production moved swiftly: story, treatments, and final screenplay were written from October through December 1940, with all twelve installments filmed in January and part of February 1941. The first episode was released to theaters on March 28, 1941, followed by an episode a week thereafter.[9]

Not to be outdone, Superman, Inc., got its star on the silver screen in 1941.

FLEISCHER'S SUPERMAN

Max and Dave Fleischer were pioneers of motion-picture animation. Max had even been awarded a 1917 patent application award for a "rotoscope," a device allowing live-action footage to be traced, frame by frame, to create realistic animation. Two years later the brothers organized Out of the Inkwell, Inc., also known as Fleischer Studios, partnering with a major studio, Paramount Pictures, to handle their releases for the next fifteen years. "Max retained the copyrights on the characters, but signed over all other rights to the films to Paramount—a decision he would later regret," notes animation historian Charles Solomon.[10]

The Fleischers were a serious rival to Walt Disney Studios. Like Disney, they experimented with combining animation and live-action and boasted star characters like the surreal Ko-Ko the Clown, vampish Betty Boop, and spinach-chomping Popeye the Sailor, based on Elzie Segar's comic strip. As with Disney, each cartoon was a short film—the unknown was whether audiences would sit through feature-length animation. Walt Disney found the answer in 1937 when his Technicolor feature release, *Snow White and the Seven Dwarfs*, was a huge box-office success.

Fleischer played catch-up with its own Technicolor feature, *Gulliver's Travels*. But while *Snow White* was in production for four years, *Gulliver's Travels* was in the works for less than half that, although the patented rotoscope was used to great effect. Paramount expected a blockbuster when *Gulliver's Travels* opened on December 22, 1939. It was not a *Snow White* phenomenon.

The Fleischers were deep in debt to Paramount and under the gun to deliver the big feature-length success their partner studio expected. And then Paramount proposed a series of *Superman* shorts. "I didn't want to make Superman," Dave Fleischer recalled. "Paramount wanted it. They called me over and asked why I didn't want to make it. I told them because it was too expensive, they wouldn't make any money back on it. The average short cost nine or ten thousand dollars, some ran up to fifteen: they varied. I couldn't figure out how to make Superman look right without spending a lot of money. I told them they'd have to spend $90,000 on each one. . . . They spent the $90,000."

Superman, Inc., entered into the agreement on August 27, 1940, and by late 1941 a poster trumpeted "Superman Is Here!" The poster for the first Technicolor animated short included the credit, "Comic Strip Created by Jerome Siegel and Joe Shuster." Fleischer's rotoscope also got a screen credit: "Stereoptical Process and Apparatus Patented. Patent Number 2054414." Bud Collyer, the radio Superman, voiced the animated hero. The short was a natural progression: hand-drawn feats from the comic pages blown up, bigger-than-life, on movie screens through hand-drawn animation.

"Some of the best animation the studio ever produced brought the dramatically staged actions of the popular comic books to life," Charles Solomon writes. "The Superman cartoons look like the lavishly budgeted films they were. The animators were able to pencil test much of their work, a luxury that had never been permitted on the Betty Boop shorts. The figures—some rotoscoped, some drawn freehand—are carefully shaded to suggest three-dimensional forms."[11]

The first animated short was celebrated in a Superman story promoted in *Action* #53: "Man of Steel becomes Man of the Movies! You've thrilled to SUPERMAN in Paramount's animated cartoons in Technicolor. . . . Now don't miss the thrillingly different adventure entitled 'Superman, Matinee Idol' in *Superman* no. 19 on sale Sept. 4th at [news]stands everywhere!" In the surreal story, Clark takes Lois to the movies but realizes the theater is showing the *Superman* serial—he must distract Lois, or she'll discover *he* is Superman! In one panel the movie screen lights up with the credit: "Copyright, 1942 *Action Comics* and *Superman* Magazines, based on the famous comic strip created by Jerome Siegel and Joe Shuster." Lois responds, "Siegel and Shuster? Who are they?" Clark thinks, "How they know so much about me is a puzzle. Perhaps they're clairvoyant!"

In 1943 DC got another of its stars into a live-action movie when Columbia released a *Batman* serial. Bob Kane flew across the continent to watch the filming, arriving in Hollywood in

Superman #19 includes Lois and Clark going to the new *Superman* movie and puzzling over the onscreen credit given to Jerome Siegel and Joe Shuster.

"SUPERMAN MATINEE IDOL," *SUPERMAN* #19 (NOVEMBER/DECEMBER 1942), P. 2, PANELS 1–6, PENCILS BY JOE SHUSTER, INKS BY JOHN SIKELA.

starry-eyed anticipation. "As I entered Columbia Studios . . . I was bursting with excitement," Kane recalled. "I anticipated seeing Batman brought to the screen for the first time, but my enthusiasm soon turned to disappointment." Kane thought Batman actor Lewis Wilson "an overweight chap" and thought no better of Douglas Croft as Robin, who was hardly a "boy" wonder. Then he asked director Lambert Hillyer about the Batmobile. "He looked at me like I was crazy for not recognizing it and said I was standing right in front of it. I did a double take, because the car that was supposed to be the Batmobile was an ordinary gray convertible. . . . Obviously, the producer lacked imagination . . . or a budget."[12]

THE SWEET SMELL OF SUCCESS

Superman artist Jack Burnley always saluted "the uniqueness of the first Superman." He first met Superman's creators at Whit Ellsworth's office in the early 1940s, at their peak of success: "I remember [Shuster] as rather small and slim, with thick-lensed glasses and a quiet, unassuming manner. Siegel was just the opposite, heavy set and voluble with an out-going personality."[13]

In 1941 quality problems continued at the Cleveland studio, including ongoing drama over Lois's look. Editorial director Whit Ellsworth drew a rough sketch of Lois in a February 19, 1941, letter to Siegel: "You used to make her more or less in this manner—slim and sleek." He criticized her hairstyle as a "rat's nest." Shading Lois's breasts to highlight them had to be avoided, Whit complained: "You know as well as I do what sort of censure we are always up against, and how careful we must be." The "vertical pen-lines" underneath her stomach elicited the crude comment that "you arrange for her to have an abortion or the baby and get it over with so that her figure can return to something a little more like the tasty dish she is supposed to be." Ellsworth told Jerry to explain to Joe and his artists the formula for drawing a pretty girl, starting with a pretty face and keeping everything consistent—a continuing complaint was that the look of characters kept changing—making her shoulders wider than her hips (Lois's hips were always too wide) and finishing with long legs. Ellsworth reported Liebowitz's dissatisfaction: "He says that in addition to making Lois look like a witch, you have apparently dressed her out of a Montgomery Ward catalogue. He suggests *Vogue*, *Vanity Fair*, and *Harper's Bazaar* as likelier spots for dress-research." Whit's bottom line: "The gal ain't being done right"[14]

Advance press for the first animated *Superman* cartoon included an article in the June 21 issue of the *Saturday Evening Post*. The popular magazine reproduced a film still of Superman straining to push back a destructive ray fired by a mad scientist, the credit reading, "Courtesy of Paramount-Fleischer Studios." The caption added, "Superman crashes the movies—a scene from his first animated cartoon, about to be released." Robert Maxwell took affront, complaining the magazine arranged with Paramount and Fleischer to reproduce the image, but did so "without our consent or permission" despite assurances they would not publish *anything* without first submitting it to Superman, Inc.[15] This lapse included the article itself. "Up, Up And Awa-a-y! The Rise of Superman, Inc.," was a high-profile piece revealing uncomfortable truths about the Superman Corporation.

On its face the article celebrated Superman. "No other cartoon character ever has been such an all-around success at the age of three," noted writer John Kobler. "No other cartoon character ever has carried his creators to such an accomplishment as Siegel and Shuster enjoy at the age of twenty-six." Superman was an "authentic culture hero. . . . Governments have taken official note of Superman." *Superman* comics were translated overseas but "banned wherever the swastika waves."

There were concerns among parents and educators about Superman's potentially negative effects on impressionable minds, but DC's editorial advisor, psychiatrist Dr. Lauretta Bender (who approved of bondage-filled *Wonder Woman*), felt the character was a positive figure of imperishable strength. Every few months Siegel visited New York for meetings about maintaining Superman as a paragon of virtue. In-house moral guidelines stipulated Superman was not allowed to destroy property (unless belonging to a villain), kill, use a weapon, or betray sexual desire.

Siegel and Shuster had begun making serious money, and Kobler credited their persistence, which, presumably to Liebowitz's frustration, they happily revealed to the writer: "It was only after anguished appeals that Siegel and Shuster finally managed, in 1940, to wangle sizeable profits for themselves: $75,000, of which $16,000 goes in staff salaries and overhead [to the Cleveland studio]."

Joe used his share to move his mother and father into a

ten-room house in Cleveland. He bought a radio-phonograph console for playing the classical music he loved listening to with his mother. Joe wanted his dad to retire, but every day Mr. Shuster dutifully headed downtown to his job as an elevator operator. Mrs. Shuster cooked their meals, although twice a week a maid came to houseclean. "None of the Shusters can quite grasp what has happened to them," the article reported.

Jerry married Bella, a high school sweetheart, and the couple was the picture of modern domesticity. Jerry had an even $20,000 in the bank and worked at home, hitting his typewriter keys to the beat of swing music records. The couple lived in "an air-conditioned, rock-wool-insulated, weather-stripped house with so many laborsaving gadgets that Bella Siegel has little to do all day except flip switches."

The article reported that although Jerry and Joe were rolling in dough, DC reaped the fortune. "How much [Donenfeld] personally pockets from Superman is a question much debated in New York publishing circles," Kobler reported, although he wrangled a startling comment from Liebowitz who "cautiously" admitted that Donenfeld paid his 1940 income tax on "more than $100,000." Superman, Inc., would net an estimated $120,000 from the first *Superman* animated film alone, while thirty-three licensed products developed within the previous six months boosted DC's estimated 1940–1941 income to $1.5 million.

Kobler reported that Siegel and Shuster were developing a "new" project, although the creators apparently failed to tell the writer the idea had been twice offered, unsuccessfully, to DC. "It may be called Superboy and will confine itself to Superman's adolescence, when his supermuscles—the mind recoils from the possibilities—were employed in practical jokes. . . . 'It will be,' Siegel explains, 'about Superman before he developed a social conscience.'"[16]

The *Post* piece was not well received at 480 Lexington. Siegel didn't help in a June 18 letter to Liebowitz that included a clipping of another unauthorized Cleveland newspaper feature on

Superman's creators. "The interview irritated me considerably," Liebowitz wrote back. "I wish once and for all that you would stop talking so that you will not jeopardize our relationship. . . . This has been arranged with you in the past—that you are not to give any interview without consent. . . . I would not want anything in the future to happen which would strain our present relationship."

The letter was stern, but absent the lecturing tone of earlier correspondence—it even opened with apologies for not writing sooner. "But at least once a month there arises an occasion for me to write, and that is when sending you the check for syndication returns." Enclosed was a substantial $2,758.94 for the syndication share, and two other checks: $325 and the requisite release agreement for Siegel and artist Leo Nowack's new creation, *Robotman*, and $500 "in line with our usual generous attitude towards you boys . . . in effect a token of feeling."

The $500 was an attempt to lighten bad news: "Under the term of our contract you were entitled to a percentage of the net profits accruing from the exploitation of Superman in channels other than magazines. These figures for last year show that we lost money, and therefore you are entitled to no royalties."[17] It was more of the "Hollywood accounting" that kept *Captain America* profits from Simon and Kirby.

"Donenfeld's companies had grossed a million-and-a-half dollars directly off Superman, and yet Jack's figures showed they'd lost money," Gerard Jones writes. "The 'boys' were up against an accountant . . . who had mastered his trade among unions, racketeers, and pornographers. . . . He wasn't going to be beaten by a couple of junior *luftmenschen* who didn't know what 'net profit' implied." The problem with Siegel and Shuster was that "they [had] never learned any codes on the street, had never made any real deals, had never known the boozy smoke-blowing world of business. They knew movies and comics and pulp stories, where words meant what they meant and good guys and bad were clearly delineated."[18]

Siegel mailed the signed Robotman release back to Liebowitz, promising a script would soon follow and noting the "excellent page rate opens new opportunities to us." Siegel's return letter did not mention the $500 but added that since the *Saturday Evening Post* article appeared, he and Joe had been "approached by literary agents, some of them among the most prominent in the country, who wish to represent us. They claim they can secure much better terms for us than we are now receiving. . . . Joe and I would very much prefer working directly with you on the matter of rates, and not have other parties negotiate our increases with us. . . . If you believe you can give us an increase at once, we will notify the various agencies who wish to handle our business affairs, that we are not interested."[19]

The desired terms weren't forthcoming, and the dance continued. There was a jocular tone to a "Dear Jerry" note from Ellsworth requesting splash pages "as interesting and intriguing as those in 'Batman' as another impulse device for kids. These days, when kids thumb thru magazines before buying 'em, all the come-on salesmanship you can pour into a story helps. So give, pal! Bestest, Whit."[20]

When Jack reported fan mail wanted Lois to discover that Clark is Superman, Jerry disagreed: "If Lois should ACTUALLY learn Clark's secret, the strip would lose about 75% of its appeal— the human interest angle. . . . I fear that if this element is removed from the story formula that makes up SUPERMAN, that the strip will lose a great part of its effectiveness."[21]

They were riding the Superman wave for all it was worth. Fun-loving Harry Donenfeld, who'd recoiled from the *Action* #1 cover, now wore an "S" chest emblem T-shirt underneath his suit that he occasionally exposed, as in Clark's already-classic reveal. Instead of skulking in the shadowy world of pornographic pulps, Donenfeld was enjoying the spotlight. The *Kansas City Star*, which carried the *Superman* strip, hailed him as "The man who built the financial biceps of Superman."[22]

Things were busy, editorially, and Whit Ellsworth hired Mort

Weisinger as associate editor and artist Dick Sprang to stockpile *Batman* pages ahead of the talent drain should the United States enter the war.[23] Ellsworth was responsible for correct copyright notices, but a mistake snuck through on the first *Superman* in his charge, issue #5 (Summer 1940). Instead of "Detective Comics, Inc.," the copyright notice read "Entire contents copyrighted 1940 by Superman, Inc." It was a major blunder, as Superman, Inc., was DC's licensing arm only, with no publication rights.

When *Superman* #6 was released, again copyrighted under Superman, Inc., someone finally caught the error. To fix the problem an amendment letter was appended to the earlier January 18, 1940, agreement letter provided between DC and Superman, Inc. The August 14, 1940, amendment allowed the Superman Corporation to take out copyrights in its own name, with rights reverting to DC at the agreement's termination. Superman stories in *Action* and *Superman* were now officially published in the name of Superman, Inc., but the amendment could not retroactively apply to the bungled copyrights.[24]

Meanwhile, *Captain Marvel* was outselling *Superman*, and Fawcett trumpeted the news in cover copy of *Captain Marvel Adventures*: "LARGEST CIRCULATION OF ANY COMIC MAGAZINE." In June 1941, the month of the *Post* article on Superman, Inc., DC sent Fawcett a cease and desist order, accusing the publisher of infringing their Superman copyright. DC also warned Republic not to release *Captain Marvel*, but the serial went into release in March 1941. The first in the series of Fleischer *Superman* cartoons was released on September 26.

THE LAWSUIT

On September 5, 1941, plaintiffs DC and Superman, Inc., sued for copyright infringement and unfair competition against Fawcett Publications, Inc., and Republic Pictures Corporation and Republic Productions, Inc. DC's legal actions against the likes of

Wonder Man had been about a single character. Now, emerging media and merchandising empires were in play and at risk.

Detective Comics, Inc., and Superman, Inc., retained the Manhattan firm of Phillips, Nizer, Benjamin & Krim, with Louis Nizer leading the fight. Fawcett Publications called in the New York firms of De Witt, Van Aken, Nast & Chapman, and Nims, Verdi & Martin, with Wallace Martin taking the lead for Captain Marvel.

New York lawyer Meyer H. Lavenstein represented Republic Pictures Corporation and Republic Productions, Inc. (hereafter "Republic"). Because of copyright questions, McClure Syndicate would be caught up in the lawsuit and retained Guggenheimer & Untermyer, Esq.

Fawcett's attorneys saw an Achilles heel in the Superman, Inc., copyright mistakes in *Superman* #5 and #6, and in the sloppy and incomplete copyright notices on the newspaper strip, such as "(Copyright, 1939)." In contrast, the daily registration for *Terry and the Pirates* in 1939, the year the *Superman* strip began, read: "Reg. U.S. Pat. Off.: Copyright, 1939, by News Syndicate Company, Inc." Fawcett argued that if *Superman* was not correctly copyrighted, then it was in the public domain and there could be no infringement. (When McClure began a *Batman and Robin* strip on October 25, 1943, copyright was correctly affixed: "Copyright 1943 by Detective Comics, Inc., Dist. by McClure Newspaper Syndicate.")

In preparation for battle, Harry Donenfeld called upon artist Joe Szokoli, son of gangster Frank Costello's favorite barber and one of Harry's prized *Spicy* artists, to alter H. J. Ward's Superman painting hanging at 480 Lexington Avenue.

"Legal prosecution of this case required DC to provide an iron-clad definition of their character's patented qualities," pulp historian David Saunders notes.

This was not so easy, because in fact Superman had slightly evolved since his first appearance. His chest emblem had grown larger. His dangling forelock had shifted to the right side of his forehead. His once spunky smile had matured into a sterner expression of patrician approval, and his friendly eyes had narrowed down to a weather-beaten squint. Donenfeld needed to alter Ward's original painting to include all of the 1942 characteristics that were legally stipulated in his copyright lawsuit. . . . For fifty bucks [Szokoli] painted the prescribed changes during a single visit to Donenfeld's office.[25]

CHAPTER 10

BATTLE OF THE CENTURY

[The plaintiffs' periodicals] contain a large amount of matter wholly original with the said authors . . . revolving principally about the figure and character of "SUPERMAN," and constitute copyrightable subject matter under the laws of the United States. . . . Captain Marvel [periodicals] were copied from the aforesaid copyrighted material. . . . FAWCETT PUBLICATIONS, INC. has derived and will derive profits and revenue and has caused and will cause irreparable damage to the plaintiffs. The said profits and revenue and the said damage are incapable of accurate computation

DC, Inc., and Superman, Inc., Complaint, 13th and 31st cause,
served September 10, 1941

LEGAL WARFARE

The complaint served by Detective Comics and Superman, Inc., against Fawcett and Republic had six counts of copyright infringement and unfair competition. The complaint charged that Captain Marvel was purposely designed to resemble Superman, creating "confusion and deception in the minds of the public, who have been led to believe that the continuity and comic strip of the defendant . . . is in fact the work or product of the plaintiffs, to the irreparable damage and injury of the plaintiffs."

The suit accused Fawcett of copying physical characteristics and "scenes, characters, incidents and pictorial delineations revolving principally about the figure and character of 'SUPERMAN'"; the plaintiffs also alleged that Fawcett had created and distributed infringing merchandise, such as the movie serial. The complaint demanded the defendants be enjoined from further infringing; pay damages and report all profits; pay court costs and attorney fees for DC/Superman, Inc.; and grant the plaintiffs whatever additional relief the court considered "just and proper."[1]

Republic attorney Meyer Lavenstein fired back in his own sworn statement on October 28, 1941, arguing the complaint failed to state *exactly* how the motion picture copied or appropriated Superman. The attorney requested that DC/Superman, Inc., furnish a "bill of particulars," a statement listing specific reasons for legal action, to "specify and identify the particular items."[2]

A lawsuit was underway that threatened a publishing and merchandising enterprise, that might even change the industry, but it was otherwise business as usual for the contending publishers. In 1941 DC spun off *New York World's Fair Comics* into *World's Best Comics*, an anthology featuring separate adventures of Superman and Batman and Robin. In *Superman* #13, a cub reporter previously seen in the background came to the fore as Jimmy Olsen, a character properly introduced on the radio show in April 1940.[3] The cover stamp, "A DC publication," and an adjoining "Ind" for Independent News, was replaced on all titles with "DC" in an inner circle, enclosed in an outer circle reading, "A Superman Publication."

Whiz #25 (December 1941) introduced Captain Marvel Jr., a.k.a. Freddy Freeman, a fourteen-year-old who hawks newspapers, as Billy Batson once did. The brainchild of coeditor Eddie "France" Herron, with art by Manuel "Mac" Raboy, Captain Marvel Jr. was featured in *Master Comics* and *The Marvel Family*. In his origin story, Freddy is crippled by the homicidal Captain Nazi but rescued by Captain Marvel, who takes him to the Rock of Eternity where the spirit of Shazam, who departed the mortal world after empowering Billy, grants Freddy the power to speak his savior's name—*Captain Marvel!*—and become Captain Marvel Jr. Freddy does not physically transform, but after a cloud-burst and lightning flash, he is imbued with super powers and clothed in a blue leotard with a yellow lightning bolt chest emblem and red cape trimmed in yellow.

Mary Marvel, the creation of Otto Binder and Marc Swayze, was introduced in 1942 in *Captain Marvel Adventures* #18, predating DC's Supergirl spinoff. Mary was Billy Batson's twin sister; her "Shazam" acronym represented mythic females: Selene (grace), Hippolyta (strength), Ariadne (skill), Zephyrus (fleetness), Aurora (beauty), Minerva (wisdom).

Although cocreator Bill Parker wrote the earliest Captain Marvel stories, Fawcett had a policy against editors writing features. In 1942 it was discovered editor Eddie Herron was secretly writing Fawcett scripts under the name "Batstone," and he was fired.[4] Herron would get his revenge as a DC witness when the lawsuit came to trial.

WAR YEARS

Joe Simon and Jack Kirby had been stars at Timely and carried their star power with them to DC. They transformed Sandman— another pulpish crime fighter who had at first dressed in a suit and fedora, wore a gas mask, and carried a sleeping-gas gun— into a costumed superhero. They did the same for another hero, Manhunter, and brought a "Dead-End Kids" spin to a new title, *The Newsboy Legion*. They had another kid-centric hit in *The Boy Commandos*, a solo title and feature in *Detective Comics* and *World's Finest*.

But Jack Liebowitz "started to panic," Simon recalled, fearing that there wouldn't be enough stockpiled pages to see DC through wartime. Simon and Kirby went into high gear to help amass the three years' worth of material Liebowitz wanted. Jerry Robinson, working in the bullpen near Kirby's drawing board, describes how Jack drew a crowd:

Others in the office would gather round to watch Jack. We had some pretty fast artists there but even they couldn't believe what he was doing. . . . A whole story all penciled by the time he knocked off for the day. It would have been impressive if it had been mediocre work, but this was Jack at his best. Joe . . . was working just as rapidly, writing and inking and laying out pages. There was a reason those guys had the reputation they had.[5]

Meanwhile, the creation they left at Timely was ready to do his duty. *Captain America* #13 (April 1942), the first issue to appear after Japan's surprise attack at the Pearl Harbor naval base, was an "All Out for America!" number, with a cover showing Cap firing an uppercut into the jaw of a demonic-looking Japanese military official, exclaiming, "You started it! Now—we'll finish it!"

"Remember Pearl Harbor" was stamped on covers, including Timely's *U.S.A. Comics* #4, with the clarion call echoed on the inside cover: "Let All America Arise, Victory Shall Be Ours, Do Your Share: Buy United States Savings Bonds and Stamps!" A grim Captain America appears in a promotion, declaring, "We'll Win! This war can only end in one way . . . in victory for America! . . . JOIN young America's fastest growing Patriotic Organization. . . . Become a Sentinel of Liberty To-Day!"[6]

Paper shortages now curtailed production, and licensing deals ground to a virtual halt. Superman, Inc., did have an item heading to market in 1942: *The Adventures of Superman*, a novel written by George Lowther and illustrated by Joe Shuster. A cover credit read, "Based on the famous character created by Joe Shuster and Jerry Siegel." It was the first comic book superhero novel and the first time a writer other than Siegel had the byline on a Superman story.[7] Other ancillary business moved forward, as McClure president Richard H. Waldo advised DC they wanted to exercise their option to renew the *Superman* daily and Sunday, under the same terms for another five years, beginning June 1, 1944.[8]

The country was at war, but Jerry Siegel remained obsessed with his quest for a partnership in Superman. It was now a festering psychological wound, his signing away his creation. "We once had fantastic hopes of being able to invest and share in SUPERMAN, INC., and being on the receiving end of bonuses that would make up for contractual inequalities but we now regard these visions as sheer fantasies," Siegel confessed in a letter to Ellsworth early in 1942. "If we had been a little more brash and had been born extraverts [sic], the financial fates would have smiled more kindly on us. Meanwhile, we're the last to deny that we're fortunate to be doing as well as we are—but we can dream, can't we?"[9]

While Siegel dreamed, Ellsworth fumed, unhappy when the Cleveland studio mailed in *Superman* dailies needing so much work that he would've returned them had pressing deadlines not forced him to assign an in-house artist to properly prepare them for McClure. "I'm particularly upset because I wrote you about the same troubles after receiving the last set," Ellsworth wrote Siegel on Superman, Inc., stationery. "It seems impossible that you look them over before sending them out; either that, or you are very complacent about the guy you invented. SUPERMAN looks like a different person in almost every picture, and worse, in each . . . SUPERMAN's face is incredibly bad in more than fifty percent of its renditions." Whit described "bad hands, bad figures and bad action" and the ongoing problem of the hero's "jock strap." The bright spot was the backgrounds, but that seemed at the expense of the figure drawings of Superman in the comic books and strips.

"All in all, the sad truth is that after all these years, SUPERMAN is not outstandingly well drawn either in the magazines or in the syndicate stuff," Ellsworth concluded. "And it is getting to the point where I feel that if at least the syndicate material doesn't show a marked improvement, we shall have to consider it 'unacceptable,' and make other arrangements to have it done. . . . Altogether, the situation is serious enough to warrant your doing some real worrying."[10]

Meanwhile, Siegel was exasperated with his partner, whose output was dwindling because of his worsening eyesight. It was a sore point with Siegel, because Ellsworth and Liebowitz some-times proposed that Jerry hire new artists out of *his* share. Siegel finally wrote to Liebowitz: "Something new all the time. Always another headache. And here's the latest. . . . Joe, the social butter-fly, has stuck his neck out again." Joe, without Siegel's knowledge, signed a girl named Geraldine Mandell to a long-term contract to pose as Lois Lane for the *Superman* movies and comic strip, an arrangement reported in the local junior high school paper. "I don't know what he told this girl but he seems to have devel-oped a genius for saying the wrong things at the wrong time to the wrong people."

Siegel shared the story in confidence and probably wouldn't mention it to Joe. "I dislike arguments, and telling him to watch his step doesn't seem to do any good." Joe was "a swell guy," and he only reported the incident to explain why he didn't want to help pay for artists.

> I created the character, and outside of the first three or four SUPERMAN magazine releases and the first several weeks of the syndicate strip, Joe hasn't drawn up anything complete. In the past he used to ink work penciled by other men, but now he doesn't even do that. . . . After paying off his men in 1941, he netted over $15,000.00. For 1942, he'll probably net at least $20,000.00 or very close to it. Why then, since he's doing so well for doing so little and with a minimum of worries, should I pitch in and pay his men for drawing up the work he is being paid for?
>
> In my mild, subdued way I've told Joe many times that if he's a smart boy he should try to avoid complications of any kind and be content with quietly making a lot of money. That if he does this, after a period of years he will be financially set for life.[11]

It was sound advice Siegel himself would fail to follow.

Among the autobiographical pieces Siegel and Shuster

occasionally created, one spoke to the factory-production grind of making comics—and Joe's dissolution as a creative force. In *Superman* #25 (November/December 1943) the Siegel and Shuster story, "Geezer: King of the Comic Books," opens with the question: "Do you take your comics for granted? Or do you wonder about the story behind the stories in the funny books? Do you ever wonder how strips came to be created? Who their creators are?" In the story Lois and Clark share a news release about German outrage over the lampooning of Nazi leaders by the American comic book superhero Geezer. The *Geezer Comics* cover depicts the muscle-bound hero, with toothsome grin and unruly red hair, riding bareback on a flying missile—a jab at a Captain Marvel image on the cover of Fawcett's *Special Edition Comics*. The muscular young creator of *Geezer* is revealed to be a corporate front man. The real creator is a bespectacled cartoonist grown lazy as a studio of writers, artists, and letterers churn out Geezer adventures. The cartoonist bears a striking resemblance to Joe Shuster.

Later in 1942 Liebowitz invited Jerry and Bella to New York to discuss Superman "art material." Siegel's reply letter noted their five-year contract would soon be up and made another participation plea:

> I think you may agree now that the comic book business is here to stay (with the possible exception of suspension purely because of war shortage difficulties) and it is no longer necessary to withhold profits from creators of strips because you want to make your fortune while you can. From all indications you are solidly entrenched in a "big business" field that will continue to grow with the years.... Joe and I would like nothing better than to always be associated with you. You can assure this by making us a real part of SUPERMAN, Inc. and by giving us a contract that remunerates us on the basis of income received and not on the basis of what you arbitrarily decide to pay out.[12]

Liebowitz had been upset with Siegel before, but this letter angered him. The situation was so serious Whit Ellsworth didn't send a letter but placed a long-distance phone call to Siegel, adding the New York meeting was delayed a week.

Siegel shot out an apology letter to Liebowitz—still pressing his demands. "I may not have worded my letters diplomatically enough," he opened. "And if I've antagonized you, I'm sorry." He and Joe "created a big money maker, for which we foolishly signed away all rights. Though you have generously increased our income far greater than signed contracts stipulate, we often have the empty feeling that our income is far below what it would be if we had been born with a little more brains. That, as you can understand, can be a source of aggravation. And it leads to sleepless nights of disgust with one's self. That is not a healthy situation, but one which can be remedied only by you . . . if you have the inclination."

Siegel's proposal "to keep our self respect" was to have a "top-notch percentage arrangement with you as a permanent part of SUPERMAN." Otherwise, he threatened, they would go elsewhere. "Frankly, the former would be preferable because the combination we have formed with you is probably the type of thing that comes once in a lifetime, if at all." Siegel reported being in touch with thirty-five promising artists, "but the main obstacle to our hiring them is that their salary demands are beyond us." If they could bring in more artists and an assistant writer, they could continue producing quality Superman material, even if he and Joe ended up in the army. Siegel concluded with a postscript: "Is all forgiven?"[13]

In July 1943 Siegel was drafted into the army; Shuster got a deferment because of his bad eyesight. Unknown to Siegel, DC had his Superboy idea in play—it was at the ashcan stage, copyrighted with a January 1942 edition featuring placeholder cover art of Batman crashing into a crime lair to rescue Robin.[14]

With Siegel in the service, writers contributing to *Superman*, *Action*, and *World's Finest Comics* included Bill Finger, Mort Weisinger, and Don Cameron, who began writing for DC in 1941. Throughout the war, Superman stories carried Siegel and Shuster's byline, including a new, unauthorized "Lois Lane, Girl Reporter" feature in *Superman*.

Many cartoonists were off to the battlefields; others served on the home front. Joe Simon decided not to wait for Uncle Sam to call and enlisted in the US Coast Guard in 1943.[15] Jerry Robinson was deemed too skinny to serve, and he never forgot the physician's comment: "Look, son, we'll call you when the Nazis get to Fourteenth Street." Robinson's close friend Bernie Klein, assigned to a combat photography unit in North Africa, died on the beaches of Anzio, a personal loss that haunted his dreams for years.[16]

Jack Kirby married Rosalind "Roz" Goldstein on May 23, 1942, and the next year, on June 21, reported for duty at Camp Stewart, near Atlanta. Kirby began in the motor pool, was reclassified as a rifleman, and in August 1944 shipped to Normandy with Company F of the 11th Infantry. Kirby was on the front lines, filling his downtime writing and sketching letters home to Roz. While fighting in the mountainous Ardennes of France during the desperate, last-ditch Nazi stratagem called the Battle of the Bulge, the unseasonably freezing winter gave Kirby a dangerous case of frostbite. In a hospital in France, he heard doctors discussing whether to amputate one or both of his feet. The tough guy from the Lower East Side walked out of that hospital on both.[17]

Will Eisner headed the art department of *Army Motors*, a technical and maintenance magazine for soldiers, where he created the cartoon character Joe Dope, a G.I. illustrating what *not* to do. After the war Eisner followed up on his arrangement with Everett Arnold. "When I got back I went to him and told him I wanted to disassociate him from *The Spirit*, and he signed an agreement in which he gave the rights back to me."[18]

THE LEGAL FRONT

Throughout the war, the Superman versus Captain Marvel lawsuit forged ahead. On November 13, 1943, Superman's lawyers provided the requested bill of particulars. Louis Nizer signed the document for exhibits showing alleged copying of Superman in *Whiz* and *Captain Marvel Adventures*, *Captain Marvel Jr.*, *Mary Marvel Comics*, *America's Greatest Comics*, and *Master Comics*. Also marked for exhibit was every published Superman appearance extant: *Action Comics* #1–66, *Superman* #1–24, Superman stories from the first twelve issues of *World's Finest*, the *Superman* daily strips in the *New York Post* from July 10, 1939, to present, Sunday comics published in the *New York Daily Mirror* from December 24, 1939, to present, Paramount's animated *Superman* films, and the radio show broadcast over station WOR.[19] The details got down to lines of dialogue, as in *Whiz Comics* #3, where Billy Batson exclaims, "This is a job for Captain Marvel," an alleged swipe of "This looks like a job for Superman."

Emotions over the lawsuit spilled into the pages of Fawcett's *America's Greatest Comics* #7 (May 28, 1943), an issue with cover-to-cover war stories as Commando Yank battled Nazis in occupied Holland and Minute Man parachuted into Berlin to recover stolen art from the palace of Nazi propaganda minister Goebbels. In a poignant ode to recent, happier times, the cover pictured Captain Marvel pointing out a scale model of a Futurama-esque city to a young boy, the copy announcing, "Captain Marvel Visits the World of *Your* Tomorrow!"

Inside, the cover story opens with a crowd exclaiming, "Hey! What's that?"

"Is it a bird?"

"Is it a plane?"

The subject of the crowd's curiosity, a man solidly on terra firma, responds, "I am *not* a plane, and I am *not* a bird! I am an *inventor*! Go away you nasty people!"

DC/Superman, Inc., was not amused. This satirical use of the famous Superman phrase was introduced as another example of stolen dialogue. The supplement of complaints included pages and pages citing examples of Captain Marvel, Captain Marvel Jr., and Mary Marvel displaying Superman-like strength, invulnerability, and flight.[20]

Pretrial depositions of witnesses provided ammunition for both sides. Defendant lawyers sought testimony repudiating DC's copyright and questioning whether the publisher actually owned Siegel and Shuster's work; plaintiff lawyers wanted testimony showing Fawcett committed intellectual property theft. Fawcett's strategy of attacking faulty copyright notices hit a wall in their deposition of McClure Syndicate's assistant treasurer and secretary, Henry O. Nimis, who was instructed by counsel *not* to answer virtually any questions, certainly nothing about defective copyright notices.

Over protest from the Superman side, Judge Bright of the Southern District for New York signed an order on October 17, 1945, directing Nimis and other witnesses to answer the questions and ordering McClure to produce for defendants' counsel all "matrices, plates and proofs now in the files of McClure Newspaper Syndicate containing the Superman cartoon strips," every plate or printer's proof used in promotional material, and McClure's written instructions to engravers for preparation of plates from the original black-and-white drawings covering *Superman* strips 1 through 169.[21] Nimis's testimony amounted to 858 transcribed pages. To put that in perspective, the next highest page count was from key deposition witness Jack Liebowitz, at exactly 342 ½ pages. Fawcett now had plenty of ammunition in its strategy of attacking DC's faulty copyrights.[22]

REPUBLIC

Pretrial depositions of five Republic witnesses—Morris J. Siegel, producer Hiram S. Brown Jr., story editor Norman S. Hall, and writers Joe Poland and Ronald Davison—began in Los Angeles County on April 9, 1945. First up was producer Brown, employed at Republic from October 1, 1938, to June 1942, when he became

World War II was raging when this vision of "the world of your tomorrow" revived memories of the bright future envisioned by the recent New York World's Fair. Fawcett was being sued by DC for copyright infringement when, in its whimsical way, it poked fun at the Superman phrase, "Look! Up in the sky . . . !" DC considered it stolen dialogue and added this fresh outrage to a supplemental bill of particulars against Fawcett.

"CAPTAIN MARVEL AND THE WORLD OF YOUR TOMORROW!," *AMERICA'S GREATEST COMICS* #7 (MAY 28, 1943), OPENING SPREAD, ARTIST C. C. BECK. FAWCETT PUBLICATIONS, INC.

a captain in the Army Air Force and was stationed at the 18 AAF Base Unit, Motion Picture Unit, in nearby Culver City.

Plaintiff attorneys demanded to know if the *Captain Marvel* serial copied *Superman*. Brown testified that when the *Superman* production abruptly ended, they had not progressed beyond the early treatment phase. Regardless, the two superheroes posed different story opportunities. "The characters in the Captain Marvel strip employ usual or ordinary human devices," Brown explained.

> "In the Superman story the plot there had to provide something superhuman to contend against Clark Kent, Superman, who is one person, and has all the characteristics of a superman, even while he is Clark Kent, so for that we devised [a mechanical] monster that had powers even greater than Superman. . . . The man who had devised this mechanical method of combating Superman in the course of our story saw the potentialities of his weapon . . . desiring to use his power to control the wealth of the world and the people of it."[23]

The *Captain Marvel* serial emphasized the hero's magical nature, Brown later elaborated: "Captain Marvel . . . is a mystic creation, and has what amounts to magic powers."[24]

Story editor Norman Hall echoed Brown's testimony: "Superman never lost his identity as such. He merely masqueraded as Clark Kent. Captain Marvel was an entirely separate entity from Billy Batson, and it took a mechanical change in the way of a flash of mystic lightning and an explosion to bring Captain Marvel into being. . . . He was a separate entity."[25]

The exchanges sometimes became surreal, as when DC attorney Walter Beck, noting Brown's testimony that Superman had no "superhuman or mystical qualities," asked the producer:

> "Would you consider ability to fly through the air at such great speed as to overtake express trains, or to dive to the depths

of the ocean and push up submarines or sunken ships and hulks, human qualities?"

"In so far as to a minor degree everybody can do those things, yes."

"Have you ever tried to fly through the air?"

"I can jump and go through the air that way."

"Let's not quibble. Have you ever flown through the air, Captain Brown?"

"No."

Beck's questioning established that Superman and Captain Marvel did not fly by flapping their arms like wings. But when Beck asked if their quality of flying was different, Brown answered, "Yes."

"In what respect?"

"In the power that made it possible for the individual characters to fly."

"I am not referring to the origin of the ability; I am referring to the quality or kind of flying. Was there any difference in the quality or kind of flying between that depicted for the character Superman and that depicted for the character Captain Marvel?"

"No."

"That is all."[26]

EXPLOITATION

One deposition that would return to haunt Fawcett's cause was Bill Parker's testimony in the summer of 1944—appropriately, he was *Captain* Parker, on leave from a secret location in the Pacific theater. Parker was asked about the stack of reference comics Ralph Daigh brought in and if, at that time, he'd known of Superman. "Yes, I had," Parker answered.[27] Parker further testified he did not study comics in writing comics, but instead "followed the methods used in writing movie scripts."[28]

C. C. Beck's deposition corroborated that he and Parker discussed Superman in the fall of 1939, with Daigh and art director Al Allard present for many such conversations. Beck admitted picking up the occasional *Superman* comic around the Fawcett office—this one "looks pretty good" or that one "doesn't look so good." At trial C. C. Beck would testify to a *mention* of Superman, not discussions.[29] The problem was that when the trial finally arrived, Parker would mount the Wonder Man defense, claiming that until the lawsuit he *knew nothing* of Superman.

Jack Liebowitz's deposition was taken in New York between August 14 and August 23, 1945. During the August 14 session, Fawcett lead counsel Wallace Martin asked Liebowitz to explain the Superman licensing business and what he meant by "exploitation of the character."

"Well, the character is licensed for various items," Liebowitz began. "At least, that was the intention when the license was granted to Superman, but the war intervened and licensing was at a standstill for the duration of the war. But at the present time we have started again to license the character."

Liebowitz verified that Detective Comics, Inc., acquired its Superman rights by purchasing the character through a contract with Siegel and Shuster. Walter Beck produced photostatic copies of the contract from September 22, 1938, and the supplemental employment agreement of December 19, 1939. Beck handed the contracts to Martin, who had the 1938 contract marked "Defendant Fawcett's Exhibit A," and the 1939 agreement "Exhibit B."

Martin asked Liebowitz about his negotiations with Siegel and Shuster.

"Well," Liebowitz began, "we bought the feature—"

"Please answer the question, Mr. Liebowitz," his attorney, Beck, interrupted. "The question is: 'Do you recall when you entered negotiations with them?'"

Martin fired back, "Mr. Beck . . . if you want to instruct him not to answer, that is all right, but I ask that you not try to guide the witness in his answer."

"I have a right to caution the witness to answer the question, instead of lumbering up the record with many irresponsive answers and then having you—"

"I will be responsible for lumbering up the record," Martin interrupted, "and I ask you not to try to guide the witness."

Beck responded, "Please don't do that, Mr. Martin. Don't say I am trying to guide the witness. I am asking the witness to try to answer your question, not to try to answer some other question."

"Well, Siegel & Shuster used to draw other features for us," Liebowitz finally responded.

"I move to strike the answer," Beck replied.

"Were any of the comic characters which Siegel & Shuster drew for Plaintiff Detective Comics, Inc., prior to the time that Plaintiff Detective Comics, Inc., acquired rights in Superman, characters similar to the Superman character?" Martin pressed.

"No."

"Did Siegel & Shuster submit to you the script for the Superman which appeared in Action Comics, the first issue, at the time of your negotiations with Siegel & Shuster for the purchase of the Superman character?"

"No."

"When was the work done, if you know, for the Superman which appeared in the first issue of Action Comics?"

"I don't know how long prior to the date of publication, but it must have been done at least a month or so before that time."

Martin, developing the argument that Siegel and Shuster created Superman independently of DC, asked if Liebowitz ever checked in with McClure. Liebowitz replied there was no such policy and assumed they were doing a good job because they had a financial interest in doing so. He also testified that artwork for the comics and newspaper strips was prepared in Cleveland and mailed to DC in New York.

Martin asked what DC had done with the original art for the *Superman* strips. Liebowitz replied that it was "the custom" to destroy them. "Well . . . we usually keep it for a year, on hand," he elaborated. "If we have sufficient room, we keep it there; if it gets too bulky, we just tear it up—sell it for wastepaper."[30]

Martin persisted: "Do you know as a matter of fact whether or not it has been destroyed?"

"It would have been destroyed, yes, because during the war we were quite anxious to supply as much wastepaper as we could. . . . We destroyed practically all the stuff that was on hand at the time." Liebowitz explained their policy was not to repeat work already used. In other words, an artist's work was the publisher's property and once published the artwork had fulfilled its purpose. It was an attitude shared by many artists who didn't see the point in hoarding "work product." They were always on to the next assignment, the next pages, the next deadline.

"Don't you know as a matter of fact that the first few issues of [*Superman*] were composed entirely of strips secured from McClure Newspaper Syndicate?"

"No, I do not know," Liebowitz said.

"You would be surprised to find that to be the fact, would you?"

"Yes, I might."

The hearing adjourned at 4:10 P.M.

Liebowitz's deposition resumed on Friday, August 16, with Martin referring to transcripts of the previous day's hearing and questions the witness had been unable to answer. Liebowitz had forgotten when negotiations for Superman rights began—January 1938—and could not provide the name and address of the *Action Comics* printer—McClure Newspaper Syndicate, headquartered in Baltimore, while *Superman* was printed by the Greater Buffalo Press in Buffalo, New York.[31]

Liebowitz had a final pretrial deposition on February 20, 1948, during which Fawcett attorney Martin returned to the subject of the solo *Superman* title's use of McClure strips. "Well, isn't it a fact, Mr. Liebowitz, that the art work which was first used in the newspaper strips, in the early strip numbers, was used in the first issues of the Superman Magazine?"

"Not to my knowledge."

It was a startling statement, given the original contract with McClure stipulated the syndicate's return of the original art "so that said drawings may be used by Detective in the publication 'Action Comics,' six months after newspaper release . . . or for any substituted magazine."

The point was a major thrust of Fawcett's legal offensive: not only did the syndicated strip have faulty copyrights, but its reuse in the comic books tainted those as well. And then there was the incorrect application of Superman, Inc., copyright on *Superman* #5 and #6.

In January 1948 a notarized statement to the court by Wallace Martin observed the plaintiff's filing in court of the ordered printer or engraver's proofs of syndicated *Superman* strips indicated that "[many] of these strips do not bear the copyright notice required by the copyright statute."

Martin's statement got down to specifics: "In order to be fully prepared for trial, it will be necessary for Fawcett to be advised of the particular panels in the Captain Marvel strips which plaintiffs will contend were copied from the Superman strips, and the particular Superman panels from which it will be contended such Captain Marvel panels were copied. This information has never been supplied to defendant Fawcett."

The implication that DC had to prove copyright infringement not just in the main but also in panel-by-panel specificity would be writ large in the final trial decision.[32]

The complaint charges infringement of comic strips and continuities involving a character named "Superman", for which plaintiffs claim copyright, by defendant's comic strips and continuities involving a character named "Captain Marvel". In order to be fully prepared for trial, it will be necessary for defendant Fawcett to be advised of the particular panels in the Captain Marvel strips which plaintiffs will contend were copied from the Superman strips, and the particular Superman panels from which it will be contended such Captain Marvel panels were copied. This information has never been supplied to defendant Fawcett. We request the Court to direct plaintiffs' counsel to supply us with this information on or before February 13, 1948.

When the original complaint was filed in 1941 numerous specimens of printers' or engravers' proofs of the Superman strips as syndicated in newspapers were filed in Court by plaintiffs. Many of these strips do not bear the copyright notice required by the copyright statute. Defendant Fawcett is entitled to know in advance of trial who supplied plaintiffs' attorneys with this particular material so that if necessary such persons can be examined before trial. We ask the Court to instruct plaintiffs' attorneys to give us these names on or before February 3, 1948.

SWORN to before me this
23rd day of January,1948.

JOHN J. HORAN
Notary Public in the State of New York
Residing in New York County
N.Y.Co.Clk's No.469 Reg.No.1016-H-9
Kings Co.Clk's No.109 Reg.No.554-H-9
Bronx Co. Clk's No.66 Reg. No.309-H-9

The DC vs. Fawcett trial was about to start, and the defendants had yet to receive specific Superman images that Fawcett had allegedly swiped. The idea that DC had to prove specific instances of infringement would become an issue at trial.

WALLACE MARTIN, TRIAL REQUEST, US DISTRICT COURT, SOUTHERN DISTRICT OF NEW YORK, JANUARY 23, 1948, NARA.

CHAPTER 11

THE ADVENTURES OF SUPERBOY

During some of the court proceedings in Westchester, Jerry would sometimes imagine Superman standing or sitting in places near him, kind of like a ghost.

BRAD RICCA
on Siegel and Shuster's Superman and Superboy lawsuit

MORE FUN WITH SUPERBOY

Late in the war Jerry Siegel was a corporal stationed in Hawaii and was still unaware that DC/Superman, Inc., was preparing *Superboy* for publication, with Don Cameron scripting the feature and Joe Shuster handling the art. Shuster, probably feeling complicit in betraying his partner, mailed an after-the-fact letter to Siegel. "[Superboy], I know, is one of your original ideas, which you tried to get Jack to put out," he sheepishly noted in his letter of October 1, 1944.

> Last summer, I hear, it was drawn up by another artist with unsatisfactory results. Since then, nothing was said about it until the assignment was given to me.
>
> I've just finished the job and have been trying to get a copy to you. Jack says it won't appear until after the war. Perhaps you could write to him and obtain a photostatic copy.[1]

Jack did not wait until after the war. It would be debated how much of Siegel's original *Superboy* script, submitted in his second

During World War II, DC went ahead with Jerry Siegel's idea for *Superboy* while he was serving overseas and *without* his permission. Siegel took DC to court and briefly won back the character, although the verdict was overturned when he entered into a disastrous settlement with DC.

"SUPERBOY," *MORE FUN COMICS* #101 (JANUARY/FEBRUARY 1945), P. 1, ART BY JOE SHUSTER. DC MILLENNIUM REPRINT EDITION, NOVEMBER 2000.

pitch, was used in the first story appearing in *More Fun Comics* #101 (January/February 1945). The feature was quietly introduced, with no Superboy cover image or mention. Only wartime paper shortages postponed plans for a solo *Superboy*.

In the inaugural five-page story, Krypton now glows "like a green star," and its inhabitants are "human beings of high intelligence and great physical beauty" but not physically super. Two Kryptonians discuss how Earth's lighter gravitational pull would allow them to leap over buildings, "almost defy gravity entirely." Scientist Jor-L—his name changed to "Jor-El"—again fails to convince the "Supreme Council" to build spaceships for an exodus to Earth, but he builds a spacecraft big enough for his infant son *and* wife to escape. Lara, her name changed from the strip's Lora, refuses to leave her husband, and as their world breaks apart, they bravely launch their child to Earth.

The spacecraft lands and the unnamed motorist remarks on the "peculiar looking contrivance." The Kents adopt the child, as in *Superman* #1. The older couple would eventually be identified as a farming couple from the midwestern town of Smallville, but that backstory is intimated here as the super boy leaps over a barn. And it is not his foster father's advice that compels Clark to keep his powers secret, as in *Superman* #1, but the self-aware boy himself: "I can't let people know how different I am! I'll just have to hold myself in check and go along like all the other kids."

Superboy was finally announced in *More Fun* #103, with tantalizing cover copy: "What was Superman like when he was a boy?" The big rollout came in the next issue—Superboy on the cover in his preteen cape and costume, selling 7th War Loan bonds, with the cover announcement, "In this issue: Superboy again!"

POSTWAR CONSOLIDATION

On May 7, 1945, Nazi Germany surrendered. America's atomic bombings of Hiroshima and Nagasaki compelled Japan's surrender on September 2. A *Life* editorial noted the war "which had been tapering off to a whimper, is instead ending with a bang." The "Atomic Age" was a rude awakening for the "dream of the return to 'normal' life." *Life* put the new reality in popular terms: "After all, this bomb has been inevitable for a long time. America's kids, fans of Flash Gordon, reacted to the news with . . . stares which seemed to say, 'What's all the excitement?' or, '*We've had it for years.*'"[2]

When Superman first appeared only "a bursting shell" could penetrate his skin. Seven years later he had evolved to withstand the atomic bomb—the cover of *Action* #101 (October 1946) depicts the Man of Tomorrow hovering above an atom bomb test, recording the mushrooming cloud with a movie camera. Comics historian Les Daniels notes that kryptonite, the green meteoric remnants of Krypton whose radiation is Superman's vulnerability, was invented in an unpublished 1940 story but was unleashed on the radio show shortly after Hiroshima and Nagasaki. "There is good reason to believe that the menace of kryptonite was symbolic of atomic energy," Daniels notes. "The symbolic radioactivity of kryptonite might have been too much for the original super hero, but he offered reassurance to his readers by repeatedly defying the blast of the actual nuclear bomb itself."[3]

The same month Superman was filming atomic tests, Captain Marvel survived an atomic blast in *Captain Marvel Adventures* #66. Captain Marvel then watches helplessly as atomic missiles are mysteriously launched, ending in global destruction. It is revealed the atomic nightmare is only a dramatization, broadcast by Whiz network over the new broadcast medium of television.

With the war over, DC began the "consolidation," as Liebowitz called it, with M. C. Gaines agreeing to a buy-out of his half of All-American Comics. With the deal completed on September 30, 1946, All-American's pantheon—including Wonder Woman, Flash, and Green Lantern—officially became part of the same corporate and mythological universe as Superman and Batman. A partnership with World's Best Publishing Company, begun with

World's Finest Comics in January 1941, was also absorbed. DC's corporate name was changed to National Comics Publications, Inc., although the "DC" acronym continued, along with the circle emblem, "A Superman Publication: DC."[4] Within a decade the Golden Age business model would be transformed.

Gaines remained at 225 Lafayette Street with a venture he called Educational Comics (EC). In the buyout Gaines got DC's *Picture Stories from the Bible* to add to a lineup that would include *Picture Stories from American History* and *Tiny Tot Comics*.

The All-American division at 480 Lexington Avenue included editors Sheldon "Shelly" Mayer and Julius "Julie" Schwartz, the latter a pioneering science-fiction literary agent hired in 1944 who would become a major DC editorial figure in the decades ahead. A new generation of DC creators got their start after the war, including artist Joe Kubert, who was in high school when he began working for Mayer at the All-American division. Kubert once summed up DC's headquarters: "It was massive. It was ritzy. That was 480 Lex. First of all, you were so impressed by the painting of Superman that hung in the office there."[5]

DC's future editor and publisher, artist Carmine Infantino, first visited 480 Lexington Avenue with artist Frank Giacoia in 1946. "Walking into the foyer, the first thing you saw was this giant painting of Superman, unbelievably huge, hanging on the wall," Infantino described.

> One corner was filled with the licensing of all the characters, toys. It was nice, clean, lovely. A comfortable couch was out in front. We were so impressed with this and we asked to see the art director. Eddie Eisenberg came out, looked at our stuff, and said, "You've got nice stuff. But we can't use you here. Go down the hall; there's a company called All-American Comics. It's a sister company, and talk to a guy named Shelly Mayer— he's the editor. Tell him I sent you." So we went down the hall, where it wasn't nice at all. The offices down there were nothing. There was just a little girl sitting in the corner; it was really

barren, a big wide-open hall. We asked for Shelly, he brought us in, and he liked what we had.[6]

DONENFELD'S DEPOSITION

A few months after consolidation, on November 12, 1946, publisher Harry Donenfeld gave his deposition at the New York offices of DC's law firm. Fawcett attorney Wallace Martin summarized his convoluted business ventures, including being president of three now-defunct companies: Merrill Publishing, Donny Press, Inc., and Tilsun Publications, Inc. Donenfeld was currently president of DC and Superman, Inc., All-American Comics, Inc., World's Best Comics, Inc., and vice president and director of Independent News Company—all located at 480 Lexington. "I make the contacts with wholesalers throughout the country who distribute all of the Independent News Company publications," Donenfeld explained. "I build the good will between the Independent News Company's publications and wholesalers."

IND had been distributing *Action* and *Superman* since they began, but Donenfeld acknowledged that prior to purchasing *Superman* he had not met Siegel and Shuster, although they had been contributing features since DC's inception.

"Well, when did you first have any contact with Mr. Siegel or Mr. Shuster?"

"When I decided to buy the Superman script. Either Gaines or Jack Liebowitz wired Cleveland for the two boys to come in, and that was the first time I met them." Donenfeld explained that he had nothing to do with the terms of negotiations of the first contract—Liebowitz took care of that.

Martin asked, "You are very familiar with these comic magazines as published in this country, aren't you?"

"In a general way."

"Well, haven't you sort of grown up with the business?"

"Yes."

"And you are probably the biggest man in the business at the present time, aren't you?"

"I object to that," Beck said. "Please don't answer it."

"He has already answered it," Martin said.

"No, he hasn't," Beck replied.

Donenfeld testified that Independent News Company distributed about fifty magazines. When Martin asked how many were published by companies in which Donenfeld had an interest, Beck interrupted: "I do not object to your asking him about any activity of the Independent News Company concerning the publications involved in this action, but I am going to object to any interrogation concerning activities of the Independent News Company concerning other magazines not involved in this action."

It was another front in Fawcett's strategy—if DC was publishing or distributing magazines with Superman-like heroes, why were they singling out Fawcett? "It is not the magazine, Mr. Beck, in which the character, Superman, has been published, but in which any character who has any similarity to Superman has been published," Martin countered, turning his attention back to Donenfeld. "Do you recall how much material Gaines sent over to you in this first instance on the Superman strip?"

Donenfeld broke down the elemental basics out of which an industry was forged: "Several strips . . . six panels . . . on a cardboard."[7]

THE STORY BEHIND THE STORIES

About three months before Siegel was drafted, he and Liebowitz traded letters that appeared to establish a mutual understanding. In the spring of 1943, a warm Liebowitz letter expressed affection for Superman's creators and hopes that their association would never end. Even if Siegel went to war, Liebowitz proposed even paying Jerry and Joe for Superman stories they had not stockpiled.

Siegel mailed a poignant reply to the man who was his boss, antagonist, and ostensible friend.

Dear Jack:
First, thanks for the stack of checks. They, combined with your nice letter, serve to effect Joe and I almost as though we had undergone a blood transfusion. New life, new impetus, surges thru our veins—and it isn't spring fever, either.

All of which serves to remind us that, in great part, we owe a great deal of our good fortune directly to you. Considering that in pre-prosperity days we used to have to wait months for $70.00 checks from Nicholson I guess it wasn't too difficult to wait a few weeks for checks that totaled over $7000.00.

. . . These occasional clashes of temperament are unfortunate, but let's be glad that they're only occasional. I think I once fumblingly tried to explain to you that the careers of Joe and I orbit about your personality and whims, and the kind words that emanate from you on occasion have upon us somewhat the same effect that the early morning's sun's rays have upon a [drooping] plant. They resuscitate—revive—and inspire.

. . . Your decision to pay Joe and I the amounts mentioned in your letters for magazine releases we do not produce is a source of great satisfaction to Joe and I and certain indication to us that you have our welfare in mind. . . . Despite the aforementioned arrangements, I shall of course continue to have an active interest in magazine releases, . . . turning out as much magazine work as I can. And I look forward to the period after the war, when our staff is reassembled again and we can return to producing complete magazine releases as heretofor [sic].[8]

By January 1946 Siegel was home, and DC/National initiated negotiations regarding his payment and role as writer for *Superboy*.[9] The publisher maintained Superboy's first appearance in *More Fun* #101 was partly based on Siegel's script, with writer Don Cameron contributing, while Joe and the Cleveland shop did the artwork. In other words, *Superboy* was an assigned work for hire, meaning DC owned it. But Superboy was personal—not only was the character Siegel's first big idea after the Superman sale, but Jerry and Bella were now parents of a son, Michael, born in January 1944, whom they'd nicknamed "Superboy."[10]

Siegel saw the publication of *Superboy*, without permission or payment, as betrayal. Apparently, Jack did *not* have their welfare in mind, and this was only the latest grievance. Years of impassioned letters and lobbying had not won a seat at the Superman Corporation. DC got rich off Superman *and* in-house copycat superheroes. The Siegel and Shuster bylines had been used, without permission or payment, on the wartime feature *Lois Lane, Girl Reporter*. And Siegel was sure that DC was "poaching" artists from the Cleveland studio, moving them to 480 Lex—even Joe relocated to New York.[11]

Siegel suffered sleepless nights worrying about his financial security, even though these were the "prosperity days." By 1947 Siegel and Shuster's total compensation was estimated at over $400,000.[12] Jerry convinced his reluctant partner to join him in a big move—a lawsuit against DC/National to return rights to Superboy *and* Superman, along with a massive $5 million settlement. Jerry was confident they would win it all.

SIEGEL AND SHUSTER SUE

Siegel tried enlisting industry support for his lawsuit. Reasoning that solidarity between the creators of DC's stars made a powerful front, he approached Bob Kane. "I was at Bob's apartment in New York the day that Joe Shuster and Jerry Siegel came over to try to talk him into getting into the lawsuit against DC," recalled Lew Schwartz, a prolific Batman artist of the period. "And Bob's father, who was a wise old Jewish guy, said, 'Listen, they guarantee you X amount of money. It's okay if you don't own it. They're paying you. Be quiet about it.' He talked Bob out of doing that, and he was smart because the money kept coming in."[13]

Kane was within his rights not to join the suit. But a more sinister version of the story has Kane heading straight to Liebowitz to break the news of the brewing legal challenge—and renegotiate his Batman deal. "Bob Kane was a *New York* Jew," opines Mark Zaid, drawing a cultural distinction between a Big City go-getter and the midwestern working-class culture of Siegel and Shuster. "Donenfeld and Liebowitz were older, sophisticated, almost Mafia-type Jews—they ate Siegel and Shuster for breakfast. But Kane pulled a fast one on DC, saying that he was a minor when he created Batman, and his contract was invalid."

What arrangements were made between Kane and Liebowitz behind closed doors has been much speculated. Paul Levitz provides a cautionary note: "Don't pay the slightest attention to any of Bob Kane's 'deals.' I have never seen one thing that has been in print that remotely resembled the truth. None of it is accurate."[14]

Whatever killer deal Kane struck, it did not include Bill Finger.

Siegel and Shuster tried enlisting M. C. Gaines, who now had no allegiance to DC. He was interested but his son, Bill, recalled his father telling him "a couple of sharp lawyers got ahold of those boys and got them malcontented." When the senior Gaines felt they were misrepresenting facts, "he dropped them like hot potatoes and that was the end of that."[15]

In 1947, the year Siegel and Shuster's lawsuit went to trial, Max Gaines was tragically killed, along with his friend Sam Irwin, while boating on Lake Placid. Irwin's son was with them when a woman's out-of-control motorboat rammed their boat, but before the fatal impact, Max managed a super-heroic act. "What he did was, he picked up this kid, and threw him in the back seat," Bill Gaines recalled, "and it worked, because this woman's boat went through where the two men were sitting and the kid would have been—at least, that's the kid's story. He was 10 years old, and that's what he said happened."[16]

The Gaines family, shocked at Max's freakishly sudden and violent death, tried to regroup. Bill, then twenty-five, had seen his first marriage fail and was entering his last year at New York University when his mother asked him to take over his father's business at 225 Lafayette. Educational Comics was $100,000 in debt, but the son grudgingly agreed to take command of what he later called "the smallest, crummiest outfit in the field," with the "weakest distributor" in Leader News.[17]

WESTCHESTER ACTION

It was Donenfeld and Liebowitz's turn to feel betrayed: the nonjury trial of plaintiffs Siegel and Shuster versus National Comics was to be heard before the New York Supreme Court in Westchester County, Judge J. Addison Young presiding. National argued they owned Superboy, an extension of their copyrighted property, Superman. Siegel and Shuster's grievances included DC passing on its contractual option for Superboy, publishing the feature without Siegel's consent, using his rejected synopsis, and not providing payment.

Judge Young's ruling on November 21, 1947, declared Superboy *was* a distinct creation and DC failed to exercise its option— Superboy belonged to the plaintiff! "It is quite clear to me . . . that in publishing Superboy the Detective Comics, Inc. acted illegally," Young ruled. "I cannot accept defendants' view that Superboy was in reality Superman. I think Superboy was a separate and distinct entity."

Young concluded, "Plaintiff Siegel is the originator and the sole owner of the comic strip feature SUPERBOY. . . . The defendants . . . are perpetually enjoined and restrained from creating, publishing, selling or distributing any comic strip material of the nature now and heretofore sold under the title SUPERBOY. . . .

The originator and owner of the comic strip feature SUPERBOY has the sole and exclusive right to create, sell, and distribute comic strip material under the title SUPERBOY."[18]

But winning back Superboy was only half the battle won, and Judge Young further ruled that Superman remained DC's property because the original rights agreement of March 1, 1938, was valid. The Superman acquisition was also covered by the December 4, 1937, DC employment contract option clause, with the transfer of rights representing DC's exercise of the option. The court further ruled that DC's direction to Siegel and Shuster to revise its original *Superman* strip submission to conform to a comic book format was in accord with legal precedent of work for hire, including an employer directing and supervising an employee's work.[19]

The plaintiffs had not won back everything, but they had established a precedent—National Comics acted "illegally" in publishing *Superboy*. Both sides had moved to appeal when, suddenly, a settlement was announced on May 19, 1948.

The settlement called for a $94,000 payment to Siegel and Shuster, a precipitous drop from the anticipated millions. But what the creators gave up was demonstrably greater than the formerly unknown possibilities of that *Action* #1 character constructed from dreams and comic strip panels pasted on cardboard.

As part of the settlement, Superboy was returned to the publisher in language that was a total reversal of Judge Young's earlier ruling: "Defendant NATIONAL COMICS PUBLICATION, INC. is the sole and exclusive owner of and has the sole and exclusive right to the use of the title SUPERBOY and to create, publish, sell and distribute and to cause to be created, published, sold and distributed cartoon or other comic strip material containing the character." Two days later, on May 21, Young entered a final consent judgment vacating his previous rulings and findings.[20]

Looming over the settlement is the shadowy figure of Albert Zugsmith, who ingratiated himself as Siegel and Shuster's legal advisor. He reportedly told the creators they had no chance in a protracted appeal and had to settle. Shuster always suspected Zugsmith of working out the settlement in cahoots with Liebowitz.[21]

The lawsuit was a disaster: most of the settlement money went to pay legal bills, the creators lost Superboy and Superman, and both were *out* at DC/National, their bylines expunged from the exploits of their creations. Mark Zaid has a critical view of Siegel, noting that in an era when creators struggled under relentless deadlines for the page rate, Superman's creators were at the top of the field, with the compensation to prove it. "There are so many court proceedings and letters that have been preserved, that you can formulate a really good picture, and that changed my attitude from sympathy," Zaid explains.

> Shuster was never one to challenge anything, very happy, apparently—Siegel pulled him in [the lawsuit]. In Siegel's letters you see that he was an arrogant, cocky guy. And by this time, DC [had] added significantly to the Superman character, which had nothing to do with Siegel.
>
> One of the things that dispels this notion that they were ripped off is that [back then] it was *all* work for hire, that was the standard practice. At $10 a page for the first *Action* they were being paid double what their peers were being paid—and they were ecstatic! They made a *ton* of money, particularly off the newspaper syndication rights. . . . So you lose a little sympathy. This guy was doing fine.[22]

Siegel and Shuster next created *Funnyman*, a slapstick crime fighter dressed in baggy pants and circus clown shoes, armed with madcap gadgetry—a boxing glove sprang from a hidden chest cavity, a fake flower squirted knockout gas. Former DC editor Vincent Sullivan, heading a new publishing line called Magazine Enterprises, gave Superman's creators a chance, even granted their dream of an ownership deal. The first issue of *Funnyman* (December 1947) proclaimed: "The creators of SUPERMAN

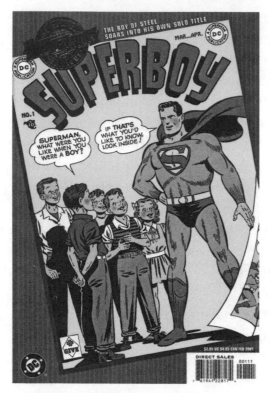

Despite a postwar drop in superhero popularity, Superboy got his own title in 1949. At this point Siegel and Shuster were gone from DC.

SUPERBOY #1 (MARCH/APRIL 1949), ORIGINAL COVER ART BY WAYNE BORING AND STAN KAYE. DC MILLENNIUM REPRINT EDITION, FEBRUARY 2001.

As a creator in-joke, the criminal mastermind Funny Face is unmasked as Jerry Siegel himself.

"CASE OF THE FUNNY PAPER CRIMES," *SUPERMAN* #19 (NOVEMBER/DECEMBER 1942), P. 13, PENCILS BY JOHN SIKELA, INKS BY ED DOBROTKA.

present their NEW HERO." But the title struggled, limping along until the summer of 1948, when it was cancelled after six issues.

Siegel's personal life was also in upheaval. He was in love with Joanne Carter, Joe's model for Lois Lane. Bella sued for divorce on July 15, 1948; Jerry and Joanne married that October. Sadly, Jerry would become estranged from his "Superboy" son.[23]

Their dreams for Superman came true, but Jerry never forgave himself for the Faustian bargain of selling Superman. Occasionally, as in the Geezer story, Superman's creators tried to tell fans what it was really like in the comics business. In addition to the self-deprecating Superman movie story in *Superman* #19, that issue also includes the "Case of the Funny Paper Crimes," featuring the masked villain Funny Face, who magically brings *Daily Planet* comic strip characters to life as giants to do his bidding. Superman captures and unmasks him.

"And who are you?" Superman asks. "You look unfamiliar!"

"That was the whole trouble! Nobody knows me! I wanted to be a celebrity—the creator of a famous comic strip. But no one would buy my strips."

Funny Face was Siegel himself.

REGENERATION

If Superman's 1938 debut was Year One for the superhero, 1948 marked the first decade. The genre revealed its innate ability to regenerate core myths and origin stories in a process of renewal that reacquainted loyal fans and primed new ones. Superman's tenth anniversary was celebrated in *Superman* #53 with "The Origin of Superman," drawn by Wayne Boring (the artist who once got disparaging comments from Liebowitz), who defined Superman's look in the coming decade.

Batman's origin was retold in *Batman* #47 (June/July 1948). Regeneration included a capacity to expand on a character's origin: "The Peril-Packed Inside Story of 'The Origin of Batman'"

NO. 80
JANUARY

ADVENTURES
A Fawcett Publication 10¢

CAPTAIN
MARVEL
IN
A TWICE-TOLD TALE
THE STORY OF HOW
BILLY BATSON FIRST BE-
CAME CAPTAIN MARVEL

Comics creators realized it was important to periodically reacquaint fans with the origins of characters. Captain Marvel's story is cleverly retold as the villain Sivana goes back in time to destroy Billy Batson and keep Captain Marvel from ever existing. The issue appeared the year DC's lawsuit against Fawcett went to trial, with Captain Marvel facing the possibility of being cancelled out of existence.

"A TWICE-TOLD TALE," *CAPTAIN MARVEL ADVENTURES* #80 (JANUARY 1948), COVER ART BY C. C. BECK. FAWCETT PUBLICATIONS.

reveals the formerly unknown killer of Thomas and Martha Wayne as Gotham gangster Joe Chill.

Captain Marvel Adventures #80 (January 1948) featured "A Twice-Told Tale," an ingenious retelling of Marvel's origin as Sivana time-travels to the past to kill Billy Batson and prevent Captain Marvel from existing. But Sivana forgets why he went back in time—until he returns to the present, where Captain Marvel is waiting.

"Omigosh!" Sivana exclaims, as the hero drags him away. "Now I remember everything! I went to the past in order to prevent Captain Marvel from ever existing! But when I got to the past, all I did was relive the same events that happened before! Curses!"

The year 1948 to which Sivana returned was a time of peril for Captain Marvel: he was finally squaring off against Superman in a courtroom battle for supremacy of the superheroes.

CHAPTER 12

THE TRIAL

The breathless anxiety of actors on the opening night of a play has been written about and depicted frequently. But it is nothing compared to the nervous excitement on the opening day of a court trial. The air is laden with anticipatory fears and hopes. Both sides have prepared for years, and now in the actual clash the strength of the contending forces will be revealed for the first time.

LOUIS NIZER
Superman's attorney, *My Life in Court*

FINAL MANEUVERING

As the Superman versus Captain Marvel trial neared, Superman attorney Louis Nizer secured former Fawcett insiders to testify. He had disgruntled former editor Eddie Herron, who, in turn, sent a telegram to former Fawcett writer Manly Wade Wellman in North Carolina, telling him to call a number, reverse the charges, and ask for Louis Nizer.

Nizer got Joe Simon, who worked on the first *Captain Marvel Adventures* with Jack Kirby. After the war Simon and Kirby had briefly reunited at DC. In 1946 Joe married Harriet Feldman, and he and Jack left for Harvey Comics.[1] When the copyright infringement suit came to trial, Simon and Kirby were at Crestwood Publications pioneering romance comics and other emerging postwar genres.

Simon got the lowdown on the copyright infringement suit in the lobby of 480 Lex, where he ran into National editor Jack Schiff, who was on his way to a meeting with lawyers on the case.

"Why are you people suing Fawcett?" Simon asked.

"Captain Marvel. He's a copy of Superman."

"So are a dozen others."

"Captain Marvel is getting too big," Schiff replied. "Donenfeld wants to make a test case of Captain Marvel. . . . Hey, you guys did the first *Captain Marvel* one-shot. Our lawyer, Louis Nizer should talk to you."[2]

Simon wasn't happy about testifying but knew they could subpoena him. He met Nizer at his law firm's office in the Paramount Building and spent days with him in preparation for testimony. "Nizer was one of the country's most celebrated attorneys, a small, dark, intense man, impeccably dressed, with the silvery voice of an orator," Simon described. He "skillfully led us in the testimony he was seeking. . . . Nizer was anticipating any and all questions the defense might come up with. He was brilliant."[3]

Louis Nizer was born in London in 1902 and came to the United States as a child. He graduated from Columbia Law School and was only twenty-four when he and Louis Philips set up a law partnership that grew into a prestigious firm. Nizer would have a long, high-profile career, specializing in copyright law and anti-trust, film, libel, and divorce cases. His celebrated clients included Johnny Carson, Charlie Chaplin, and Salvador Dalí. He was a close friend and supporter of New York mayor Fiorello La Guardia and a leader in Jewish philanthropic circles.

Nizer was fiery and eloquent—a raconteur. Once when presenting Sara Delano Roosevelt, President Franklin Roosevelt's mother, at a banquet, he declared, "A beautiful young lady is an act of nature. A beautiful old lady is a work of art. I introduce you to a work of art." Another time he wryly recalled one of many divorce cases he'd handled: "I was cross-examining a lady, who was accused of infidelity, and after close questioning, she broke down and screamed: 'What you say isn't true. I have been faithful to my husband dozens of times.'"

Nizer was a formidable courtroom adversary because of his

skill, passion, and preparation. Nizer wrote "A Lawyer's Prayer," which included, "I would pray, O Lord, never to diminish my passion for a client's cause, for from it springs the flame which leaps across the jury box and sets fire to the conviction of the jurors." Superman versus Captain Marvel was a nonjury trial, so Nizer's flame had to set fire to one person, the district judge, Hon. Alfred C. Coxe.[4]

UNBEARABLE TREPIDATION

In his best-selling autobiography, Nizer describes pretrial signs of "unbearable trepidation" manifesting in clammy hands, sweaty brows, and flushed cheeks, each lawyer knowing opposing counsel would aim for the smallest chink in their armor. "The setting of the courtroom drama is also awesome," he writes, describing the high-paneled, walnut-grained walls of most federal courts, opposing tables for lawyers and assistants for the plaintiff and defendant, the elevated platform and desk where the court clerk sat and marked documents into evidence, the jury box, and the nearby chair where witnesses took their oaths and testified.

"And towering above all on a magnificently carved platform is the Judge's chair," Nizer observes. "It is built like a throne with a huge brown leather back topped by graceful wooden carving. Behind that chair is a high wall designed in paneled wood with the seal of the Federal government engraved into the walnut. And at one side stands a huge silk American flag with gold fringe, the only brilliant touch of color in the austere surroundings."[5]

National Comics Publications, Inc., v. Fawcett Publications, Inc. (hereafter *National Comics/DC v. Fawcett*) began on March 9, 1948, and finished on March 31. The trial lasted sixteen days, and an estimated 249 exhibits were entered into the record from plaintiff DC and 142 from defendant Fawcett, including runs of comic book titles, correspondence, contracts and licensing agreements, promotional and in-house material, and enlarged photostats of comic book art. Pretrial court rulings and depositions ran to 2,600 transcribed pages; the trial produced an additional 1,795 pages of testimony from more than twenty witnesses.[6]

In his opening arguments Nizer emphasized Superman was such an "unusual, unique and fantastic type of cartoon that it had been rejected by other publications. . . . We have one thing to be thankful in this case—that there was no subtlety about the situation. They made a replica of Superman." Only in his use of a magic word, a "thin disguise," was Captain Marvel different. Fawcett copied Superman, right down to a fan club promotion. "That was unfair competition, and they went about that quite brazenly and in detail. We got out a special button and a card, and they immediately followed with the same kind of button and card."

Nizer dismissed Fawcett's contention of potentially invalid copyright registrations as existing "on the periphery of this entire litigation and they are practically of no consequence." "The real issue," he contended, "is whether they have copied our original concept and depicted it, and on that issue we feel that we will submit evidence that will overwhelmingly show that they did." Nizer warned they would seek "accounting and injunctive relief" for eight years of "deliberate copying."[7]

WHIT TESTIFIES

The testimony of Whit Ellsworth, stretching from March 9 to March 11, allowed Nizer to elicit a litany of Fawcett offenses: Captain Marvel not only duplicated the character of Superman, but also that of alter ego Clark Kent by making Billy Batson an orphan and a journalist; *Whiz* features included Scoop Smith, a daring newspaper reporter suspiciously similar to *Action Comics'* own newsman, Scoop Scanlon; Fawcett put a Captain Marvel

Clark Kent can't seem to find a phone booth as he ducks into this nondescript alley to make his big change. It was an editorial rule that Clark Kent always appear in costume when doing his super feats, a point made in the copyright trial against Fawcett. In this 1942 story he comes close to flying as he goes, "Up—up and away!!"

"MUSCLES FOR SALE!," *SUPERMAN* #17 (JULY/AUGUST 1942), P. 4, PANELS 4–6, ART BY JOHN SIKELA.

emblem in the upper left corner of its covers, copying Superman's cover emblem.

Nizer even charged that Captain Marvel's duality was another Superman swipe. Under Nizer's questioning, Ellsworth explained Liebowitz forbid showing Clark Kent doing fantastic feats so that the comic could maintain the illusion of a weak man transitioning to meet the "superhuman problem or this evil problem that requires him to be super human." After defeating his foe, Superman reverted to his powerless persona. "Of course this [is] a device . . . to give the reader an opportunity to identify himself with a real person such as Clark Kent and then, vicariously of course, with the super-creature who can take care of every sort of problem that the ordinary man cannot."

Nizer returned to Superman's duality while questioning Ellsworth on March 11: "In a small number of panels, in all these years, have they ever shown any such action without that costume?" Ellsworth explained: "I think it is obvious [Superman] is a dual personality. We never see Superman and Clark Kent at the same time, any more than we see Billy Batson and Captain Marvel at the same time, or any more than we ever see Jekyll and Hyde at the same time. This is the dual personality, but it is the same character." (Of course, Clark and Superman were the same being, while Billy Batson and Dr. Henry Jekyll underwent a transformation to become their other selves.)

During his cross-examination of Ellsworth, Fawcett attorney Wallace Martin echoed Siegel's complaint that DC had published other superheroes for years, contradicting its claims that Fawcett was undermining "the distinctiveness of their character [Superman]."

The comic book superheroes had been around a decade, but Wallace Martin, among others, could be forgiven for not understanding the medium's visual language. At one point, trying to draw similarities between Superman and in-house DC superheroes, Martin asked Ellsworth if Batman could fly. Fans knew Batman, having no super powers, could not fly, but the imagery

The visual language of superheroes was so new that attorney for the defense Wallace Martin asked DC editor Whit Ellsworth: "Does Batman fly?" Batman's aerial acrobatics—swinging from silken cords over impossible spaces, cape flung open like wings—begged the question. In this 1945 story Batman does fly "like a human bat," with *two* parachutes as backup!

"PUNCH AND JUDY!," *BATMAN* #31 (OCTOBER/NOVEMBER 1945), P. 11, WRITER BILL FINGER, PENCILER JERRY ROBINSON, INKER GEORGE ROUSSOS.

Q Well, did the front office tell you?   A Obviously, if I put it in Superman it was Superman that was the publisher.

Q When you say "the front office" whom do you mean? A I mean Mr. Leibowitz. He is our general manager.

Q Is it a fact that Mr. Leibowitz told you the form of the copyright notice which you used in issue No. 5 of the Superman magazine?   A You mean verbatim, word for word?

Q Well, either word for word, or information from which you formed your judgment to put this copyright notice in.   A I presume that is true, sir, if that is the way it went in.

Q Do you recall talking to Mr. Leibowitz about it? A I have talked to Mr. Leibowitz about a great many things, so I presume that I talked to him about that, as having to do with publication.

Q Including the copyright notice? A Possibly.

Q Do you know whether or not Superman, Inc. undertook to publish this magazine entitled "Superman Magazine" as the result of any contract or assignment by Detective Comics, Inc. to Superman, Inc.?   A I was not taken into confidence on business matters in that connection, Mr. Martin.

Q Then your answer is no, is that right? A That is

Whit Ellsworth gets tripped up in cross-examination over the mistaken copyright notice in *Superman* #5, an error that loomed large in the trial.

ELLSWORTH CROSS-EXAMINATION BY MARTIN, MARCH 11, 1948, TRIAL TRANSCRIPT, P. 294, NARA.

of the masked hero impossibly swinging across vast spaces from silken cords, or of leaping off rooftops with his cape unfolding like wings, begged the question.

"Do you know whether anybody representing Detective Comics, Inc., or Superman, Inc., ever discussed with the originator or artist producing the Batman character as to whether or not that character should be portrayed as flying through the air?" Martin asked.

"Do you understand the question?"

"I understand the question, yes," Ellsworth replied. "The answer is no."

"You seem to be quite sure in your own mind that that character has never been portrayed as flying through the air."

"That is correct."

"Well, from your examination of the Batman character, would you say that all the feats which were performed by the Batman could be performed by a human[?] Is that what you mean?"

"With slight exaggeration, naturally, to fit the exigencies of romantic narrative."

"Well, of course, if you exaggerate human powers, you run into the superhuman powers, don't you?"

"Not necessarily."

Fawcett got better traction on the faulty copyrights, arguing that early issues of *Superman* were tainted by inclusion of syndicated strips with invalid copyrights—two stories in issue #2 alone had a run of strips 67–90 and 91–126, as displayed in Fawcett Exhibit N.

Martin addressed the mistaken Superman, Inc., notice in *Superman* #5, the first issue for which Ellsworth prepared copyright as new editor. Martin established that Ellsworth inserted copyright notices by direction of the "front office"—which meant Liebowitz—but couldn't pin him down to a specific direct order. "I presume that I talked to [Liebowitz] about that," Ellsworth said.[8]

SIMON TAKES THE STAND

On March 9 Joe Simon settled his long, lanky frame in the witness chair. Nizer asked him to recall his first meeting to discuss a *Captain Marvel* magazine with art director Al Allard. "[Allard] said it was a takeoff on Superman. I asked him how he could get away with it, and he told me that it was no concern of mine nor his; that he just wanted to put out the best magazine he knew how and he wanted me to do the best art work I could."

Allard provided photostats of *Captain Marvel* images so Simon and Kirby could draw samples in the likeness established by C. C. Beck. After their sketches were approved, Allard took Simon and Kirby to Bill Parker's office to pick up the scripts. Eddie Herron was also there, Simon recalled.

"We were unusual in this respect: we were in the habit of changing [the] script to improve the cartoon, having been writers and editors in the field ourselves. And Mr. Parker said no, we definitely couldn't change the script. So I thought that was strange and I told him I didn't see what objections he would have to our improving the script and the final story, and he said well, they are following a definite pattern there. . . . They have taken the formula from Superman; Superman is selling and they don't want this to be any better or worse than Superman. . . . As a matter of fact, I might add that he told me—I don't know whether I should say this or not."

"Tell us everything that happened," Nizer urged.
"He said in his opinion Superman stinks."
Wallace Martin cross-examined Simon when he returned to the witness stand on March 15. Fawcett's lawyer asked Simon to

describe the kinds of heroic comics characters he had worked on. First up was Captain America.

"What kind of character is Captain America?" Martin asked.

"He was a soldier. He put on a star-spangled costume and became a detective." Under questioning, Simon explained the character wore a tight-fitting costume, but didn't have a cape.

Nizer objected, calling the questioning "irrelevant."

"I don't know what the purpose is, except to test his credibility," Coxe added.

"Did Captain America do superhuman feats?" Martin continued.

"No, he didn't. He didn't fly, or he didn't leap through the air."

"Did you ever draw a character which did superhuman feats?"

"Objection, sir, as immaterial," Nizer pounced.

"Sustained," Coxe ruled.

"If your Honor please, shouldn't we be able to test his credibility?" Martin explained he wanted to see if Simon had been inspired by other super characters that might have dived or flown through the air.

"I have done a lot of characters," Simon replied, "but if any of them did dive through the air or fly through the air it was for a reason. For example, I once did a character named Blue Bolt. He was a Flash Gordon type of character, who lived on another planet and he leaped high in the air, but that was explained because of the fact that the planet on which he lived was smaller and it was the natural gravitation which allowed him to do such a thing."

"He leaped great distances through the air?"

"Well in such a climate, and with the scientific factors, even if you walked you would sail through the air."

"Did he wear a tight-fitting costume?"

"I object to that, your Honor," Nizer announced.

"He has already answered—I don't see that we are getting anywhere with it," the judge said.

Martin asked if the character wore a cape.

"He wore a long cape down to his ankles."

Nizer continued his objections, until an exasperated Martin

turned to the judge. "Well, if your Honor please, we are trying to test the credibility of this witness's testimony by showing that he draws not only characters having these [superhuman] traits but he draws them for the plaintiffs."[9]

Simon had underlined the creative influences pervading the medium—Flash Gordon's and John Carter's model of powers inherent in gravitational effects directly inspired Blue Bolt. But his testimony corroborated the plaintiff position that Fawcett deliberately copied Superman.

FAWCETT INSIDERS

Plaintiff witness Manly Wade Wellman was a newspaper reporter in Wichita, Kansas, before coming to New York in 1935 to write magazine fiction. By 1939 he was caught up in the post-Superman boom, with Bill Parker hiring him to contribute to *Ibis the Invincible*. Towards the end of 1940 he was called into Parker's office, where editor Eddie Herron was present. Parker explained they were planning a solo *Captain Marvel* title—was Wellman interested?

"Superman was at that time the one at the pinnacle in the business," Wellman testified. "It was in the comparatively early days of such comics. He said, 'Follow Superman. It is selling well and going along like a ball of fire; that is what we want.'" Wellman was given Superman comics to study and while poring over them noticed a recurring peculiarity—when meeting a challenge, Superman kept a "running fire" of flippant "wisecracks."

"I thought at the time it was unpleasant to me and I thought it might be unpleasant to the general reader, and said as much. I said, 'This doesn't strike me as being in character with the sort of man you want to present as Captain Marvel, a big, rugged, courageous, heroic person; he might be more serious and dignified. Suppose we get away from this.' No, said Bill Parker, that goes in. . . . They wanted it, and in it went. . . . I wrote them in a hurry; I think I wrote them in four days, a script a day. I brought them in, they were accepted and paid for."

Wellman studied Superman feats he could apply to Captain Marvel that would be "illustratable," from crushing a gun to crashing through walls and knocking down buildings. Plaintiffs' Exhibit 3-A, featuring panels from an *Action* #12 story, displayed an example of Wellman's copycat research. In the story Superman declares war on reckless drivers, starting by visiting the lot where traffic violators' cars are stored—and he *destroys* them. Superman next demolishes the Bates Motor Company factory for making dangerous vehicles by using cheap, inferior materials. Wellman testified that panel 3 on page 9, which shows Superman pushing over pillars and causing the factory to collapse, "struck me as being illustratable . . . the general notion of a powerful destructive force contained within one single body."

Wallace Martin opened his cross-examination by asking Wellman why he couldn't have written original scripts.

"I was fairly limited to the Superman character as—well, research material."

"Didn't you consider that an insult to your writing ability?"

"Well, may I answer that rather fully? I was at that time in need of money. . . . War was threatening, and, indeed, came later, and I wanted some money because I intended to go into military service. I didn't get very far doing that, and at that time I thought I could. I hoped to have activated my reserve officer's commission. I wanted to leave a little money for my wife and child. No, I didn't like it. I wrote it rather under protest, and rather anticipated that something like this would be asked about and that my part in it would be questioned."

Martin jumped on that: "What do you mean by that now? Will you just explain? You rather anticipated what?"

"At the time it struck me as strange that there was that much of a copy—"

"Did you rather anticipate—"

"Will you permit him to finish before you ask another question?" Nizer interrupted. "May I respectfully request that he be permitted to finish[?]"

"Were you finished?" Martin asked.

"No, I was not."

"Well, go ahead."

"What I was trying to say in my own words, if you allow me, is this: At that time, this was back in 1940, it struck me as a little irregular, maybe more than irregular, and I thought at that time that my part in this whole thing would be questioned, and at that time I didn't know that I would write others and that I wouldn't have war service." The witness then made a cryptic remark: "I put a code in this script, an acrostic code, because I wanted to remember this specific situation and the fact that I wrote these scripts and discussed them later with the one who was there at the time."

"You anticipated you might have to testify in litigation; is that what you mean?" Martin asked.

"I didn't know about litigation. I didn't know how far it would go, but I thought the thing would be questioned, and as the years went by I forgot a little about it, because I had expected such a situation as this to arise earlier."

Wellman insisted that he had not gone to the plaintiff to offer his services in exchange for testimony. In 1942, after discovering he was too old to have his army commission activated, he estimated writing half a dozen scripts for DC, but never a *Superman* script, and was no longer writing for Fawcett. "I didn't particularly please them. I didn't like it at the time."[10]

Eddie Herron appeared for the plaintiffs on March 11 and 12. He testified to having been "co-editor or assistant editor" in Parker's office on the twenty-second floor of the Paramount Building. Herron declared that copies of DC Comics, Quality Comics Group, and Timely Comics were around the office, adding,

DC lawyers and witnesses contended that Fawcett studied *Superman* comics for super feats that were "illustratable." In *Action Comics* #25 (June 1940), Superman brought a falling plane safely to earth. It might have been coincidence, but in a 1941 *Whiz* tale, Captain Marvel spectacularly duplicated the feat, rescuing this plummeting Pan American Airways *Yankee Clipper*.

CAPTAIN MARVEL UNTITLED STORY, *WHIZ COMICS* #12 (JANUARY 1941), P. 3, ART BY C. C. BECK.

"Well, he [Parker] looked through the Superman comics and I assume through some of the others."

Martin moved to strike that comment, and the judge agreed. Martin hit Herron on his pseudonym "John Batstone," for which he received checks "contrary to the established rules of Fawcett Publications." The defiant Herron added that another alias was "Otto Dinger."

"I was responsible for everything that appeared in these magazines—everything, Mr. Martin," Herron testified on March 12. "I was Mr. Beck's boss and the writer's boss, the boss of the whole art department. I was the one [who] built the stories with the writers, checked the art work on them and everything else. I was in complete control of these magazines."

Herron declared it was Fawcett editorial policy to copy Superman. "Mr. Daigh wanted Superman feats, and I went out and got them. . . . He made direct reference to Superman being a good seller and getting his feats into the magazine." Herron noted a scene in *Action* #24—a would-be suicide tries driving off a cliff, but Superman seizes the car's rear bumper and swings it back around to solid ground, shoving his right fist into a spinning rear tire to blow it out. "Now this is the sort of scene that I would refer to in looking for Superman feats for Captain Marvel. I would go through the books and I would find out what it was that Superman was doing that was really superhuman. Not just deflecting a bullet, because that was becoming fairly common."[11]

LIEBOWITZ TAKES THE STAND

When Jack Liebowitz testified, Wallace Martin returned to his first Superman negotiations with Siegel and Shuster, drawing an objection from Nizer and a "sustained" from the judge. Martin explained he was trying to make the point that Siegel and Shuster acted as independent contractors, not as work for hire. The contractual agreement, the $130 exchange of rights, "was merely a purchase of certain strips, that is all it was; and it included nothing but these particular 13 pages of strips, and they paid so much a page for it."

Martin then referred to Liebowitz's March 1, 1940, letter replying to Siegel's concerns that DC was imitating Superman, in which the executive advised Siegel to address his communications to Detective Comics, Inc., not Superman, Inc., as the latter was promoting licensing outside of the comic books.

The judge asked Martin what the question had to do with the case.

"It has to do with it, if your Honor please," Martin replied. "The position is taken here that Superman, Inc. was in a position to be the proprietor of this strip, and it is our contention that they never were in a position to be proprietor because they were merely there as the licensing agent, and this is a statement by this witness, the manager of the business, to Siegel, to that effect."

"The contract itself says Superman shall have those rights," Nizer responded. "It is in evidence."

"You will have to construe that contract, and these facts have a bearing on that construction," Martin said.

"It could not be available to you in any event, sir," Nizer replied.

"I will sustain the objection to the question," the judge ruled.

Martin continued, "Is it not a fact, Mr. Liebowitz, that on September 28, 1938, you wrote Mr. Siegel advising him . . . when Superman reaches the same popularity as Dick Tracy, Orphan Annie, Skippy, Mutt and Jeff, and dozens of other topnotch features, you will be in a position to ask for more money?"

"Objection, sir," Nizer said.

"Sustained."

"If your Honor please, this witness has testified from the very beginning Superman was the most popular strip on the market. Now here is a letter dated September 28, 1938, [that] tells Siegel it is not, and contradicts his testimony."

"What difference does it make if it is not as popular a strip?" Coxe asked.

"That is the whole position of the plaintiffs. They take the position from the very beginning that it was the most popular strip on the market."

Martin returned to DC's agreements with Siegel and Shuster: the March 1, 1938, assignment of Superman rights; the contract of September 22, 1938; and the supplemental employment agreement of December 19, 1939. "There was never any kind of agreement between Superman, Inc., and the author and artist of the Superman strip, Siegel and Shuster, was there?"

"No sir; never a contract with Superman, Inc."

Martin turned to the copyright issue, announcing they were offering into evidence a book of photostats of the *Superman* strip: "We offer it for the purpose of showing a number of things, including the use of improper copyright notices."

Under Nizer's questioning, Liebowitz testified that he had no knowledge of copyright problems. During their *Superman* negotiations with Paramount, McClure Syndicate even gave assurances "that everything in accordance with our contract was being lived up to and the copyrights were in proper order."[12]

Further trial testimony explored the beginning of the comics business and the mythical roots of costumed superheroes. Nizer got Captain Marvel's cocreators on the stand and turned up the heat, while the question of copyright infringement turned back on the plaintiff, with uncomfortable testimony on aspects of the character that might have been plagiarized by Superman's creators.

CHAPTER 13

PROGENITORS

We have in both Superman and Captain Marvel essentially a
hero, and one might almost say a demigod. He is a creature
of very special and immense endowments. He has bound-
less strength, extraordinary speed and agility. He has the
power of flight. He is invulnerable to wounds of practically
any sort. . . . The figure is a familiar figure in literature. We
have instances of it, of course, in mythology.

> Columbia professor HARRISON STEEVES
> defense witness, *National Comics/DC v. Fawcett*

TESTIMONY OF EVERETT M. ARNOLD

The birth of the comic book business was spotlighted when
Everett M. "Busy" Arnold, publisher of the Quality Comics Group,
was sworn in as an expert witness for the plaintiffs. From 1933 to
1937 Arnold was vice president and sales manager for the Greater
Buffalo Press of Buffalo, New York, which eventually printed comic
books such as *Superman* and magazine sections for Sunday and
daily newspapers. Attesting to the industry's economic impact and
the growth of the newspaper tabloid comics insert he pioneered
with Will Eisner, Arnold estimated Greater Buffalo Press and its
subsidiary, the Great Lakes Color Printing Company (of which he
was president), had five hundred employees and an annual volume
of Sunday color magazines and color comics sections of up to six
hundred million.

In the early summer of 1937, when Arnold entered the comic
book business, there were about six titles, only two of which
featured original material, and both were published by Harry

Donenfeld, he testified.[1] Arnold's now-thriving Quality Comics Group alone had seventeen titles, including *Police Comics*, *Feature*, *Hit*, *Crack*, and *National*. With the lifting of wartime paper restrictions, his comics line by 1947 had 31.5 million copies in circulation, with expectations of 40–45 million for the current year.

Under friendly questioning from Nizer, Arnold recalled first seeing *Superman* as an unsold feature. "[Siegel and Shuster] submitted it to me and I rejected it and sent it back to them, and that was the first time I saw Superman. The reason I rejected it was I thought the character was too unique, the idea was utterly fantastic, and in those days we were not used to the dynamite in comics that we have at the present time. Unfortunately I rejected it."

"Will you state in the light of your experience as a producer and publisher of comics magazines for all these years, your opinion with respect to the possibility of confusion to a prospective purchaser of *Action Comics* and *Whiz Comics*?"

Martin objected, but the judge allowed Arnold to answer. Adults were "more fixed in their habits," he explained, and they made specific purchases like *Life* or the *Saturday Evening Post*, whereas children spontaneously bought comics because of compelling cover art and other impulsive factors. "I would say there is plenty of confusion." Superman and Captain Marvel were

"practically twin comic features. . . . They both do the same deeds. Bullets bounce off their chests. They jump across the ocean. They jump up in the sky and bat planes down. Shells can burst on them and do no harm to them. In fact, Superman and Captain Marvel can get out of any situation because they can't be hurt in any way. They are both unique in that respect. As far as I know, they are the only two in the comics magazine field that are like that. . . . These two characters are very similar in appearance. They do the same miraculous feats. The shots in the magazines are pretty close."[2]

Arnold claimed his own inside-Fawcett knowledge, gleaned early in 1943 during a three-hour lunch with Quality editor John Beardsley and C. C. Beck. Beardsley had shared the editorship of Fawcett's comics line with Otto Binder before both resigned on May 12, 1942, Binder for the freedom of freelancing, Beardsley to join Quality.[3] Beardsley was at the lunch to offer Beck the job of Quality art director.

"Mr. Beck indicated he was not too satisfied with Fawcett, he had never been given proper recognition," Arnold testified. "[Beck] further discussed Captain Marvel and said that it was not a character that he liked, because it was, as he termed it, an imitation of Superman, and that was not the type of character that he liked to portray." Beck submitted several early sketches for Captain Marvel, but Fawcett executives told him "the character was not close enough to Superman, and he had gradually made it as close as possible to Superman."

At the lunch Arnold asked Beck why he was talking that way—Fawcett was already facing DC's copyright infringement suit. The artist replied, according to Arnold, "Why everybody copies Superman. We copy it and everybody else. Now our main difference is that we employ the use of the word SHAZAM. . . . And both Mr. Beardsley and I laughed and said we didn't think that was enough difference."

Arnold continued: "Then Beck pointed out that one of my features, The Doll Man, was greatly like Captain Marvel [and] Superman. I indignantly denied that and stated in no uncertain terms The Doll Man was not a superhuman type of character, it was altogether different from Superman. Shortly thereafter the luncheon was broken off." Beck declined Beardsley's job offer, Arnold added, because Fawcett was allowing him to set up an art studio with Pete Costanza.

Beck vehemently denied Arnold's account of the lunch and allegations that he copied Superman.

Wallace Martin took over cross-examination, asking Arnold about alleged similarities between the debut covers of *Action* and

Whiz, including each car having a tire spin off. "I think the artist when he drew it had the Superman shot in front of him," Arnold maintained.

Superman imagery copied in *Captain Marvel*, Arnold testified, included breaking open a steel door and batting down airplanes. The suitable-for-framing cover of *Superman* #6 (September/October 1940) had Superman posing with his signature underneath: "Very Truly Yours, Clark Kent (Superman)"; the subsequent cover of *Whiz* #16 (April 1941) had Captain Marvel posing with the signature, "Yours Truly, Captain Marvel." Another exhibit was the cover of *Action* #21 (February 1940), showing Superman catching a shell before it hits a battleship; the cover of *Whiz* #10 (November 1940) shows Captain Marvel catching a missile before it hits a sailboat.

Superman's "dynamic, dramatic action itself" was being copied, Arnold concluded. "I don't believe the publishers of Superman could in the first few issues give all of the Superman qualities that later they endowed Superman with. . . . It took them quite a little while to build up all these superhuman qualities that Superman possessed[,] probably a year or a year and a half later."

Martin turned to Exhibit 123, which showed panels depicting both characters smashing a steel door. "You can see that the artist, each of them, gave his own expression to the idea of hammering down a door, can't you?"

"Well, if you can call it his own expression; I call it lifting," Arnold answered.

"You have no trouble in using the word 'lifting,' do you?"

"No. I am an expert at it."

"Isn't it a fact that in these two pictures which you examined and so glibly told counsel that they were lifting or copying—"

"I object to that," pounced Nizer.

"Let me finish the question," Martin replied.

"No. I object now to the use of the phrase 'glibly.'"

"Mr. Nizer is going to sit down," the judge announced.

"In all these answers which you have given to counsel's questions in which you stated they were copied or in which you stated they were lifted you were referring to the idea portrayed in the picture, weren't you?" Martin asked.

"Yes, primarily."

"You didn't intend to say that one was a facsimile of the other, did you?"

"Well, it wasn't a tracing, if that is what you mean."

"What you meant to say was that in each instance different artists were attempting to portray the same idea?"

"The artist who did certain of these Captain Marvel shots was employing the Superman technique. As far as possible he was trying to create the illusion in the minds of children that Captain Marvel was doing the same deeds that Superman had done and does at the present time, but the action itself might be slightly different."

It was Martin's turn to ask that Arnold's opinion be struck from the record. The judge let it stand and denied a further request that Arnold's descriptions of "copying" and "lifting" be struck. Under Martin's questioning, Arnold contended that other than Superman, only Captain Marvel exhibited "a combination" of super-human powers. Even an image of the miniature Doll Man in defendants' Exhibit W, showing the character flying through the air and socking an opponent in the jaw, was not a superhuman feat—the little hero was just "a bundle of dynamite."[4]

"I DIDN'T KNOW ANYTHING ABOUT SUPERMAN."

Since December 1945 Bill Parker had been employed as Fawcett feature editor for *Today's Woman*, "a magazine for young housewives," as Parker described it. Now a trial witness under oath, Parker testified his "bowing acquaintance" with comic books began in the early part of September 1939.

Nizer pressed him on Wellman's earlier testimony. "Did you ever say to Mr. Wellman, 'Well, follow Superman?'"

"No I did not. Obviously his mission was to follow Captain Marvel."

Nizer asked, and the court agreed, to strike everything after the word "no."

"Did you ever say to Mr. Wellman, 'Follow Superman, it is selling well and going along like a ball of fire; that is what we want'?"

"No, I did not."

"Did you ever discuss the character of Superman with Mr. Wellman?"

"No, I did not."

Nizer turned to the stack of comics that Parker was given as reference.

"Mr. Daigh gave me a pile of assorted comic magazines and told me to look through them and get a feel of comic magazines," Parker explained, contending he had *never seen Superman*. "I never read a Superman comic strip . . . to this day."

Nizer asked whether *Superman* was among the comics provided.

"I don't recall the Superman feature in that pile of magazines."

"Do you deny that, sir, that there was? Or do you mean you cannot say one way or the other?"

"I cannot say one way or another."

"You won't deny that that is so?"

"No, I cannot deny that."

"And you had the heavy duty of becoming for the first time an editor and getting out a new comics magazine which would be the first one that your company was going to publish; isn't that so? You knew that?"

"Yes."

"This was the first, wasn't it? *Whiz Comics* was the first [comics] magazine of the Fawcetts?"

"That is right."

"Now never having read one, never having seen one and having had no experience with them, did you then study through the pile of comics magazines which he gave you?"

"No, I didn't."

"You didn't?"

"No."

"You violated his instruction to study up on these magazines which he gave to you; is that it?"

"Yes, I did."

"And you went ahead, based on your complete inexperience, to submit a story and synopsis, without even looking at the magazines which he asked you to study; is that right?"

"No, I said that I looked at them. I glanced through them very rapidly."

"I thought a moment ago you said you violated his instruction and did not look at them. Which is correct?"

"You asked me if I studied them."

"You are drawing a distinction between looking at them and studying them?"

"I thought you were making a point of that, that distinction, and that is why I was careful."

"Yes, I want you to be careful, and I do not want to trick you. I want the facts. You mean you looked through them but did not study them; is that what you mean? Am I stating fairly the distinction you wish to make?"

"Yes."

Parker explained that to his "best recollection" it was *probably* around the time he wrote his Captain Thunder synopsis for Daigh that he received the comics but couldn't recall. Parker reiterated that it wasn't until the lawsuit that he knew of Superman.

The following day Parker was back on the stand. Nizer sprang a trap by referring to court transcripts of Parker's testimony of the previous day. "So isn't it fair to say that yesterday you testified that except for seeing it in the lawyer's office you don't recall ever having seen Superman to this day?"

"That is a complete misrepresentation of what I testified and it is obvious that you are simply trying to twist my words. I said I couldn't recall having seen it, meaning I couldn't recall a specific incident, when I had seen it prior to the time that this discussion arose. I might have seen a copy of the magazine on a newsstand and not been aware of it. I can't testify that I didn't see it. How can I testify that I didn't see anything? You can't testify to a negative statement, condition, can you? . . . I can repeat that statement truthfully. I don't recall seeing it."

"At the time that Mr. Daigh gave you the 20 comics magazines did you know of the character Superman?"

"No. To the best of my recollection, I didn't."

Nizer was ready with transcripts of Parker's 1944 testimony, quoting page 67, when the exchange referred to the time immediately after Daigh gave him the comics magazines: "'Q: Had you known of the character Superman at that time?' 'A: Yes, I had.'"

Nizer asked Parker if that had been his answer.

"I guess I did if it is in that deposition."

"And do you want to take back the answer you made a moment ago, that you are positive you didn't know?"

"I didn't say I was positive I didn't know about him."

"Well, do you want to retract it?"

"Do I have to preface everything I say to you by 'I don't recall,' or some other word? I will be glad to do it if that is what you wish me to do."

"All I wish you to do is to tell the truth."

"That is what I am trying to do, tell the truth."

"I am asking you to search your memory as fairly as I know how. You answered you did know of the character of Superman when you testified that in 1939 he gave you these magazines, and I ask you whether you want to retract the answer you gave a moment ago that you didn't know it?"

"I must have known of him if I stated so in my previous testimony," Parker answered, denying having discussed *Superman* with Daigh or knowing *Superman* was a best-selling feature. "I was only interested in my own magazine."

Nizer brought out Parker's 1944 deposition, turned to pages 142–143 and quoted his testimony that Superman's success was "rather a matter of common knowledge."

"Do you recall making that answer in 1944?"

"No, I don't recall it."

Nizer walked to the witness stand and held out the transcript of Parker's deposition. "Well, do you deny that you made that answer?"

"Obviously I can't deny it if it is in there."

"And you swore to it?"

"I swore to it."

"And you signed it?"

"Yes, I did."

"And you made no corrections of it?"

"I don't recall making any corrections."

Nizer read from page 142, quoting Parker's statement that "naturally I was interested in the larger selling magazines in the field."

"So you were naturally interested, weren't you, in what your competitors were doing in the field? Isn't that a fact?"

"There again is an interpretation of the words 'interested

in.' You mean by it I was interested in copying Superman, which I never did. I mean by it that I was generally interested in the circulation. . . . I was unable to form a critical opinion of Superman, not knowing anything about the character or the story."

"Now, let us have it now. You mean then when you said, 'I didn't know anything about Superman,' you meant merely you didn't know about the specific stories and plots in Superman? Is that what you just meant by that distinction?"

"I imagine that is what I meant."

"You imagine?"

"Yes."

"Stop imagining."

"Why don't you read me the whole thing and see what led up to this?"

"That is your entire answer, 'I didn't know anything about Superman.' I read it to you. Will you stop arguing with me, because I don't want to argue with you either. I am doing my duty. I would like to know whether in the last answer you meant to draw the distinction between not knowing the specific plots in Superman but knowing something about Superman otherwise as a character, as a superhuman character, or whether you meant in that answer that you didn't know anything about Superman. Which is it?"

"I meant I didn't know anything about Superman. I should have prefaced it with this: As I recall I didn't know anything about, or to the best of my recollection; if that is what you wish me to do, then I will do so. It is obvious what I meant."

Nizer asked if Parker ever proposed "a comics character who would combine the best aspects of Mandrake the Magician and Superman?"

Parker didn't recall, until Nizer produced a piece of stationery, "Memo from the desk of Bill Parker, Fawcett Publications," dated November 22, 1939. Parker remembered the memo—after Nizer had him read it.[5]

C. C. BECK TESTIFIES

Charles Clarence Beck took the witness chair, girding himself to stand his ground against the relentless Nizer.

"Mr. Beck, there has been testimony that over the years Superman was drawn to appear progressively and increasingly taller and heavier, and likewise Captain Marvel was drawn to follow the same progression in appearance. Is it or is it not true that Captain Marvel was made to follow Superman?"

"It is not true. . . . Captain Marvel was made to be a character resembling no one but himself, a creation of mine."

Nizer noted a Parker memo that asked Beck to create a heroic character with "perfect powers which were to exceed any character that had yet been used in fiction or in mythology." Beck did not recall it until Nizer produced transcripts of Beck's earlier testimony discussing that memo.

"Superman was mentioned in the discussion which followed this memorandum, wasn't he?"

"Probably, sir." But other than the "heroic figure" concept, Beck denied having lengthy discussions about Superman or that Captain Marvel's lightning bolt chest emblem was inspired by Superman's "S" chest logo.

Beck admitted seeing Superman in 1939, referring to "the big half-page opening panel" of *Superman* #1. He acknowledged there were *Superman* magazines at Fawcett's offices, and he "looked at three," but "read" only three pages of one.

> "So you read one and you looked at two others? Is that what you now tell his Honor?"
>
> "That is what I say now, yes."
>
> "Isn't it a fact that it was Mr. Parker who asked you to read the *Superman* magazine in his office?"
>
> "No. I don't remember him saying that."
>
> "Did you pick it up of your own volition?"
>
> "I picked it up for a couple of minutes while I was waiting to get his attention."

didn't you?   A Yes.

Q And at that time, in the fall of 1939, weren't
there Superman magazines in the Fawcett offices? A Yes.

Q And those were both Action Comics magazines
with Superman in them and Superman magazines with Superman
in them; isn't that so?   A I don't know. I don't know
what ones he is in. I didn't know until very very
recently.

Q Well, without knowing the names, you say you
knew that there were Superman magazines?   A I knew that
there was one there, because I testified to having seen
part of one page of one Superman story, and that is all
I ever did see.   I don't know what magazine it was in.

Q You say you remember testifying that; did you
read your testimony in the deposition over the weekend?
A No sir.

Q What is that?   A No.

Q When was the last time that you saw it? A Oh,
about two weeks ago, I guess.

Q Did you go over it with Mr. Martin?   A No.

Q Well now, without reference to what you previously
testified, is it or is it not a fact that you saw the
Superman magazine in the fall of 1939 in the Fawcett
offices?   Is that a fact?   A I saw one page.

Q Did you see any magazines, plural?   A I can't

DC attorney Louis Nizer argued that there was plenty of Superman talk—and
Superman comics—around the Fawcett offices to inspire their infringement. He
cross-examines C. C. Beck on the point in this page of court transcripts.

BECK CROSS-EXAMINATION, MARCH 22, 1948, TRIAL TRANSCRIPT, P. 994, NARA.

Beck declared his drawings of Captain Marvel came *before* looking at any Superman comic. "That is why I think that I made the drawings first and then, while waiting there, I glanced at this magazine."

"Well isn't it a fact that you and Parker discussed Superman many times in the fall of 1939?"

"We didn't discuss him. We mentioned him to each other. We had no discussions about the character at all."

Nizer turned to page 51 of Beck's pretrial deposition, quoting Beck's testimony that he and Parker *discussed* Superman "many times in the fall of 1939."

"I say the same today as I said then, that there was a mention of Superman."

"Now we come back to the fact that you mentioned him."

"Well, when we started in 1939 I recall very little mention of Superman at all. As I answered these questions in 1944, I meant after we got going. There would often be a *Superman* magazine in the place, and I believe I said in 1944 what I am saying now; that we were not entirely unconscious of it. . . . We knew it was coming out. We had many magazines around the place, but never had any time to read them. . . . I only looked at the ones that I enjoyed."

"Did anybody warn you not to read the *Superman* magazine?" Nizer asked.

"Only the kids," Beck replied defiantly. "They said it was a waste of time."

"You didn't think it was a waste of time on the part of the editor to pick it up to show it to you, did you?"

"I wasn't hired to tell editors what to do."

"This kind of incident in which the editor showed you the new issue of *Superman* magazine occurred many times, didn't it?"

"Maybe less than a half dozen."

Nizer referred to Allard's deposition, when Fawcett's art director testified that he talked about Superman with Beck in the fall of 1939.

"Does that refresh your recollection that Mr. Allard, the art director, discussed Superman with you at that time?"

"Not a bit."

Nizer asked about a Fawcett survey to ascertain the relative merits of Captain Marvel to Superman. Beck replied it was meant for "the boys" in the art department.

> "You mean to say that you did not read any [*Superman* comics] at the time you were making an analysis of your magazines and the Superman magazines?"
>
> "Sure."
>
> "You stated this morning that you were never interested in Superman, and didn't care what happened about him. Don't you think that this indicates a keen interest—making an analysis between the Superman magazines and Captain Marvel?"
>
> "The interest was in finding the biggest strip. We thought perhaps it was Superman, and we found to our satisfaction it was Captain Marvel."
>
> "You felt that there was a race going on between those two, didn't you?"
>
> "No, I just said we were—"
>
> "When you reported to [the art department] that Captain Marvel had passed Superman did a cheer go up?"

"No," Beck answered.[6]

It was the bosses in the penthouse offices who wanted a Superman; Parker and Beck wanted a new kind of superhero. That was Beck's contention, years later.

GLADIATOR

A mythological context was presented when Columbia professor of English Harrison Steeves appeared as an expert witness for the defendants. A wary Nizer asked that the professor not "read a lecture," but Coxe allowed him to "testify in [his] own way."

"The characteristic treatment of the hero in literature is the regard of him in the first place," Steeves said.

> "He is not only a person of superior attainments but is a person of superior conscience, devoting his life to the welfare of his people. One characteristic feature of most of these treatments is what folklore call the enfant; that is the bringing up of the child, the strengthening of his body through the process of education and exercise, and the education particularly in matters of the spirit. He is the champion of his race, a representative of good against evil.
>
> "You find that very characteristically in the story of [King] Arthur. Arthur came into the world from an unknown source. He is floated in upon the sea. He is adopted by a pair of benevolent noble parents, and he is educated . . . in the tradition of service to humanity."

Steeves referenced the German myth of Siegfried and the mythical Irish hero Chulainn before turning to the contemporary example of Philip Wylie's *The Gladiator*. Super-powered Hugo Danner "shows very close parallels in detail after detail to the substance of this story Superman. I can particularize there."

Nizer objected; the judge allowed Steeves to continue but cautioned him to be brief.

> "In *The Gladiator* you have the common treatment of the child's feats. Even in the cradle the child shows extraordinary strength, and in his growing childhood he discovers his own power. He can leap from trees, run like an express train. . . . He can pull up big trees, hurl rocks, and all of this impinges on his conscience, ultimately, with the sense of responsibility . . . and his father explains to him that here is a set of endowments that must be used in the good of humanity."

Nizer again objected. The judge warned the professor he was going into too much detail but let him proceed.

"Of course, he flies. Taking it for granted that flight is used in the general sense of locomotion through the air—he hasn't wings—he has extraordinary endurance, extraordinary agility."

Nizer objected a third time, declaring that unless the witness followed the judge's admonition to be brief, he would have to go into a lengthy cross-examination. The judge allowed Steeves to proceed.

The professor described Danner's ability to bend a railroad rail or a gun barrel, haul a tank, bust holes in walls, pull off iron gates, lift an automobile, and outlined his invulnerability to revolver, machine gun, and cannon fire. Steeves placed Hugo in the heroic tradition but with significant differences: *Gladiator* provided an insight into forces shaping the twentieth-century superhero.

"In the first place the powers of The Gladiator far transcend any of the powers that the old heroes were endowed with, except perhaps the gods; and in the second place . . . it is a very important consideration that for the first time in *The Gladiator* within my knowledge *these powers are exerted upon the modern technological life* [author's emphasis]. . . . There is not a very substantial change from the range of aptitudes and action from a hero of the classic ages down to the beginning of this century, but the important thing with regard to *The Gladiator* is that . . . all of contemporary automotive transportation, highly mechanized industry, highly organized business, and most particularly all elaborate and recondite technology is brought into the compass of this book. And the interest of the hero's life and the effects of his life repose very substantially in that fact, that this is a story of a hero against a background of modern technology."

Of the two rival superheroes, Steeves offered his opinion that "the feel of the two men is different to the eye, conceding the fact that they are both men of enormous size and of course with the ability of acrobats or professional strongmen. In matters of costume, Superman appears always with the blue wrist to ankle tights. That is the conventional uniform of the acrobat, the circus acrobat or gymnast."

Nizer moved to strike that comment. Judge Coxe let it stand.

Superman had X-ray vision, a new power added since his creation, giving him a quality of "omniscience." A dual personality did *not* apply to Superman but might to Captain Marvel. "[Billy] Batson is a magnificent boy," Steeves declared, and the boy's utterance of the magic word allowed the "conjunction" between the boy and Captain Marvel, "an absolutely separable and separate personality."[7]

When Billy said the magic word, was he replaced by a different being or did he transform into a mightier version of his own self? The professor believed the latter. "A female character . . . is introduced into the action, but Captain Marvel's attitude towards her is always an attitude of fluttering bashfulness. The explanation of that is obviously that here after all is a boy's heart and a boy's mind in a man's body, and his romantic sentiments have not been awakened."

Martin announced "cards" in evidence showing similarities between *Gladiator* and *Superman*. Nizer objected; the court asked to see them. "We think it portrays very graphically what we allege in our complaint, namely, that the story of Superman was copied from *The Gladiator* and was not original so far as the idea of the Superman character is concerned," Martin declared.

The judge sustained the objection, but cards were marked for identification.[8]

The issue might have been resolved if Wylie had sued for copyright infringement. Wylie biographer Frederick Keefer writes:

One of the main challenges to Wylie in writing *Gladiator* was the need to devise spectacular feats for Hugo to perform and then to make them seem probable. Our exposure to the

Superman comic strip unfortunately obscures the originality of many of these inventions, which, according to Wylie, as well as recent scholars, were "borrowed" from *Gladiator*. Hugo hurtling across a river in a single leap, bounding fifty feet straight up in the air . . . lifting an automobile by its bumper and turning it around in the road—all of these were, in 1930, fresh and new and very exciting to read about.[9]

WRAP-UP

On March 23 judge and counsel for defendant and plaintiff attended an afternoon screening of all twelve episodes of *Adventures of Captain Marvel*. Two days later Republic counsel Meyer Lavenstein appeared before the court to announce he was talking settlement with Nizer.

More witnesses rounded out the trial, including illustrator Dean Cornwell, who appeared as expert witness for the defendants. Over Nizer's objections, Cornwell testified he saw no instances of copying. "I am not interested in comic books, and I am looking at the pictures as pictures"; Cornwell added that the popular image of Superman expanding his chest and breaking his chains was similar to a sketch by the American Bureau of the Federation of Labor that was originally "an allegory symbolizing labor being freed."[10]

Under oath, Fawcett writer Otto Binder described meeting Eddie Herron in wartime service, early in 1943. Nizer objected, but the judge allowed him to testify.

"He told me that he had been approached by [Donenfeld] to testify in their behalf and what would I think of his accepting their offer for money and work in reference to that testimony."

Nizer moved to strike, but the judge let it stand.

Martin asked if Herron had told Binder he would accept the offer.

Nizer objected. The judge announced, "Of course, you haven't laid a foundation for it, but still I will take it."

"Well, I was given the impression that he had decided to," Binder said.

"I move to strike it out," Nizer interrupted.

The judge agreed, closing the Pandora's Box he just opened.[11]

The trial concluded on March 31, 1948, but Judge Coxe's ruling would not be handed down until 1950. In the intervening years, Fawcett and National were busy responding to the convulsive postwar market.

CHAPTER 14

JUDGMENT DAY

Happily, I did not learn of the Superman versus Captain
Marvel law suit until years later. It would have done me
no good to discover two of my idols, staunch believers in
direct action, bent over, hands cupped to lips, whispering
in the ears of their lawyers. No one should have to grow up
that fast.

JULES FEIFFER
The Great Comic Book Heroes

DIVERSIFICATION

In 1949 *Captain Marvel Adventures* celebrated its hundredth issue
with "Dr. Sivana and the Plot Against the Universe," a full-length
"comic novel." The epic features Sivana's takeover of the Rock of
Eternity, another retelling of the origin, and includes appearances
by Tawny the talking tiger and Shazam's spirit, whose "Shazamim"
bracelet allows him to adopt an "ethereal form."

Captain Marvel was celebrating his milestone, but a postwar
sales slump in superhero comics generated industry-wide diver-
sification. At Fawcett this included a six-issue *Jackie Robinson*
series celebrating the African American ballplayer who in 1947
broke professional baseball's barrier against black players. New
genres included crime comics; publisher Lev Gleason's *CRIME
Does Not Pay* was one notorious example.

In 1949 DC/National published *Superboy* #1 but was diversi-
fying into the romance field being pioneered by Simon and Kirby.
Titles included *Girls' Love Stories* and *Secret Hearts*. In 1950
National's licensing of celebrity images began with *The Adventures*

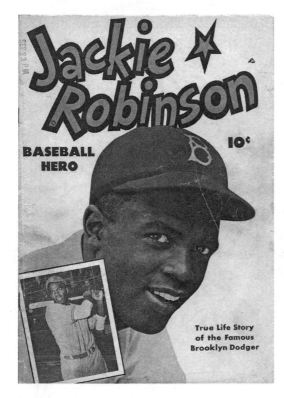

BASEBALL HERO

10¢

True Life Story
of the Famous
Brooklyn Dodger

In 1949 Fawcett released a comic book series about Jackie Robinson, the first African American to break major league baseball's racist "color barrier." With a postwar drop in popularity of superheroes, publishers were looking for new genres to exploit, including sports, romance, horror, and crime comics.

JACKIE ROBINSON #1 (1949), FAWCETT PUBLICATIONS.

of *Bob Hope* #1. In 1950–1951 DC introduced science-fiction titles *Strange Adventures* and *Mystery in Space*. Funny animal comics included *Animal Antics* and *Funny Folks*. In 1952 came *Our Army at War*, the title that later featured war-weary Sgt. Rock and his "combat-happy Joes" of Easy Company.

THE RULING

Judge Coxe made his ruling on April 10, 1950, summing up the litigation as National Comics' complaint that Fawcett stole their copyrighted character and engaged in unfair competition. Fawcett's principal defense was noninfringement based on invalid copyrights and the absence of unfair competition. Although not noted by the judge or followed up in the main legal issue of infringement, Fawcett had raised intriguing questions at odds with the work-for-hire assumptions of the era: Were Siegel and Shuster actually freelance contractors? Had they created Superman independent of DC?

Coxe ruled there was no evidence of unfair competition by Fawcett or Republic, so it was on to the main event of alleged copyright infringement.

The trial established that the first six *Action* Superman stories, published from June to November 1938, were reprinted in the first three issues of *Superman* by Detective Comics, Inc. Fawcett lawyers argued this resulted in loss of copyright. The judge agreed this would be so, if not for the fact that *Superman* "contained substantial new and original matter, in addition to the 'Superman' stories, which made them 'new works subject to copyright' under Section 6 of the Act." He concluded all issues of *Action* were properly copyrighted in the name of Detective Comics, Inc., and those rights were not lost because some stories were reprinted in *Superman*.

Coxe dismissed Fawcett's contention that *Superman* copyrights taken in the name of Superman, Inc., were invalid and agreed that the amended agreement of August 14, 1940, authorized Superman, Inc., to take out copyrights to *Superman* comics in its own name. But Coxe noted the copyright misappropriation of "Superman, Inc.," in *Superman* #5 and #6 could not "operate retroactively to validate the copyrights."

The judge cited the Wonder Man precedent that had determined Superman was an original character. However, evidence of actual copying was conflicting. There had been testimony that C. C. Beck admitted Captain Marvel was a Superman copy, but Beck denied it. Expert witnesses on both sides offered contradictory testimony, and there *were* differences. But he concluded, "I am satisfied from all the evidence that there was actual copying."

He turned to McClure's messy copyrights: some carried no notices, others incomplete information, and still others were blurred or barely discernable. National claimed errors in copyright were the syndicate's fault and did not bind them to legal consequences. Coxe disagreed, characterizing their arrangement—assignment of artists, division of sales proceeds, return of original artwork to DC for republication—as a joint venture, or "joint adventure," as he put it: "As the agreement was one of joint adventure, the errors and omissions of McClure are chargeable to Detective, for the rights and obligations of joint adventurers are substantially those of partners, and each participant in a joint adventure is an agent for the others."[1]

In an astonishing ruling, the judge declared, "I find that, with very few exceptions, the copyrights upon the McClure syndicated newspaper strips are invalid, and that therefore these strips have been dedicated to the public."

The judge raised the possibility that invalid copyrights on strips used in *Action* corrupted the comic, even though the magazine itself had proper copyright:

> The question remains whether the publication of this large number of syndicated newspaper strips without proper copyright notices resulted in an abandonment of the copyrights on the strips published in "Action Comics." . . . The syndicated newspaper stories were not identical with the "Action Comics" stories. But they were so nearly similar that, if they had been published by a stranger, they would clearly be held to be infringements of the copyrights in the "Action Comics" stories. If a copyright owner authorizes or permits the republication of its copyrighted material without copyright protection, it forfeits, i.e., abandons the copyright.

Coxe ruled, "I find, therefore, that the publication of the McClure syndicated newspaper strips without proper copyright notices resulted in the abandonment by plaintiff of the copyrights on the 'Action Comics' stories."

Fawcett and Captain Marvel had won!

National Comics/DC appealed, as did Fawcett, given that Coxe had also ruled they *were* plagiarists: "In view of the finding already made that there was 'actual copying' by defendant Fawcett of plaintiff's cartoon strips, I am not deposed to make any allowances to Fawcett for attorney's fees." Republic defendants were charged only as "contributory or secondary infringers" who had not copied the plaintiff's comics, and the judge provided $1,000 to Republic as an attorney's fee.[2]

APPEAL VERDICT

The appeal before the US Court of Appeals for the 2nd Circuit was not argued until May 4, 1951. Judges Chase, Frank, and Hand heard the appeal, with the verdict delivered by Chief Judge Learned Hand, a man once discussed as a potential Supreme Court nominee.

Learned Hand graduated with honors from Harvard Law School and ran, unsuccessfully, in 1913 as Progressive Party candidate for Chief Judge of the New York Court of Appeals. In 1924 President Coolidge appointed him to the Court of Appeals for the 2nd Circuit, which he had presided over as chief judge since 1939. Hand had gone into semiofficial retirement but remained active, with a heavy workload, when he considered the appeal in the matter of *National Comics Publications, Inc., v. Fawcett Publications, Inc.*[3] Coincidentally, Hand's older first cousin, Judge Augustus Hand, made the precedent-setting ruling in the Wonder Man appeal.

Justice Hand's ruling on August 30, 1951, agreed with the dismissal of DC's claims of "misappropriation" and "unfair competition." Hand also agreed Fawcett copied Superman with the same "degree of detail" as in *Detective Comics, Inc., v. Bruns Publications* (*DC v. Bruns*), adding, "It takes scarcely more than a glance at corresponding strips of *Superman* and *Captain Marvel* to assure the observer that the plagiarism was deliberate and unabashed." Nizer and his team would seize upon that statement.

McClure *had* been negligent in providing complete copyright notices, but the fact that they continued publishing the strips and affixing a copyright notice, however imperfect,

is conclusive evidence that it wished to claim a copyright upon them; and indeed it would have had no conceivable purpose in allowing its rights to lapse. . . . This confusion has led to the erroneous conclusion that because McClure with Detective's supposed acquiescence may have been negligent in protecting the copyrights upon many of the strips in suit, Detective abandoned its right to copyright all pictorial portrayals of the exploits of Superman. Since it did nothing of the kind, the case can be disposed of only by determining the validity of the copyright on each strip separately.[4]

The notion of *separately* determining copyright validity on each strip probably gave Louis Nizer pause.

Hand agreed that publication of the 1938 *Action* material in the 1939 issues of *Superman* did not forfeit copyright and limited his opinion to the September 22, 1938, contract between McClure and Detective Comics, Inc. "The judge, apparently without suggestion from either party, construed this agreement to be a 'joint venture,' and for that reason held that McClure's failure to affix the 'required notices to the strips had the same effect upon the copyrights in suit as though McClure were the proprietor.'" Hand agreed that McClure was "proprietor" of the copyrights, but it wasn't necessary to decide whether the contract constituted a joint venture, "incidentally one of the most obscure and unsatisfactory of legal concepts."

The 1938 contract with McClure stipulated that at its termination all rights reverted to Detective Comics—but only if DC held exclusive title. "In final confirmation of this interpretation is the clause in which McClure assumed 'to provide Detective with all the original drawings so that said drawings may be used by Detective in the publication *Action Comics* six months after newspaper release.' That is the language of a proprietor, who assumes power to license another to copy the 'works.'"

At issue with *Superman* #5 and #6 was forfeiture because the copyright notice listed the corporation as Superman, Inc., when that entity was the licensing arm of Detective Comics, Inc. Hand noted that Section 21 of the Copyright Act did not excuse an insufficient notice, but he added that there was no need to invoke that section "for we think that the notice was sufficient because of the relation of Superman, Inc., to Detective. It was a corporation having the same officers, directors and shareholders as Detective, which appointed it in January 1940, as its 'exclusive agent to exploit Superman.'" The interests of both "were precisely the same."

As with his cousin's comment in the Wonder Man case, Learned Hand was bemused at the contested material: "In the case of these silly pictures nobody cares who is the producer—least of all, children who are the chief readers; the strips sell because they amuse and please, and they amuse and please because they are what they are, not because they come from Detective. To allow the first producer of such pictures to prevent others from copying them, save as he can invoke the Copyright Law, would sanction a completely indefensible monopoly."

Learned Hand reaffirmed Superman as unique in his "different magical feats." A copyright never extends to the "idea of the work, but only to its expression," he observed. This was the precedent in the Wonder Man appeal, in which Augustus Hand had ruled that no one could monopolize the idea of a "Superman who is a blessing to mankind," but the "arrangement of incidents and literary expressions" could be copyrighted and susceptible of infringement.

In a blistering reproach to Fawcett's strategy of spotlighting faulty copyright notices, Hand declared the appeal judges were "unwilling to allow a bare-faced infringer to invoke an innocent deviation from the letter that could not in the slightest degree have prejudiced him or the public." Hand cited *Fleischer Studios, Inc., v. Ralph A. Freundlich, Inc.*, in which Fleischer's Betty Boop copyright notice omitted "Inc." That mistake was dismissed as "trivial," Hand noted, "and surely the measure of triviality is not whether on its face the mistake seems important, but whether it is in fact."

Thus, Hand ruled the "judgment reversed; and cause remanded for further proceedings with the foregoing opinion."

As for Republic, Hand warned: "Republic in its brief appears to suppose that, because its photoplay differed from *Superman* in essential details of plot and in general pattern, it did not infringe. Nothing could be more mistaken; a plagiarist can never excuse his wrong by showing how much he did not plagiarize. In so far as Republic copied the details of those strips which Fawcett had copied from *Action Comics* or *Superman*, it infringed."

But it was up to DC to identify the *Superman* exploits that Republic reproduced to satisfy the doctrine of *DC v. Bruns*: "On the new trial the court will have to decide what valid copyrights Republic did infringe. . . . On this record we cannot dispose of the claim." The movie studio declined to continue the fight, entering into a separate settlement agreement with DC/National on May 6, 1952.

Round 2 to Superman, but a *new trial* was required for "determining the validity of the copyright on each strip separately."

Although the trial had compared specific examples of alleged swipes, the new trial echoed concerns Fawcett attorney Martin had expressed "of the particular panels in the Captain Marvel strips which plaintiffs will contend were copied from the Superman strips." The retrial in the US District Court for the Southern District of New York was ordered on the main issue of copyright infringement, with Judge Vincent L. Leibell presiding.

SECOND TRIAL

Thomas A. Diskin, of De Witt, Van Aken & Nast, stepped in as new lead counsel for Fawcett. In a motion on March 24, 1952, Diskin made no mention of their previous victory being overruled or of the judgment that Fawcett was a "bare-faced infringer." Diskin emphasized the dismissal of the unfair competition charge and stuck to the contention that flawed copyrights left Superman in the public domain.[5]

At an appearance before Judge Leibell on May 19, 1952, Nizer likened Fawcett's infringing to Bruns Publications:

"How much clearer can Judge Learned Hand have been in disposing of that question of the fact of copying, particularly when we have Judge Coxe making a finding of fact which is explicit and in full detail? . . . If your Honor still has doubts on that question, we are at the crossroads of a decision which will seriously affect the new proceedings, because that goes right to your Honor's suggestion which we feel, respectfully, is quite improper, that we now give them detailed figures of every strip and of every panel."[6]

Superman's counsel was so outraged it formally requested the appeals court to explain their ruling that Fawcett infringed and petitioned the district court to issue an injunction against them. In a *per curiam* opinion (one issued by an appellate court or multiple judges), filed on June 10, 1952, Justices Hand, Chase, and Frank left the matter of an injunction to the district court but affirmed they *did* mean to say Fawcett infringed, "a necessary finding" given Fawcett's contention they had not. But the appeals court had not ruled *which* strips were infringed so as to be "actionable" under *DC v. Bruns*.

Each such comparison really involves the decision of a separate claim; there is no escape from it. The plaintiff may put in suit as many strips as it pleases, but it must prove infringement of each, or it will lose as to that strip. In saying that Fawcett was an "unabashed" infringer we meant no more than that there were some such instances. Whether the strips so copied were protected by a valid copyright we did not say.

The plaintiff has the burden of proving as to any strip it puts in suit that it was validly copyrighted; but we leave it open whether Fawcett has the burden of proving whether any copyright, once proved to have been validly obtained, was later forfeited.[7]

Jack Liebowitz was not about to accept the burden of proving anything. He delivered a sworn affidavit on November 14, 1952, asking for "instant application" for a court order directing that Fawcett file a surety bond with the clerk of the court in the amount of fiscal damages the court deemed proper. If Fawcett defaulted, the court would grant a preliminary injunction, patterned after *DC v. Bruns*, restraining Fawcett from printing, publishing, promoting, and selling any magazine or book with a costumed character exhibiting Superman-like powers. Liebowitz stated the grounds for the request was "the *inevitability* [author's emphasis] of a final judgment in plaintiff's favor."

Liebowitz calculated that from 1940, when Fawcett "launched its infringing magazines" to the 1948 trial, Fawcett sold 200 million copies. Based on the ten-cent retail price and the usual publisher's take of a little over five cents, he estimated $11.5 million in gross sales and a minimum of $2.3 million in profits. Four years later, Fawcett had accrued an additional $3,833,000 gross sales and profits of $766,000.

"Fawcett has already launched its 1953 infringement year," Liebowitz observed. The January issues of *Captain Marvel Adventures* and *Whiz Comics* currently on the newsstands

reek from cover to story . . . with further "bare-faced" plagiarism of the Superman cartoon. . . . Fawcett is continuing its flagrant piracy on the theory that the day of judgment may be long delayed by it—and, it is not beyond the realm of possibility that under then existing financial conditions Fawcett might be unable to pay the amounts awarded, or be in a position to bargain for reduced payment. Surely, the Court is not as helpless as Fawcett believes to blunt the consequences and risks of the delays attendant upon litigation.[8]

In response, the court directed Fawcett to provide a gross profits statement for magazines featuring Captain Marvel and Captain Marvel Jr. from September 1, 1951 through November 1952.

In the ensuing affidavit, Thomas Diskin reported three of the five magazines showed *losses*, as estimated by the comptroller of Fawcett Publications: *Whiz Comics* lost $3,188.12; *Master Comics* had losses of $2,471.07; *Captain Marvel Jr.* was $6,421.39 in the red. During the same period, *Captain Marvel Adventures* had gross profits of $41,780.53 and *The Marvel Family* grossed $17,053.61. Gross profits totaled $46,753.56, but direct and indirect costs would reduce that figure. Halfway through the affidavit's litany of losses, Diskin delivered a shocker:

[Notices] have been sent in the publishing trades to distributors that commencing in April, 1953 the defendant Fawcett Publications, Inc. will cease publication of three of the above five publications, which will include MASTER COMICS, CAPTAIN MARVEL, JR., and WHIZ COMICS. This information is furnished to the Court since the Court has stated that it intended to project a figure based on the profits up to September, 1953.[9]

Like the corner of a battered heavyweight, Fawcett was throwing in the towel.

DAY OF JUDGMENT

Emilio Squeglio graduated high school in 1947 and headed straight into his first real job at Fawcett "in between the production department and the bullpen," he recalled. Al Allard, who hired him, warned the lawsuit heading to trial might affect the comics division. "I don't know how long we're going to last," Allard admitted.

In addition to his regular duties, Squeglio created life-size cutouts of Captain Marvel and Superman for courtroom exhibits. "I was in court a couple of times, shuttling back and forth, watching Nizer kill the thing we loved the most," Squeglio recalled. "Fawcett did good books and were perfectionists when it came to making and selling comic books. Fawcett knew how to do it better than anybody else, and that's why DC was so jealous of them. We were doing far better than they were. Captain Marvel was outselling Superman by leaps and bounds. That's why DC sued them—they didn't want the competition."[10]

The legal war was settled without a new trial. On August 14, 1953, Judge Leibell's five-page judgment decreed Fawcett and its subsidiaries and affiliates were "perpetually enjoined" from producing and selling a Superman-like character in any medium. The judgment did not constitute an admission that Fawcett Publications, Inc., copied or infringed, a face-saving bit of boilerplate. But Fawcett agreed such language "shall not at any time affect the enforceability of the injunctive provisions contained in . . . this judgment."

Judge Leibell signed the judgment, and Donenfeld signed for National Comics Publications, along with the name of plaintiff's law firm; Fawcett Publications VP Roger Fawcett signed, along with the name of his law firm.[11] The settlement included Fawcett paying $400,000 in damages.

The injunction did not apply to Republic Pictures Corporation and Republic Productions, Inc., as they had settled the previous year, although a "Supplemental Stipulation and Settlement Agreement," signed on August 14, 1953, was added to the original settlement and letters of May 6, 1952. If Republic violated the agreement, its exclusion from Leibell's judgment would not prevent National Comics from seeking redress with the 2nd Circuit Court.[12]

Fawcett was not prohibited from publishing comic books, but

the company decided to get out of the business, also terminating a growing licensing empire. National's lawsuit achieved what scheming Sivana and his evil ilk could not. Captain Marvel—the World's Mightiest Mortal, the Big Red Cheese, Shazam's hand-picked champion—was no more.

The last issue of *Whiz Comics* was #155. *Captain Marvel Adventures* closed out at #150. The cover by Kurt Schaffenberger for the 89th and final issue of *The Marvel Family* pictured white silhouettes of a vanished Captain Marvel, Captain Marvel Jr., and Mary Marvel. A boy looking on exclaims, "Holey Moley! What happened to the Marvel Family?" A cover blurb declared, "And Then There Were None!"

SUPERDUPERMAN!

Bill Gaines represented the next-generation comic book publisher. When he took over his father's faltering Educational Comics, its titles included *Picture Stories from the Bible*, *Picture Stories from American History*, and *Tiny Tot Comics*; under young Gaines, EC became Entertaining Comics and published titles like *Tales from the Crypt*, *Frontline Combat*, and *Weird Science*. And there was *Mad* magazine, an EC humor comic edited by the visionary Harvey Kurtzman. *Mad* #4 (April/May 1953) featured *Superduperman!*, a funhouse mirror reflection of the Superman versus Captain Marvel lawsuit that set *Mad* on its course as satirical arbiter of American culture.

It was rare to see superheroes caricatured and lampooned, and under the penciling and inking of Wallace "Wally" Wood, readers enthusiastically responded to a fantastical, funny faceoff between Superduperman and "Captain Marbles." The title character's secret alter ego of the *Daily Dirt* newspaper copy boy Clark Bent endures a pathetic existence cleaning office spittoons and suffering rejection from curvaceous reporter, Lois Pain. Bent becomes Superduperman when the city is terrorized by the "unknown

The legal warfare between Superman and Captain Marvel was satirized in an early issue of *Mad*. It was so unusual to see a superhero parody that *Superduperman!* set *Mad*'s satirical course, influencing future creators such as artist Dave Gibbons.

"SUPERDUPERMAN!," MAD #4 (APRIL/MAY 1953), P. 7, ART BY WALLY WOOD. EC.

monster," revealed as *Daily Dirt* boy reporter Billy Spafon, who transforms into mighty Captain Marbles by uttering "Shazoom" for Strength, Health, Aptitude, Zeal, Ox, power of, Ox, power of another, and Money.

Marbles is attired in Marvel's familiar cape, costume, and colors but has a dollar sign for a chest emblem. Captain Marbles casually smokes a cigarette and starts yakking, even as his rival drops a safe on his head, followed by an entire building. Captain Marbles sits in the rubble, counting cash spilt from the smashed safe, concluding, "To heck with this Captain Marbles gimmick! The only important thing is the good ol' do, re, mi . . . lettuce . . . kale . . . shekels . . . Get it? Cash!" Superduperman finally gets Captain Marbles to throw a wild punch that explodes into his own face. The triumphant hero flexes a bicep for Lois Pain, revealing he is Clark Bent—"Whata burner on you, huh?" But the gal reporter slaps him silly. "So you're Superduperman instead of Clark Bent!" she shrugs, striding over the fallen hero in her high heels. "Big deal! Yer *still* a creep!"

DC threatened *Mad* with a copyright infringement lawsuit. "Kurtzman knew that the future of *Mad* lay in doing satires and parodies, and he was not about to let the success of his new comic be threatened," writes *Mad* historian Maria Reidelbach. "Gaines consulted Marty Scheiman, his advisor Lyle Stuart's lawyer, about the situation. Scheiman suggested that they simply ignore the threat and continue with their parodies, which they did, without further problems."[13]

DC/National was busy, anyway, conquering the emerging medium of television. Although Columbia released the licensed live-action serial, *Atom Man vs. Superman* in 1950, serials were going the way of the pulps. (In 1949 *The Shadow*, the first pulp superhero, ended his publishing run.) Whit Ellsworth, consultant on DC/National's movie serials, transitioned to a live-action Superman movie as a production lab for a potential TV pilot. Liebowitz sent Robert Maxwell to California to organize the production, while Mort Weisinger became editor of *Superman* comics in New York.

Superman and the Mole Men proved costs could be cut for television without losing the fantastic illusions, including hand-drawn animation of Superman flying. The casting was perfect—veteran actor George Reeves, with his broad shoulders and strong jaw, looked physically convincing as both Superman and bespectacled

Clark Kent. Phyllis Coates was Lois Lane, but she left after the first season. Her replacement, Noel Neill of the original serials, became the definitive Lois for many fans.

The Adventures of Superman TV show debuted in 1952. Each episode opened with a voice-over recalling the radio show opener, this time with a decidedly pro-America finish for the Cold War era: "Yes, it's Superman, strange visitor from another planet who came to Earth with powers and abilities far beyond those of mortal men. Superman, who can change the course of mighty rivers, bend steel in his bare hands, and who, disguised as Clark Kent, mild-mannered reporter for a great metropolitan newspaper, fights a never-ending battle for truth, justice, and the American way!"

In 1953 DC/National released a twenty-five-cent one-shot inspired by the 3-D trend in movies: *Superman: Three Dimension Adventures* featured off-registration art that, when readers slipped on the attached 3-D "Super Glasses," appeared "in startling 3-D Life-Like Action!" The 3-D comic was also notable for the work of artist Curt Swan, a fill-in for Wayne Boring. "We only put out one 3-D *Superman*, but [editor Mort] Weisinger was quite happy with my work on it, and soon after that he put me on *Superman* steady," Swan said. "I guess I was pretty far off base when I predicted, back in 1945, that comic books were only a passing fad and would never survive the '40s."[14]

But there was a harbinger of a tumultuous decade ahead. Timely Comics had maintained an in-house staff of salaried writers, artists, and production people—until 1949, when Martin Goodman reportedly discovered a huge stash of surplus art, possibly stockpiled from the war. That discovery, and changes in New York State employment tax laws, saw Goodman fire his in-house, salaried "bullpen."

Overnight, Timely artists like Syd Shores, Mike Sekowsky, Joe Maneely, Dan DeCarlo, and Carl Burgos were freelancers, scrambling for work at the page rate.[15]

CHAPTER 15

CRACKDOWN AND CRASH

> If I were asked to express in a single sentence what has happened mentally to many American children I would say that they were conquered by Superman.
>
> FREDRIC WERTHAM
> *Seduction of the Innocent*

SEDUCTION OF THE INNOCENT

As Captain Marvel and Fawcett Comics exited stage left, a tidal wave swept the industry, a perfect storm of a depressed postwar market for superheroes, long-simmering concerns that comics negatively impacted impressionable kids, and the lurid content of postwar crime and horror comics stoking the fires of comic book burnings. A lot was at stake—comic books were now an industry that generated $100 million a year.[1]

The voice of anticomics forces coalesced in Dr. Fredric Wertham, a respected psychiatrist who had worked at the Phipps Psychiatric Clinic at Johns Hopkins University and had been a senior psychiatrist at Bellevue Mental Hygiene Clinic. In 1946 Wertham opened a clinic for the underprivileged in Harlem and became interested in the effects of comic books on youth.

In 1948 Wertham was featured in a sensational article in *Collier's* magazine, "Horror in the Nursery," about the negative impact of violent comics on children. He would emerge as de facto leader of the anticomics movement, seemingly taking up the task as an obligation, given the "unhealthy" qualities of psychiatrists and educators sitting on the advisory boards of comics publishers: "One must distinguish between those psychiatrists who actually work with children and the psycho-prima donnas who sit on committees and decide the fate of children from a distance. The fact that some child psychiatrists endorse comic books does not prove the healthy state of comic books. It only proves the unhealthy state of child psychiatry."

The article ended with Wertham declaring, "The [comics] publishers will raise a howl about freedom of speech and of the press. Nonsense. We are not dealing with the rights and privileges of adults. . . . We are dealing with the mental health of a generation—the care of which we have left too long in the hands of unscrupulous persons whose only interest is greed and financial gain."[2]

Wertham's crusade culminated in his 1954 book, *Seduction of the Innocent: The Influence of Comic Books on Today's Youth*. He attacked crime and horror titles, appalling racial stereotypes, and superhero power fantasies, particularly the "Superman-Batman-Wonder Woman group" that was "superendorsed" by educators and psychiatrists. Werthem argued that Superman, with his big "S" on his uniform—("We should, I suppose, be thankful that it is not an S.S.")—encouraged youth to be "receptive to the blandishments of strong men who will solve all their social problems for them—by force."

Wertham described Batman and Robin as dressing up in "their special uniforms" to have violent encounters with "an unending number of enemies." Robin was a handsome boy, his uniform accentuating his bare legs: "He often stands with his legs spread, the genital region discreetly evident." Bruce and Dick Grayson lived in luxury at Wayne's ancestral manor, which boasted lovely flowers in vases and a butler who served the crime fighters. Bruce was often shown in a dressing gown, reclining on a couch with Dick close at hand. "It is like a wish dream of two homosexuals living together," Wertham famously concluded.

Of "Superwoman," a.k.a. Wonder Woman, Wertham added:

William Marston, who created the lie detector *and* Wonder Woman, must have had a ball writing this sequence as his heroine undergoes a "slave subjecting treatment." The Amazon's adventures were full of bondage and submission fantasies, raising the ire of anticomics crusader Fredric Wertham, who called Wonder Woman "the exact opposite of what girls are supposed to want to be," in his 1954 book, *Seduction of the Innocent.*

WONDER WOMAN #3 (FEBRUARY/MARCH 1943), UNTITLED STORY, P. 10, ART BY H. G. PETER.

"She is physically very powerful, tortures men . . . is the cruel 'phallic' woman . . . the exact opposite of what girls are supposed to want to be."[3]

Wertham was criticized for not applying academic rigor to his provocative thesis that comics turned kids into delinquents. There was no control group to test his theory, while his focus group included kids who were already disturbed, some of whom happened to read comics. Regardless, the uproar got Congress's attention. The US Senate Subcommittee to Investigate Juvenile Delinquency, chaired by Senator Robert C. Hendrickson, opened its televised hearings at Foley Square Federal Court in New York on April 21, 1954.

Bill Gaines volunteered to testify. He and artist/editor Al Feldstein were proud of Entertaining Comics, which arguably boasted the most talented roster ever assembled, including Feldstein, Harvey Kurtzman and Will Elder, Wally Wood, Johnny Craig, Reed Crandall, Jack Davis, Joe Orlando, Bernie Krigstein, John Severin and his sister, colorist Marie Severin, Al Williamson, and others. EC controlled copyrights and licensing but was otherwise a refuge of artistic creativity. "EC treated their artists with respect, which was almost unique in the industry," Michael T. Gilbert writes in *Alter Ego*. "The page rate was among the best in the business, and the editors encouraged artistic individuality."[4] Gaines was also ahead of his time in loving original comics art and preserving it.

THE HEARING

Gaines approached the Senate subcommittee with righteous fury, and not just because EC was among the committee's targets— constitutional freedom of speech was at stake. The night before his appearance, Gaines crafted an opening statement with friend and advisor Lyle Stuart that argued: "The truth is that delinquency is the product of the real environment in which the child lives and not of the fiction he reads. . . . The problems are economic and social and they are complex."[5] Gaines, who was taking Dexedrine, stayed up all night writing the statement. The next day the committee didn't get around to him until late afternoon, and by then the Dexedrine had worn off and an exhausted Gaines was no match for his professional inquisitors.

One exhibit famously used against him was EC artist Johnny Craig's cover for *Crime SuspenStories* #22, which pictured a man with a bloody ax holding a woman's severed head by her long blonde hair, the lower half of her body sprawled on a tile floor. Senator Estes Kefauver asked if Gaines thought the image in good taste. "Yes, sir, I do, for the cover of a horror comic," he replied. "A cover in bad taste . . . might be defined as holding the head a little higher so that the neck could be seen dripping blood from it and moving the body over a little further so that the neck of the body could be seen to be bloody." Ironically, the original idea *was* exactly that.

Recalling the televised hearings, Joe Simon summed up the consequences of Gaines's answer: "We knew we were in trouble." Simon did feel "those horror comics went too far. . . . Some of it was richly deserving of the fate that they wound up with." The problem was it looked like the excesses would take down the entire industry. "That was the end. I never thought comics would amount to much after that."[6]

Among the defenders of comics were its main consumers, including fourteen-year-old David Pace Wigransky, deemed an authority for his collection of five thousand comic books. In a letter published in the *Saturday Review of Literature*, Wigransky explains that kids know when they were reading "imaginary violence." Besides, he argues, "if Wertham is looking for bones to pick, let him read the Bible. . . . You could read it [violence and depravity] in the best books that are published, but why are you picking on comics?"[7]

The industry feared legislative intervention and censorship. It didn't help that newspaper-strip stars Milton Caniff and Walt

Kelly, representing the National Cartoonists Society at the Senate hearings, made a distinction between strips and comic books, condemning the latter. Dr. Wertham's testimony also carried gravitas, given he had testified in a school segregation case cited in the landmark *Brown v. Board of Education* ruling by the US Supreme Court on May 17, 1954.

STAMP OF APPROVAL

That June the Senate committee reconvened to conclude its investigation. Chairman Hendrickson declared that publishers, distributors, and dealers who eliminated crime and horror comics "shall receive the acclaim of my colleagues and myself. A competent job of self-policing within the industry will achieve much."[8]

"Self-policing" arrived with the Comics Code Authority (CCA), administered by the Comics Magazine Association of America and headed by Charles F. Murphy, a former judge. The code laid down the law: using the words "horror" or "terror" in a title was forbidden, as were stories that showed lust, bloodshed, or gore; even concepts like "scenes of horror" and "gruesome crimes" were prohibited. Anything that could "stimulate the lower and base emotions" was *verboten*. Policemen, judges, and government officials were to be respectfully presented, moral behavior encouraged, and the sanctity of marriage upheld. In *The Ten-Cent Plague* author David Hajdu characterizes the code as "an unprecedented (and never surpassed) monument of self-imposed repression and prudery."[9]

Authority-approved comics carried a cover stamp with the CCA logo and "Approved by the Comics Code Authority" (designed by DC logo artist and letterer Ira Schnapp, purported creator of the *Superman* logo). DC produced a 1955 comics pamphlet (illustrated by Win Mortimer) explaining how the Authority scrutinized every panel and advertisement for offensive material. Every day Judge Murphy consulted with his staff on borderline cases, such as a comic book scene based on Robert Louis Stevenson's *Treasure Island*, for which Murphy rules, "I won't pass it. We can't show one pirate stabbing another, even if Stevenson did write it."

"Only when a publisher has conformed to all the criticisms made by the reviewers does his magazine earn the coveted seal of approval," a fictional comics seller concludes. With the stamp, "I'm giving my customers a wholesome form of entertainment in good taste!"

The censorship board had no legal authority, but fear was enough—most distributors only handled code-approved comics.[10]

One of Wertham's targets, that Amazon princess he called "Superwoman," was already being domesticated after William Moulton Marston died of lung cancer in 1947. Editor Sheldon Mayer recalled of Marston, "We fought like hell," but ruefully noted that when it came to writing *Wonder Woman*, "there was just one right guy, and he had the nerve to die." Mayer had to keep the popular character going, imitating the style he once criticized. "I was a pale imitation of Marston," he admitted.

Robert Kanigher took over as editor and writer of the feature during the CA era, when conventional notions of femininity, romance, and formulaic superhero adventure replaced bondage fantasies and the series' mythical spirit. The domestication of Wonder Woman is illustrated on the cover of *Sensation Comics* #94 (November/December 1949), which shows gallant Steve Trevor carrying Wonder Woman across a stream, her red boots replaced by demure, lace-up yellow sandals. As Clark pined for Lois, who swooned for Superman, alter ego Diana Prince longed for Steve Trevor, who was enamored of Wonder Woman.[11]

The code made life miserable for creators. In 1953 Simon and Kirby started their own company, Mainline Publications, and in 1954 released a Western hero, Bullseye, a sharp-shooting masked man who battles Indians and outlaws. "I knew we were dead when I saw them whiting out the tomahawks in the Indians' hands,"

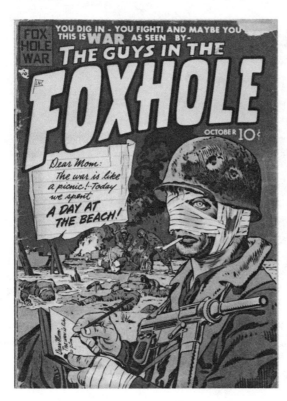

War comics were propaganda vehicles during World War II; postwar comics by creators who actually went to war were dramatically different. This title, with its sobering cover by Jack Kirby, a veteran of the Battle of the Bulge, says it all. The publisher, Mainline Publications, Inc., was a company started by Kirby and his partner Joe Simon. But a perfect storm of bad economics, censorship crusades, and a changing marketplace soon put dozens of publishers out of business, Mainline among them.

THE GUYS IN THE FOXHOLE #1
(SEPTEMBER/OCTOBER 1954),
COVER ART BY JACK KIRBY. MAIN-
LINE PUBLICATIONS, INC.

recalled Kirby. "They were attacking the settlers armed with nothing."[12] The tomahawks disappeared in *Bullseye* #6, the series was cancelled by issue #7, and Mainline was defunct by 1956. With the industry in turmoil, Simon went into advertising, but Kirby decided to stick with comics.

Bowing to the inevitable, Bill Gaines cancelled his horror titles in September 1954. Lev Gleason's violent *CRIME Does Not Pay* tried to survive by making the "Does Not Pay" bigger, but the publication went under the following year.

EC tried a "New Directions" line in 1955. *Impact* lasted five issues, carrying the code for all except the first issue, which featured a masterpiece: "Master Race," Bernie Krigstein's story, told in a unique graphic style, of a Nazi death camp commandant encountering a camp survivor on the subway. *Ace's High*, about air combat in World War I, lasted five issues. The highbrow *Psychoanalysis* lasted four issues. *Piracy*, a swashbuckling

EC challenges the US Air Force to tell the truth about Unidentified Flying Objects in this special "Flying Saucer Report" issue. After its disastrous Senate subcommittee hearings, EC tried to rehabilitate itself with a serious "New Directions" line and highbrow titles like *Psychoanalysis*. It soon cancelled all titles except *Mad* and made that publication into a magazine to bypass the censorious Comics Code Authority.

WEIRD SCIENCE-FANTASY #26 (DECEMBER 1954), COVER ART BY AL FELDSTEIN. EC COMICS.

pre–New Directions title about pirates and adventure on the high seas, made it to seven. Gaines did a code-friendly makeover of *Weird Science-Fantasy*, retitling it *Incredible Science Fiction*. It lasted four issues.

Bad blood between EC and the Code Authority boiled over with the story "Judgment Day!" in the final *Incredible Science Fiction*, issue #33 (February 1956). Written by Al Feldstein, drawn by Joe Orlando, and colored by Marie Severin, the story first appeared in pre-Code *Weird Fantasy* #18. A tale about tolerance, seemingly a Code-worthy subject, has an Earth astronaut visit Cybrinia, a planetary experiment in automaton self-replication and self-rule, seeking inclusion in Earth's Galactic Republic. The astronaut, wearing a space helmet throughout the visit, observes all robots are identical, but the orange-colored ones have subjugated blue ones. Cybrinia is denied membership, but the astronaut leaves a message of hope—learn to live together

In "Judgment Day," written by Bill Gaines and Al Feldstein, an Earth emissary leaves the robot planet Cybrinia with the hope that by becoming more tolerant they will gain admission into the Galactic Republic. When the tale was to be reprinted in *Incredible Science Fiction* #33, Charles Murphy, head of the new Comics Code Authority, balked at the dark-skinned astronaut in the final panel. Gaines published the story—with an extra-large "Approved by the Comics Code Authority" stamp—and departed the comic book industry.

INCREDIBLE SCIENCE FICTION #33 (FEBRUARY 1956), ART BY JOE ORLANDO. EC.

and the universe is yours. On the flight home the astronaut removes the helmet, revealing a black man, and "the instrument lights made the beads of perspiration on his dark skin twinkle like distant stars."

Al Feldstein personally presented "Judgment Day" to Charles Murphy. The former judge got to the surprise last panel and told Feldstein, "No. You can't have a Negro." A furious Gaines threatened to expose the Authority as racist, and Murphy relented. EC could publish the story—*if* it removed the perspiration on the astronaut's face. In what Feldstein calls Gaines's "last act as a comic-book publisher," he phoned Murphy to say "fuck you" and published the story without changes, complete with CA stamp. Gaines cancelled all titles save one, and for that he floored the gas pedal and did a full, rubber-peeling turnaround, taking *Mad* from comic book to magazine, bypassing the Comics Code entirely. The new magazine's mascot and cover subject would be Alfred E. Neuman, a big-eared kid with a gap-toothed grin whose slogan was "What—me worry?"[13]

Mad continued Gaines's policy of artistic expression, retaining many EC stars. Jack Davis was a *Mad* regular, his future artistic output ranging from mainstream magazine covers to movie posters. *Mad* contributor Joe Orlando eventually became a DC executive, bringing his artist's perspective to the executive suites. Wally Wood, a major *Mad* contributor, would go on to many successes. Artist William Stout salutes Wood, in particular, for starting *witzend*, a "prozine" started in 1966 that allowed professionals to express themselves outside the censorious limits of the code. "With his publication of *witzend* #1, Wally Wood sowed the first seeds of the modern creator-owned comics movement. Simultaneously, Wood foreshadowed the idea of total artistic freedom in comics that became the hallmark of the underground comix that were soon to follow."[14]

EC Comics inspired the next generation, including underground and mainstream artist Trini Robbins, who recalled, "Wally Wood was the first artist I knew by name. I started reading EC's because they had Wood's work in them."[15] EC influenced two future creators growing up in England, writer Alan Moore and artist Dave Gibbons. "Well, I studied art in the pages of EC reprints [laughs] and DC and Marvel comics; that's the only place I studied art," Gibbons confesses.

"Superduperman!" inspired Gibbons on an early Superman story with Moore in *Superman Annual* #11 (1985). "When Alan and I did the *Superman Annual* together, the kind of feeling that we wanted to give Superman was that sense of him being solid and lit—which isn't the way Superman is always drawn. He tends to be drawn as a kind of colored outline. The only thing we talked about when we did that Superman story . . . was very much the 'Superduperman' parody. . . . I love the feeling of weight and bulk and substance that Wally Wood gave the characters in 'Superduperman.'"[16]

Mad, both as a comic and a magazine, was always forbidden fruit. Future underground comix and rock-poster artist Richard "Rick" Griffin recalled his father once gave him a dime to buy a comic at a drugstore, and he chose *Mad* #22. "There was something unusual about the format of this book," Griffin recalled. "The strange use of doctored photographs mixed with weird art struck me as rebellious and antiestablishment. It gave me a fantastic, disorienting effect."[17]

Mad was still a comic book when a kid named Robert Crumb saw the cover of *Mad* #11—a grotesque Basil Wolverton image of a "Beautiful Girl of the Month" that mimicked the cover design of *Life* magazine. For the startled Crumb, that cover was a "significant moment. . . . Seeing this rude, insulting lampoon of the great *Life* was a revelation."[18]

"IT WAS A NIGHTMARE."

In 1952 Will Eisner was still working on the syndicated *The Spirit* comics insert, mentoring Jules Feiffer and Wally Wood, the latter drawing a space-age storyline that landed the Spirit on the moon. But *The Spirit* was nearing the end of its run, and Eisner was looking for the exits himself. Eisner had set up American Visuals in 1948, a company that adapted comics story-telling to other fields. *PS, The Preventive Maintenance Monthly*, was a comics magazine for the US Army for which Eisner worked as artistic director from its inception in 1951 through its end in 1971.

Eisner told writer David Hajdu about a 1953 cocktail party where he was enjoying a delightful chat—until the man asked what he did for a living. "I write comic books," Eisner replied. "How dreadful for you," the man said, walking away.

"I had had it," Eisner recalled. "It was very dispiriting. You were held in disdain if somebody knew what you did. . . . I wasn't the only one trying to do something good—there was Harvey [Kurtzman], and a lot of the people at EC and some others were very creative and serious about what they were doing. But nobody cared outside of comics. I felt that nobody was paying attention, except the readers, and they were mostly kids, so nobody took them seriously."

"Everybody was punished," Carmine Infantino confessed to Hajdu. "It was like the plague. The work dried up, and you had nowhere to go, because comics were a dirty word. You couldn't say you were a comics artist, and you had nothing to put in your portfolio. If you said you drew comic books, it was like saying you were a child molester. It was a nightmare"[19]

Fawcett, EC, Mainline—other publishers followed them into oblivion. Victor Fox's line ended in 1951 after taking a scandalous turn, featuring women "bound and gagged, tied to racks, threat-ened with whips and branding irons, molested by freaks and degenerates," writer Maurice Horn notes. Hillman Periodicals, whose star was wartime aviator Airboy, was done by 1953. The comic book line of venerable United Features Syndicate, which began in 1936 with *Tip Top Comics*, closed in 1955. The follow-ing year, Lev Gleason Publications ended.[20] In 1957 the collapse of American News Company, the nation's biggest newspaper and periodical distributor, wiped out half the comics companies remaining from 1952.[21]

One tragic story was the fate of Bob Wood, formerly editor of Gleason Publications' *CRIME Does Not Pay*. He struggled to find work, drank heavily, and by the summer of 1958 was reduced to "hawking sleazy gag cartoons to third-rate men's magazines to earn a meager living," recalled Joe Simon, who had no work for Wood when he came calling. That September, Bob Wood locked himself in a Gramercy Park hotel room with Violete Phillips, secretary at a Madison Avenue advertising agency, for a days-long drinking bender culminating in Wood clubbing the woman to death with an electric iron. New York tabloids ate it up: "Gramercy Park Gets the Horrors: Editor of mag called 'Crime Does Not Pay' murders ad woman in a hotel tryst," read one headline. After Wood served a prison term for manslaughter, his corpse was found dumped on the New Jersey Turnpike, Wood reportedly having paid the ultimate price for his gambling debts.

Art Spiegleman has a poignant memory of EC artist Bernic Krigstein. Spiegleman, who in 1980 began serialization of *Maus*, his landmark autobiographical account of his father's Shoah experiences and the first graphic novel to win a Pulitzer Prize, had been fascinated by Krigstein's "Master Race" story, making it the subject of a college term paper in 1967. In the early seventies Krigstein had been out of comics for years when Spiegleman visited at the artist's studio on East 23rd Street, bringing along his "Master Race" paper.

"As I began reading, he entered into the analysis avidly, acknowledging a reference to Futurism in one panel, to Mondrian in another, denying a reference to George Grosz in yet another," Spiegleman recalled. "It was as if messages he'd sent off in bottles decades earlier had finally been found.

"He yanked me further into his studio and pointed at the walls. 'Look!' he roared. 'You see these paintings?' I saw several large, molten, and lumpy Post-Impressionist landscapes in acidic colors. *'These are my panels now!'* His voice betrayed all the anguish of a brokenhearted lover."[22]

EMPIRE BUILDING

During the Comic Book Depression, *The Adventures of Superman* television series provided a platform that kept Superman—and superheroes—viable. In retrospect, superheroes were experiencing their first major period of purge and renewal. But through it all, a passionate fandom would emerge.

Michael Uslan was born in New Jersey in the early fifties. His sibling, Paul, was four years older and the first to bring comics into the house, as well as the athlete of the family. Michael was the last picked when choosing sides for a game, the kid most likely to strike out at the plate. "I was a reader and I sought refuge in my world of superheroes," Uslan recalls. "I found acceptance in that world and that probably propelled me into collecting comics in the fifties and early sixties. Collecting comics was the most *alienated* hobby. I didn't know anyone other than my friend Bobby who was into superheroes and collecting comic books. Comic books were under major attack—it was believed they caused juvenile delinquency. But my mother told me that I learned to read before I was four from comics!"

Comics could be seen at the local barber shop, Uslan recalls—battered old Golden Age and fifties comics, coverless, logos cut off—tattered but tantalizing talismans of a forbidden world. Michael recalls the seminal childhood moment when his father gave his older brother change to buy comics at Irv's Candy Store. Michael got to pick two. One was Sheldon Mayer's little kid cartoon from DC, *Sugar and Spike*, the other a copy of *Superman*, a familiar world thanks to the TV show.

DC/National solidified itself as the number one comics publisher during the decade. In 1956 National absorbed Busy Arnold's once successful Quality Comics, adding two popular properties created in 1941: Plastic Man, Jack Cole's freakishly elastic superhero; and Blackhawk, leader of the high-flying Blackhawk Squadron (credited to Chuck Cuidera, Bob Powell, and Will Eisner). Among Quality's titles was the war comic *G.I. Combat*, which DC kept publishing.[23]

In 1956 Superman, Inc., was replaced by the Licensing Corporation of America (LCA), the brainstorm of Jay Emmett, Jack Liebowitz's twenty-seven-year-old nephew. In the new and expansive business model, LCA would license not only in-house comics icons but outside properties as well.

On the distribution side, DC's Independent News Company filled the vacuum left by the collapse of American News Company. As with LCA's new business model, IND branched out beyond comics to distribute high-end glossy periodicals, including the new men's magazine *Playboy*. DC threw a lifeline to the sinking comics industry—with terms attached. One who grabbed it was Martin Goodman, whose comics line was going under. "What happened was: Martin Goodman made one of the big publishing decision mistakes that was ever made," Stan Lee recalled.[24]

In late 1951 Goodman had decided not only to publish comics but also to distribute them. He left his longtime distributor, Kable News, and set up Atlas News Company. His Timely Comics line now bore the logo of a white globe with the word "Atlas." The postwar superhero downturn caused the cancellation of *Human Torch*, *Sub-Mariner*, and *Captain America* in 1949, but Goodman brought them all back under the Atlas banner in *Young Men* #24 (December 1953). The revival was brief—the Timely titans were gone within two years. But Atlas was still doing fine. After having laid off in-house artists in 1949, Goodman had begun hiring them back. In addition to Timely talent like Bill Everett, Carl Burgos, and Joe Maneely (who tragically died in an accidental fall between commuter train cars in 1958), promising young artists were emerging, like John Romita and Steve Ditko. And then, in

In the close of Marvel's "monster-mag" era, this excerpt from a story written by Stan Lee and drawn by Steve Ditko for *Amazing Adult Fantasy* presents mutant Tad Carter—who bears an uncanny resemblance to Peter Parker, a.k.a. Spider-Man, the character Ditko would draw in the next, and final, issue. The Mutant, with an echo of Hugo Danner, can read minds and fly, and he joins his fellow mutants in hiding to await the future when they can emerge. That came in 1963 with Marvel's super-powered mutants *The X-Men*.

"THE MAN IN THE SKY!," *AMAZING ADULT FANTASY* #14 (JULY 1962).

1957, Goodman inexplicably shut down his distribution system and signed with American News Company—months before the venerable distributor went out of business.

DC/National would distribute eight Atlas titles a month, with Goodman spreading them out by making each a bimonthly. "IND," for Independent News, replaced the Atlas icon. The covers would also include "MC"—Marvel Comics.

Goodman again reduced costs by relying on freelancers working at page rates, with mainstay editor Stan Lee one of the only salaried employees. For a while the company limped along on stockpiled pages. There was improvement by the end of 1957, with new stories in the works and Goodman convincing IND to raise his quota from eight to ten bimonthly titles.[25]

The stars of Goodman's struggling Atlas/Marvel line were monsters with names like Dragoom, Groot, and Goom, prowling code-friendly titles like *Journey into Mystery* and *Strange Tales*, and light fare like *Millie the Model*. Stan Lee edited the titles, overseeing freelancers like Dan DeCarlo (famed for his *Archie* work), Steve Ditko, Dick Ayers, Don Heck, and Jack Kirby, the latter back with Goodman despite the bitter split over Captain America. But MC was in a creative stasis, and the overworked Lee was considering other career options.[26]

JERRY AND JOE/JACK AND HARRY

Like many of his colleagues, Joe Shuster was struggling. A decade into his exile from DC, he found work in pornographic periodicals, drawing images for stories of sexual sadism in *Nights of Horror*. Shuster was not credited, but his vignettes display characters with uncanny resemblances to the Superman stock company—a reefer-toking Jimmy Olsen clone, a Luthor lookalike gleefully ensnaring Lois Lane's double in ingenious torture traps, a Superman figure whipped by another Lois dead ringer. Decades later the inimitable Shuster style popped out when writer/editor

Craig Yoe happened on a used books stall and a box full of *Nights of Horror*.

"The revelation that Joe had a secret identity who created porn will upset some people," Yoe writes. "But this imperfection, if his alter ego is that, makes him far more a person of interest—someone we, with our own flaws, can relate to." Yoe adds, "Joe became a warning for creators to not undersell their ideas, and the poster child for starving artists."[27]

Jerry Siegel was struggling, too, but got steady work in 1959 with an unlikely publisher—DC/National—writing Superman stories. Joanne Siegel, showing fierce determination, essentially shamed DC into taking him back by threatening Jack Liebowitz with publicizing the financial plight of Superman's cocreator. Siegel, now forty-five, got the standard page rate and none of the raises, perks, and "token-of-feeling" checks of the glory days. His and Joe's bylines were long gone, and his current work was not credited. Superman editor Mort Weisinger "treated Siegel with no special deference or acknowledgment whatsoever," Martin Pasko notes.[28]

But Siegel brought an explosion of creativity to Superman, joining a creative team that included former *Captain Marvel* writer Otto Binder. "It was here, stripped of all identity, that Jerry Siegel perhaps did the best work of his writing career," Siegel and Shuster biographer Brad Ricca writes. "For though he invented Superman with Joe, it was here that so many elements of the modern Superman came into full being." The period saw the creation of Superman's cousin Supergirl, Bizarro and Brainiac, the Legion of Super-Heroes, Krypto the Superdog, and others.[29]

By the autumn of 1961 National Comics changed its corporate name to National Periodical Publications, Inc. With *Seduction of the Innocent* fears still fresh in the minds of worried parents and educators, the name-change downplayed comics, although the DC logo remained. Liebowitz surveyed a time-tested company boasting icons with ancillary-merchandising appeal and thriving licensing and distribution divisions and decided to take the company public. His caveat was that Harry Donenfeld, with his rumored mob connections, step down to avoid potential inquiries from the Justice Department and Security and Exchange Commission. Donenfeld did his duty and became a silent partner while Liebowitz became company president.

Before the successful public offering, Harry's wife Gussie died. Harry, free to marry his mistress, appeared happy preparing for the wedding and honeymoon cruise. But the power struggle had been "ugly," and "rumors also swirled of arguments with Liebowitz and with mob connections," writes Gerard Jones. No one knew what to make of what happened a week before the wedding, when Harry's son Irwin found his father alone in bed, barely breathing. Had Harry fallen and hit his head? He suffered damage to his speech and memory but was well cared for until he slipped away in 1965. In the comics, there was no obituary or mention of DC's publisher.[30] Harry finally got his due during DC's fiftieth anniversary, making the list of "Fifty Who Made DC Great."

SHOWCASE

DC's Licensing Corporation of America had an early success when it won the license for author Ian Fleming's James Bond, the fictional British secret agent with the "007" licensed-to-kill classification. In 1963 United Artists released the first Bond movie, *Doctor No*. DC's licensed tie-ins included a UK reprint of a *Classics Illustrated* adaptation of *Dr. No* that appeared in *Showcase* #43 (April 1963).

"People laughed when [Jay Emmett] secured the rights to James Bond at a time when it was merely a series of novels for adults and just being popularized in *Playboy* (distributed by Independent News)," Martin Pasko writes. "DC's *Dr. No* comic book, marketed as a movie tie-in, didn't set the world on fire, but as the Bond movies went 'boffo,' Emmett built a multimillion-dollar toy, trading card, and apparel business (those James Bond trench coats!). . . ."

One of the most successful of DC's early Licensing Corporation of America deals was for author Ian Fleming's secret agent James Bond. Timing was perfect; it coincided with the release of a film adaptation of *Doctor No*, the first of dozens of Bond movies to come. LCA merchandising included this *Showcase* tie-in for the movie.

SHOWCASE PRESENTS DOCTOR NO #43 (APRIL 1963), COVER ART BY BOB BROWN. DC.

Within a decade of its formation, LCA would be as highly valued a division of National as Independent News."[31]

Showcase was another next-generation creation, this time from Irwin Donenfeld, who replaced Ellsworth as editorial director in the mid-1950s. Irwin, who made a science of studying sales patterns, sensed opportunity in a down market, proposing a title that would experiment with new ideas and characters, where every issue was a surprise—maybe even the next hit property. *Showcase* began in 1956 as a bimonthly helmed by rotating editors. The first issue featured "Fire Fighters"; an editorial page explained the goal was to give readers what *they* wanted, and readers requested a firefighter feature.[32] The next issue, "Kings of the Wild," showcased outdoor animal adventures. The third was devoted to US Navy Frogmen. All three were failures.

Julius "Julie" Schwartz, editor of *Strange Adventures* and *Mystery in Space*, was next up as editor for *Showcase* #4. He recalled someone—it might have been himself—suggested reviving the Flash, a character Schwartz had edited at All-American. The initial reaction was negative, given the character had been cancelled in 1949. But someone argued that the average age of comic book readers was from eight to ten years, meaning a new generation was unfamiliar with the original character. This was a golden opportunity to reintroduce and update the character with a new origin, secret identity, and costume. Schwartz got the green light to bring him back and went to work with writer/editor Robert Kanigher, artist Carmine Infantino, and inker Joe Kubert.

The new Flash was Central City Police Department scientist Barry Allen, introduced while working alone in his lab on a stormy night. "I distinctly remember how Flash would gain his super speed," Schwartz explained. "Jay Garrick got it by inhaling heavy water, right? But I wanted something more logical, more scientific. So I suggested a bolt of lightning hit the chemicals that splashed over Barry Allen. Since a bolt of lightning is 186,000 miles per second, that's a reasonable way to do that."[33] Jay Garrick, the original Flash, had worn a mythically inspired Mercury-winged helmet, a red top, belt, and blue pants; Allen's space-age costume popped out of a ring, expanding into an aerodynamic red body suit with yellow trim and a lightning bolt chest emblem. The updated Flash ushered in the "Silver Age," the second great era of the superheroes. *Showcase* left firefighters and frogmen behind, successfully resurrecting other Golden Age superheroes like Green Lantern in *Showcase* #22 (1959).

In 1959 *The Brave and the Bold*, a DC/National title featuring medieval knights and Vikings, was retooled as a *Showcase*-type title. Schwartz also wanted to update All-American Comics' *Justice Society of America*, the team-up title cancelled in 1951. "Society" sounded like a social club to Schwartz, so "Justice League of America" was born. The cover of *Brave and the Bold* #28 featured Flash, Green Lantern, Wonder Woman, Aquaman, and the Martian Manhunter battling a gigantic starfish, "Starro the Conqueror," in the first of three straight *Brave and Bold* "auditions." Irwin Donenfeld gave Schwartz sales numbers and fan reaction for each Justice League appearance. By the third issue, Irwin didn't write a figure or rating—it was an exclamation point!

"I had to get to work, to put out the [new] magazine I'd assumed," Schwartz recalled. The title would have unexpected consequences, triggering the next stage in the evolution of comic book superheroes.[34]

CHAPTER 16

RESURRECTION AND RENEWAL

And so was born "The Fantastic Four!!" And from that moment on, the world would never again be the same!!

The Fantastic Four #1 (November 1961), origin-story copy

MARVEL AGE

In 1947 Martin Goodman had collected his periodicals, including his comics line, under the umbrella of Magazine Management Company, headquartered at 625 Madison Avenue. By the late fifties, Goodman's he-man magazines, including *For Men Only*, *Action for Men*, and *Man's World*, were going strong, but Atlas/Marvel was producing no more than a third of the value of his other periodicals.

In 1964, when a young man named David George joined Magazine Management's editorial staff, the Marvel line was on a dramatic upswing. "The first time I met Martin Goodman, I was virtually petrified," George recalled of the publisher who had seen his beloved comics line make a complete turnaround. "The silver-haired, bespectacled man had a certain presence about him that silently commanded respect. I remember how he often wore dark glasses, even when he strolled the corridors, and this seemed to render his persona almost Mafia-like. He could look at you and utter the fewest of monosyllabic words, and the effect would be chilling." But George believed his boss was "an honorable, decent man." Goodman shared his personal Depression-era stories of riding the rails and sleeping in boxcars, and George never forgot the late work night when his boss invited him into his carpeted corner office to chat over 101-proof Wild Turkey poured from Goodman's well-stocked bar.[1]

The "Marvel Age" truly began in 1961, when Goodman's instincts again began paying off. He learned of strong sales for DC's *Justice League* and asked editor Stan Lee for a team-up title. For the artist's half of the equation, Lee turned to Jack Kirby.

Since the breakup of the Simon/Kirby team, Jack had been freelancing, contributing his foursome of death-defying adventurers, Challengers of the Unknown, to *Showcase*. He teamed with Wally Wood on *Sky Masters of the Space Force*, a syndicated strip about astronauts braving the frontier of space. *Sky Masters* abruptly ended in February 1960, after DC/National editor Jack Schiff, having ostensibly served as Kirby's agent, claimed the creator owed him commission money, sued, and won. The reportedly modest settlement was still tough for a freelancer. Worse, the falling out with Schiff closed off work at offices of the industry leader. "Shipwrecked at Marvel," is how Jack put it, according to Mark Evanier.[2]

Jack Kirby's Atlas/Marvel years marked an astonishing period of creativity that changed the comics industry and popular culture. Stan Lee described his collaboration with Kirby as a smooth transition from the grind of monster comics, as Lee ran with Goodman's assignment of creating a *Justice League*-type title: "I would create a team of superheroes if that was what the marketplace required."

Kirby remembered things differently than the ebullient editor. Kirby described walking into Marvel's office sometime in 1961 and seeing Stan Lee crying as office furniture headed out the door— Goodman was finally cancelling the struggling comics line. "I told them to stop," Kirby recalled. "I told Martin we could turn the company around if he'd just hang in there."

Kirby was exaggerating, but "only by a little," Evanier writes. Goodman came close to closing his comics line in 1957, when his distributor went out of business, and by 1961 Marvel's prospects were still uncertain.[3]

In the pulp era compelling cover art was key to an impulse buy, as in DC's *Action Comics* #1 (1938). Not a word of copy aside from the title, not even the character's name—the image said it all. Worried publisher Harry Donenfeld felt a muscleman in cape and tights lifting a car and smashing it was "ridiculous . . . crazy." But the kids believed, making Superman an overnight star and convincing rival publishers there was a market for comic books and a new kind of hero—*super* heroes. Superman's creators Jerry Siegel and Joe Shuster signed over rights to DC for $130 (the page-rate price for the debut story). They remained page-rate employees, albeit the highest paid in the emerging industry, and had a share in a *Superman* syndicated newspaper strip. But even as Superman became his own corporation—Superman, Inc.—Siegel and Shuster's dreams of determining the destiny of their creation were fading.

ACTION COMICS #1, FACSIMILE EDITION, COVER ART BY JOE SHUSTER, "CELEBRATE THE CENTURY" SERIES, US POSTAL SERVICE COMMEMORATIVE, FIRST DAY ISSUANCE, SEPTEMBER 10, 1998, CLEVELAND, OHIO.

The making of *Superman* and *Action Comics* #1 is chronicled in chapter 2, "World of Tomorrow."

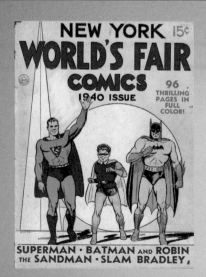

DC's competitors had to come up with unique creations to avoid copyright infringement lawsuits. Jerry Siegel was not happy, believing the superhero concept was his and Joe's exclusively and that even DC was profiting off their idea by creating new superheroes. DC's leading stars, Superman and Batman and Robin, shared this *World's Fair Comics* cover (but not the adventures inside). The fair's theme, "Building the World of Tomorrow," earned Superman the enduring moniker, "The Man of Tomorrow!"

NEW YORK WORLD'S FAIR COMICS (1940), COVER ART BY JACK BURNLEY. DC COMICS.

For more on the New York World's Fair and comics tie-ins, see chapter 2, "World of Tomorrow." For a visit to the Superhero Summer of 1939, see chapter 6, "The First Generation."

The seminal Golden Age of Comics was raw and gritty, and work was often dashed off to meet impossible deadlines. But the mostly young, unschooled creators were forging a new myth and medium, sparking flashes of genius in the process. Will Eisner created *The Spirit* as lead feature of publisher Everett "Busy" Arnold's innovative "comic book section" newspaper insert and worked a deal whereby he would own his character, making him one of the few early creators to control his creation. The nascent comics business had rumored mob connections, fly-by-night operators, and cutthroat business practices that conspired against young creators, while those in the executive suites reaped the fortunes. Eisner knew the rough-and-tumble side, having been an early comic book packager and embroiled in the first superhero copyright infringement lawsuit, thanks to a Faustian bargain he and partner Jerry Iger made with unscrupulous publisher Victor Fox.

THE SPIRIT, PHILADELPHIA RECORD COMIC BOOK SECTION (SUNDAY, JULY 20, 1941), COVER ART BY WILL EISNER.

For the scoop on Victor Fox's attempt to cash in on the Superman phenomenon, see chapter 5, "Superman versus Wonder Man"; Eisner's creation of the Spirit is spotlighted in chapter 6, "The First Generation," under the subhead "Summer of '39."

Joe Simon and Jack Kirby cocreated *Captain America* for Timely Comics, sealing the royalty share agreement with a handshake. *Captain America* was a smash success, but Simon and Kirby discovered publisher Martin Goodman was cheating them out of the promised royalties. The creators bolted to DC, but their creation stayed at Timely: it was standard practice that publishers owned a property unless a contract said otherwise. (Joe Simon later lamented that artists are terrible businessmen.) On the cover of the last Simon and Kirby *Captain America*, the star-spangled hero checks into the Hotel of Horror to rescue sidekick Bucky.

CAPTAIN AMERICA #10 (JANUARY 1941), COVER ART BY JOE SIMON AND JACK KIRBY. TIMELY COMICS.

For the full story on Captain America's creation, the ensuing legal intrigues, and Simon and Kirby's break with Timely, turn to chapter 8, "Patents and Patriots," under the subhead "The Coming of Captain America."

Shazam is an ancient wizard who chose orphan Billy Batson as his successor. By uttering the wizard's name, Billy becomes Captain Marvel. Created by editor Bill Parker and artist C. C. Beck to lead Fawcett's new comic book line, Captain Marvel's world was one of magic and whimsy, in contrast to Superman's science-fiction origin and the pseudo-scientific rationale for his powers. But Parker and Beck gave their hero a Superman-esque costume of cape and tights and the same all-around powers of super strength and speed. DC claimed Fawcett followed the Superman blueprint so closely that it created confusion in the marketplace, even copying Superman's fan club and distinctive cover logo, as seen here in the "Captain Marvel Club—Shazam" cover logo. (Note the pre–Pearl Harbor "Be an American" stamp at lower right.) Competitive tensions between the two publishers, fueled by the lucrative merchandising empires generated by each character, led DC to sue Fawcett in a marathon copyright infringement lawsuit that would last more than a decade.

CAPTAIN MARVEL ADVENTURES #4 (OCTOBER 31, 1941), COVER ART BY C. C. BECK. FAWCETT PUBLICATIONS.

The behind-the-scenes account of Captain Marvel's creation is detailed in chapter 6, "The First Generation," under the subhead "Captain Thunder." The *National Comics/DC v. Fawcett* lawsuit and trial are covered in depth in chapters 10–14.

When the United States entered World War II, superheroes pitched in, from promoting war bonds to fighting Axis forces. (TOP LEFT) Here the Human Torch and Toro blaze through an Axis chemical weapons lab in a typically ingenious cover by Alex Schomburg. (TOP RIGHT) An omnipotent Superman straddles the world as he collars Hitler and a racist stand-in for Axis Japan (possibly Hideki Tojo, Japan's military leader and prime minister). DC uses the opportunity to hail the "World's Greatest Adventure-Strip Character!" (BOTTOM) Captain Marvel invades Nazi Germany to train the "Honesty Ray" on Hitler and his flustered henchmen: Hermann Göring, commander of the Luftwaffe, and Joseph Goebbels, minister for propaganda. Fawcett doesn't miss a chance to proclaim the title "Largest Circulation of Any Comic Magazine."

MARVEL MYSTERY COMICS #59
(OCTOBER 1944), TIMELY COMICS.

SUPERMAN #17 (JULY/AUGUST 1942),
COVER ART BY FRED RAY. DC.

CAPTAIN MARVEL ADVENTURES #21
(FEBRUARY 12, 1943), COVER ART BY
C. C. BECK. FAWCETT PUBLICATIONS.

Follow the superheroes, and their creators, into World War II in chapter 10, "Battle of the Century," under the subhead "War Years."

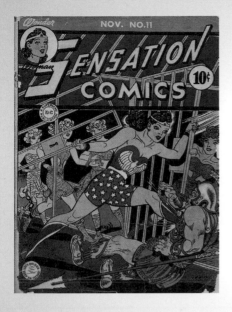

The kids who plunked down dimes for their favorite superhero comics fueled the phenomenon—but many parents, teacher groups, and guardians of decency were wary of the pulp medium. Even though DC's editorial policy maintained Superman as a chaste upholder of American values, critics felt the genre implanted unhealthy power fantasies in developing minds. Wonder Woman, ostensibly a superhero character for girls, had fans attracted to its kinky sexual undertones. Creator Dr. William Moulton Marston saw his Amazon princess as "psychological propaganda for the new type of woman." In response to criticism that his feature embraced sexual perversions, Marston replied, "The only hope for peace is to teach people who are full of pep and unbound force to enjoy being bound." This jailbreak cover story describes Wonder Woman's visit to planet Eros, where women love bondage and find happiness in prison.

SENSATION COMICS #11 (NOVEMBER 1942), COVER ART BY HARRY G. PETER.

Wonder Woman is discussed in depth in chapter 7, "Superman, Inc.," under the subhead "Wonder Woman." For the moral crusade against superheroes, see chapter 15, "Crackdown and Crash," under the subhead "Seduction of the Innocent."

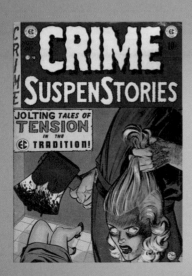

By the 1950s an anticomics crusade culminated in televised Senate subcommittee hearings investigating juvenile delinquency and its supposed link to comic books. Exhibit A was *this* "jolting" cover from Entertaining Comics (EC). Publisher Bill Gaines testified that the cover was appropriate for a horror comic—it would only be in bad taste to show the severed neck.

CRIME SUSPENSTORIES #22 (MAY 1954), COVER ART BY JOHNNY CRAIG. EC COMICS.

Details on the Senate subcommittee hearings and their aftermath appear in chapter 15, "Crackdown and Crash."

Martin Goodman's Timely Comics had run its course, and his comics line was kick-started as Atlas Comics, which introduced new titles such as *Yellow Claw* (a stereotypical Fu Manchu–esque supervillain), boasted an Atlas News Company distribution arm, and featured veteran Timely talent such as editor and writer Stan Lee and new artists like Joe Maneely, Steve Ditko, and John Romita. And then Goodman miscalculated. He ditched Atlas News Company and signed with American News Company just before the venerable distributor went out of business. Goodman was forced into a distribution deal with DC's Independent News Company (IND), with onerous terms that barely kept Atlas afloat.

YELLOW CLAW #1 (OCTOBER 1956), COVER ART BY JOE MANEELY. ATLAS COMICS.

Read all about what Stan Lee called "one of the big publishing decision mistakes that was ever made" in chapter 15, "Crackdown and Crash," under the subhead "Empire Building."

Goodman's struggling line bore the cover acronyms "IND" and "MC," for Marvel Comics. (Goodman also continued the pulp practice of keeping titles under separate companies to cover his tracks legally.) MC made a specialty of code-approved "monster mags" like *Strange Tales* and *Tales of Suspense* featuring morality plays with twist endings, but they were a pale reflection of the horrors EC once served up. In this late Marvel monster-era cover tale, a cowering watchman has raised the temperature in a scientific facility, thawing out a creature found in the Arctic ice. Seemingly inspired by the premise of the 1951 film *The Thing from Another World*, this creature is not a monster to be feared and attacked but an enlightened being from another world. Foolish humans!

TALES OF SUSPENSE #27 (1962), COVER ART PENCILS BY JACK KIRBY, INKS BY DICK AYERS. MARVEL COMICS.

For more on pre-superhero Marvel, see chapter 15, "Crackdown and Crash," under the subhead "Empire Building."

(ABOVE) In 1956 DC replaced its Superman, Inc., licensing division with the Licensing Corporation of America, with plans to license in-house stars *and* outside properties. DC also realized a new generation was unfamiliar with its seminal superstars, so editor Julius Schwartz brought back Golden Age speedster the Flash, updated with a new origin story and costume in *Showcase* #4. The Flash was a smash, and *Showcase* became a vehicle for reviving DC's superheroes of old. The original Justice Society superhero team was updated as the Justice League of America with an audition in *The Brave and the Bold*, which had become a "showcase" title. The Justice League tryout was a huge success, and the concept soon got its own title.

THE BRAVE AND THE BOLD #28 (MARCH 1960), COVER ART PENCILS BY MIKE SEKOWSKY, INKS BY MURPHY ANDERSON.

(BELOW) Editor Stan Lee felt comics as a profession had hit a dead end and was contemplating a career change when Martin Goodman, learning of super sales numbers for the Justice League, asked him to come up with a superhero team. Lee's creative juices got flowing, he partnered with artist Jack Kirby, and they made history with *The Fantastic Four*. The first issue reintroduced Timely's Human Torch, and Sub-Mariner followed with issue #4. More important, the title showed superheroes as flawed mortals, whose super powers were often more burden than blessing.

THE FANTASTIC FOUR #1 (NOVEMBER 1961), COVER ART PENCILS BY JACK KIRBY (INKER NOT CONFIRMED).

The introduction of the Justice League is noted in chapter 15, "Crackdown and Crash," under the subhead "Showcase." The story of how the Fantastic Four saved Marvel, and maybe the comic book superhero genre itself, opens chapter 16, "Resurrection and Renewal."

Marvel introduced the racially and ethnically diverse *Sgt. Fury and His Howling Commandos* in 1963. (TOP LEFT) On the debut cover, the man visible in the far background, blowing his horn and waving his weapon overhead, is Howler Gabriel Jones, an African American. (TOP RIGHT) It was so unusual to have a dark-skinned character in a mainstream comic that Gabe is mistakenly pictured here as white, as he is in a double-page "Meet the Howling Commandos" feature from issue #1. (BOTTOM) The colorization error in *Sgt. Fury* #1 was corrected in the series continuity and in reprints.

SGT. FURY AND HIS HOWLING COMMANDOES #1 (MAY 1963), COVER ART PENCILS BY JACK KIRBY, INKS BY DICK AYERS.

"MEET THE HOWLING COMMANDOES" EXCERPT, *SGT. FURY* #1, PENCIL ART BY JACK KIRBY, INKS BY DICK AYERS.

MARVEL MASTERWORKS: SGT. FURY (VOL. 1, 2013).

For the origins of Fury and the Howlers—and Marvel's Big Bang and seminal expansion of its universe—see chapter 16, "Resurrection and Renewal."

(ABOVE) In the seventies the Vietnam War and the political scandal of Watergate convulsed US culture, pushing comics towards "relevance." Even rugged Sgt. Rock and Easy Company got profoundly topical, with some stories ending with the phrase: "Make War No More." In this *Rock* story, the fine line between killing and committing atrocities in war was explored—the cover even made the cover of the *New York Times Magazine* (May 2, 1971) in the article "BWEEEEOW! WHRAAAM! Comic Books Become Relevant."

"HEAD-COUNT," *OUR ARMY AT WAR* #233 (JUNE 1971), COVER ART BY JOE KUBERT.

(BELOW) Superheroes discovered that combating racism, political corruption, and other social ills wasn't as easy as catching bank robbers. Green Lantern and Green Arrow were paired to confront the big issues and sometime had no answers. Here they look on helplessly as an environmentalist named Isaac dies for our sins.

"... AND THROUGH HIM SAVE A WORLD..." *GREEN LANTERN* #89 (MAY 1972), COVER ART BY NEAL ADAMS.

For more on the relevancy revolution and the move toward mature themes, refer to chapter 18, "Masters of Invention," under the subhead "Transformation."

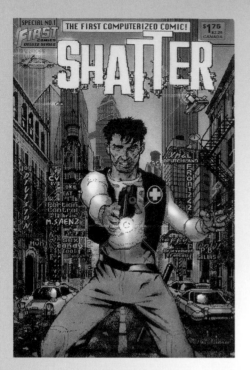

In the eighties, comic books underwent a seismic shift in storytelling, production values, and distribution (as newsstands and mom-and-pop outlets were replaced by the direct-sales market and comic book shops). At the dawn of the digital era, *Shatter* claimed bragging rights as "The First Computerized Comic!" Publisher First Comics was one of many emerging "independents" bringing innovation and adult themes. (Note the absence of the Comics Code stamp.) *Camelot 3000* was not only DC's first "maxiseries," it was a trailblazer in utilizing better printing and production values and the first title distributed solely through the direct-sales market, bypassing the Comics Code and allowing creators to explore mature themes.

SHATTERA #1 (JUNE 1985), COVER ART BY MICHAEL SAENZ. FIRST COMICS, INC.

CAMELOT 3000 #1 (DECEMBER 1982), COVER ART BY BRIAN BOLLAND. DC COMICS.

The arrival of the technology that created *Shatter* is documented in chapter 18, "Masters of Invention," under the subhead "Market and Technology"; the precedents of *Camelot 3000* appear under "Transformation."

As superheroes approached the half-century mark, the archetypal myth got a major renovation, beginning with the two-part Alan Moore Superman story, "Whatever Happened to the Man of Tomorrow?" (TOP LEFT) The Superman that generations had known since 1938 ended with the *Action* #583 conclusion of Moore's story. (Editor Julius Schwartz is among the rooftop crowd waving farewell.) (TOP RIGHT) *Superman* was rebooted with a six-part miniseries and started over with a new *Action* #1 and *Superman* #1. (BOTTOM) Meanwhile, timed for DC's fiftieth anniversary, a half century of storytelling surrounding its mythic universe was streamlined into a cohesive continuity in the twelve-part maxiseries *Crisis on Infinite Earths*, issued from 1985 to 1986.

ACTION COMICS #583 (SEPTEMBER 1986), COVER ART BY CURT SWAN AND MURPHY ANDERSON.

SUPERMAN #1 (JANUARY 1987), COVER ART PENCILS BY JOHN BRYNE, INKS BY TERRY AUSTIN.

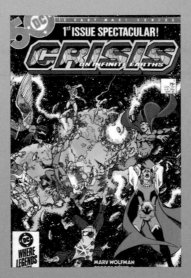

CRISIS ON INFINITE EARTHS #1 (APRIL 1985), COVER ART BY GEORGE PÉREZ.

The reshaping of a mythic universe is explored in chapter 19, "Evolutionary Imperative," under the subhead "The Last Superman Story."

American comics were no longer insular, and by the eighties an appreciation of comics publishing flourished in Europe and Japan. First Publishing brought Kazuo Koike and Goseki Kojima's manga masterpiece *Lone Wolf and Cub* to American readers in a series featuring high production values, including Frank Miller cover art. A few years earlier Miller had released his futuristic masterless samurai epic *Rōnin* for DC, a milestone title copyrighted "by Frank Miller Inc."

LONE WOLF AND CUB #1 (1987), COVER ART BY FRANK MILLER. FIRST COMICS, INC.

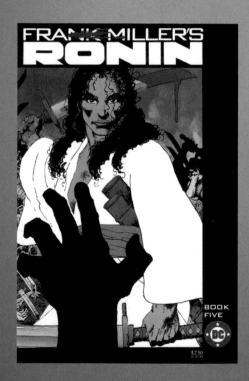

FRANK MILLER'S RŌNIN #5 (MAY 1984), COVER ART BY FRANK MILLER, COLORED BY LYNN VARLEY.

The digital revolution in comics and the making of Miller's *Rōnin* are chronicled in chapter 18, "Masters of Invention."

Independent publishers led the way in creator-owned characters. The late Dave Stevens owned the Rocketeer when the character debuted in Pacific Comics' *Starslayer* #2 (April 1982). (TOP LEFT) For the comic book adaptation/tie-in for the Walt Disney Pictures *Rocketeer* movie (1991), Stevens did the flag-waving cover, and artist Russ Heath handled the interior art. (TOP RIGHT) Paul Chadwick's copyrighted character *Concrete*—a speechwriter whose brain has been transplanted by aliens into a hulking host body—tests the limits with a solo Everest climb in the Dark Horse Comics series. (BOTTOM LEFT) First Comics and creator Howard Chaykin shared the copyright for the dystopian *American Flagg!* (BOTTOM RIGHT) Eclipse Comics trademarked *The Black Terror*, but the story was copyrighted by Beau Smith and Charles Dixon and art copyrighted by Daniel Brereton.

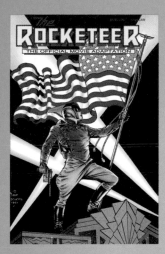

THE ROCKETEER: THE OFFICIAL MOVIE ADAPTATION (1991). W. D. PUBLICATIONS, WALT DISNEY COMPANY.

CONCRETE #9 (SEPTEMBER 1988), COVER ART BY PAUL CHADWICK. DARK HORSE COMICS.

AMERICAN FLAGG! #1 (OCTOBER 1983), COVER ART BY HOWARD CHAYKIN. FIRST COMICS.

THE BLACK TERROR, "SEDUCTION OF DECEIT BOOK 1" (OCTOBER 1989), COVER ART PAINTING BY DANIEL BRERETON. ECLIPSE COMICS.

For more on the creative renaissance of the 1980s and '90s, see chapter 19, "Evolutionary Imperative," under the subhead "For Mature Readers."

The new millennium featured major publishing events and shakeups of superhero universes, with movies a major factor in the surge of superhero popularity around the world. Marvel's seven-issue *Civil War* series, published 2006–2007, was billed as "A Marvel Comics Event." The story posits a federal law, the Superhero Registration Act, to unmask and regulate superheroes. Tony Stark/Iron Man leads the forces in favor, while Captain America champions the resistance. The movie *Captain America: Civil War* (2016), fifteenth in the Marvel Cinematic Universe series, adapted the premise of the comic book series. In 2011 DC cancelled its entire lineup and staged a massive relaunch under the banner "The New 52!" This included yet another reset for *Action Comics*, with a Prologue (issue #0), followed by issue #1. Superman is reintroduced in T-shirt and jeans.

"THE RETURN OF THOR," *CIVIL WAR* #3 (SEPTEMBER 2006), SECOND PRINTING VARIANT COVER, PENCIL ART BY STEVE MCNIVEN, INKS BY DEXTER VINS WITH MARK MORALES AND STEVE MCNIVEN.

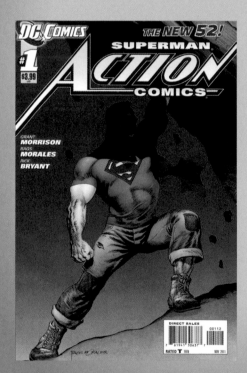

ACTION COMICS #1 (NOVEMBER 2011), COVER ART BY RAGS MORALES.

An overview of event comics, and the role of movie making in making superheroes international icons, is detailed in chapter 19, "Evolutionary Imperative."

As comics pushed further into the new millennium, superheroes began hitting serious milestones. For DC that included the trio that had endured as the longest continually published superheroes: (TOP LEFT) Wonder Woman hit her 600th issue with artist Adams Hughes's variant cover homage to the Amazon's first cover appearance in *Sensation Comics* #1 (1942). (TOP RIGHT) In 2018 *Action Comics* hit the landmark #1000 issue plateau (including pre-reboot continuity), with variant covers including this World War II setting by Michael Cho. Batman and *Detective Comics* hit the milestone #1000 in 2019. (BOTTOM) The Joker celebrates "80 years of chaos," *DC Previews* proclaims. Not just a villain but an enduring character, two different actors have won Oscars playing the Joker: Heath Ledger won a posthumous supporting actor award for *The Dark Knight* in 2009, and Joaquin Phoenix won Best Actor in 2020 for *Joker*.

WONDER WOMAN #600 (AUGUST 2010).

ACTION COMICS #1000 (JUNE 2018).

DC PREVIEWS, #22 (FEBRUARY 2020), COVER ART BY GREG CAPULLO.

The evolution and significance of DC's triumvirate of heroes—Superman, Batman, and Wonder Woman—are highlighted in chapter 19, "Evolutionary Imperative." For the price of legacy, consider the special copy of *Action* #1 that opens chapter 22, "Legacy."

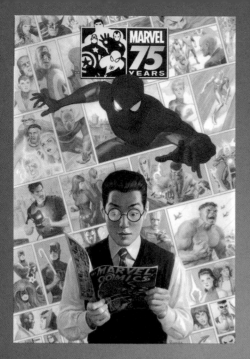

Young Peter Parker marvels at the comic book that started Timely/Marvel myth-making in this hardcover edition presenting some of the best stories in seventy-five years of publishing. In recent decades superhero mythology has been overhauled and deconstructed, its retro-conventions celebrated. In 1994 writer Kurt Busiek and artist Alex Ross chronicled the sweep of the Marvel Universe in *Marvels,* as documented by news photographer character Phil Sheldon. The classic has been reprinted ever since, most recently in the *Marvels Annotated* series.

MARVEL 75TH ANNIVERSARY OMNIBUS (2014), COVER ART BY PAOLO RIVERA.

MARVELS ANNOTATED #4 (AUGUST 2019), COVER ART BY ALEX ROSS.

The story of *Marvels* is presented in chapter 22, "Legacy," under the subhead "Marvels."

THE MARVEL METHOD

What was later called "the Marvel Method" for creating a comic book story seems to have begun around the time of Kirby's arrival, but it was born of necessity as harried editor Stan Lee juggled the editorial and scripting needs of all the titles. With no time to meticulously script and art-direct every panel of every story, Lee plotted story ideas with artists who were given the freedom to decide the panel-by-panel action and visual flow. They turned in completed pages, Lee accepted or rejected the work—Lee would say that work was rarely rejected—and the inker inked the pencils (unless it was Steve Ditko, who inked his own pencils); Lee provided dialogue and text, and the pages went on to the letterer, colorist, and printer.

The method was similar to Simon and Kirby brainstorming a story, scripting "on the board," and making margin notes. "As Stan Lee himself noted on many occasions, 'plotting' with Kirby could often be accomplished in a matter of minutes, and in later years might be done via a brief call with Kirby telling Lee what he intended to provide for the next issue," notes a future legal brief from Mark Evanier and others. "As Kirby worked, he would not only draw out the story and invent new characters where needed, he would write extensive margin notes, including suggested caption and dialogue, so that when Lee dialogued the balloons, he would know what story points Kirby felt should be made in each panel."

As a freelancer, Kirby was always working to support his family. A night owl, Kirby usually worked through dawn at his home in Long Island, down in the basement studio he called the Dungeon.[4]

The Lee/Kirby team-up title starred a young brother and sister, Sue and Johnny Storm, scientist Reed Richards, and pilot Ben Grimm. The original concept had them rocketing to Mars to beat the "Cosmonauts" of the Soviet Union into space. Lee, vastly overrating Soviet capabilities at the peak of the Cold War Space Race, declared in a rare surviving synopsis: "At the rate the Communists

Marvel emerged as a brand with this house ad appearing in most of the May 1963 cover listed titles. Instead of the inscrutable "MC" on the cover, beginning with the May issues the vertical Marvel Comics Group box—designed by Steve Ditko—appeared in the upper left corner of each magazine with an image of the title character. The astonishing period of creativity that began with The Fantastic Four in 1961 saw 1963 close out with Marvel adding to its roster: *Sgt. Fury And His Howling Commandos, Dr. Strange, The Avengers,* and *The X-Men.*

HOUSE AD, MAY 1963, ART CREDITED TO JACK KIRBY AND STEVE DITKO.

are progressing in space, maybe we better make this a flight to the STARS, instead of just to Mars, because by the time this mag goes on sale, the Russians may have already MADE a flight to Mars!" The heroes would, indeed, "fly to the stars."

The Fantastic Four #1 (November 1961) saw the foursome's flight into the unknown bombarded by "cosmic rays," forcing a rocky return to Earth, where each discovers they have been fantastically transformed. Richards's body has become elastic, and he takes the name Mister Fantastic. Johnny can burst into flame and fly and becomes the Human Torch. ("I took that from . . . one of Timely Comics' first books called *The Human Torch*," Lee later explained.) Sue can turn invisible and calls herself the Invisible Girl. Ben has become a hulking slagheap-skinned monster with super strength, adopting the name a startled Sue blurts when she sees him—Thing. Set in fictional Central City, by issue #3 the foursome had costumes and a secret "skyscraper hideout." By issue #4 the town is identified as New York. By issue #6 their very public headquarters is identified as a tower above the thirty-third floor of the fictional midtown Baxter Building.

The key to the Fantastic Four was their emotional chemistry, led by the monstrous Thing who was "not really a good guy," the synopsis notes. "The rest of the foursome always fears the Thing will go out of control and do great harm with his super strength. The Thing even wants to win the Invisible Girl from her true love, Mister Fantastic."[5]

In the third issue the Thing and Johnny Storm have a bitter confrontation, and by the next issue the upset and confused teenager, on the run and trying to blend in with the lost souls of the Bowery, grabs a bed in a flophouse. He picks up a 1940s *Sub-Mariner* comic, and a few regulars brag that an old "stumble-bum" at a nearby table is as strong as Sub-Mariner was supposed to be. The shaggy, bearded man refuses to play along, sending them flying before falling into a chair, trying to remember his identity. The other lost souls are ready to fight, but Johnny intervenes, firing up his right forefinger and, with perfect control, shaves the stranger's long hair, moustache, and beard—revealing Prince Namor, the Sub-Mariner.

Hoping to revive the amnesic super being, the Torch returns Sub-Mariner to the sea, restoring his memory. Namor discovers his undersea capital deserted and in ruins, glowing with radioactivity from atomic bomb tests. Vowing vengeance, Sub-Mariner attacks New York, and a reunited Fantastic Four must stop him.

In short order, the *Fantastic Four* brought back two of Timely's triad—one reimagined as a very human Torch and Sub-Mariner in his prime—while rewiring and reengineering the superhero mythology, jolting a moribund industry still in economic recovery out of its doldrums and galvanizing a new generation of fans. The new Marvel heroes would be all in for justice, but as in the Timely era, superpowers were more burden than blessing.

The Fantastic Four marked the beginning of a growing pantheon of Marvel superheroes. The comics celebrated the star team of Stan "The Man" Lee and Jack "King" Kirby, even as creative tensions were building between them. "There would later be disagreement over the sequence of events that brought forth the new heroes," Mark Evanier writes. "[For the *Fantastic Four*] Lee would say he figured out the story and characters, typed up a plot outline . . . , selected Jack to draw it, and handed him the basics of the first issue. Kirby would say that wasn't how they ever worked—that even on short, unimportant romance stories, there'd be a plot conference, and then he'd be sent off to pencil pages as he saw fit, with or without typed plot. He'd say he came up with the characters and even point to how similar the origin was to *Challengers of the Unknown*." Evanier notes, "Among those who worked around them at the time, there was a unanimous view: that *Fantastic Four* was created by Stan and Jack. No further division of credit seemed appropriate. Not on that, not on all the wonderment yet to come."[6]

For young comics fan Michael Uslan and his friend Bobby, *Fantastic Four* #9 was *it*. The cover featured a gloating Sub-Mariner looking on as the foursome is evicted from the Baxter

Building and a cover blurb asks, "What happens to comic magazine heroes when they can't pay their bills and have no place to turn?"

One glorious day Uslan's mother drove her son and his friend Bobby from New Jersey into New York for a tour of DC's offices at 480 Lexington, where they met Murphy Anderson, Bill Finger, and production department personnel like Jack Adler, who happily answered the questions of the dazzled fanboys.

Also on the itinerary was a visit to the Baxter Building. They searched midtown for the famous skyscraper, but nobody had heard of it, even a police officer. Michael's mother finally called Marvel and got Stan Lee's secretary, Flo Steinberg. "Oh, the Baxter Building is not real," she said. "Stan and Jack invented it." Marvel didn't do tours, but she invited them to come by the Marvel office at 655 Madison Avenue "and we'll work something out." Uslan had brought a Golden Age Timely, *All Winners* #18, and left with Lee and Kirby's signatures on it. It was one of those "magical days," Uslan recalls, piercing the veil and meeting the mythmakers.

A new relationship was dawning between publishers, talent, and fans. As in the days of old, publishers would offer fan clubs, but the next-generation fans would help shape the narrative of the medium through their own fanzines, clubs, and collector's gatherings. Fans like Alan Moore and Dave Gibbons would emerge as next-generation creators. Other fans would become executives and publishers, getting a foothold in the industry in their teen years, including Jim Shooter, who sold his first comics script to DC and went on to become editor in chief at Marvel and subsequently, a comics publisher.[7]

HEROES—ASSEMBLE!

By 1962 Marvel monster comics were on the way out, and Lee wanted to feature a superhero in *Amazing Adult Fantasy*. "The sales of the superhero magazines were soaring, which meant that

AAF . . . was having an uphill battle bucking a trend," Lee writes in his book, *Origins of Marvel Comics* (1974). He recalls the decision to cancel the retitled *Amazing Fantasy* with issue #15: "I can still remember discussing my sinister little scheme with Martin Goodman. . . . Everybody knew about Superman—so the time had come for a competitor to make the scene; and what fun it would be to call him Spider-Man."[8]

Years later Lee recalled events a bit differently, especially his pitch to Goodman about a super-powered teenager with problems. "Martin said, 'Stan, you're losing it. That's the worst idea I ever heard. . . . First of all, you can't call a hero Spider-Man. People hate spiders. Secondly, you can't make him a teenager. Teenagers can just be sidekicks. And finally, problems? Don't you know what a superhero is? They don't have problems. They're superheroes.'"

Anyway, *Amazing Fantasy* was being cancelled, and the Spider-Man story moved ahead. Lee wanted Kirby to do it, but his heroic style didn't fit the character of Peter Parker, a brilliant but lonely high school student being raised by his Uncle Ben and Aunt May—Steve Ditko was the perfect artist to capture the poignancy of the character. At a science exhibit on radioactivity, Parker is bitten by a radioactive spider and miraculously endowed with the proportionate strength and agility of a spider. He then cashes in as a masked performer in the wrestling ring and as a costumed TV performer. Hiding behind his mask, Parker could care less when he lets a fleeing crook escape—until, soon after, that criminal murders his beloved Uncle Ben. The closing text notes a "legend is born" as the distraught youth learns the hard way that "with great power there must also come—great responsibility!"

"And the book sold fantastically," Lee noted. "So a couple months later when the sales figures were in, Martin came to me and he said, 'Hey Stan, you remember that Spider-Man idea of yours that we both liked so much? Why don't we make a series of it[?]'"[9]

Creations credited to Lee and Kirby include a World War II

series, *Sgt. Fury and His Howling Commandos*, which began with an issue cover-dated May 1963 and was promoted with the tagline, "'Seven Against the Nazis!' Another Big One from the Talented Team That Brings You the Famous 'Fantastic Four!'" Years before the multiethnic *Dirty Dozen* commandos of book and movie fame, Sgt. Nick Fury's ragtag commandoes were a mix of backgrounds and ethnicities, including Jewish, African American and Italian American, a rebel-yelling Southerner, and an Ivy Leaguer. Gabriel Jones, the black commando, went into combat wielding a gun and, like his namesake angel, blowing his trumpet. It was so unusual in 1963 to depict a dark-skinned character that Gabe was colored white in almost all his appearances in *Sgt. Fury* #1, a mistake corrected by the next issue and in reprint editions.

Artist John Severin recalled that sometime in the late fifties he enjoyed coffee and cigars with Kirby, who, fresh off *Sky Masters*, envisioned a new syndicated strip and asked Severin if he wanted to partner on it. "The story would be set in Europe during WWII," Severin described. "The hero would be a tough, cigar-smoking Sergeant with a squad of oddball G.I.s—sort of an adult Boy Commandos. Like so many other grand decisions I have made in comics, I peered through the cigar smoke and told him I really wasn't interested in newspaper strips. We finished cigars and coffee and Jack left, heading towards Marvel and Stan Lee."[10]

During the sixties the spy genre popularized by James Bond movies and *The Man from U.N.C.L.E.* TV series (a show Stan Lee enjoyed) was a huge success. *Sgt. Fury and His Howling Commandos* was also a hit, and Lee decided to give Fury a post-war career as a secret agent, complete with an eye patch over his left eye. Kirby drew a run of the early *Nick Fury, Agent of S.H.I.E.L.D.* ("Supreme Headquarters International Espionage Law-Enforcement Division") in *Strange Tales*, a monster title now starring the reinvented Johnny Storm/Human Torch. James Steranko, whose cinematic style had fandom buzzing, followed up with his own breakthrough work on Agent Fury.[11]

Complicating the question of who created what is the unsung

role of Lee's brother, Larry Lieber. His credited work includes writing and scripting *Rawhide Kid*, but he was also an uncredited writer's assistant to his brother, turning Lee's plots into traditional scripts for artists. "Stan made up the plot, and then he'd give it to me, and I'd write the script," Lieber told Roy Thomas. Years later, Lieber described his work as a classic "panel-by-panel" breakdown of Stan's synopsis.

Lieber's uncredited contribution alters the all-encompassing definition of the artist's singular role in the Marvel Method since Lieber wrote key stories, including the origin tales and earliest first appearances of Thor, Ant-Man, Iron Man, and a solo Human Torch series. He also came up with the alter egos: Don Blake (Thor), Tony Stark (Iron Man), Henry Pym (Ant-Man). "Thor was just another story," Lieber recalled. "I didn't think about it at all. Stan said, 'I'm trying to make up a character,' and he gave me the plot, and he said, 'Why don't you write the story?'" In his *Origins of Marvel Comics*, Lee acknowledges his brother wrote Thor's origin, but stressed that "the basic concepts would be mine."

By 1963 Marvel had released two team-up titles that would become epic multimedia franchises: *The Avengers* was a roll call of recent superhero creations—Thor, Iron Man, Ant-Man, Wasp, the Hulk. The second team consisted of super-powered teens; Lee later explained he had seemingly exhausted every means of transforming ordinary mortals into super beings—cosmic and gamma rays, ingestion of chemical concoctions, the bite of a radioactive spider. "I took the cowardly way out. I said I'm going to just say they were born that way." Lee called them "the Mutants," young people who kept their genetically endowed powers secret but developed them at a private school for "gifted youngsters" presided over by the wheelchair-bound telepath Professor Xavier.

Goodman loved the concept but not Lee's name for the team.

He said, "That's a terrible name. Nobody knows what the word mutants means." . . . I thought about it. And I thought

Professor X, Xavier. And the mutants have extra powers. For some reason I thought I could call them the X-Men. So I went back to Martin. He said, "Oh, that's a good name." And as I walked out, I thought, if nobody knows what a mutant is, how are they going to know what an X-Man is? But I had my name, so I wasn't about to make waves.[12]

In 1963 the third Timely hero returned. On the dramatic cover of *Strange Tales* #114, the Human Torch throws a fireball that is blocked by the shield of a star-spangled costumed hero. A blurb announces: "From out of the Golden Age of Comics into the Marvel Age, CAPTAIN AMERICA Returns to Challenge the Human Torch!" The surprise ending reveals it was not Cap, but the Torch's adversary, the Acrobat, in disguise. An end caption announced the story was a test: Did readers want Captain America to return?

Jack Kirby drew the story, with inks by Dick Ayers, the first time in almost a quarter century Kirby publicly worked on his cocreation. Some four to five months later, Jack was back with Cap, this time for real, in *The Avengers* #4 (March 1964). Lee's story reveals that during their last World War II mission, Steve Rogers and Bucky Barnes failed to stop a booby-trapped airplane that exploded over water, presumably killing Bucky. Rogers is miraculously dropped into an ice floe in a state of suspended animation. *Avengers* readers first see him encased in ice and worshipped by Eskimos; suddenly Sub-Mariner appears and tosses the frozen idol into the sea, where the block of ice drifts into warmer waters and melts. The Avengers, patrolling the area by submarine, spot the floating figure and pull into their craft a young man whose outer layer of tattered clothing reveals a familiar shield and the red, white, and blue uniform underneath. Twenty real-time years removed (bypassing the brief time in the fifties when Cap and Bucky fought Communists), Captain America awakens as a patriotic relic in a strange new world.

DC/National, while reintroducing and updating its own Golden Age heroes, reengineered its superhero mythology to align past and present in a "multiverse." In *The Flash* #123, "Flash of Two Worlds," the Barry Allen Flash performs a rare public exhibition of his powers, vibrating so rapidly he crosses into Earth Two, a parallel dimension where he meets retired counterpart Jay Garrick, who is now twenty years older. Allen explains he knew of Garrick's exploits because of stories real-life writer Gardner Fox wrote in *Flash Comics*. "Obviously, when Fox was asleep, his mind was 'tuned in' on your vibratory Earth!" Allen concludes. "That explains how he 'dreamed up' The Flash! The magazine was discontinued in 1949."

"Amazing!" says Garrick. "That's the very year I—The Flash—retired."

The concept of Earth One and Earth Two was revisited two years later in *Justice League of America* #21 and #22, with the new League meeting its Justice Society of America counterparts on Earth Two.

With over two decades of comics publishing between DC and Marvel, there now came the mutual realization that there might be a market for not only the old characters but also the classic stories. Both publishers would connect in earnest with modern fans and promote creators as stars. Stan Lee became the exuberant pitchman and showman of Marvel, providing insider updates in the comics via "Marvel Bullpen Bulletins" and "Stan's Soapbox" columns that signed off, "Excelsior!" At DC, Julie Schwartz began publishing addresses of letter-page writers, as did Marvel. From there a nationwide fan network developed.

The year *The Fantastic Four* began, so did the reader-created fanzines, starting with Jerry Bails and Roy Thomas's *Alter Ego*. "Produced with the technology of the times, the early fanzines look incredibly crude . . . but in many ways they previewed the community of the World Wide Web," writes Paul Levitz, who as a New

York teenager in 1971 published and edited the mass-circulation fanzine *The Comic Reader*.

Some fanzines were historically focused, ardently telling the story of previously anonymous creative talent or researching vanished comics companies. Others were filled with indexes, laboriously building databases searchable only by eye. Identifying each other through published letter columns and the fanzines, amateur press alliances were formed—essentially usegroups in print, with a monthly exchange of information, gossip, and discussion between like-minded people. The spread-out and disconnected individuals who cared deeply about comics were now connected.[13]

Fans were taking an active role in the industry. Michael Uslan recalls a letter from Scott Taylor of Westport, Connecticut, in *Justice League* #42 proposing that instead of calling the current era the "Second Heroic Age"—and since everyone was agreed on the "Golden Age of Comics"—this had to be the "Silver Sixties." It wasn't much of a leap to come up with the enduring "Silver Age of Comics."

And there were the early comics fan conventions, such as the New York Con at the crumbling Broadway Central Hotel (described in the introduction). The gathering included the event that Uslan believes triggered the decade's comics boom—an auction of old comics that included *Action* #1. "The *Action* #1 sold for $40 dollars, and the news articles picked up on the story and began interviewing geeky collectors like me and the rest is history," Uslan notes. It's all about context, he adds: in the sixties $40 was an astounding sum to pay for a comic (over $300 in 2020 dollars). An *old* ten-cent comic fetched many times its cover price in an era when comics had not yet achieved their intangible monetary value as collectibles.

Uslan was in the seventh grade when he embarked on a journey to learn all he could about comic books and superheroes after seeing *Alter Ego* #7 (October 1964) and reading the cover article, "The Saga of the Marvel Family." He learned that the main Captain Marvel writer, Otto Binder, lived in his home state of New Jersey. Uslan wrote Binder to see if he and his pal Bobby Klein could come interview him, Binder happily agreed, and Uslan's dedicated parents drove them all to Binder's home. "Otto was my first mentor in comics, the one that explained the history of the comic book industry, the publishers, how it all came to be, how comics are made—he was my guru, my Yoda, my Obi-Wan," Uslan says. "Otto put me in contact with C. C. Beck and Fawcett Comics editors Wendell Crowley and Will Liberson. And it just continued to open up the world to me. . . . It felt like we were in this secret fan club, what a handful of us were reading, and doing fanzines."

Uslan credits his parents for being there for both their children and, in his case, being the rare parents who supported his comics obsession. "My mom was the one who raised us in the trenches when my dad was at work. She said that when you make a commitment you honor it and stick to it, no matter how difficult." Lillian Uslan actually read her son's comics, concluding there was nothing wrong with them. In fact, Michael's teachers told her he had the best vocabulary in the class and was very creative, which they felt came from reading comics. In one of his self-described "best deals ever," Michael agreed to his mother's terms about comics: he could collect and keep them as long as he kept them neat and agreed to also read books, newspapers, and magazines.

"My dad made us understand you need to find your passion in life, and make that your work, so that throughout your life, even on a rainy morning, you can't wait to go to work," he reflects. Joseph Uslan was a stonemason who dropped out of school when he was sixteen to go to work to help his parents during the Depression. When Joseph moved his family to a new house in 1962, their son's comics had expanded beyond the limits of his bedroom closet. Joseph never parked his car in their new one-car garage, instead building floor-to-ceiling shelves that wrapped around three walls for his son to stack his collection.

Michael Uslan learned that Jim Halperin, who was about six months older, was starting *Flame On*, a mimeographed and stapled fanzine, for which the pay rate for contributors was zero. What was not to like? He carried the same fanboy passion to DC, where he got paid $125 a week and around $20 a page to write comics: "I would have done it for free," Uslan says. (Halperin became a comics auction specialist and cochairman of the board of Heritage Auctions.)

When Stan Lee announced he was open to being interviewed for fanzines, Uslan and Bobby Klein sent him a ten-page Q&A questionnaire, with a self-addressed stamped envelope that Lee used after answering the list of questions. It was later, when Uslan was teaching the first accredited course on comics at Indiana University and Lee called to ask how he could help, that another comics mentor became a friend and colleague.

Fanzines found a surprising fan in Dr. Fredric Wertham, whose final book, *The World of Fanzines: A Special Form of Communication*, was published in 1973. "It seems that all the comic-reading kids . . . Wertham was sure were going [to] be ruined by their hobby, had turned out all right after all," observes comics historians William Christensen and Mark Seifert.

> They had grown up to create a medium of communication that, in Wertham's words, "constitutes a vivid and vital kind of interchange of thoughts and opinion. . . . Fanzines show a combination of independence and responsibility not easily found elsewhere in our culture. . . . [Fanzines] are worthwhile and constructive. Communication is the opposite of violence. And every facet of communication has a legitimate place."[14]

The growing fandom market included mail-order services for vintage comics. One circa-1974 catalogue, *The Super Catalogue* from Passaic Book Center in New Jersey, listed *Fantastic Four* #1 for a hefty $60, while *Superman* #6 could be had for $50. The catalogue included advertisements for Steranko's new, must-have

The History of Comics, prints by fantasy artist Frank Frazetta, and Passaic's own reprints of EC black-and-white original art, "designed to be colored by you, if you like!"[15]

In 1960 DC published the first *Giant Superman Annual*, a twenty-five-cent special hailed as "An All-Star Collection of the Greatest SUPER-Stories Ever Published!" Batman, Flash, Wonder Woman, and others would also get reprint-heavy annuals. "There's some indescribable quality about the eighty-page annuals and giant-sized comics of the '60s," DC creative director Richard Bruning wrote in 1998:

> They had a tremendous impact on the buyers and readers of the time, containing as they did numerous stories from earlier adventures in varying art styles. . . . The comic books available to you at the time were whatever came off the racks of . . . the local corner Mom 'n' Pop store, battered copies handed down from a friend or sibling or maybe the occasional great find at a flea market. . . . So, anytime any comic offered you previously published stories, it was a real treat—a glimpse into a character's past that was otherwise unobtainable.[16]

In 1966 Marvel began reprinting Timely tales in *Fantasy Masterpieces* #3, a title already reprinting Atlas/Marvel's recent monster and thriller tales. Timely was absorbed into Marvel's continuity stream: "From the Golden Age of Marvel" read the words above the title. Inside, an announcement declares, "Starting this month, every sizzling issue of *Fantasy Masterpieces* will headline one of the great costumed heroes from the Golden Age of Marvel!! So, for the most sensational start of all, here he is . . . exactly as he appeared in the 1940s . . . CAPTAIN AMERICA."

Well, not *exactly* as he first appeared—there had been no Comics Code Authority when Cap's adventures were full of ghoulish villains, horrific violence, and ghastly murders. Unsuspecting young readers did not know the Golden Age reprints had images redrawn and text rewritten to earn code approval.

A groundbreaking introduction to the Golden Age was car-toonist Jules Feiffer's affectionate tribute, *The Great Comic Book Heroes*, published in hardcover by the Dial Press in 1965 (preceded by an article of the same title in *Playboy*). Nostalgia was the book's intention, Feiffer explains, but when "it hit a generation of young readers, it served to validate the seriousness of their interest as opposed to the condescension you'd normally expect from grown-ups or from the culture."[17]

Feiffer's book opens with wry essays and features the ultimate "secret origins" reprints of Superman and Batman, Flash, Green Lantern, Captain America, and Plastic Man as well as the chilling first Joker story, a Human Torch and Toro (his flaming sidekick) tale, and excerpts from Wonder Woman, the Spectre, Hawkman, and Sub-Mariner. Captain Marvel, now twelve years gone, had six panels reprinted from the *Whiz* origin: "More can not be printed without unsettling the settlement between Clark Kent and Billy Batson," a footnote explained. "We thank J. S. Liebowitz, President of National Periodical Publications, Inc., for permission to reprint, for historical purposes, the following matter."

The final reprint featured a non-super-powered crime fighter as forgotten as his creator, strangely out of place among his costumed contemporaries. The splash page of the *Philadelphia Record* comic book section from Sunday, July 20, 1941, begins: "This is a story of the East, where mere wars cannot penetrate into the shadowy world that exists beneath the sun-baked bazaars. . . . Where truth laughs at fiction and death is not the end." Letters towering like pillars above an exotic Damascus street scene spell SPIRIT; the dapper, domino-masked hero, clad in white hat and suit, stands atop the letters, arms and blue-gloved fists akimbo.

"The book was taken seriously, so the form gained a new lease on life and new respect, none of which interests me particu-larly, except in what I did to redeem Will Eisner's career," Feiffer explains. "That was, for me, a major interest in that this was a guy who was no longer heard of, was completely forgotten, had forgot-ten himself and was no longer doing comics. I was happy that, in a sense, I was able to bring him back from the dead or, at the very least, from exile."[18]

After decades running his own company, Eisner returned to comic books in a big way, picking up on his dream of comics as a medium for sequential art with untapped storytelling potential. Eisner helped pioneer the American graphic novel in 1978 with *A Contract with God: And Other Tenement Stories.*

POP ART

In 1965, the year of Feiffer's book, there were signs superheroes were being taken seriously by more than Third Eyes subculture. An *Esquire* article on college student rebels included the Hulk and Spider-Man among "28 People Who Count" on college campuses (a list that also included Malcolm X, Fidel Castro, Chuck Berry, Bob Dylan, Stanley Kubrick, and James Bond).[19]

The comics, particularly daily strips, formed a familiar visual language, from word balloons to the benday dots of the four-color printing process. The medium was literally being cut up and deconstructed by modern artists. For example, in the mid-to-late 1950s artist Jess Collins specialized in "paste-ups" of random visual images, including a collage series of *Dick Tracy* newspaper strips.[20] The "pop art" movement found comics a font of inspiration. California artist Mel Ramos's superhero-inspired paintings included, in 1962 alone, *Batmobile, The Joker,* and *Dr. Midnight.*

Painter Roy Lichtenstein cribbed from comic books, copying panels, usually from DC war and romance comics, and transforming them into pop art. In 1963 his oil painting *Image Duplicator* was inspired by a Kirby panel from that year's *X-Men* #1 picturing a close-up of mutant supervillain Magneto's staring eyes bracketed by a head covering recalling a Greek Corinthian helmet. The artwork's title summed up Lichtenstein's technique.

Ironically, in 1947 army boot camp officer Irv Novick had been asked to appraise the artistic potential of young private

Lichtenstein. Years later, with Lichtenstein a celebrated pop painter and Novick a page-rate artist at DC/National, their divergent paths intersected in Lichtenstein's *Whamm!*, a 1963 painting reproducing a Novick panel from an *All-American Men of War* story showing a jet fighter blowing up an enemy plane, emphasizing the explosion and Gaspar Saladino's lettering. A Museum of Modern Art "High & Low" exhibition in 1990–1991 called the work a "jet-fighting . . . fantasy of the future," likening the explosion's "curvaceous flame" to something out of a Hiroshige woodblock print.[21]

Comics creators weren't so admiring. "Roy Lichtenstein's *Blam!* painting is based on one of my panels from an old DC war comic," said artist Russ Heath. "Roy got four million dollars for it. I got zero."[22] Had pop art crossed the line from inspiration to appropriation? "We were pissed off," recalled comics artist John Romita Sr. "A lot of guys wanted to get together and file a class-action suit against Lichtenstein."[23]

BATMANIA

In 1964 master adapter Julius Schwartz became *Batman* editor and began a course correction for a classic hero who had strayed from his masked-avenger roots. In *Detective Comics* #326 Batman and Robin are captured by an alien "animal hunter" and exhibited in an extraterrestrial zoo. The crime fighters were brought back to Earth with the next issue of *Detective* and in *Batman* #164, as Schwartz introduced his "New Look" Batman. The makeover included tweaking Batman's costume by encasing his black bat chest emblem in a yellow oval and introducing a sleek new Batmobile. "The original Batmobile has had its day!" Bruce Wayne tells Dick Grayson as he unveils the new car in *Batman* #164. "The trend now is towards sports cars—small, maneuverable jobs."

The first New Look *Detective* story, written by John Broome, with art by Carmine Infantino and inks by Joe Giella, included a teaser: "We're going out on a limb with our prediction that next issue's 'Gotham Gang Line-up' will stir up more excitement—and *controversy*—than any *Batman* story ever published!" Bill Finger wrote the story wherein Schwartz proposed that loyal Alfred sacrifice his life to save Batman and Robin. "I knocked off Alfred the Butler and replaced him with Dick Grayson's Aunt Harriet," Schwartz explained. "I wanted a story with some real sock and second, there had been muttering about three men living together—so I decided to move a woman into the Wayne Mansion."

Around this time producer William Dozier decided Batman and Robin might make an entertaining television series. "I was happy he liked our new Batman—but one of my changes backfired," Schwartz added. "Dozier wanted to have Alfred the Butler in the series, and I had to figure out a way to revive a dead Alfred."[24]

With color television coming to the mass market, the *Batman* TV series was promoted "in color" when it debuted on January 12, 1966. Decades before computer-generated imagery and animation (CGI or CG) revolutionized superhero movies and TV shows, *Batman* was a perfect vehicle. The character didn't have super powers requiring expensive special effects, and its visual panache was made for the new color broadcast medium, a comic book come to life with its colorful costumes, brightly lit sets, tilted camera angles, and optically added pop-art fight scene exclamations: *Pow!* It had tongue-in-cheek, "campy" humor, including "Holy" exclamations from Robin actor Burt Ward such as "Holy Return from Oblivion" and "Holy Priceless Collection of Etruscan Snoods." Decades later, media coverage of superheroes *still* use variations on the "Holy" exclamation.[25]

Life chronicled the ensuing "Batmania" with a cover featuring actor Adam West in his Batman costume leaping against a white background studded with New Look oval bat symbols. The copy reads, "Batman makes a mighty leap into national popularity." The article proclaims, "Supermadness! The entertainment world offers it up on all sides, and the public gobbles it up. Batman conquers TV. Kids swing Batman capes in the backyard, and Bat products are everywhere. . . . The whole country is going deliberately, and profitably, nuts." There was an animated TV show, *The New Adventures of Superman*, and even a Broadway musical, *It's a Bird . . . It's a Plane . . . It's Superman.*[26]

The TV phenomenon pushed *Batman* comics into sales numbers not seen since the Golden Age. In 1966, in *Detective* #356, Schwartz finally brought Alfred back from the dead as an amnesic villain called the Outsider.[27] That issue included a full-page ad for a *Batman* movie from 20th Century Fox starring the TV cast. The copy promised: "For the First Time on the Motion Picture Screen in Color."

The *Batman* series lasted three seasons but burned bright. It would also be derided by legions of fans. During the first season, Michael Uslan realized that *Batman* was a *comedy*—the world was laughing at Batman! "The *Batman* TV show gave high society types the right to laugh at Batman and ridicule comics! I was about fifteen when the show came on the air, and, again, it's in the context of the times. I embrace the show *now* because today there are so many different interpretations of Batman. But back then the TV show was the singular interpretation of Batman for the whole world, and it was making a joke out of it."

Uslan felt a sense of obligation to the creators and their character to counter the campy TV spoof. By then he had met Bill Finger and Bob Kane and would go on to meet Jerry Robinson, another mentor. "I was in our den and made a vow that somehow, someday I would show the world the *true* Batman, the creature of the night created in 1939. But I was a blue-collar kid from New Jersey, my dad was a mason, and my mom was a bookkeeper. I couldn't buy my way into Hollywood. So how do you jump the Grand Canyon?"

Meanwhile, the comics industry was changing. Earlier in the decade the price of a comic rose from ten to twelve cents, DC/National went public, and Marvel Comics began pulling ahead as sales leader. The old publishing companies that birthed and nurtured the first superheroes were vanishing; a new and bigger corporate structure was absorbing superhero mythology.

In 1968 Kinney National Services, a company specializing in parking lots and funeral parlors, acquired DC/National, their first venture into the entertainment field before purchasing the Warner Bros. movie studio. Enfolding National Periodical's famous characters into what would become the Warner Communications Company meant synergistic production of in-house properties for publishing, movies, and merchandising. In 1970 Jack Liebowitz retired, comfortably ensconced on the board of Warner Communications.[28]

Also in 1968, Martin Goodman sold his Magazine Management Company, including his Marvel line, to Perfect Film & Chemical Corporation, a Long Island–based conglomerate that soon changed its name to Cadence Industries. The new corporate owners realized slipshod pulp publishing practices—all those Marvel characters created by freelancers without contracts—made their increasingly valuable assets vulnerable to claims. A future legal document chronicled it thus: "In the 1970s Cadence/Marvel started demanding that artists such as Jack Kirby sign agreements such as the 1972 Agreement [with Kirby] assigning to Marvel all previous Kirby work published by Marvel. . . . Cadence was seeking to 'clean up,' if not completely rewrite, Marvel's past to protect what had become recognized as valuable intellectual property."[29]

Meanwhile, out of the spotlight of the *Batman* TV phenomenon, the drama of first-generation comic book creators seeking to claim their creations was playing out, thanks to the cyclical terms of US copyright law that arrived like a returning comet—the initial twenty-eight-year copyright term for Golden Age superheroes was up for renewal, starting with Superman in 1966.

STAN, WALLY, STEVE, AND JACK

Artist Gil Kane praised the Marvel Method as "extremely liberating" in striking a creative balance between story and art, as opposed to the tradition of writers dictating panel-by-panel instructions for artists to slavishly follow. In truth, the Marvel Method made writers and artists cocreators and collaborators, but that wasn't the reality. Kirby had a hand in almost all of Marvel's superheroes but owned a financial stake in none; likewise Steve Ditko and his signature work on Spider-Man and the mystical Dr. Strange, "Master of Black Magic" (as he was first introduced). While Ditko labored in his New York studio and Kirby worked long nights in his Dungeon on Long Island, Lee held court at Marvel's New York office, meeting media representatives and celebrities like filmmaker Federico Fellini. As Marvel's public face and writer/editor, Lee was credited (sometimes through no fault of Lee's), as the sole reason for Marvel's success. In the pulp tradition, Marvel freelancers churned out the work, along with a page-rate voucher that Stan Lee approved and passed on to Marvel's bookkeeping department for processing.

Wally Wood had come to Marvel, where he contributed to *Avengers, The Mighty Thor, X-Men*, and *Fantastic Four*; he seemingly found a home with *Daredevil: The Man without Fear*. But the run was brief. "[Wood] was never convinced by the 'Marvel method' and years later he would satirize it harshly," notes an exhibition catalogue essay. "Kirby, Ditko and Wood wanted to tell their own stories without editorial interference and this triggered [Wood's] departure from Marvel. Wood maintained that if the artist was developing the idea he should be paid for it. . . . When Lee saw that the artist was ready to quit he offered him the job of writing on *Daredevil*. Wood put his name on the script for #10, but he already made up his mind."[30]

Wood's decision to leave was probably confirmed by what happened to his issue #10 cover depicting Daredevil on a rooftop, confronting the villainous foursome of Cat Man, Ape Man, Bird Man, and Frog Man. The Comics Code Authority ruled that Wood must alter his original, which showed Cat Man carrying off a beautiful woman and the others moving in with villainous intent.

Steve Ditko believed the Marvel Method made him integral to the storytelling and wanted his credit to reflect that. He got his wish in "The Mystery of the Man in the Crime-Master's Mask," *Spider-Man* #26: "Painstakingly Plotted and Drawn by Steve Ditko." The plot credit would stay until the end of Ditko's run with *Spider-Man* #38. (The only exception was the issue #31 credit reading, "Magnificent Artwork by.")

"The idea that there could be more than one 'author'—that perhaps there couldn't be a single 'creator' when the Marvel Method was used—never came up," authors Fred Van Lente and Ryan Dunlavey observe in *The Comic Book History of Comics*. "It didn't take long for tensions between Lee and his primary artistic 'co-authors' [Kirby and Ditko] to reach the breaking point."

A rare look at the Marvel Method was a three-page feature in *The Amazing Spider-Man Annual* #1 (1964), "How Stan Lee and Steve Ditko Create Spider-Man!" The Ditko illustrated story pictures Lee jolted awake in the dead of night, a lightbulb glowing overhead with a brilliant idea. In the ensuing story session with "Stevey Boy," Lee proposes doing twelve panels per page as Ditko leans back in his chair and groans, "Waddaya mean *we*?? I do the drawing while you practice signing your name all over!" After a contentious session, a caption notes: "After the usual friendly story conference, Stan gives Steve the script and then leaves to have a similar fight with Jack Kirby! Meanwhile, Steve begins work on the new Spider-Man tale."

Steve Ditko made Spider-Man the star of the Marvel Age. But Stan, quoted in a 1966 magazine article, seemed dismissive:

> I don't plot Spider-Man any more. Steve Ditko, the artist has been doing the stories. I guess I'll leave him alone until sales start to slip. Since Spidey got so popular, Ditko thinks he's the genius of the world. We were arguing so much over plot lines I told him to start making up his own stories. He won't let anybody else ink his drawings either. He just drops off the finished pages with notes at the margins and I fill in the dialogue. I never know what he'll come up with next, but it's interesting to work that way.[31]

Ditko left Marvel soon after, and Kirby would follow.

"By the late '60s Jack Kirby looked around and saw that he had resurrected a company that even then was patronizing him," Janet Bode chronicles. "Since his arrival, Marvel's monthly output had quadrupled from eight to 32 titles, with sales surpassing archrival DC—Marvel had become number one. . . . A new generation of fans, instead of dropping comics as teens, remained loyal through college and beyond. . . . Kirby continued to receive his usual [page] rate."[32]

In 1970 the "Marvel Bullpen Bulletin" page in September cover-dated issues featured one of the strangest installments of "Stan's Soapbox." The editor seemed to be in self-deprecating shock:

Remember a few years back when Steve Ditko suddenly left the hallowed halls of Marvel to seek his fortunes elsewhere? Well, at the time of this writing (early in March), Jack Kirby has unexpectedly announced his resignation from our surprised but stalwart little staff. . . . That's where we're at— understaffed, under-manned, and under-fed—but as bushy-tailed and bewildered as ever! So watch for the fireworks, friend, as we turn ourselves on, knock ourselves out, and do ourselves in to prove once again that, while we may not be the biggest, we're still the boldest and the best!

Excelsior

CHAPTER 17

COPYRIGHT WARS

I submitted the appropriate paperwork [for rights to Captain America], but didn't include Jack Kirby because he was working for Marvel at the time, on projects that included Captain America. I thought it would constitute a conflict of interest. . . . My lawyers notified Marvel, and that's when they sued us. Their contention was that we had created the character while working in the [Timely] office on staff, so it was company property.

JOE SIMON
My Life in Comics

He wants the copyright and it looks like you're out. [Said to Jack Kirby.]

MARTIN GOODMAN
quoted in Sean Howe, *Marvel Comics: The Untold Story*

JERRY TALKS TO LAWYERS

Among Jerry Siegel's major contributions during his return to DC were memorable "Imaginary Stories," those "what if?" tales outside canon and continuity. Martin Pasko observes their popularity "was both a vindication for Siegel's bruised ego and a liberation of his imagination. In his heyday, he had sometimes found his bigger ideas being shot down amid fears that they would inhibit the character's exploitability. . . . He could even write the best-remembered Imaginary Story of them all: 'The Death of Superman.'"[1]

Jerry Siegel invested his emotions into Superman, and deep psychological probing isn't needed to divine the truth behind "The Death of Superman," a grim tale of brutal betrayal illustrated by Curt Swan for *Superman* #149 (November 1961). Lex Luthor gains Superman's friendship, and the Man of Tomorrow, in his idealistic faith in redemption, is played for a sucker as he's slowly drawn into Luthor's deadly embrace. When Luthor springs his trap, an innocent, unwitting Superman slowly dies from kryptonite radiation. "He wriggled and twisted like a worm on a hook!" Luthor gloats at a gangland banquet celebrating Superman's death.

It had not been a happy homecoming for Siegel. Mort Weisinger was notoriously difficult to deal with (except with his close friend, Julie Schwartz), but the editor reveled in disparaging the man whose creation launched the industry. One story has Weisinger announcing he had to go to the can and wondering if he could borrow one of Jerry's scripts to use to wipe his ass. Years later, the crusty Weisinger gave Siegel his due. Of all the Superman writers, he said, "Siegel was the best emotional writer of them all."[2]

In 1963 Siegel began talking to lawyers in preparation for a copyright renewal fight for Superman. Siegel was fired, this time for good. Siegel's challenge was denied, but he appealed with pro bono counsel, awaiting the ruling in California, where he and Joanne relocated in 1968.[3]

Siegel and Shuster had lost their Superman byline; now, like fallen royalty, their names were being stricken from the record. *Superman* #183 (January 1966), a special "80 pg. Giant," reprinted the *Superman* #19 story featuring Lois and Clark attending a movie theater playing the first *Superman* cartoon. In the panel where *Action* and *Superman* copyright notices appear on screen, the original Siegel and Shuster credit was expunged. Lois's original comment, in which she wondered who Siegel and Shuster were, was replaced with "I don't believe I've ever seen those magazines."

In October 1966 Joe Simon filed suit in New York State Supreme Court, claiming authorship of Captain America and seeking "an accounting, damages, and injunctive relief" against Martin and Jean Goodman and Magazine Management Company; Krantz Films, Inc.; RKO Gen., Inc.; and Weston Merchandise Corp.

The following year Simon filed suit in US District Court for the Southern District of New York against the Goodmans and their affiliates. Simon sought injunctive relief to prohibit the publisher from applying for renewal registrations of "the Works" and a declaratory judgment that Simon, as author under the provisions of the Copyright Act, had "sole and exclusive right to the renewal term of the copyright."

The tone in the legal summaries was markedly different from the condescending judicial comments of earlier comic book actions. Timely Publications and Timely Comics, Inc., were recognized as having published the first issue "of the *now iconic* [author's emphasis] Captain America Comics in December 1940."

Simon's state and federal suits claimed that since he had no written agreement with Timely, just a handshake deal, Simon "orally assigned his interest in Captain America Comics and the Captain America character . . . to Timely."[4]

Jack Kirby had been his partner in creating the patriotic superhero, so why wasn't Kirby mentioned in Simon's lawsuit? Simon claimed a conflict of interest, as Jack was still at Marvel, working on a new run of *Captain America*. "Marvel also told Jack that I was trying to cut him out, and he became upset," Simon recalled.[5]

It certainly seemed like betrayal to Kirby. Goodman proposed a deal with him: if he sided with Marvel, the publisher would match any future settlement it made with Simon. Kirby signed a deposition on July 12, 1966, stating, "I felt that whatever I did for Timely belonged to Timely as was the practice in those days. When I left Timely, all my work was left with them."[6]

In the state action, Goodman's lawyers argued Simon had been an "employee for hire." In the federal action, Goodman's counter-claim declared Timely owned the "Works" and asked that Simon be enjoined from applying to renew a copyright he didn't own.[7] During this phase of suit and countersuit, children's author and illustrator Theodor Seuss Geisel, popularly known as Dr. Seuss, was suing the *Liberty* magazine archives of the Liberty Library Corporation for rights to "Dr. Seuss's Merry Menagerie," a cartoon series Geisel created for the magazine in the 1930s. Geisel won the first round, but on appeal Liberty Library's ownership was upheld. With that precedent, Simon's lawyers declared they had no chance—Joe had to settle.[8]

Simon entered into a settlement agreement with Marvel in November 1969 (the comics company having transferred owner-ship from Goodman to the corporation soon known as Cadence Industries). Simon now agreed he had been "an employee for hire," and Marvel was assigned all "right, title and interest" in Captain America. The respective state and federal courts dismissed Simon's filings.[9]

"We got some money, but not a hell of a lot," Simon recalled. "I had to turn the copyrights over to Marvel. After that I was more careful than ever to renew copyrights when they came due. . . . The conclusion was a tough thing to swallow."[10] Comic book creators were not businessmen, and few had the resources to underwrite marathon litigation against the emerging global entertainment companies. Changes to the Copyright Act were coming, but an abiding verity was the David-and-Goliath scenario of lone free-lancers seeking to enforce rights against major corporations.

"It's the American way!" attorney John Mason says, ironically. "In our system, each side bears its own costs, which means the side with the most resources can tilt the playing field. I've sued Walmart and gone up against other big companies on behalf of struggling artists, so, yeah, it's a real fight and a real problem."[11]

Copyright cases considered under the 1909 act relied on a single sentence devoted to defining "work for hire." Around the renewal period for Golden Age creators, a "test" for establishing copyright ownership emerged through two seminal cases. The first—*Lin-Brook Builders Hardware v. Gertler*, heard before the 9th Circuit Court of Appeals in 1965—held that in the absence of a contractual agreement, the presumption was copyright vested in the party at whose "instance" the work was induced and at whose "expense" it was created. In *Brattleboro Pub. Co. v. Winmill Pub. Corp.* (1966), the 2nd Circuit Court of Appeals held that if the intent of the parties could not be determined, copyright would vest in the employer.

In a subsequent legal article, Thomas M. Deahl II assailed the instance and expense test, particularly the 2nd Circuit's "consistently inconsistent" application of it, especially the "expense prong." Citing *Nimmer on Copyright*, a widely cited multivolume work on copyright law, Deahl called the expense aspect the

> most troubling and unpredictable. As discussed by Nimmer, this prong should examine the cost of the creation, "rather than the cost of publication" because this would make all published material work-for-hire. . . . Further, the Second Circuit stated that though the work may not have been at the expense of the hiring party, if the work was at their instance it would be considered a work for hire. Without establishing hard set boundaries, in determining what constitutes as being at the hiring party's instance and expense, there will be no resolution in enhancing the predictability of copyright litigation.

Deahl called the test "an injustice to comic books."[12]

Meanwhile, Goodman stopped a copyright challenge from Sub-Mariner's creator by giving Bill Everett a loan with a wink-wink understanding that it need not be repaid, according to fanzine pioneer and Marvel's future editor in chief Roy Thomas, then a Marvel staff writer. Writer Jon Cooke cites another Goodman "loan" of $2,000 on May 22, 1968, from Magazine Management Company to Kirby, who was relocating with his family to California.[13]

Carl Burgos consulted lawyers about the Human Torch

The original Human Torch sacrifices its android self to save the Fantastic Four—and ensure Marvel's ownership of the original character's copyright.

"THE TORCH THAT WAS!," *FANTASTIC FOUR, KING-SIZE SPECIAL* #4 (NOVEMBER 1966), P. 18, PANEL 5, PENCIL ART BY JACK KIRBY, INKS BY JOE SINNOTT.

copyright, which was up for renewal in 1967. But on the newsstands in August 1966, cover-dated November, Burgos's android Torch was reintroduced in a fiery clash with Johnny Storm's Torch in *Fantastic Four* "King-Size Special" #4, only to see Burgos's creation sacrifice himself to save others. Sue Storm laments, "The original Human Torch! Reborn—only to die again!" The reappearance coincided with the character's first appearance exactly twenty-eight years before. "The original Torch had been revived long enough to ensure [Marvel's] copyright claim," writes Marvel historian Sean Howe, who adds the maneuver might explain the scene that summer when Burgos's daughter, Susan, discovered her father in their backyard destroying the comics and memorabilia of his Golden Age career. "I grew up believing that he came up with this fabulous idea, and that Stan Lee took it from him," Susan Burgos recalled.

Like many a wronged creator, Burgos's bitterness cut deep. In the early 1970s, when a young comics artist asked Burgos for advice, the creator warned him to stay away from the industry, adding, "If I'd known how much trouble and heartbreak the Torch would bring me, I would never have created him."[14]

SIEGEL AND SHUSTER V. NATIONAL PERIODICAL PUBLICATIONS, INC., ET AL.

Jerry Siegel's fight over the expiration and renewal of Superman copyright was finally heard before District Judge Morris E. Lasker in the US District Court for the Southern District of New York.[15]

The court was mindful that this was no ordinary intellectual property fight. At issue was control of a world-renowned icon. Judge Lasker, in his ruling on October 18, 1973, opened with a poignant statement:

> Although Clark Kent, generally known as Superman, is happily capable of solving all problems without going to court, his creators and exploiters, mere mortals like the rest of us, are not so fortunate. Jerome Siegel and Joseph Shuster are Superman's creators. They seek a declaration that they, and not the defendant National . . . are entitled to the copyright renewal rights of the renowned comic strip. National counterclaims for a declaration in its favor. . . . We find, on the material facts as to which there is no genuine issue, that National is the owner of the copyright renewal term and grant the motion.

Lasker ruled the 1947 Superboy/Superman settlement in the New York State Supreme Court was binding on the current action. "Furthermore, the issues which plaintiffs want to litigate in this action could have been raised in the Westchester action, and consequently are barred by *res judicata* as well." (*Res judicata* translates as "the matter has already been judged.")

Lasker acknowledged the plaintiffs' contention that copyright renewal existed to give the creator a second chance at a property whose marketability was uncertain at its creation. But, the judge countered, Siegel had ceded that point when the Westchester settlement granted DC *all* rights to Superman and Superboy: "Plaintiffs certainly knew by 1947, if not before, that Superman was an extraordinarily marketable man, as well as one of unusual powers. . . . The fact that this language makes no specific reference to renewal rights militates as much as if not more strongly against plaintiffs than defendants, in whose favor all rights to Superman were confirmed on the face of the various agreements." Lasker further ruled Superman a "work for hire," affirming the Westchester judgment that determined Siegel and Shuster had devoted "exclusive artistic services" to their employer, who supervised and directed the work. "These elements were indisputably present in the relationship between plaintiffs and Detective."[16]

Siegel forged ahead, appealing before the US Court of Appeals, 2nd Circuit. The appeal was argued on November 7, 1974, before Chief Judge Irving Kaufman and circuit judges Anderson and Mulligan.[17]

Judge Mulligan's ruling on December 5 *overturned* the work-for-hire judgment: "Superman and his miraculous powers were completely developed long before the employment relationship [with DC] was instituted. The record indicates that the revisions directed by the defendants were simply to accommodate Superman to a magazine format. We do not consider this sufficient to create the presumption that the strip was a work for hire."

Siegel won another battle but lost the war, thanks to the Westchester ruling following him like a curse. "Accordingly, we affirm the dismissal of the complaint, but only on the grounds that the 1947 state court action . . . precludes the plaintiffs from contesting ever again that all rights in Superman, including the renewal copyright, have passed forever to defendants," Mulligan ruled. "Since we hold that the state judgment action determined that the defendants owned all of the rights to the Superman strip without reservation, the doctrine of res judicata is properly applicable."[18]

SHAZAM!

An era ended in 1973, as National Periodical Publications moved from 480 Lexington Avenue to the new Warner Communications building at 75 Rockefeller Plaza. Artists were now entering the executive suites: Carmine Infantino had risen from editorial and art director positions to become publisher of DC/National, and former EC artist Joe Orlando added "editor" to his resume.

A creative jolt was needed at DC, given that Marvel led the industry by a wide margin. Denny O'Neil summed up their differences: "Briefly and oversimply, DC was classical, Marvel was romantic. DC was well-made plots, clear artwork, a comforting predictability: a Mozart concerto. Marvel was improvised story lines, high energy, surprise: a Charlie Parker saxophone solo."[19]

Paul Levitz's leadership on *The Comics Reader* fanzine led to his writing scripts at DC, including a long run on *Legion of Super-Heroes*. He became an editorial assistant in 1973, succeeded Julius Schwartz as *Batman* editor, and in 1980 began an eventful tenure in DC's executive ranks. Levitz believes Infantino was the first working comics creator to hold a business-oriented executive job. "There have been working creatives, like Stan Lee, that had creative leadership roles," he adds, "but Carmine was the day-to-day business leader of the company, and I think that was the first time that had ever happened with one of the larger companies."[20]

Joe Orlando observed that DC had been "getting their asses kicked in by Marvel at the newsstands" but never bothered figuring out *why*.

Carmine and I became very good friends. In the course of our friendship we discussed our philosophy of comics and what we thought about them, how they should be done, and why DC was taking second place to Marvel. It seems that the editors at DC were so institutionalized, coming off all these wonderful accomplishments—taking credit for the invention of the super-hero and maintaining it. . . . DC had sued Fawcett over Captain Marvel and won. They felt invincible.

Orlando credited Infantino with breaking up DC's staid "gentle-man's club" and with being an artist's editor, soliciting talents like Dick Giordano, another editor/artist from Charlton Comics who came to DC and brought along Denny O'Neil, Steve Ditko, and others.[21]

One of Infantino's personal projects was resurrecting Captain Marvel. "The 'Big Red Cheese' not only rivaled Superman; from time to time he actually surpassed the sales of Superman's titles," Infantino recalled. "So all these years later, around 1970, I decided to bring the character out of mothballs. I called Fawcett, who were now just publishing books, not comics. I negotiated a deal and acquired the rights to publish the character."

Since his banishment to comic book limbo, Captain Marvel had many strange incarnations. When Fawcett ended its comics line, it left London-based comics publisher L. Miller & Son at a loss—Captain Marvel, licensed through Fawcett, was one of their most popular American superhero imports. Undaunted, the publisher called on writer/artist Mick Anglo to create an imitation. Anglo introduced Micky Moran, a boy who transforms into Marvelman by saying "Kimota" ("atomik" spelled backwards), and Dr. Sivana is reborn as Gargunza. They debuted in *Marvelman* #25 (February 1954), a seamless transition from the Captain Marvel continuity that lasted until 1963, as did an adaptation of Captain Marvel Jr., *Young Marvelman*.[22]

In 1966, during the first superhero copyright renewal period, Carl Burgos and Myron Fass, a publisher and former Timely artist, secured rights to the abandoned "Captain Marvel" name, with plans to create Marvel characters to compete against Martin Goodman. But the publisher felt the "Marvel" name should be his. Goodman offered $6,000 for name rights, but Fass refused. In 1967 Goodman called their bluff by changing the title of issue #12 of *Fantasy Masterpieces* to *Marvel Super-Heroes* and heralding "The Coming of Captain Marvel!" This was not Fawcett's superhero. Gene Colan's cover art pictured a tall masked man in a green helmet and white space suit trimmed in green, with a green Saturn emblem emblazoned on his chest: "Captain Mar-Vell," a member of the Kree race and commander of an "intergalactic space fleet."

Otto Binder tried reviving the Captain Marvel concept for Milson Publishing Company in 1967, with young Tod Holton donning a magic green beret to become Super Green Beret, a Marvelesque hero fighting the Vietnam War. None of the whimsy of old was to be found in the jungles of Nam—*Tod Holton: Super Green Beret* lasted two issues. That year Burgos and Fass took a loss and sold Goodman the Captain Marvel name rights for $4,500. A solo *Captain Marvel* title began in 1968, with a proclamation above the title: "Marvel's Space-Born Superhero!"

DC/National continued its plans to resurrect Captain Marvel: a settlement with Marvel allowed use of the name, but not as a title. The new series was named after the magic word, with editor Julius Schwartz contributing an exclamation point: *Shazam!*[23] Edited by Schwartz, drawn by C. C. Beck, and written by Denny O'Neil (as lead writer), it was shaping up as an A-list effort. Beck sounded the first discordant note: "DC contacted me and I agreed to do the artwork, not without some misgivings. 'I'll be happy to draw Captain Marvel again,' I told them. 'But do you think a comic character who was a big hit 30 years ago will appeal to readers of the '70s?'"[24]

Captain Marvel was immediately installed in the top tier of DC's pantheon, alongside Superman. The once-bitter Golden Age rivals appeared together on the cover of *Shazam!* #1 (February

1973). A smiling Superman (figure drawn by Nick Cardy, face rendered by Murphy Anderson) stood stage left, pulling back a curtain to reveal Billy Batson saying the magic word, accompanied by a thunder cloud and lightning bolt; standing stage right, Beck's grinning superhero.[25]

O'Neil's story, set in real-time, revealed that twenty years before, Captain Marvel, Mary Marvel, and Captain Marvel Jr. were honored at an outdoor ceremony when they and assembled friends were trapped and lifted into outer space by a Vortex Transporter Paralyzer Beam emitting from the Sivana family's orbiting spacecraft. In space, Sivana seals them in a globe of Suspendium and is about to send them into infinity, but crashes into the globe. For twenty years they all orbit in suspended animation until the sun awakens Captain Marvel, who frees them.

An early problem with *Captain Marvel* was DC's refusal to let Beck have as his assistant Don Newton, a young artist and Captain Marvel fan he was mentoring. "They'd lose control. . . . They were afraid I was going to set up a Harry Chesler shop and send them a bunch of junk and stuff," Beck grumbled.[26] Otherwise, Beck declared that his first six stories captured the "old humorous, lighthearted approach," praising writers O'Neil and Elliot S. Maggin in a letter dated November 27, 1973: "DC has given me authority to change scripts as I see fit to keep the stories in the old style. We take sly digs at hippies, rock music, mod clothes by making Billy and Marvel, with their 1940s attitude, just slightly confused and bewildered in the '70s."

But Beck suddenly soured on the project, leaving after ten issues. He *now* insisted the whimsical spirit of old was lost in translation: "Instead of being the World's Mightiest Mortal, Captain Marvel was being the World's Biggest Clown and all his friends and enemies from the '40s were being treated as foolish, ridiculous characters who were good only for laughs because of their quaint costumes and old-fashioned beliefs."[27]

Shazam! artists included Bob Oksner and original Captain Marvel artist Kurt Schaffenberger (who did the last cover of *The*

Once unthinkable, Superman welcomes Captain Marvel, his bitter Golden Age rival, back from comic book limbo. DC bought the rights to Fawcett's dormant franchise, but Marvel now held rights to the Captain Marvel name. A compromise allowed DC to use the name, but not as a title: hence the use of the magic word—*Shazam!*

SHAZAM! #1 (FEBRUARY 1973), COVER ART BY C. C. BECK, SUPERMAN BY NICK CARDY, WITH MURPHY ANDERSON. NATIONAL PERIODICAL PUBLICATIONS, INC. (DC).

Despite the smiling welcome into the DC family accorded Captain Marvel, fans knew there was a deep animosity between the former Fawcett star and Superman, the latter of whom won their battle for supremacy during the Golden Age. This 1976 *Justice League of America* cover pictures the face-off fans clamored to see, but the story inside failed to deliver the promised fireworks. The Superman vs. Captain Marvel theme would be touched on in future titles.

"CRISIS IN TOMORROW!," *JUSTICE LEAGUE OF AMERICA* #137 (DECEMBER 1972), COVER ART BY ERNIE CHAN.

Marvel Family). Beck's pupil, Don Newton, fulfilled his dream of drawing Captain Marvel, closing out the series with issue #35. The artist could emulate his mentor in his cartoony "Beck style," but he made Captain Marvel realistic and heroic, drawing the ire of the cantankerous Beck, who wrote Newton a scathing letter about the terrible "new look."

But Newton studied the beloved Fawcett and *Shazam!* stories, concluding each had good and weaker efforts. "In my opinion, any character that has survived for several decades has had to evolve, Mickey Mouse being a classic example," Newton explained. "When DC offered me the chance to draw Captain Marvel, I was delighted to hear [editor] Jack Harris say that he should be drawn in a more realistic, contemporary style. . . . Captain Marvel's plastered-down hair dated him badly, so I gave him a newer 'dry look.' As the trend today in comics is to show greater muscular detail, I now make his costume look as if it is painted on him. I draw him as realistically as possible, and use more shading to define his muscles."[28]

Newton continued *Shazam!* in *World's Finest Comics*. A live-action *Captain Marvel* TV show began a three-season run on September 1, 1974. DC would continue developing Captain Marvel projects. "I guess it worked out okay for DC in the long run," Infantino concluded. "There was a *Shazam!* TV show, and DC got full rights to the property, and the once-forgotten character continues to show up to this day."[29]

SIEGEL STRIKES BACK

There was finality to the ruling rejecting Siegel's Superman copyright renewal appeal, but he wasn't licked—he wanted to take his case to the United States Supreme Court. But in April 1975 his lawyers informed him that if he ended his litigation, National was prepared to offer a financial settlement. Siegel agreed to wait for National to do the right thing.

Siegel and Shuster were no longer part of the industry, and two savvy fans—Alan Light, publisher of *The Buyer's Guide for Comics Fandom*, and *Buyer's Guide* columnist Murray Bishoff—were unhappy. Bishoff wrote a critical account of fans neglecting Superman while longing for Captain Marvel's return, a character Siegel considered "a direct copy of his creation," as Bishoff noted. "That makes me wonder, if fans gave the Siegel and Shuster Superman (1938–1947) the same nostalgic acclaim they give Captain Marvel, how different things might be today."

Shel Dorf, founder of the annual San Diego Comic-Con, invited Jerry and Joanne Siegel to attend the August 1975 con as special guests. Bishoff and Light arrived "with great anticipation," Bishoff recalled, where they met Siegel and his wife on the convention floor for an interview. "I found Jerry Siegel to be a deeply injured man emotionally," Bishoff wrote. "He was bitterly *disappointed*, let down by those he had trusted."

At the convention banquet Siegel was among Inkpot Award honorees, the Comic-Con's annual award for excellence in comics, animation, and related fields of popular culture. The crowd cheered as an all-star group photo saw Jerry Siegel standing alongside Will Eisner, Jack Kirby, Gil Kane, Stan Lee, Jim Steranko, Bob Clampett, Daws Butler, and June Foray. "I was so happy for him for this was what I had hoped would happen," Bishoff recalled. "Yet he was so quiet. He later told me the moment was so emotional for him that he simply could not speak. It was from this experience at the San Diego convention that Jerry Siegel got the strength to get back in the fight. For the first time he had felt the support he always should have known from fans. A little over two months later, he went to the national press with his story."

What prompted an angry Siegel to tell his story—a "5,000-word diatribe," Bishoff called it—was news that Warner Communications planned to return Superman to the silver screen in one of the most ambitious live-action productions ever. *Superman: The Movie* would test the power of corporate "synergy," with DC/National providing the iconic character and Warner Bros. Studios producing the movie under the big tent of Warner Communications.[30]

The deal was major news in the Hollywood trades and definitely news to Siegel, who was still awaiting the promised financial settlement. In response Siegel released a blistering press release to media outlets titled "A Curse on the Superman Movie!"

> It has been announced in show business trade papers that a multi-million dollar production based on the Superman comic strip is about to be produced. It has been stated that millions of dollars were paid to the owners of Superman, National Periodical Publications, Inc., for the right to use the famous comic book super-hero in the new movie. The script is by Mario Puzo, who wrote The Godfather and Earthquake. The film is to have a star-filled cast.
>
> I, Jerry Siegel, the co-originator of Superman, put a curse on the Superman movie! I hope it super-bombs. I hope loyal Superman fans stay away from it in droves. I hope the whole world, becoming aware of the stench that surrounds Superman, will avoid the movie like the plague.

It had been over thirty years since Siegel wrote Jack Liebowitz that he and Joe "orbit about your personality and whims." Shorn of illusions, and with Donenfeld gone, Siegel trained his fire on Liebowitz and the "money-mad monsters" at DC/National. "Jack Liebowitz, a member of the Board of Directors of Warner Communications, stabbed Joe Shuster and me, Jerry Siegel, in the back."

> [Liebowitz] ruined our lives, deliberately, though Joe and I originated Superman, which enriched Liebowitz and his associates. . . . Superman has been a great money-maker for National Periodical Publications, Inc., which is owned by

Warner Communications. . . . Liebowitz proceeded to violate our good faith, which he had aroused with his written and verbal . . . promises of integrity upon his part; he dealt with us unfairly, in violation of his promises to protect our interests. . . .

I can't flex super-human muscles and rip apart the massive buildings in which these greedy people count the immense profits from the misery they have inflicted on Joe and me and our families. I wish I could. But I can write this press release and ask my fellow Americans to please help us by refusing to buy Superman comic books, refusing to patronize the new Superman movie, or watch Superman on TV until this great injustice against Joe and me is remedied by the callous men who pocket the profits from OUR creation. Everyone who has enjoyed our creation Superman and what he stood for, those of you who believe that truth and justice should be the American Way, can help us.[31]

The press release generated the desired media coverage. The *New York Times* described the sixty-one-year old creators as "nearly destitute." Joe was nearly blind and rooming with his bachelor brother in Los Angeles; Siegel supported his family on a $7,000 annual salary as a clerk typist for the State of California. Bill Gallo, president of the National Cartoonists Society, expressed shock at their treatment. Jay Emmett, now a Warner vice president, commented, "We have no legal obligation, but certainly we feel that from a moral point of view we should do something and we have worked out a pension-type plan."[32]

The news coverage was a variant on the need for Superman to come to the rescue, but it was comics creators who arrived to save the day. Jerry Robinson, whose post-*Batman* career included editorial cartooning, led the fight with new-generation artist Neal Adams. Robinson and Adams pressed Warner Communications to financially support Siegel and Shuster *and* return their bylines. "That was the only way to restore their dignity, after all they'd been through," Robinson reflected. "It's every artist's moral right to be credited for his or her work. That's unquestioned in Europe, but not here."[33]

Adams and Robinson secured support of the National Cartoonists Society and the Association of American Editorial Cartoonists, writers Norman Mailer and Kurt Vonnegut, and print and broadcast journalists Pete Hamill and Mike Wallace. Siegel and Shuster appeared on the *Today Show*; there was coverage on *CBS Evening News*. "Publicity was our most effective tool," Robinson explained. "The movie was in production, millions of dollars were at stake. We had to act quickly to take advantage of the pressure that the media coverage brought to bear."[34]

Robinson personally conducted final negotiations with Jay Emmett. They agreed to a financial package of $20,000 a year for life for each cocreator. But credit was a sticking point. "Just because Shakespeare isn't copyrighted, you don't take his name off the plays," Robinson argued. Emmett maintained that applying a creator's credit on toys and other licensed products was not physically practical, and Robinson gave him that one. Warner agreed to restore Siegel and Shuster's credit to Superman comics and, after strong advocacy from Robinson, the movie as well.

Siegel and Shuster were flown to New York to sign the agreement. Afterwards, Robinson and his wife hosted a reception at their Upper West Side apartment, with special guests including Mailer, Vonnegut, Feiffer, Eisner, and *New Yorker* cartoonist Sam Gross. Robinson and Adams promised *CBS Evening News* an exclusive, and the party gathered around the TV to watch news anchor Walter Cronkite close the broadcast with the Superman story. "Today, at least, truth, justice, and the American way have triumphed," Cronkite intoned.

"Everyone raised their champagne glasses in a toast to Jerry and Joe, and many of us had tears running down our faces," Robinson said.[35]

SUPERMAN: THE MOVIE

Superman, directed by Richard Donner, was budgeted at $55 million, which at that time made it the most expensive production in movie history. The casting of Marlon Brando as Jor-El generated positive publicity. A two-year Superman search led to twenty-six-year-old Christopher Reeve, a virtual unknown whose credits included a role in the daytime TV drama *Love of Life*. Publicity reported the tall, broad-shouldered Reeve was getting into Superman shape with body builder Dave Prowse, who had played the villainous Darth Vader in the recent box-office phenomenon *Star Wars*. The *Star Wars* connection included composer John Williams, who won an Oscar for his *Star Wars* score and would be nominated again for his *Superman* score. Production designer John Barry, also a *Star Wars* Academy Award winner, would win a BAFTA Award (British Academy of Film and Television Arts) for Best Production Design/Art Direction on *Superman*.

Superman: The Movie was released in 1978, the fortieth anniversary year of *Action* #1. Another fantasy box-office blockbuster, it generated over $300 million worldwide. Sequels followed that would themselves be rebooted and reimagined in the decades ahead.[36] The movie was Hollywood's Holy Grail—a franchise. John Calley, head of Warner Bros., described the costs and complexity of popular filmmaking as a "very dangerous game. . . . If you're able to create a franchise, you know a very big piece of business is available to you every few years."

Calley explained:

> We didn't make *Superman* as an exploitive sci-fi, comic book thing. It was done with a seriousness that said to audiences, "We believe in this and we want you to, as well." I'd always loved the Saturday matinee adventure serials, and I'd read *Superman* as a kid, but I hadn't awoken one morning with a number and a formula. I was making twenty-five to thirty

movies a year, so I was scratching and looking all the time. *Superman* seemed plausible, then it worked because Dick Donner was remarkable and inventive. He started a genre.[37]

1976 COPYRIGHT ACT

In the works since 1955, the Copyright Act of 1976 was passed by Congress, signed into law by President Gerald Ford, and went into effect on January 1, 1978. The new act was the result of a comprehensive congressional review process—the first major revision of copyright law since 1909—and considered revisions accounting for forms of mass communication and intellectual property issues that hadn't existed sixty-seven years before or had been in formative states.

Attorney John Mason notes the 1976 Act federalized copyright. Until then each state had copyright offices. He explains: "In an information economy like ours, Congress thought we needed a uniform, cohesive, and sophisticated federal copyright law and not have a state legislature mucking around in it. It had become too convoluted and unwieldy. So now you cannot bring a copyright case to any state court."

Significantly, the new act was a response to "the continual erosion of authors' rights subsequent to the 1909 Act," as noted by a 2002 decision in *Marvel v. Simon* that reversed an earlier decision for Marvel and favored Simon's ability to legally pursue his claims to authorship of Captain America. "It allowed authors to terminate the rights of a grantee to whom the author had transferred rights in the original work . . . *notwithstanding any agreements to the contrary*" [author's emphasis].[38] The new law included an "extended renewal term" of an additional nineteen years; the key Section 304 "termination provision" allowed claims "effected at any time during a period of five years beginning at the end of fifty-six years from the date copyright was originally secured." Mason explains: "Congress saw this problem of work made for hire, the courts struggling to address it in the absence of legislation. There is now a statutory definition written into the '76 act."

The new act described work for hire as "a work prepared by an employee within the scope of his or her employment; or . . . a work specially ordered or commissioned for use as a contribution to a collective work . . . if the parties agree in a written instrument signed by them that the work shall be considered a work made for hire."[39]

The new act's exception for its artist-friendly termination provisions was if the work had been "for hire," as defined by the new act. But pre-1978 cases, such as the Golden Age cases, would be governed by the 1909 act, including application of the controversial "instance and expense test."

Still, lawyers could argue the precedent of the new act. "Remember, usually later laws are implemented to better or supplement existing laws," Mason adds. "So a smart lawyer who is trying to argue that the later law benefits his client, even when it doesn't apply, might explain it was created to balance an inequity."[40]

Attorney Marc Toberoff, who would represent the heirs of Superman's cocreators and Jack Kirby, emphasizes the significance of the termination provision. Originally Congress noted a creator's work had to be published to establish value, but when it became a success, the creator would be bound to a previous contract. "The renewal copyright was to give the author, or the family, if the author had died before the renewal term, a second life when the market value was known," Toberoff explains.

Copyright is to provide financial incentive for authors to create, the same way patent law provides financial incentive for inventors to invent, and exclusivity over the works to then license to others.

Then, in a notorious case, *Fred Fisher Music* [*Co., et al., v. M. Witmark & Sons*, 1943], the Supreme Court held that when an author goes into a publishing deal for the initial term, they could sell their renewal expectancy in advance, even though the renewal term is [decades] off. So, of course, the renewal term became the condition of any publishing deal, gutting the whole renewal scheme. So in the 1976 Act, Congress enacted the termination right, which is an extraordinary right, cutting through contract principles to allow the author or heirs to terminate without cause prior assignments and get back the copyright. The sole exception to this termination right is when it is work for hire. So, of course, the first thing the other side will claim is it's a work for hire, which is subject to this vague instance and expense test. This test is essentially being used to gut this very important termination right, which is the most important right of an author under the Copyright Act, outside of the copyright itself.

In the comic book cases to come, Toberoff would represent his client's interests but also seek to overturn the instance and expense test, making it his mission to change copyright law.

The '76 act provided that Golden Age creators would have *another* chance to reclaim their creations, starting with Superman in 1994.[41]

CHAPTER 18

MASTERS OF INVENTION

Don't do what you can trace. Don't trace what you can paste up. Then draw the fuck out of what's left.

HOWARD CHAYKIN'S paraphrase of Wallace "Wally" Wood's wisdom, in his introduction to Wood's *Cannon* collection

You can publish your stuff episodically on a digital platform for people to read instantly, then bring out the collection in the [print] equivalent of a graphic novel. Big companies like DC are doing print and digital on the same day. [Digital technology] is changing the whole model of comics, and it is the way things are going. I know tradition is important, but guys, we've had automation, we've had the digital revolution. We are going forward, so we are going to change. So, serve the change, don't stand in the sea with your arms out trying to stop it, because you ain't going to do it.

DAVE GIBBONS

HIRED HANDS

Siegel and Shuster's package from Superman's corporate owners—bylines restored, compensation for life—was a one-time deal that didn't include a share in merchandising or movie grosses and required the creators to concede that DC owned the Superman copyright; neither did it extend throughout the industry. In the settlement's aftermath the creators were saying all the right things, usually. In 1983 Jerry and Joanne Siegel and Joe Shuster were interviewed for *Nemo*, a new comics history magazine. During a closing comment, Jerry revealed, "It has been very frustrating for Joe and me to have been off the character that we originated and loved for so many years. We are grateful that in our senior years— we're both almost 69—that the corporation which owns Superman is treating us well."

"We have a good relationship with DC and Warner's," Joanne added.[1]

Other superstars were not so fortunate. It might have been coincidence, but in 1970, the year Kirby departed Marvel, the first volume of Steranko's *History of Comics* was released and dedicated to Jack Kirby, "without whom there may not have been any comics to write a history about." When Kirby departed Marvel, he was happily welcomed to DC by Carmine Infantino—a huge event for a fandom often split into rival Marvel and DC camps. It would not be a seamless fit, but Kirby had the creative freedom to create his own mythological "Fourth World," an epic exploring the worlds of New Genesis and Apokolips in *The New Gods*, *The Forever People*, *Mister Miracle*, and even *Superman's Pal Jimmy Olsen*.

Kirby's departure from Marvel arguably began in 1967 with a Fantastic Four storyline introducing Galactus, an omnipotent being who roams the universe, consuming the energy of planets. In Marvel Method style, the plot reportedly began with Lee's proposal to Kirby: "Have the Fantastic Four fight God." Lee later declared he had the name Galactus, the plot, and a fully developed story in mind. He then left it to Kirby, who descended into the Dungeon to complete his pages.

Lee later recalled:

But when I looked at the artwork, I saw there was some nutty looking naked guy on a flying surfboard. And I said, "Who is this?". . . [Kirby] may have called him the Surfer. But he said, "I thought that anybody as powerful as Galactus who could destroy planets should have somebody who goes ahead of him, a herald who finds the planets for him. And I thought it would be good to have that guy on a flying surfboard.". . . I loved it. And I decided to call him the Silver Surfer, which I thought sounded dramatic. But that was all. He was supposed to be a herald to find Galactus his planets. But the way Jack drew him, he looked so noble and so interesting that I said, "Jack, you know, we ought to really use this guy. I like him.". . . But that's how it happened—accidentally. I mean, I had nothing—I didn't think of him. Jack—it was one of the characters Jack tossed into the strip. And he drew him so beautifully that I felt we have to make him an important character.

You see, if there's a story where the hero goes, let's say, to a nightclub . . . the artist has to draw other people in the nightclub. So the artist is always creating new characters. . . . The artist in every strip always creates new characters to flesh out the strip and to make the characters living in the real world.[2]

The being that rode the cosmic waves was a rare overnight sensation. Mark Evanier later wrote of the Silver Surfer: "One of the most popular of all Marvel heroes had popped up where no one expected. Just like that. . . . Both men became possessive about the character Stan sometimes cited as his favorite."

In 1968 the Silver Surfer got his own title. Lee wrote the origin story but assigned the artwork to John Buscema, not Kirby. "Jack saw the Surfer as a creature formed of pure energy, one who had never been human," Evanier added. "In Stan's story, the Surfer had been a man on another planet who sacrificed human form to save the woman he loved. . . . Kirby especially didn't like that he hadn't been given first refusal on doing the new book. His idea had been taken away from him in every possible sense."[3] By 1970 Lee was moving against Kirby's conception of the character's inherent pacifism, planning "The Savage Silver Surfer."

Lee assigned Kirby to pencil a prelude in *Silver Surfer* #18, a story that ended with the announcement, "Next: The Savagely

Riding the cosmic waves, the Silver Surfer was introduced in *Fantastic Four* #48 and quickly became a star—and a point of creative tension between creator Jack Kirby and editor/writer Stan Lee. The cosmic figure in the background is the Watcher, who first appeared in *Fantastic Four* #13.

FANTASTIC FOUR #72 (MARCH 1967), COVER ART PENCILS BY JACK KIRBY, INKS BY JOE SINNOTT.

Sensational NEW Silver Surfer." The final two pages, done in pencil and pen and ink with graphite by Kirby and inker Herb Trimpe were among the original art included in "Masters of American Comics," a 2005 traveling exhibition originating at the Hammer Museum and the Museum of Contemporary Art in Los Angeles. The exhibition catalogue noted that without Kirby's involvement the *Silver Surfer* comic failed, apparently one of the reasons Lee planned to turn the Silver Surfer savage. The final two pages show Kirby's creation zooming through space, a volcanic fury building, the final page filling with a close-up of the face of an anguished Surfer crying, "No longer mine a lonely voice, pleading peace in a world of strife! From this time forth, the Silver Surfer will battle them on their own savage terms!"

"Kirby turned this page into graphite fury. . . . Look at the horrific anger of a fully betrayed face," Glen David Gold observed in an exhibition catalogue essay. "Kirby's last piece of art from his glory days at Marvel. There is no one in costume here, just a Kirby cipher standing in for all the hurt done him. . . . And that's the kind of resonance that makes the artwork actually matter—the connection of the epic and the emotional. Kirby felt it, he had the Surfer feel it, and then readers felt it too."[4]

In January 1970 Marvel's corporate owner (that is the year Perfect Film & Chemical Company changed its corporate name to Cadence Industries) began tightening up its ownership of the company's intellectual property, including getting former freelancers under contracts favorable to Cadence. The contract offered Kirby was onerous, with no pay raise, nothing guaranteed (not even credit), and no legal recourse. Kirby wanted to negotiate, but the company refused to talk to his attorney.

Kirby did get a call from a corporate rep who gave the artist two choices: sign or get out. "Jack protested: He was too important to be treated this way," Evanier recalls. "The caller told him he was nuts. Stan Lee created everything at Marvel and they could get any idiot to draw up Stan's brilliant ideas. At least, that's how Jack would remember the conversation. Kirby hung up on him, phoned Infantino, and changed companies."[5]

Previously, when Goodman's Magazine Management Company had been writing the paychecks, they were stamped with a legend acknowledging the signee accepted the publisher's terms. This lasted until around 1978, when the Copyright Act of 1976 went in effect; after that the backs of checks from the newly titled Marvel Entertainment Group acknowledged the endorser accepted, among other terms, "that all payee's works are and shall be considered as *works made for hire* [author's emphasis], the property of Marvel Entertainment Group."[6]

There was the sense of artists as "hired hands."

Wally Wood, in his EC glory days, presented "My World" in *Weird Science* #22, a manifesto illustrated with primordial jungles, gleaming cities of the future, rocket ships in space, terrible wonders of alien worlds—visions of the strange, beautiful, and violent. The final panel showed a smiling young man at a drawing board, a cigarette dangling from his lips, looking at the reader and declaring, "My world is what I chose to make it. My world is yesterday . . . or today . . . or tomorrow. . . . For my world is the world of science-fiction . . . conceived in my mind and placed upon paper with pencil and ink and brush and sweat and a great deal of love. For I am a science-fiction artist. My name is Wood."

Wood's career ranged from EC and *Mad* to Marvel and DC; his creations included *T.H.U.N.D.E.R. Agents* for Tower Comics and *witzend*. The National Cartoonists Society, among others, had honored him. Wood's page rate was $38 at EC, and he earned the highest rate in the business—$200 a page—at *Mad*.[7]

But Wood was treated like another hired hand. His work was in practically every edition of a series of *Mad* reprint paperbacks licensed between EC and New American Library's Signet Books, but he never received royalties. Wood didn't own *T.H.U.N.D.E.R. Agents*. Years later, with serious health problems, Wood had no health plan or pension. "By now, [Wood had] seen how the industry used and discarded people just like him," Michael T. Gilbert writes.

"I'm through with comics—for other people, anyway," Wood declared in 1978, three years before he ended his life. "All I know is comic artists have been ripped off for so long they don't even know they HAVE rights. No medical care, no retirement benefits, no reprint money. . . . I think everyone gets into the business because they love it, and somewhere along the line, when they're wised up, find themselves trapped in it, too old to start a new career. . . . Everyone in the business has given away ideas for page rates, which then become the property of the company."[8]

Bill Finger struggled, writing comics for the page rate until his death. He wrote a couple episodes of the *Batman* TV show, while Bob Kane reportedly negotiated a huge fee. In the early seventies, Finger met Kane in Central Park and they talked about the past. Finger, who looked "peaked" to Kane, confessed he never met his potential. "I had to agree," Kane recalled. "Bill could have become a great screen writer or perhaps the author of a best-seller instead of hacking out comic book stories anonymously. How sad—a great talent wasted."

Paul Levitz admired Bill Finger's work—in the days when scripts, like art, were tossed after publication, he snagged and kept a few Finger scripts to study. He was there for the veteran story-teller at the end. "I effectively wrote Bill Finger's last script as a young assistant editor. I let him take a check for two scripts when he was only able to deliver one. He passed away before being able to deliver the last one, so I had to deliver it."[9]

Finger died in New York, age sixty, on January 18, 1974. "Bill Finger was a contributing force to *Batman* right from the beginning," Kane acknowledged. "He was an unsung hero. . . . I often tell my wife, if I could go back fifteen years, before he died, I would like to say, 'I'll put your name on it now. You deserve it.'" Kane's excuse was, "I never had complete control over the *Batman* strip, and the editors placed increasing limits on what Bill and I could do."[10] Kane showed remorse, but not enough to fight for a posthumous credit for his partner.

There were a few successful comics creators who worked on their own terms. One was Dick Sprang. He met Bob Kane once, when they were introduced at 480 Lexington by the man who hired him, Whit Ellsworth. "We said hello, glad to meet you, and that was it," Sprang recalled. "We never met again or corresponded."

Sprang's dream was to keep working on *Batman*, but from untrammeled spaces out West.

> I dislike cities and crowds. My great love is exploring the remote canyons of the southwest, running its rivers in my own boat, and researching in the field the trails of the early western scientific and pioneer expeditions.
>
> As to my interpretation of a script, I was given complete autonomy. I had proved myself in this regard during my New York years. Whit Ellsworth told me early on that he and the other editors liked the way I interpreted a script, and they liked the fact that I always (barring drastic illness) got my work in

on time. He said that with these two attributes, I could rest assured that I could be a Batman artist for as long as I pleased, working from anywhere in the country that had a post-office. This was a solid fact; when I quit of my own volition, I had drawn the character for more than twenty-five years.[11]

Sprang began his freelancer's dream in the late 1940s after moving to Sedona, Arizona. He would first receive a script in the mail. If it was from the "superlative" Bill Finger, it might have reference images attached, or a note from editors Jack Schiff and Murray Boltinoff, or even Mort Weisinger if it was a *World's Finest* team-up involving Superman with Batman and Robin. Sprang did his pages, mailed them to New York, and before the arrival of the next script was off on a new adventure. His backcountry companions might include his wife, field guides, movie scouts, river pioneers, and others sharing his love of desolate places.

Sprang was particularly drawn to Glen Canyon, a 170-mile expanse of the Colorado River that was his "Brigadoon, a wonderland known only to a lucky few," he reflected. "We liked wild places. That's why we sought them out. We had a spirit of getting beyond the furtherest hill on the horizon to see what was there. It was as simple and uncomplicated as that."[12]

GENERATIONAL CHANGE

In the seventies writer Denny O'Neil and artist Neal Adams brought Batman back to his lone avenger roots after the lingering hangover of the campy TV show, establishing the foundation for a grittier Dark Knight in the comics and big-budget Warner movies to come. The reboot included the Joker, who had devolved from psycho killer to madcap prankster.

"The Joker's Five-Way Revenge!" in *Batman* #251 (September 1973) opens with Adams's sinister, wide-eyed Joker returning to Gotham City, laughing maniacally as he drives through the night

The Joker returns to Gotham as his old, maniacal self in this story by writer Denny O'Neil. Artist Neal Adams recalls their work on Batman was a creative statement, a return to a "more realistic, more gritty" Dark Knight.

"THE JOKER'S FIVE-WAY REVENGE!," BATMAN #251 (SEPTEMBER 1973), P. 1, ART BY NEAL ADAMS.

amid rain and lightning. O'Neil's text warns: "And from the greater dark of a past filled with evil . . . comes a terrifyingly familiar face! . . . There is death abroad this night!" This was the return of the psychotic mastermind of *Batman* #1 who left a joker playing card with victims whose faces were contorted into ghastly death grins from his lethal toxin.

"We all kind of got it," Adams concluded. "It was as if the memory of DC Comics went along with the statements that both Denny and I were making, that we want it to be more realistic, more gritty."

Paul Levitz puts the new beginning in the context of a medium becoming popularly accepted, no longer the target of book burners and censors. "The creative people had sort of spontaneously reacted to what both Denny and Neal were doing on their projects. . . . It was kind of a 'Declaration of Freedom and Intent.' It was, 'Oh, we can sign our names proudly to something.'" Levitz characterizes the revival as "a generational change. This was the moment of recovery from Wertham."

The shift included Bob Kane moving on. "Until that point, Kane's contract was still to produce a certain number of pages," Levitz explains. "And that was a major piece of how he was making money off Batman. And then about when the deal was renegotiated so that he got other financial benefits, he was allowed to sort of ride off into the sunset professionally." But Kane left behind his solo byline.

In the late seventies, when Levitz became editor of the *Batman* titles, DC began developing a more cohesive mythology for the Gotham crimefighter that would eventually include the whole of the DC universe. Levitz would play a major role, rising from manager of business affairs to vice president of operations to executive vice president. In 2002 he became president and publisher.

"I tried to pull the *Batman* books together in a way that had not been the case previously, with one official history, one official logic and mythology," Levitz explains.

In the later years I was one of a number of executives involved in the decisions as to where the company was going. But at no point in DC's history did I view myself as the font of creative direction for the company. I believe that would be a bad job description, certainly a bad one for me. I viewed my gig as defining the rules of the sandbox for each of the editorial leaders who led our various groups and imprints, that the different lines should reflect the creative views of the editors.

Part of my job in the mid-seventies was I took over files and records [from the old company controller]. I got to see a lot of artifacts, licenses for things like Jackie Gleason and Bob Hope [comic books], things for various litigations. A lot of creators in the field did not have access to any of the business information in the old days, when these were family companies. To some extent the bosses of this earlier generation were generally Jewish entrepreneurial guys prone to take every body-blow the business [dealt out], when it felt like the world was about to end—and some days it was very convenient to not pay people as much. A different world!

Around the same time, Michael Uslan was in law school and while working at DC also saw evidence of the fly-by-night nature of earlier pulp publishing. In the summer of 1972 he was told by former comics colorist and DC executive Sol Harrison to clean up the "DC Closet," a disorganized space crammed with corporate records, lawsuit materials and legal papers, cease and desist letters, ashcans, even a black-and-white George Reeves Superman suit. "Sol said I could take notes. I saw all the original papers on the takeover [of DC by Donenfeld], I learned that *Superman* #1 had three printings."

During the 1970s DC retained Mark Evanier to determine approximate dates of past publications. Outside of significant issues, notably Superman in *Action Comics*, it was difficult to determine a "run of the mill" title's publication dates from the 1930s and 1940s. Often, Evanier concluded, dates were "mere guesstimates" by the publisher, with scheduled dates of publication often varying based on printing and delivery delays and other factors.[13]

Young creators were coming into the business who had grown up with comics and superhero archetypes and mythology, and they would begin deconstructing and reshaping it. "When I first came to the USA in 1973, I came to New York to try to break into comics, completely unsuccessfully [at the time], but that's what I tried," Dave Gibbons reflects.

What I wanted to see was not the Empire State Building or the Statue of Liberty. I wanted to see the fire hydrants on the streets because [England] had nothing like that. I wanted to see the water towers on top of the downtown buildings because that's what Steve Ditko used to draw in *Spider-Man*. Later, when I came to do things like *Watchmen*, both me and

Alan [Moore] reflected this view we had of America as a kind of mythical place with things of wonder.

One of the things that was really attractive about American comic books, growing up in postwar England, was their color and vibrancy and sense of this rich consumer culture that was far more exciting than the culture we had, a kind of Babylon on the other side of the Atlantic Ocean. I was fascinated by the ads in the comics for things like Tootsie Rolls or the so-called footlockers full of [toy] soldiers. On family vacations in England we used to go to Norfolk, where there were a lot of US Air Force bases in the fifties and sixties, and I got to know some American kids, and they had lots of American comic books. So, there was the sense of this wonderful culture that was a step removed.

I was just at the prime age when the Silver Age started, when DC revived all those super heroic characters and Stan Lee and Jack Kirby created all the Marvel characters. It was a wonderfully exciting time to be a comic fan. To me, the cover of *Brave and Bold* #28, which was the first Justice League of America, with all these heroes piling into this giant starfish, was like the moment of the Big Bang and I was actually there for that.[14]

MARKET AND TECHNOLOGY

By the time artists like Gibbons and Moore were ready to work their magic, comic books were ready for sophisticated storytelling and adult themes, a creative advance largely made possible by a new "direct sales" market that encouraged independent publishers and innovations at the big publishers, with digital technology replacing machine-age production.

In Harry Donenfeld's era, a distribution network delivered titles to newsstands and grocery and department stores, with unsold copies fully returnable to the publisher. By the eighties there was synergy between the emerging direct-sales market and the rise of stores devoted to comics and related merchandising. The direct-sales market allowed retail orders of specific titles and quantities from a publisher at a lower price, but copies were not returnable. Distributors and retailers now had an incentive in pushing the titles they ordered, while unsold copies became the basis of a back-issue collectibles market.

One of America's first comics stores was the San Francisco Comic Book Company, a hole-in-the-wall storefront in San Francisco's Mission District opened in 1968 by comics collector Gary Arlington. The store became a focal point for the underground comix movement in the Bay Area and beyond, a countercultural reaction to mainstream superheroes and the Comics Code Authority.[15]

A milestone in nonmainstream comics, and a new front against the Comics Code, was Robert Crumb's *Zap Comix* #1, published in San Francisco in 1968, complete with a counterculture version of the CCA stamp. "I loved it when I saw on the first *Zap*, 'approved by the ghost writers in the sky,'" recalled Victor Moscoso, one of "the magnificent seven" *Zap* artists, as Crumb called them. "Fuck you, Comics Code Authority. . . . Now, since we were distributing through the head shops and the poster shops, we didn't have to deal with the normal system of distribution which DC, Marvel, and Archie comics had to deal with. They were subject to the Comics Code Authority. We did whatever we wanted to on our pages."[16]

Mainstream direct-sales comics stores would cater to every fandom interest, offering the latest from Marvel, DC, and a growing number of independent publishers—Pacific Comics, First Comics, Dark Horse, Eclipse, Image, and others—as well as vintage back issues, toys, and other merchandising. Most important, direct sales could circumvent the Comics Code, throwing off the shackles of censorship.

In 1982 Eclipse Enterprises presented *Destroyer Duck*, an anthropomorphic duck criminologist battling the ruthless Godcorp, Ltd.—its corporate motto, "Grab It All, Own It All,

Robert Crumb, along with a pregnant wife, sold the first issue of *Zap Comix* on street corners in San Francisco's Haight-Ashbury district. The self-published Crumb title soon attracted an all-star team of underground artists, including Victor Moscoso, who loved the subversive, "Approved by the Ghost Writers in the Sky" stamp in the upper right corner.

ZAP COMIX #1 (1967), COVER ART BY ROBERT CRUMB.

Drain It All," a stand-in for every company that ever abused an artist. There was no code stamp on the cover; instead a notice read: "Special Lawsuit Benefit Edition #1." Contributing artists, including Jack Kirby on the title story, provided work gratis to assist creator Steve Gerber's legal battle over ownership of Howard the Duck, a character he created for Marvel. "ECLIPSE ENTERPRISES has not only pioneered a new approach to creator's rights in comics (and thus attracted many talents who now refuse to work for the 'major' publishers), it has also demonstrated a *commitment* to the creators' share in the enterprise by publishing *Destroyer Duck* and *taking no profit for itself*," Gerber wrote, with emphasis. "Your goodwill, and that of the comics' creative community, are what Eclipse hopes to earn as a result."[17]

The mechanics of publishing—the four-color production process for photographing art, making production plates, rolling presses at printing plants—was also being transformed. In the late eighties, colorist Steve Oliff led a pioneering digital colorization effort on Marvel's Epic division English translation of Katsuhiro Otomo's *manga* (comics) masterpiece, *Akira*. First published in Japan in 1984 as a long-running black-and-white series, Marvel and Otomo wanted the English version in color. A prestige project, Oliff proposed doing the colorization on the computer. Marvel agreed, provided it looked good and wasn't too expensive.

Two days after Christmas 1987, Oliff received a Federal Express delivery that included an IBM 286 12mhz box with an AT&T Targa graphics board, the operating system and software, a monitor, and a "handmade heat diffuser to cool off the math co-processor." There was a one-page sheet of instructions.

Oliff uploaded discs of scanned black-and-white *Akira* art into his computer; three months later he downloaded the final colorized work to disc. "The system chugged like an old farm truck," Oliff recalled. "The software was buggy and the machine was erratic. It really needed that heat diffuser, because when it overheated (every day, some days many times a day), it froze, and I'd lose everything up to the last save."

Oliff and his "Olyoptics Computer Crew" worked on the serialization from 1988 into the mid-nineties. "I wanted *Akira* to look like nothing else," Oliff added. "I tried to do something new every issue. I was rewarded for my efforts when I won the Harvey Award for best color in 1989 for *Akira*. The computer age was on. There was no turning back."[18]

In 1985 Mike Saenz created *Shatter* for First Comics, billed as "The First Computerized Comic." The art was created using a Macintosh, Apple's breakthrough personal computer released the previous year. "It took artist Michael Saenz to turn a nifty piece of hardware into the most revolutionary storytelling tool since the motion picture camera," editor Mike Gold wrote at the time.[19]

In 1990 Pepe Moreno's *Batman: Digital Justice* was created on a Macintosh II. Compared with the Mac used on *Shatter*, this computer was eight times faster and boasted an estimated sixty-four times the internal memory and four hundred times the storage capacity. "Pepe conceived and executed his work directly on the monitor with the electronic medium in mind," explained consultant Mike Gold. "He used a wide variety of tools to bring the book to life: CAD [computer aided design] programs, vector illustration, 3-D modeling, text effects, and such paint programs as Image Studio, Studio/8 and Photo Shop."[20]

The earliest born-digital comics like *Shatter* and *Digital Justice* used computers to create content for print media. The next breakthrough was using the electronic medium to create and distribute digital comics. Dave Gibbons was an early convert, having used digital lettering and coloring tools for years. For Gibbons it "felt instinctive" to draw on a tablet and see the image on his computer screen.

On a computer you don't have to get a brush and black things in—you click on the "paint bucket" [application] and it fills with black. One time I was drawing and I'd filled in an area with black. I rotated the screen to draw something else. I put my arm down, and said, "Oh, shit!" I pulled my arm back because

I thought I'd smudged it, which is impossible, of course. But it was that level of distinctiveness and naturalness. . . . I've spent [so much time] with pens that didn't work because the ink was clogged up, getting things lost in the mail. You don't need that. You want to focus on the creativity. Anything that helps you tell the story is a good thing.[21]

TRANSFORMATION

In the early 1970s another season of cyclical change was under-way at DC. *Superman* #233 (January 1971) was announced as "A Return to Greatness." Superman was no longer vulnerable to kryptonite, and Clark Kent had left print media to become a TV broadcaster for the Galaxy Broadcasting System, a corporation headed by megalomaniacal Morgan Edge. Denny O'Neil and Neal Adams injected new energy not only into Batman but also into a Green Lantern and Green Arrow team-up that addressed social issues—the watchword was "relevance"—while writer Len Wein and artist Bernie Wrightson introduced a modern monster in *Swamp Thing*.

The Nixon administration asked Stan Lee to do an antidrug series, and Marvel responded with the story arc of *Amazing Spider-Man* #96–98 (May–July 1971), which did *not* receive the Comics Code stamp of approval—the code's draconian rules forbid even *mentioning* drugs. But times were changing, and the code would become increasingly irrelevant.

But the biggest change came in 1976 in the executive suites, when Jenette Kahn became DC's publisher, one of the era's rare female executives. It was a historic moment in the male-dominated comics world. "Kahn had never read Jack Liebowitz's playbook," Martin Pasko writes. "She didn't know you were sup-posed to tell people that the name of your company had been changed to National Periodicals because people like [Senator] Estes Kefauver thought comics were four-color Communists. She thought DC should be proud of what it was, and changed the company's name to what people had actually been calling it since 1937: DC Comics."[22]

The biggest change came as Kahn and her colleagues noted that although the mythology had been evolving, the medium itself had not. It was the same pulp publishing format and in its third decade of being ruled by the Comics Code. But a paradigm shift was coming. In France high production values and sophisticated storytelling were on display in the pages of *Metal Hurlant*, a glossy, adult science-fiction comic that in 1977 was translated into English and released in the United States as *Heavy Metal*.

There was emerging awareness of creator rights, including treating artwork as an artist's property. Kahn declared, "The return of artwork is an artist's inalienable right." In 1978 DC contractually guaranteed artists the return of their work and payment for artwork damaged or lost under the publisher's care. Putting it all in context, Michael Uslan recalls tours of Marvel and DC where original art was chopped up and distributed as souvenirs (although fans like Uslan weren't content on leaving with anything but complete pages). "I once asked Joe Simon whatever happened to the art for *Captain America* #1, and he laughed and said, 'Michael, I think we used it to clean up the ink blots, put our coffee cups on, put out our cigars and cigarettes.' After [pages] came back from the engraver, it was on to the next thing. Nobody thought it had any value, except for a few, like Joe Kubert, who asked for the pages back."

Paul Levitz, who has donated cartons of his scripts to the growing comics collection at Columbia University, adds that writers, too, were guilty of trashing a script when its usefulness was over. Levitz certainly did not hang on to "research tools" such as outline notes and "legal pad scribblings." The archives of Bill Finger, Wally Wood ("Wood was legendary for his archives," Levitz says), and others were usually lost or thrown out. It began changing in the 1970s when it became industry practice to return art to creators and a subsequent market developed in original art. "In the earlier days it was a way of making a living, it wasn't art with a capital 'A,'"

The adult comics storytelling of France's *Metal Hurlant* got its American version in *Heavy Metal.*

Levitz notes. "There's a famous story on Eisner's *Spirit*, that they used the pages of original art to separate and protect the printing plates because the metal in the plates made them more valuable than the artwork."[23]

It was also clear that creators could no longer give away their creations. Kahn could relate—between graduating college and coming to DC, she helped create three magazines but was denied an ownership share in the most successful, a "bitter loss," she later wrote. "I shared the artists' and writers' indignation at what were considered to be the comic book industry's feudal conditions and felt morally bound to change them," she wrote. "With Paul Levitz and Joe Orlando, my two most valued colleagues, we set out to do just that."

"Collectively, we understood that our market was changing," Levitz adds.

In marketing terms you would define it as comic book's product life cycle shifting. The original product that was the comic book in America was ubiquitously available, low priced, [a] casual purchase, largely entertainment for children, and was suddenly being replaced by something you would define as a "shopping good," something you had to go out of your way to get. So the audience was going to be older, was going to have a more sophisticated point of view of what they wanted and perhaps, we thought, be willing to pay more for a better product.... We believed we were moving into an era where credits would be more important, star power with the creators more relevant, and we took a lot of steps to prepare ourselves for that. We developed the first really broad royalty program in the business to align the creator's interest with ours. We looked at how to build that new distribution system to funnel a lot of money through to the retail environment to try and make it healthy and sophisticated. We looked into better printing and production methods, and that was one of the things that came into being with *Camelot 3000*.[24]

The twelve-part *Camelot 3000*, released in 1982, was DC's first "maxiseries"; the first issue cover was emblazoned: "The Time Has Come." The series still had the print ads comics always carried—issue #1 spots included the Lego Expert Builder Series, BubbleYum bubble gum, and Life Savers candy—but it was printed on higher-grade Baxter paper. The story, by writer Mike Barr and artist Brian Bolland, set the popular King Arthur legend in a future imperiled by invaders from outer space and featured an interracial and interspecies Round Table. Sir Tristan was a man trapped in a woman's body, King Arthur a cuckold, and a gunslinging US president bore an uncanny resemblance to Ronald Reagan.

"Distributing the series solely through the direct market, rather than through the traditional newsstand market meant that it was not subject to approval by the Comics Code Authority," Barr notes, "which led to such innovations as Sir Tristan, a character who could not have appeared in a Code comic at that time. That said, having added a transsexual knight, lesbianism, incest and various other

Code-breaking plot points, I felt I had pushed the envelope about as far as it would go at the time. . . . In many ways CAMELOT 3000 was like a first child for DC, in that the company learned valuable lessons . . . which would come in handy for later offspring."[25]

Kahn concluded of *Camelot 3000*, "The specter of newsprint still haunted it. We were seized with what our comics might look like on that glistening stock [for *Metal Hurlant*], how nuanced and compelling our artwork could be if realized with the telling subtleties and gradations of paint instead of mechanical color. That world was thousands of miles away, but it was our future."[26]

CHANGING THE RULES

Kahn saw creators' rights and innovative publishing like *Metal Hurlant* as "touchstones . . . [that] laid the groundwork for a new comic book landscape." She looked to artist/writer Frank Miller, who broke into comics at Gold Key in 1978 and had done innovative work on *Daredevil* for Marvel, as one of the "key architects" of a potential renaissance. When she took a lunch meeting with Miller, DC's creators' rights policies had been in place for five years, and Kahn felt the company had been true to its principles. In what she hoped was an atmosphere of trust, she offered Miller a dream scenario—if he could create any kind of comic book, what would it be? Better still, she promised to make it happen. Miller began musing about a *ronin*, a masterless samurai, when Kahn interrupted—as a devotee of Japanese samurai films she knew what *ronin* meant. From there they began discussing story ideas "with the happy fervor of two zealots sharing the same faith," she recalled. Miller's story, *Rōnin*, echoes the spirit of feudal Japan as a disgraced samurai on a quest for honor navigates a future of sentient computers in a dystopian New York.

The first step was having Paul Levitz break down costs for glossy paper stock and consider all production issues necessary for a new type of comic book. In the end, Kahn recalled, they got everything except the cover spine—that came later, with Miller's *The Dark Knight Returns*. DC committed to a direct-market release for *Rōnin*. The assigning of copyright was the final hurdle. Kahn later wrote:

> [Copyright] was the last bastion of the comic book companies' dominance and for that reason tremendously symbolic. Frank used his cachet to make owning the copyright a condition of writing and drawing RONIN and in doing so helped change the balance of power between comic book companies and talent. . . . With RONIN, Frank ushered in a new era of comics, setting the standard not just for a new kind of storytelling and full color art, but for creators' rights as well. . . . In the process, he demonstrated that the direct market . . . would support quality and innovation and make other works possible.[27]

"It changed the rules," Miller reflected in 1985. "It showed me that comics have endless possibilities. I'd like to think of *Ronin* as the first of a new kind of comic book that will begin to appear more often. I had to adapt my writing and drawing styles for the improved format. The primary difference was that on the better paper the coloring became a vital part of the story. The tones that colorist Lynn Varley created for *Ronin* are much more subtle and compelling than anything that could be achieved in the standard formats."[28]

When the first of six *Rōnin* installments appeared, without a single advertisement or the Comics Code stamp, the publishing information included "Copyright © 1983 by Frank Miller Inc." The series had back cover blurbs, with *Camelot 3000* author Mike Barr's review best summing up the breakthrough: "Comics have recently taken great leaps in printing and production values, yet remain caught in an editorial stasis. Frank Miller's *Rōnin* is the first comic to fully utilize—as opposed to exploit—the editorial freedoms open to it. . . . With *Rōnin*, I have seen the future of comics, and it works."[29]

THE KIRBY PETITION

But while a creator-driven future seemed on the horizon, there were still messy creative battles. Michael Dean, writing in the *Comics Journal*, observes that DC "had gradually come a long way toward improving its relations with creators," contractually stipulating return of artwork in 1978 and providing a "small share" of reprint royalties. Marvel followed DC's example for royalties and return of artwork, although artists still signed a one-page release. Irene Vartanoff had begun cataloguing a Marvel warehouse full of haphazard stacks of envelopes stuffed with original art, many pages of which had been disappearing out of that warehouse and other storage venues and often ending up for sale at comics conventions and elsewhere.

In 1984 a one-page release for return of Marvel pages stipulated the work had been for hire and Marvel owned worldwide copyright. But when Jack Kirby asked for the return of his estimated eight thousand Marvel pages, he was offered only eighty-eight pages and presented with an onerous four-page agreement binding himself, his heirs, and their representatives. The document stipulated that the release of the artwork acknowledged no claim to ownership, and it restricted the use of his art. One clause noted: "To the extent, if any, that all copyright rights and all related rights in and to the Artwork are not owned by Marvel . . . the Artist hereby irrevocably grants, conveys, transfers and assigns its entire worldwide rights, title and interest therein to Marvel."

Kirby would not sign. He wanted his art returned without conditions, but he faced long odds, as Janet Bode reported in a *Voice* article:

> Marvel, in fact, has a lot to protect: more than 500 worldwide licensing arrangements, games, action toys, home furnishings, apparel and the like; 250 half-hour TV episodes in production; and its normal, 40-odd, monthly titles that give it a

75 per cent share of the U.S. comic book market and a large piece of the international market. The books are translated into 16 languages and distributed in more than 25 countries.

Kirby's colleagues, including publishing executives, rushed to his support. A letter signed by Jenette Kahn, Dick Giordano, and Paul Levitz declared, "Jack Kirby is one of our industry's greatest innovators and contributors. We are all in his debt. His artwork, like that of all the hundreds of other artists who have received their pages back from the publishers, is his morally and by industry practice for the past twelve years." A 1986 "Kirby Petition" demanding Marvel return Kirby's art was signed by a Who's Who that included Neal Adams, C. C. Beck, Robert Crumb, Burne Hogarth, Harvey Kurtzman, Frank Miller, Diana Schutz, Julie Schwartz, Jerry Siegel, Art Spiegelman, Dave Stevens, and Gary Trudeau.

Marvel dropped its demands, substituting a short form rewritten to accommodate Kirby. "Jack got just about everything he wanted," Greg Victoroff, Kirby's attorney, told the *Comics Journal*. The artwork returned to Kirby in 1987 amounted to 1,900 pages, far short of the artist's output, but a vast improvement on the original offer.

But Kirby *still* had to sign Marvel's "work-for-hire" release.

There was a twist in the battle for Kirby's art. Mark Evanier told the *Comics Journal* the bitter fight truly began when the exasperated artist told Marvel they were vulnerable to copyright claims. "The [initial four-page] Kirby release was apparently a result of Marvel's heightened concerns with respect to Kirby's numerous, and now famous, creations," Evanier and others added in a subsequent legal brief. The irony was that Kirby was bluffing. "It was the only way he could get their attention," Evanier explains. "And somebody at Marvel over-reacted." In the early 1970s Kirby had decided that "financially and emotionally" he was not prepared for a marathon copyright battle.[30]

But Marvel *was* vulnerable. Kirby had worked on almost all

of the star heroes of the Marvel pantheon and had coequal billing with Stan Lee on the seminal stories. And under the copyright law of the day, it was arguable that Kirby, working without
contract and as a freelancer, was the creator of those valuable
properties.

CHAPTER 19

EVOLUTIONARY IMPERATIVE

Like traditional folk tales, [superhero sagas] must evolve. If they don't, they may become irrelevant to the real world they mirror, and thus lose their power to satisfy and amuse; they risk degenerating into mere curiosities instead of remaining vital fiction.

DENNY O'NEIL
"Postscript," *Batman: A Death in the Family* (November 1988)

There's no type of fiction that comes close to comics for the layers of storytelling. This is mythology, but it's not mythology that's refined slightly over time. It's mythology that's constantly evolving.

AXEL ALONSO
quoted in "Modern Marvel," *New York Times*, March 27, 2011

WATCHMEN AND *THE DARK KNIGHT*

In 1983, the year of *Rōnin*, writer and artist Howard Chaykin produced *American Flagg!*, one of the early titles from First Comics. Set in 2031, the story features Reuben Flagg, a former TV star (he played vice cop Mark Thrust of the Sexus Rangers), who is drafted into the Plexus Rangers, a force for the Plexus Corporation that rules America after a series of upheavals forces the government to relocate to Mars. In a retrospective essay, novelist Michael Chabon observes that although Chaykin wasn't the first to create a dystopian American future, "no one had ever crammed those elements all together before, in quite the way that Chaykin did here: the post-nuclear, post-global-collapse, post–Cold War, corporate-controlled, media-overloaded, sex-driven, space-traveling . . . freak-o-rama that was to be life in 2031."

Similarly, Chaykin was not the first to make inventive use of word balloons, panel arrangements, and parallel narratives, but his unique storytelling technique inspired others. It is hard to imagine, Chabon declares, *The Watchmen* and *The Dark Knight Returns* without *American Flagg!*

Watchmen, a twelve-part DC series from Alan Moore and Dave Gibbons, ran from 1986 into 1987. It was a publishing event, and critical acclaim included a subsequent listing on *Time* magazine's "100 Best English-Language Novels since 1923." The original idea was to take superheroes that DC had recently acquired from the Charlton Comics Group—such as Blue Beetle (a Fox Comics creation from 1939), Captain Atom, and the Question—and place them in a self-contained world. But DC editor Dick Giordano, formerly an executive editor at Charlton, had a "paternal affection" for them and "really didn't want to give his babies to the butchers, and make no mistake about it, that's what it would have been," writer Moore explained in 1986. "Our intention was to show how super-heroes could deform the world. . . . Just their presence there would make the difference."

Giordano suggested they create their own superheroes, a decision Gibbons later acknowledged was "hugely liberating. . . . We could now create our own embodiments of these basic types. . . . More importantly, their world would be fashioned to fit one of the basic premises of Alan's story, that human society itself would be deformed by the presence of a superpowered being."

The key example is Dr. Manhattan, a scientist accidentally de-atomized in a lab test chamber, who reappears as a godlike, blue-skinned being capable of rearranging atomic structure. "He doesn't take over the country or make people subservient to him, but just his presence there makes everything begin to change. . . . If you equate Dr. Manhattan with the atomic bomb, the atom bomb doesn't take over the world, but by being there it changes everything," Moore added.

The new generation of *Watchmen* costumed heroes includes nocturnal crusader Nite-Owl, who with the costumed Silk Spectre takes the flying "Owlship" out of mothballs and into combat; the vigilante Rorschach, who wears a mask of ever-changing Rorschach-test patterns; the Comedian, a flag-waving killer who fancies himself the American Dream personified; and brooding billionaire Ozymandias, who has a terrifying plan for making peace on Earth.

As Moore and Gibbons prepared to create *Watchmen*, Gibbons had "an epiphany" that it

> was not a super-hero book as such, but rather a work of science fiction, an alternate history. Accordingly, I was particularly determined to make *Watchmen* look different from super-hero comics of the time and proposed the nine-panel grid that is the backbone of its visual narrative. That lent it a classic look, harking back to the Spider-Man work of Steve Ditko, the EC comics of Harvey Kurtzman, and the style of many European comics. It also allowed Alan a very precise control over pacing and the juxtaposition of story elements.[1]

Watchmen is set in the era of its release (the late eighties), but in an alternate reality where an elderly Richard Nixon is US president. A backstory explores the absence of Dr. Wertham and censorious government committees, resulting in the ascendance of EC Comics. The public *fears* superheroes like Dr. Manhattan, but because superheroes are working for US interests, government propaganda officially promotes superhero comics as "all-American entertainment," as Moore explained in 1987. "Basically, the government was giving a clean bill of health to comics and even endorsing them. . . . Consequently, with the super-heroes in the world of *Watchmen* generally being objects of fear, loathing, and scorn, the main super-heroes quickly fell out of popularity in comic books, as we suggest. Mainly, genres like horror, science fiction, and piracy, particularly piracy, become prominent—with EC riding the crest of the wave."

The irony of EC pirate titles dominating the mainstream was expanded on with a *Watchmen* side feature ostensibly reprinting a chapter of a 1984 book, *Treasure Island Treasury of Comics*, with knowing alternate universe references to stellar EC pirate artist Joe Orlando being lured to DC Comics: "Orlando, having been successfully tempted away from his well-received run of 'Sargasso Sea Stories' in EC's *Piracy* [EC's actual "New Directions" title] by National editor Julius Schwartz, was regarded as a star amongst pirate artists, and a prize catch."[2]

Despite the movement towards creators' rights, the *Watchmen* copyright was held by DC Comics, Inc., with all characters "trademarks of DC Comics, Inc." In an *Atlantic* article recounting struggles of comic creators, Asher Elbein notes, "And who can forget Alan Moore, who produced the seminal graphic novel *Watchmen* under an agreement that the rights would revert to him when it went out of print, only to find that DC had no intention of allowing that to happen."

Alan Moore once attended a comic book convention in Grenoble, France, and discussed the vagaries of creation with Harvey Kurtzman, then suffering from Parkinson's disease. "I remember that he said that *Watchmen* was 'a damn fine piece o' work,' and I know that it's one of those memories that I'll still be clutching at pathetically when I'm old and spent," Moore reflected.

I remember that he seemed surprised when I told him that *Watchmen* wouldn't exist if he hadn't skewed my perception of the super-hero genre with works like "Superduperman." He looked amazed, almost bashful, unbelievably enough, and said, "Well how about that?" . . . I told him about working for DC, how you know they're going to end up owning your creations going in the door, but how at the time you assume,

(Left) Accidentally locked into a test chamber and bombarded by "particle cannons," Jonathan Osterman is seemingly obliterated—until he manifests as the godlike being they call Dr. Manhattan in the *Watchmen* saga. (Right) Dr. Manhattan initially serves as a tool of US interests; he's shown here routing the Communist Vietcong in Vietnam. In the *Watchmen* world "superheroes" are figures of fear, not beloved public icons.

WATCHMEN #4 (OF 12) (DECEMBER 1986), P. 10, AND P. 20, PANEL 1, ART BY DAVE GIBBONS.

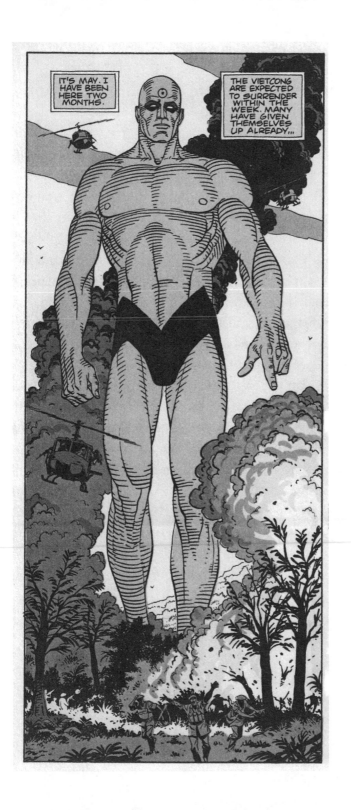

with the total folly of youth, that it isn't important; that you will always have an inexhaustible supply of good ideas. He nodded. "That's true. What you said about assuming that you'll always have ideas, that's very true."

Although Frank Miller's *Rōnin* was copyrighted in his name, DC similarly held copyright and trademarks on Miller's breakthrough Batman saga of 1986. *The Dark Knight Returns* was announced in a house subscription ad featuring Miller art of Batman standing alongside a lithe blonde Girl Wonder: "Batman and Robin as You've Never Seen Them Before[:] Frank Miller, Klaus Janson, and Lynn Varley at their gritty best." This was a "new graphic novel format," a forty-eight-page, square bound, four-issue set printed on high-quality paper and not available through newsstands, with only 1,200 copies available by subscription.[3] The notice had the feel of something special, even important, in popular culture.

In Miller's story an older Bruce Wayne comes out of crime-fighting retirement to retake a decaying Gotham City, whose mean streets are ruled by violent freaks called the Mutants. Robin is a girl, the Joker a mass murderer. Two-Face, former district attorney Harvey Dent (who had half his face disfigured by acid), is healed but remains emotionally scarred. An unnamed President Reagan flexes military might—and superhero power—on behalf of America: "We've got God on our side . . . or the next best thing, anyway," the president states, referring to Superman, who gives old friend Bruce Wayne a warning: If "somebody in authority" orders him to bring in the Dark Knight, he will. "When that happens, Clark, may the best man win," Bruce sneers.

In *Dark Knight* Miller burrowed into psychological depths where rarely even a spade of earth had been turned since Bill Finger revealed the tragic secret of how Batman came to be nearly a half century earlier. It was also a historic take on Superman— the champion of "Truth, Justice, and the American Way" was not a free, altruistic agent but was weaponized to serve his adopted nation's strategic interests.

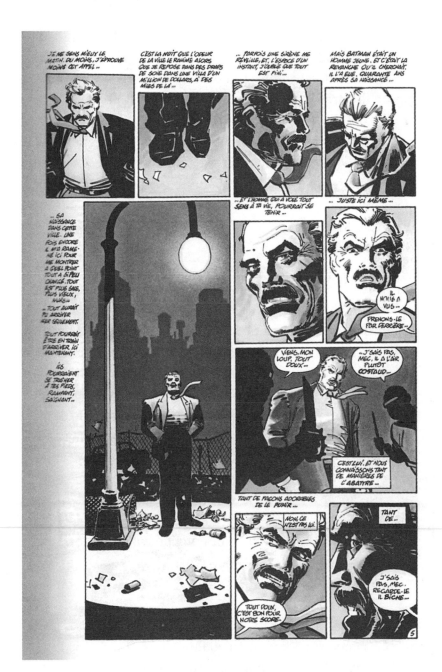

In this French edition of Frank Miller's landmark *The Dark Knight Returns*, an older Bruce Wayne returns to the spot where he watched his parents being murdered during a holdup—and finds nothing has changed.

BATMAN I. LE RETOUR ET LE TRIOMPHE (1986), P. 5, PENCIL ART BY FRANK MILLER. DC COMICS, INC./AEDENA.

Exploring the deeper meanings behind superhero archetypes was a generational perspective, Gibbons says. "[Before us] a lot of illustrators had done comics to make money before they became magazine illustrators or fine artists; a lot of writers were writing this rubbish until they could write a screenplay or novel—but my generation, we *wanted* to do comics! So when we came into it in the sixties we brought all this excitement, all this knowledge, rather than the people in the forties and fifties who had never read comics growing up and it was just a job, providing cheap entertainment for kids."

Gibbons adds:

It's no coincidence that Alan Moore and I came up with *Watchmen* at more or less exactly the same time as Frank Miller came up with *The Dark Knight Returns* take on Batman. I think the characters by that time had become so familiar that people were beginning to get tired of them again; all the possible stories seemed to have been done and were being recycled. I suppose what we really did with *Watchmen* was to say, if these characters were real what would they be like? We came upon it as adults who knew the background, and we were doing it for the direct market, which by definition was for comic fans. We knew we didn't have to explain all the background about Nite-Owl having a cave full of gadgets—everybody got the Batman reference. We had our archetypal characters who related to things that people knew, so they knew what we were trying to subvert.[4]

From Batman's debut in 1939 it had taken almost a decade for the Gotham crime fighter to coalesce into the classic folklore figure recognized by even nonfans: the millionaire and his ward operating out of the Batcave underneath the ancestral manor, assisted by the loyal butler, complemented by the Batmobile and his crime-fighting tools, summoned to action by the Bat-signal shining from the roof of police headquarters. As Dick Sprang explains, not only a legion of artists but also Golden Age editors and writers, including Whitney Ellsworth, Jack Schiff, and "the outstanding Batman writer, Bill Finger," set the character's "permanent integrity."

> When recent drastic conceptual changes of Batman and Robin occurred under the hands of contemporary editors and artists, the character had become a legend so fixed in continuity that startlingly fresh visual and psychological changes were accepted by the more skeptical and cynical newer generation of readers with very little objection, although many old-time fans yearned for the image of the classical Batman.

Sprang, long retired when Miller's *Dark Knight Returns* was released, noted in 1988: "I admit this [Miller's Batman] image is more powerful and forbidding than our Golden Age image, and fits the anti-hero image. But having spent 25 years drawing the old Batman, I have a simple affection for our early depiction of the character. My opinion is personal and prejudicial."

Sprang concluded: "He had a special flavor. For me, he was vulnerable, unlike Superman. He could be overpowered, wounded, and thus identified with. The guy was human. . . . To the artist he wasn't just a dumb macho hero battling his way through a mob of dumb crooks. His super powers resided in the thrust of his intellect and athletic ability. He commanded respect as a wary and resourceful avenger looming out of the night."[5]

THE LAST SUPERMAN STORY

In the mid-1980s DC embarked on its ambitious makeover of a universe that had been inexorably expanding since Superman's Big Bang birth in 1938, generating characters and storylines from Golden Age to Silver Age to Bronze Age (considered to cover the years 1970–1985). Aligning nearly a half century of storytelling continuity was the challenge of *Crisis on Infinite Earths*, a twelve-part maxiseries by writer Marv Wolfman and artist George Pérez that ran from 1985 through 1986. It was the first comics "crossover," a storyline referenced in multiple titles. *Crisis* changes included the deaths of Supergirl and of the Barry Allen Flash (Allen's acolyte Wally West, "Kid Flash," accepts the mantle as the new Flash).

"A lot of things were changing in comics during the mid-1980s," notes comics writer/editor Paul Kupperberg. "The way things had been done for the previous fifty or so years had come under the scrutiny of a slew of creators who were finding new ways to do things." There was Miller's *The Dark Knight Returns* and Moore and Gibbons's *Watchmen*, revisionist takes on a classic character and the superhero mythology, respectively, while *Crisis* "was literally reshaping the DC universe itself," Kupperberg concludes, with the post-*Crisis* era offering "the perfect opportunity to revamp or relaunch a host of DC's top-tier heroes."[6]

First up was the seminal superhero, and the Superman canon as it was developed in nearly a half century came to a conclusion with a two-part story, "Whatever Happened to the Man of Tomorrow?" The tale began in *Superman* #423, cover-dated September 1986, and simultaneously concluded that same month in *Action Comics* #583. The two-part conclusion marked not only the end of the Superman continuity but also the demise of DC's two flagship titles, with editor Julie Schwartz closing out his editorial supervision of the Man of Tomorrow.

Schwartz had approached Jerry Siegel about writing the "last" Superman story, but although he was eager to do it, there were "legal problems," Schwartz recalled, that couldn't be resolved in time. The writer selected was an obvious choice—Alan Moore, who was already stretching the bounds of the mythology. For the first part, appearing in the "historic last issue" of *Superman*, the talent included Curt Swan's pencils being inked by George Pérez; the *Action* conclusion teamed Swan with Kurt Schaffenberger.

The story is told through the memories of Lois Lane, as told to an inquiring *Planet* reporter. The story marks a final, bizarre team-up of Lex Luthor and Brainiac, who die at the conclusion. Other perennial antagonists appear and die, including Bizarro, but so do Jimmy Olsen, Lana Lang, and even Krypto the Superdog. At the end it is revealed that the onslaught of Superman's greatest foes has been orchestrated by the magical being from the fifth dimension, Mr. Mxyzptlk. This isn't the mischievous imp of old—the character is revealed in the terrifying form of a dark sorcerer bored with eternity, who dedicates millennium-length mood swings to good, evil, or indifference. In their final encounter, Superman kills the being. Having broken his most solemn vow to never kill, Superman exposes himself to gold kryptonite, which ends his Kryptonian ability to process Earth's yellow sunlight into super powers. The story concludes with the possibility that a powerless Superman has changed his civilian identity and, having married Lois and started a family, is enjoying a happy retirement.

Alan Moore declared his intention at the outset in *Superman* #423: "This is an Imaginary Story. . . . Aren't they all?"

In an essay ending the two-parter in *Action* #583, consulting editor E. Nelson Bridwell concludes: "And now we come to an end—and a beginning. This issue's story didn't happen—yet it gives a happy ending to our years with the Metropolis Marvel. New hands will be at work on the first and greatest of the superheroes. We'll see a lot of changes. And yet, deep down, he'll still be the same hero Jerry and Joe gave us in *Action* #1."

Superman's renewal began with a six-issue *Man of Steel* miniseries, leading into the 1987 launch of a new *Superman* #1 series continuity led by writer/artist John Byrne. "In one of the boldest moves in comic book history, DC decided that its most famous icon was in need of a makeover," a DC history records. "The idea was simple. Keep the core themes and elements of Superman's character that had made him popular . . . but trim around the edges by removing the outdated concepts and sometimes preposterous situations. The result was a streamlined new Man of Steel that stayed true to the character's personality, but was tailor-made for a modern audience."[7]

In the aftermath of *Crisis*, Wonder Woman was also "scheduled for an overhaul," George Pérez recalled. The Amazonian princess had already gone through her own regenerative cycles. In 1968 Denny O'Neil stripped Wonder Woman of her powers and remade Diana Prince into a modern woman wearing contemporary fashions. The makeover only lasted twenty-five issues—even *Ms.* magazine publisher Gloria Steinem protested the loss of a feminist icon (one featured on the July 1972 first issue of *Ms.*, complete in bustier and star-spangled tights).

Pérez inquired about an artist for the post-*Crisis* Wonder Woman, but no one had stepped up—so he did. Pérez began working with editor Karen Berger and writer Greg Potter, with Jenette Kahn and Gloria Steinem providing "a feminist perspective that helped direct this series," Pérez said. Changes included ending the guise of Diana Prince. "The turning point, however, really came when Karen, Greg and I agreed that what made Wonder Woman unique was both her feminism and the Amazon legends with their roots in Greek Mythology. This mythical and mystical angle definitely made Diana something other than a 'female Superman.'"

"Along with her colleagues Superman and Batman, Wonder Woman formed a triumvirate of the longest-lasting super heroes in American comic books, and that record continues today," Les Daniels wrote in 2000. "Nobody else even comes close."[8]

FOR MATURE READERS

In 1980 Marvel came out with *Epic Illustrated* and in 1982 its Epic Comics imprint began releasing titles *without* Comics Code approval. In 1989 DC began its alternative Piranha Press imprint (marked "For Mature Readers" and not code-approved). Star creative teams descended further into the bottomless depths of Batman's dark mythology, with projects including *Batman: Year One*, by Frank Miller and artist David Mazzucchelli (1986–1987), the one-shots *Batman: The Killing Joke*, by Alan Moore and Brian

Bolland (1988), and *Arkham Asylum*, by Grant Morrison and Dave McKean (1989).

In 1986 Kahn mailed a form letter to DC freelancers announcing what, for some, was a controversial move—editorial guidelines as to what content would be suitable "for mature readers." DC had shown its willingness to bypass the Comics Code

> when your material warranted it. . . . As a result, we are poised on the brink of a new era in comics. This year, it is undisputably [*sic*] clear that comics are no longer just for kids. . . . If a 10-year old child picked up *Swamp Thing*, his or her parents would have a right to be concerned, even disturbed. The work deals with mature themes . . . so we labeled it "Sophisticated Suspense." . . . We believed that the covers on *Watchmen* and *Dark Knight* signaled their levels of sophistication. We didn't always label, but we always had sensitivity to mature material.[9]

Howard Chaykin's four-part DC-licensed adaptation of the pulp avenger *The Shadow* got the "for mature readers" cover stamp in 1986. Chaykin's three-part *Blackhawk*, published by DC in 1987 in the new square-bound format reserved for prestige projects, was full of political nuance, violence, sex—"Yes, I got Blackhawk laid," Chaykin admitted—but did not get the "mature readers" notice.

In a subsequent interview Chaykin said he'd gotten no complaints about *Blackhawk*. Before the sales success of *The Shadow* and Miller's *Dark Knight*, DC considered them "dogs" commercially, in Chaykin's opinion. "I don't like mainstream and mass-market comic books very much. . . . I am, unfortunately, also very much in love with genre fiction. . . . I think the real intention of the ratings system was to put us in our places. . . . I did not take [the ratings] as personally as those of my friends who seemed to feel that it was a conspiracy to de-nut them."

Paul Levitz recalls the labeling debate as not affecting the direction of comics, calling it a "blip in the late eighties." There certainly was no interest in an industry-wide rating system analogous to the motion picture rating system. "It made a lot of noise for about a minute and a half," he says. "A number of the important leading creators at the time were very much against that sort of labeling. It's a legitimate debate, whether [a rating system] was a necessary step, but in the end [creators] decided it didn't hamper them. The marketplace evolved over time; there began to be ways to easily understand the difference between what was a children's comic and what was not a children's comic."

A renaissance in storytelling and format was underway across the comics spectrum. Some creators evoked the spirit of pulp fiction and matinee cliffhangers, producing genre pieces about primordial lost worlds and fantasy kingdoms. Artist P. Craig Russell's career began in the 1970s, and his work included adapting novelist Michael Moorcock's sword-and-sorcery series *Elric of Melniboné*, the fairy tales of Oscar Wilde, the mythical world of Robert E. Howard's Conan the Barbarian, and classic opera, notably Richard Wagner's *The Ring of the Nibelung*.

In 1981 writer Mike Baron and artist Steve Rude unleashed *Nexus* in Capital Comics (followed by First Comics and Dark Horse Comics), a hero of the future who receives super powers from the Merk, an alien entity; in exchange Nexus must periodically kill a mass murderer, enduring the nightmarish dreams of the suffering victims until he executes judgment.

In 1982 artist Dave Stevens went back to the sunny Los Angeles of 1938—Superman's birth year—for *The Rocketeer*, a story about a young daredevil aviator with a gorgeous pin-up model girlfriend who discovers a rocket pack and, outfitted with a streamlined art deco helmet, enters a world of high-flying intrigue. "All I wanted to do was insinuate this little, tiny story into the minds of the comics reading public and leave the impression that the reader had come across something that might have been printed fifty years ago, divorced completely from anything current," Stevens explained. "I wanted to build a feeling around the Rocketeer character that was sort of Paul Bunyanesque, that was Americana, a grassroots hero

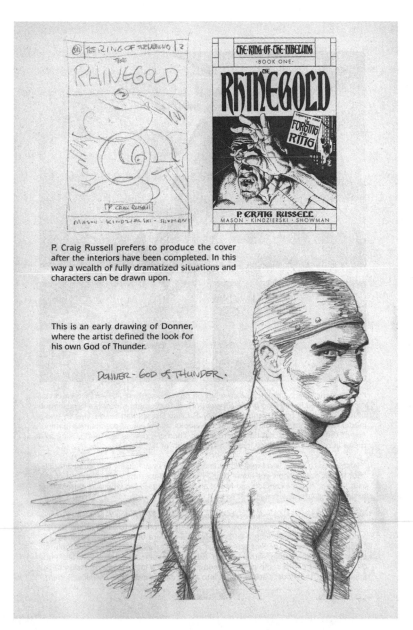

P. Craig Russell prefers to produce the cover after the interiors have been completed. In this way a wealth of fully dramatized situations and characters can be drawn upon.

This is an early drawing of Donner, where the artist defined the look for his own God of Thunder.

DONNER - GOD OF THUNDER.

P. Craig Russell was among many comics artists bringing an artistic renaissance to the medium. This excerpt from a "Sketch Book" section of Russell's epic adaptation of *The Ring of the Nibelung* provides insights into the artist's creative process. Such behind-the-scenes creative secrets have become a common feature of comics, particularly in deluxe graphic novel editions.

THE RING OF THE NIBELUNG, BOOK ONE: THE RHINEGOLD, CHAPTER 2: "THE FORGING OF THE RING, MARCH 2000," FEATURE OF DONNER, P. 9. DARK HORSE COMICS, INC.

that really didn't exist. That's what a myth is, something bigger than life that really isn't the guy; it's just something that happens when the public finds out about it, takes hold of it and runs with it. It makes the character more than he could have been on his own—an icon."

Mary Wollstonecraft Shelley's *Frankenstein* was presented in 1983 as "A Marvel Illustrated Novel," with Shelley's text complemented by Berni Wrightson's fantastical illustrations. (The novel is in the public domain, but the art is copyrighted in Wrightson's name.)

By the 1980s American comics were welcoming in the world. In 1987 First Comics began its English-language run of writer Kazuo Koike's and artist Goseki Kojima's manga series *Lone Wolf and Cub.* That same year, Eclipse Comics, based in rural Forestville, California, introduced such manga titles as *Mai: The Psychic Girl* by writer Kazuya Kudo and artist Ryoichi Ikegami.

Xenozoic Tales began publishing in 1987 though Kitchen Sink Press. *King Kong* fan Mark Schultz's saga conjures a world post–ecological cataclysm where humans emerge from subterranean shelters to a planet repopulated by strange creatures and dinosaurs of prehistory; the ensuing struggle for survival is seen through the eyes of seductive scientist Hannah Dundee and rugged man-of-all trades Jack Tenrec.

In 1990 Eclipse published Jon J. Muth's four-part *M*, a prestige, square-back adaptation of German director Fritz Lang's disturbing 1931 film of the same name about a whistling pedophilic serial killer. Muth felt the horrifying subject required "that gray area of ambiguity" of black-and-white photography. In that predigital era the photographic medium was as close as he could get to "objective imagery," but it still kept readers outside the story, he felt. In the tradition of classic illustrators and painters, Muth "cast" people as his characters, dressed in costume and posed in settings with props, for the photographic reference that inspired his artwork.

"I used silverpoint, literally drawing thousands of little lines with silver," Muth explained. "Then I added graphite, powdered charcoal applied with a brush, and pastel. In the final chapter, where the story reaches its climax, I worked in oil paint on prepared paper." Muth changed nothing in his photographic references—even if a photo was badly shot or blurry, he drew from it. While working in the photorealistic technique, he noticed something unexpected happening: "No matter what, if any, feeling the photograph elicited, when I duplicated a photograph by drawing it, the drawing extracted a different range of emotions than the photo. This happened though I tried to be as faithful to the photograph as possible. The overarching ambience in the book is one of grief and loss and longing. This was a discovery, and not by design."[10]

A DEATH IN THE FAMILY

Death was a rare and unwelcome intruder in the comics. Milton Caniff shook up the nation on October 16, 1941, when his brave female character, Raven Sherman, died in the lonely mountains of China in that day's installment of *Terry and the Pirates*. Years later, newspaper columnist Ray Orrock shared Caniff's memory of going to his office the day after Sherman's death. The elevator operator, who usually greeted the celebrated cartoonist with a cheery "good morning," was silent. When Caniff got off at his floor, the operator muttered, "Murderer!"[11]

Batman editor Denny O'Neil could relate. In 1988 he gave readers the power of life or death over Robin in the four-part "A Death in the Family" storyline in *Batman* #426–429. This was not the Boy Wonder of old—Dick Grayson had moved on as leader of the super group the Teen Titans—this was a *new* and controversial figure among fans, Jason Todd. Conversation in DC's offices dovetailed negative fan reaction to Todd and the idea of returning Batman to his lone-avenger roots. Thus was born what O'Neil called the "telephone experiment." *Batman* #427 ended with a Joker time bomb explosion seemingly killing the "Jason Todd"

Robin, but the inside back cover had this notice: "Robin will die because the Joker wants revenge, but you can prevent it with a telephone call." Between September 15 and 16, fans in the United States and Canada could call either of two telephone numbers: "The Joker fails and Robin lives" or "The Joker succeeds and Robin will not survive." O'Neil was ready with two endings for the fateful *Batman* #428.

"We received 10,614 calls," O'Neil reported. "The final tally: 5,271 for [Robin surviving], 5,343 against. Hail and farewell Jason Todd."

Robin, whatever his alter ego, had been integral to the Batman narrative for nearly a half century—one "Robin lives" vote was from O'Neil. Only seventy-two votes decided the character's fate, but the editor didn't expect the massive media coverage the stunt provoked—or being personally blamed for Robin's death. In a postscript for a paperback collection of the series, O'Neil wrote that for superheroes to stay relevant they had to keep evolving. "So, please consider the death of Jason Todd part of an occasionally bumpy process."[12]

O'Neil later reflected, "It changed my mind about what I do for a living. Superman and Batman have been in continuous publication for over half a century, and that's never been true of any fictional construct before. . . . They have become postindustrial folklore, and part of this job is to be the custodian of folk figures."[13]

BATMANIA II

Since he was eight, Michael Uslan had dreamed of writing a *Batman* story, and by the mid-seventies he had achieved it. In 1976 he was fresh out of law school and working at United Artists as a movie production attorney when he returned to his vow to bring a dark and serious Batman to the world. "For almost four years, I was networking like mad, learning how to produce, finance, and distribute motion pictures. I was getting the credentials I needed to go to Sol Harrison, who by then was president of DC, and say I want to buy the rights to Batman and make this dark and serious movie."

The success of *Superman: The Movie* showed the potential of superhero movies done seriously, and Uslan partnered with a Hollywood veteran that could make his Batman dream come true. Benjamin Melniker had been at MGM since 1939, and as an executive vice president and chairman of the studio's film selection committee he was involved in green-lighting such classics as *Ben-Hur* (1959), *Dr. Zhivago* (1965), and *2001: A Space Odyssey* (1968). He brought gravitas to the quest to negotiate a *Batman* option deal with DC Comics.

"I never thought at the time that comic books would be as dominant as they are today," Melniker recalled. "I remember meeting Michael in my office and he was so excited. . . . His sheer passion gave me the strong feeling it could be possible. When one goes in to make a deal on a character like *Batman* you know you're in a big deal. The negotiation was very substantial and took a long time to negotiate—paying $50,000 in 1979 for an option was a very substantial deal."

Lillian Uslan's adage to her sons—when you make a commitment, honor it and stick to it, no matter how difficult—was tested across the next decade. Uslan recalls a round of meetings in 1979 that he and Melniker took with big studio executives, striking out each time. They came to the last studio on their list, and the executive was interested—*if* they cast TV Batman Adam West. Uslan was crestfallen: the whole point was to make a movie about the grim avenger of old, not the campy TV show. Looking at Uslan, the executive added, "Son, it is better to have a movie than no movie at all."

"I just said no, no way," Uslan recalls. "After that meeting, Ben and I were sitting on a bench on the studio lot and I was just despondent. Then Ben says, 'It's ironic, Michael, that the final No came from you.' Then Ben said, 'You know what you are—you are Batman's Batman, you're his protector and defender. You have this commitment.' Ben was my dad's age and his sage counsel at that moment reenergized me, was an inspiration to keep going."[14]

Uslan and Melniker successfully brought their Batman option to the production company of powerhouse producers Jon Peters and Peter Guber. Screenwriters and potential directors came and went until 1988, when the producers brought aboard Tim Burton, a young director with a graphic visual style, and screenwriter Sam Hamm.

Warner Bros. would make the movie, with the synergistic groundwork between the studio and DC laid in the autumn of 1982, when Jenette Kahn met with a Warner team led by executive vice president Mark Canton. In a six-page follow-up letter to Canton, Kahn summarized her thoughts, reiterating her support for the villain being the Joker, a "bizarre genius" and master of chaos forming a "Yin/Yang duality" with Batman, the paragon of "perfect control." She added:

> A point which I made in the beginning of our meeting and which cannot be overly stressed is that our own library of Batman lore is often contradictory, irrelevant, and frequently includes not just the insipid and idiotic, but also the totally unpublishable (which, of course, never deterred us). Forty-three years of history is a lot to justify.
>
> Therefore, what's important to us at DC is not that the movie reconfirms an action that occurred in panel 4 page 16 of *Detective* 92 but rather that it embraces and in many cases expands upon the elements, tone, and direction that now guide us in producing over 1,200 pages of Batman material a year. Many of these components we have drawn from the earliest characterizations of Batman. Others we have added or rethought as times and tastes and even we ourselves have changed.

"Batman's mystique" was his lack of super powers and compelling alter ego, Kahn emphasized. Wayne was so wealthy he never worked—even Superman worked! "In his smoking jacket and silk ascot, with Alfred, his butler, anticipating every need, Bruce represented another world as mysterious and compelling as the Batman himself." His substantial inheritance did not diminish "the almost artistic purity of his drive. . . . [The] public Bruce Wayne persona is, in our opinion, as important to Batman as Clark's is to Superman . . . the dual identities reveal the true essence and poignancy of each character."

Kahn made the distinction that "Superman adopts the bumbling awkward Clark as his secret identity most of all to hide his powers. Batman, however, cultivates the arch urbane dilettante Bruce Wayne most of all not to hide his powers (after all, he has none) but to mask his true character. So driven is the real Bruce Wayne, so wired, so taut, that he cannot afford to assume a public face that people would take seriously."

Kahn noted that over ten years earlier DC had tried a Batman makeover that changed Bruce Wayne from indolent playboy to dynamic financier and director of the Wayne Foundation. They had since realized this was a mistake, "severely undercutting the essential dichotomy between the public Bruce Wayne and the Batman. In the comics now we are moving him out of the glass tower in the center of the city, leaving Wayne Enterprises and the Foundation in someone else's capable hands, and emphasizing the superficial playboy image of old."

Kahn concluded:

Whereas Superman is a sunny character, the Batman's domain is one of pitch-black rooftops, alleyways, and dark grim streets. As his cape billows about him in ever-changing folds, he is as mysterious and elusive as the shadows that secret him. The Batman (like Dracula, though one hesitates to draw the analogy) becomes alive with the night. It is then that he can drop all pretense, then that he can stalk his prey. When he pursues criminals, his senses are at their keenest, his reflexes most acutely tuned, his mind a cutting edge, his courage and daring and stamina untinged by fear.[15]

Sam Hamm's screenplay was developed during a screenwriter's strike; some of his storyline was discarded (his original screenplay included Robin), and other screenwriters added their flourishes. But Hamm's story took Batman seriously, featuring the origins of Batman and the Joker, turning them loose, and following the antagonists on their collision course. The mood was established at the outset with Hamm's description of the 1989 Gotham:

The City of Tomorrow: stark angles, creeping shadows, dense, crowded, airless, a random tangle of steel and concrete, self-generating, almost subterranean in its aspect—as if hell had erupted through the sidewalks and kept on growing. A dangling fat moon shines overhead, ready to burst.[16]

Production designer Anton Furst, who won an Oscar for *Batman*, explained in a *Cinefex* interview that movie cities often look as if a single person designed them. "But New York or any other real metropolis looks as if it is something that has been designed by thousands of architects over hundreds of years. So we went for a potpourri of different styles within the same complex, being careful to control it so that in the end we would have a cohesive composition." He included "everything from the early brownstone buildings to modern brutalism, gothic architecture to Italian futurism."[17]

There was universal approval of Jack Nicholson's casting as the Joker, but Burton's Batman selection of Michael Keaton, popularly considered a comedian, kindled fan fears of a campy production. To counter the negative reaction, a trailer showcasing Batman, Joker, and a dark and dangerous Gotham was screened in Los Angeles in November 1988, and was in wide release by Christmas, way ahead of the scheduled summer 1989 release. Long before Internet and social media, word of mouth and the fandom grapevine got multitudes heading to their local theaters just to see the trailer. Fans were appeased—and stoked for the opening. The publicity campaign became a model for movie marketing.

Warner's Licensing Corporation of America fanned interest with over a hundred movie-licensed products. "By the start of the year there was a feeding frenzy that we took advantage of, and to a certain extent fueled," Rob Friedman, Warner president of world-wide advertising and publicity, said ahead of the theatrical release. *Newsweek* called the second coming of the Batman phenomenon, "A summer struggle for the dark soul of a mythic American hero—and a boom in Bat-products."[18]

Batman was released on June 23, 1989, the character's fiftieth anniversary year. *Batman* excitement enhanced the value of Warner Communications through summertime merger intrigues with Time, Inc. Shareholders were scheduled to vote when Paramount, Inc., made a $10.7 billion cash tender offer for Time. The August 1989 *Manhattan, inc.* cover article, "Greed and Ego in Gotham City: Time Inc. Lurches On," featured David Levine illustrations of Warner chairman Steve Ross as Batman, Paramount rival Martin Davis as the Joker, and the "dynamic duo" of Time chairman Dick Munro and president Nick Nicholas suited up as twin Robins. Ultimately, the merger won, creating Time Warner, Inc. DC Comics was now part of the world's biggest media entertainment company.

Batman was a box-office phenomenon, with a domestic take of $251,188,924, while foreign markets added $160,160,000—61.1 and 38.9 percent, respectively. The domestic versus international ratio would soon dramatically reverse. "*Batman* 1989 was the revolutionary step that changed Hollywood, for better or worse, that changed comic books and superheroes," Michael Uslan declares. "Its impact is not measured by box-office numbers, but how it transcended borders and cultures."

"Comic-book-style movies—and I include *Star Wars* and the four million things in development—I'd be interested to see if

"Batmania" described the nationwide fervor generated by the campy *Batman* TV show. It was Batmania II when director Tim Burton's brooding, atmospheric take screened in movie theaters around the world in 1989. This Japanese magazine cover featured a chummy pairing of actors Jack Nicholson as the Joker and Michael Keaton as Batman. Motion pictures were the perfect vehicle for exporting America's comic book superheroes to international audiences.

DAYS JAPAN (1989).

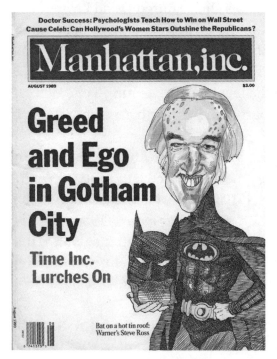

The *Batman* movie coincided with intrigues involving DC's corporate owner, Warner Communications. This *Manhattan, inc.* cover article went full-on Batmania as Warner head Steve Ross gets suited up as Batman himself.

MANHATTAN, INC. (AUGUST 1989), COVER ART BY DAVID LEVINE.

they mature the way that comics themselves have matured," Sam Hamm said in 1989. "They're in their adolescence now, just on the brink."[19]

MARVEL MOVIES

Marvel was setting the pace in publishing, but its movie deals, individually farmed out to various studios, were outright failures or rights were stuck in legal limbo. *Captain America*, a 1990 production, was not released theatrically in the United States. "Dismayingly awful adaptation of the great Joe Simon–Jack Kirby comic books," judged Leonard Maltin, whose *Movie Guide* gave the picture its worst rating.[20]

In 1996 Marvel declared bankruptcy but was rescued by Toy Biz owner Ike Perlmutter, who brought in new CEO Peter Cuneo and chief operating officer Bill Jemas; Joe Quesada became Marvel Comics editor in chief and Avi Arad headed Marvel's film and television division. Marvel now began coproducing and exerting creative control over its films. In 1998 there was unexpectedly good box office for *Blade*, based on Marvel's vampire hero, followed by the success of *X-Men* in 2000, successes that launched two franchises.

Spider-Man rights remained a tangled web, with Sony Pictures, MGM, and Paramount holding competing claims. Sony had tried to purchase Marvel during the bankruptcy but now focused on acquiring *Spider-Man* movie rights. John Calley, now head of Sony, wanted a *Spider-Man* film in the serious spirit of his earlier *Superman*. Yair Landau, president of Sony Pictures Digital Entertainment, went after a deal as executive vice president for corporate development. Calley hailed him as "relentless" in his successful negotiations with Avi Arad.

But making a deal with Arad was "half the equation," Landau noted. "The other half was solving the situation with MGM and Paramount. The rights had been contaminated by a series of companies that had gone under." Such was Carolco Pictures' Spider-Man claim, but when that studio went bankrupt, Spider-Man rights were among the assets absorbed by MGM. Sony held separate rights to MGM's James Bond franchise, and during litigation over Bond rights, it was decided to settle by swapping icons: Sony turned over Bond rights and in return received MGM's Spider-Man interest. "As part of our settlement we essentially won half the [Spider-Man] rights," Landau recalled. "They ended up with clarity that we weren't going to make a Bond film, and we ended up with Spider-Man." With MGM settling and Sony successfully making a deal with Arad, the studio overcame Paramount's claim, consolidating rights. "None of this had anything to do with the creative take. . . . This put us in a position to have those conversations," Landau added.

Avi Arad hailed the timing as *Spider-Man* went into production through Sony's Columbia Pictures studio, along with its in-house Sony Pictures Imageworks visual effects division—computer-generated imagery had come of age.[21] The visual effects work supervised by *Star Wars* veteran John Dykstra was key to bringing the web-slinger to life, but it also fed life into the superhero film genre. CG technology, in the hands of artists and storytellers, was the means by which fantastical comic book imagery could be faithfully adapted to a live-action picture.

Spider-Man, directed by Sam Raimi, starred Tobey Maguire as Peter Parker/Spider-Man; Kirsten Dunst played Peter's girlfriend Gwen Stacy; and Willem Dafoe played the villainous Green Goblin. The 2002 release generated over $800 million in global box office, cementing Marvel's cinematic turnaround. Marvel was now "flexing big muscles," *Newsweek* reported. Upcoming Marvel movies included *X-Men 2* and *The Hulk*. "Both films are expected to build on the success of *Spider-Man*," *Newsweek* business reporter N'Gai Croal reported, focusing on the consumer ripple effect, including sales of almost two million *Spider-Man* videogames. "The movie helped push the revenue of Marvel and its publishing, licensing and toy divisions to $290 million last year, up from $181 million in 2001. Marvel's stock, trading near $4 last fall, is now above $10."[22]

BILLION-DOLLAR BUSINESS

By 2005 Marvel Studios was making its own films in a deal allowing creative control and financing in partnership with marketing and distribution by Paramount Pictures.[23] That year Marvel Studios began reclaiming film rights to its other properties, including Lee and Kirby's Silver Age creation, the Black Panther—a.k.a. T'challa, ruler of the technologically advanced African kingdom of Wakanda—from Columbia and Artisan Entertainment. By November Iron Man returned from New Line Cinema. In 2006 Hulk rights reverted from Universal after the studio failed to go into production on a sequel to director Ang Lee's *Hulk* (2003). That year rights to Thor reverted from Sony, as did Black Widow from Lions Gate Entertainment.[24]

In 2006 Perlmutter promoted studio vice chairman David Maisel to chairman, and Kevin Feige became president of Marvel Studios. Marvel was going into production on *Iron Man* with a $140 million budget, Jon Favreau as director, and Robert Downey Jr. as Tony Stark/Iron Man. The May 2, 2008, release, distributed by Paramount, blew up expectations with over $585 million in global box office, 45.6 percent of it from foreign markets.[25]

Iron Man was the beginning of a vision for Marvel movies that got a serious boost when the Walt Disney Company purchased Marvel Entertainment for $4 billion in September 2009. "The surprise acquisition points to the film industry's biggest issue at the moment: access to capital." The *New York Times* continues:

> Marvel told investors in May that it would self-finance a third of each [*Iron Man* and *Hulk*] film—something that would be much easier with Disney's muscle behind it. The purchase essentially made Disney a partner with other studios that had

long-term deals to make or distribute Marvel movies, but the goal was to eventually reclaim those properties.

Marvel has aggressively exploited its most popular characters through motion pictures, video games and consumer products. But Disney sees an opportunity to plug Marvel into its vaunted marketing and distribution system.

Comic books still powered the brand—Marvel vice chairman Peter Cuneo told investors they had "the most profitable print publishing business in the world."[26]

Marvel Studios' endgame was to make films featuring individual heroes, building momentum for a massive *Avengers* team-up production. "While the notion of a superhero team-up is fairly common in comic books, it's been a difficult thing to arrange on the big screen," Ray Subers writes in a Box Office Mojo article.

DC Comics has tried for many years to assemble Batman, Superman, and a handful of other characters in a *Justice League* movie, but that has had numerous false starts and is currently on the backburner. . . . Prospects for Marvel's *The Avengers* didn't seem much better.

That all changed in May 2008. . . . *Iron Man*'s extraordinary success made *The Avengers* a viable option, and even after *The Incredible Hulk* earned an underwhelming $134.8 million, Marvel still moved ahead with bringing the other elements of the franchise to life.[27]

Each film had fans waiting through long end-credit crawls, because before fading to black there would be a dramatic teaser scene for the next scheduled Marvel movie. As Marvel comics had superheroes interacting and guest-starring in each other's adventures, the cinematic adaptations brought individual franchises into an interconnected mythology called the "Marvel Cinematic Universe."

As intellectual property attorney Nicole J. S. Sudhindra reflects,

"Comic books, once associated with geeky adolescent boys and low-budget entertainment, now are linked to celebrities and big money. What's changed since the dawn of the concept in the 1930s? Movies!"[28]

Jack Kirby worked on—he would say *created*—most of the Marvel characters that would be generating billions in global box office. Jack wasn't there to see any of it—the "King" died of a heart attack at his home in Thousand Oaks, California, on February 6, 1994.

CHAPTER 20

SUPERMAN AND CAPTAIN AMERICA ON TRIAL

Ruling Gives Heirs a Share of Superman Copyright: In a Setback to Time Warner, Federal Judge Awards Unspecified Amount to Family.

New York Times headline, March 29, 2008

THE DEATH OF SUPERMAN

Superman turned fifty in 1988, and in synergistic style the March 14th issue of *Time* (the magazine was part of Time Warner) celebrated with cover art by John Byrne and Jerry Ordway of Clark Kent ripping open his shirt, revealing his bold "S" emblem uniform. Siegel and Shuster were not marking the milestone with interviews or public celebrations—decades of courtroom battles had taken their toll, *Time* reported. They had that annual stipend, but Superman's estimated value was more than $1 billion. Tom Andrae adds a poignant assessment: "They are just in such pain over this situation"[1]

When Superman turned sixty, and with a new millennium approaching, the US Postal Service's "Celebrate the Century" series featured a Superman first-day issue in Cleveland on September 10, 1998, complete with a faithful reproduction of *Action Comics* #1. But a major makeover—"energy-based" powers and new costume—drew howls of criticism. A *New York Times* editorial was philosophical about the now-familiar transformative cycle vital to a character's longevity: "The new Superman bristles with electricity and, instead of merely leaping tall buildings, transmits himself through phone lines. To court the Internet crowd, the writers have dumped all the human frailties on Clark while turning Superman into a kind of Cyberman. . . . But stripping away the cape and jazzing up the suit were logical steps in dismissing the old and ringing in the new. . . . The change could give him a new lease on superherohood."[2] But the radical costume change and energy powers were brief, and Superman returned to his classic self.

The death of Superman was chronicled in issue #75 (January 1993) of the new *Superman* continuity. A DC promotional publication declared, "It's not a dream or a hoax."[3] His was a mythically glorious warrior's death, defeating the monstrous alien invader Doomsday and saving Metropolis before dying in the arms of his beloved Lois. The funeral procession saw Ma and Pa Kent and DC's superheroes following the casket carried by pallbearers Batman, Green Lantern, Flash, Aquaman, Wonder Woman, and Robin. The "Death of a Hero" issue included a black armband and tear sheet of the *Daily Planet* obituary. Along with an astounding three-million-copy print run, Superman's apparent death generated global publicity.

"We had a way to bring Superman back," editor Mike Carlin revealed. "We just thought that we had to make the story even bigger. Now that the world was watching, if he just sat up in his coffin and said, 'Hi, I'm back,' it would have been a bad payoff to a very big story."

During postmortems a Gallup poll weighed in on the future, or lack thereof, of the Man of Tomorrow: "According to the latest Gallup Poll, 60 percent of total adults polled want to see the slain Kryptonian brought back to life; a quarter (25 percent) see him as a faded superhero whose time has passed," reported the *Los Angeles Times*. Superman's resurrection took months, with appearances by four pretenders, including a Superboy and cyborg Superman, before the real Superman returned—"with boosted sales," Les Daniels notes.[4]

Superman was deep into its comics reboot when the hero himself ostensibly died in issue #75. Superman had "died" several times previously, as these cover stories attest.

"DOOMSDAY!," *SUPERMAN* #75 (JANUARY 1993). SUPERMAN CATCHES THE FATAL PLAGUE VIRUS-X AND HAS PREPARED HIS LAST WILL AND TESTAMENT. *SUPERMAN* #156 (OCTOBER 1962), COVER ART PENCILS BY CURT SWAN, INKS BY GEORGE KLEIN.

Jerry Siegel's brief return to DC produced this bitter tale of betrayal. "The Death of Superman" was an "Imaginary" story, but as writer Alan Moore once wrote, "Aren't they all?"

"THE DEATH OF SUPERMAN," *SUPERMAN* #149 (NOVEMBER 1961), COVER PENCILS BY CURT SWAN, INKS BY GEORGE KLEIN.

Superman catches the fatal plague Virus-X and has prepared his last will and testament.

"THE LAST DAYS OF SUPERMAN!" *SUPERMAN* #156 (OCTOBER 1962), COVER ARTIST CURT SWAN.

Joe Shuster missed Superman's death and resurrection, having passed away in Los Angeles on July 30, 1992.

Jerry Siegel died in 1996, but his Superman quest lived on. Jerry's daughter, Laura Siegel Larson, stated it was "his dying wish, for his family to regain his rightful share of Superman." She called it a "cautionary tale for writers and artists everywhere," given the "David and Goliath struggle against Warner Bros."[5]

JERRY'S DREAM

As a child Marc Toberoff never read comics and was not allowed to watch television. His "German-Jewish intellectual" mother expected him to devour the works of Freud and Karl Marx. He'd heard of Superman, but it wasn't until he represented the Siegel heirs that he got his crash course in comics history.

"These two kids in high school came up with this idea, a metaphor for immigrants assimilating, this idea of universal appeal that the schlumpiest person could feel they're Superman underneath," Toberoff recounts.

> And they finally got this publisher of schlocky girlie magazines who owned printing presses to throw it on the presses, and they signed a publisher's release without a lawyer. Superman became a sensation and that publisher was soon living in a huge mansion in Westchester [County] and they were still being paid by the page. And they went to court in '47 and lost, had no participation in their creation and were blacklisted from the industry and lived near the poverty line, working menial jobs. It was almost a curse for them. My clients, the wife of Jerry Siegel and their daughter, lived in Superman's shadow.

In 1997, years before Toberoff's involvement, Joanne Siegel and Laura Siegel Larson exercised their termination rights over Superman under the 1976 Act, the termination notices having an effective date of April 16, 1999. By 2001 a settlement seemed imminent that not only included Superman, but also Siegel creations Superboy and Spectre. On October 19, 2001, Siegel counsel sent a six-page letter to Warner Bros. general counsel John Schulman summarizing the substance of the settlement discussions. Schulman replied with a five-page letter on October 26, 2001, that reviewed the summation, enclosing "a more fulsome outline of what we believe the deal we've agreed to is," adding that Warner Bros. was preparing the "draft agreement" that arrived on February 1, 2002. From there the deal went off the rails. Warner claimed they had an agreement, while the Siegels felt the draft agreement had changes from the initial settlement proposals. Toberoff says the proposals were "different in material respects" and represented "the dark arts of studio accounting. At that point [Siegel] terminated settlement."

Joanne Siegel wrote Time Warner's COO Richard Parsons on May 9, 2002, declaring that when reading the proposed draft agreement she felt they had been "stabbed in the back," reiterating that it "contained new, outrageous demands that were not in the [earlier] proposal. . . . We have no deal and this contract makes an agreement impossible."

A shocked Parsons replied by letter that the draft agreement "accurately represented the agreement previously reached" between the parties. No matter, on September 21, 2002, Joanne Siegel fired her current counsel and enlisted Marc Toberoff, then representing the Shuster heirs. That day she wrote DC president and publisher Paul Levitz that she was ending negotiations with DC and its parent company. On October 8, 2004, Toberoff filed a new action on behalf of Joanne Siegel and Laura Siegel Larson.

In 2006 the Siegels recaptured rights to Superboy, although legal challenges were underway when a blockbuster ruling in *Siegel v. Warner Bros. Entertainment, Inc.*, came down on March 26, 2008, in the Los Angeles courtroom of Judge Stephen G. Larson, of the Central District of California: Siegel's heirs had won a share in the Superman copyright and were owed compensation starting from the 1999 termination date. "After seventy years, Jerome Siegel's heirs regain what he granted so long ago—the copyright in the Superman material that was published in *Action Comics*, Vol. 1," the judge ruled. Larson dismissed the settlement issues from over six years before. "One need only review the language of the parties' correspondence . . . and the number of material differences between the terms relayed in the October 19 and 26, 2001, letters and the February 1, 2002, draft to reach the conclusion that the parties failed to come to an agreement on all material terms."

In Larson's ruling Time Warner retained its international rights, but a new trial was required to determine "an apportionment of profits." If the ruling survived appeal and reversion of rights was extended to the Joe Shuster estate in 2013, the heirs would control the billion-dollar property through 2033—or longer, if Congress extended the copyright term. "After 2013, Time Warner couldn't exploit any new Superman-derived works without a license from the Siegels and Shusters," Toberoff told the *New York Times*.

"I have lived in the shadow of this my whole life," Laura Siegel Larson told the *Times*. "I am so happy now, I just can't explain it."[6]

But the ruling applied to the first issues of *Action Comics*, while subsequent Siegel and Shuster work were judged works for hire. "This meant a potential split in the Superman universe," the *Hollywood Reporter* noted. "Siegel (and his co-author Joe Shuster) would reclaim many of Superman's defining character-istics, including his costume, Clark Kent and the origin story. But Warner . . . would retain other elements, including Lex Luthor and Kryptonite. The Siegel estate appealed, allowing both parties to resubmit to a higher authority." In 2012 Warner Bros. filed a 117-page brief to hold on to *all* Superman rights.[7]

The Shuster side was complicated. After Joe died in 1992, his sole heirs, brother Frank and sister Jean Shuster Peavy, entered into a separate agreement by which DC agreed to pay Joe's debts and provide the siblings $25,000 annually for life. In exchange they agreed to end litigation. The 1992 agreement letter from DC president and publisher Paul Levitz stated that their signing it "fully settles all claims to any payments or other rights and remedies ... hereafter existing regarding any copyrights, trademarks, or other property right in any and all work created in whole or in part by your brother, Joseph Shuster." The letter added that by signing they agreed "not to assert any claim or right, by suit or otherwise, with respect to the above, now and forever." If they violated terms, payments would cease, and they would have to refund money previously paid. The letter was dated August 1, 1992; Frank and Jean Shuster Peavy signed on October 2, 1992.

The problem was that at the time the agreement was signed, only spouses, children, and grandchildren could hold a creator's termination rights, and Joe's meager estate had not even been probated. In 1998 the Copyright Term Extension Act extended termination rights to an author's estate in the absence of heirs. In 2003 Mark Peary, Joe Shuster's nephew and the son of Jean and William Peavy, was an alternate executor under Joe's will, and he petitioned to probate the Shuster estate. He was made executor in 2003, which included power to terminate prior transfers of his uncle's copyright—and that year, the Shuster side exercised that power. (To clear any confusion, Mark adopted the slightly altered "Peary" as a stage name, according to Brad Ricca in *Super Boys*.)

The legal tussle over Superman took on the decorum of a brass-knuckle bar brawl. In 2010 DC Comics brought a declaratory judgment against Toberoff; his company, Pacific Pictures Corporation (PPC); Jean Peavy and her son; and the Siegels.[8] In a scenario out of an espionage thriller, internal Superman case documents were stolen from Toberoff's office and anonymously sent to Warner Bros., an incident that led to a federal probe. Warner subsequently filed a federal suit in Los Angeles alleging Toberoff improperly persuaded Siegel and Shuster's heirs to deprive the studio of Superman rights. Although Warner returned the stolen Superman documents, Toberoff, writing in the third person, charged the lawsuit improperly used the "large pile of privileged documents that were brazenly stolen from Mr. Toberoff's law offices and mysteriously arrived at Warner Bros.' doorstep in the midst of this billion-dollar litigation."

One of the documents, described in the *Hollywood Reporter*, was a May 13, 2003, letter from Michael, Jerry Siegel's estranged son from his first marriage—the original Superboy—to his half-sister, Laura. Michael was due a share of potential proceeds and warned Laura about getting involved with Toberoff, alleging that he and "super-agent" Ari Emanuel had a "secret agenda" to control Superman.

"This doesn't necessarily mean that Toberoff did anything wrong," *Hollywood Reporter* concludes. "It's more than possible that a judge will see Toberoff's work as garden-variety client solicitation rather than a shady business arrangement, and it's also reasonable that a judge will see the Siegels and Shusters teaming together as nothing more than some form of collective bargaining unit. . . . As they say in the comics business, *to be continued.*"[9]

Joanne Siegel pushed back in a December 10, 2010, letter to Jeffrey L. Bewkes, chairman and CEO of Time Warner, Inc., protesting "harassment of us that will gain you nothing but bad blood and a continued fight." She and her daughter were exercising their rights under the Copyright Act, and, in response, Time Warner "has chosen to sue us and our long-time attorney for protecting our rights. . . . Laura and I are legally owed our share of Superman profits since 1999. By paying that bill in full, as you pay other business bills, it would be handled as a business matter, instead of a lawsuit going into its 5th year."

Joanne's letter added that she had a heart condition and her cardiologists had so informed Time Warner attorneys. When they subjected her to a second deposition, she could only conclude the purpose was harassment. Sadly, Joanne passed away in Santa Monica on February 12, 2011, having seen a measure of vindication in her fight for Jerry's dream.

In 2011 there was another major DC reboot—transformative cycles were coming faster now. "The New 52" restarted continuity for each title with a #1 issue, including, yet again, first issues of

Action and *Superman*. The new *Action Comics* #1 was "the cornerstone of the entire DC universe," with the Man of Tomorrow retaining his cape but clad in a tight T-shirt with "S" chest emblem, work jeans, and boots.[10] Was it in the tradition of updating characters? Or was DC redefining a new Superman, one with original characteristics impervious to legal attacks from Siegel and Shuster's heirs?

In 2012 Judge Otis D. Wright II of the Central District Court of California ruled Shuster's heirs had no right to Superman. Frank had since passed, but Jean Peavy forfeited any claims when she had signed the 1992 agreement. Judge Wright ruled, "By taking advantage of [the agreement], she exhausted the single opportunity provided by statute to the Shuster Heirs to revisit [the issue]."

Judge Wright's ruling allowed "Warner and DC Comics to move forward with plans to mine Superman as they see fit," the *New York Times* reported. "A blockbuster-style movie, 'Man of Steel,' is set for release in June and the studio hopes to make sequels." But Toberoff was carrying on his appeal of the Shuster case, and he contended the pension agreement *did not* waive the termination rights.

On the Siegel front, Laura Larson wrote an open letter in 2012 to Superman fans, citing the ruling that Siegel's heirs had recaptured Superman copyrights and were entitled to profits since April 1999:

> Angered and alarmed by this defeat, Warner Bros. resorted to a despicable old trick: diverting attention from the legal merits of our case by personally attacking our long-time lawyer, Marc Toberoff. Through DC, the media giant filed a lawsuit against Mr. Toberoff, my family and the Estate of Superman's co-creator Joe Shuster, falsely claiming "unfair competition" and that Toberoff interfered with an out of court offer that Warner tried to push on my mom and me in early 2002. . . . Warner Bros. possesses documents stolen from my attorney's

office which mysteriously ended up on the desks of three top Warner executives.

Larson's letter noted that while Warner attorneys had gotten millions, Toberoff would not be compensated unless he won, calling the charge that Toberoff was trying to control Superman "ridiculous." "What Warner Bros. apparently doesn't realize is that despite their tremendous power, I will NEVER give up on my parents' dream of rightfully restoring my father's rights to his family. Would Superman, the embodiment of 'truth, justice and the American way,' let Warner Bros., DC Comics, and their gang of attorneys get away with this? Not for an instant!"[11]

THE ADVENTURES OF JOE SIMON

The year 1996 marked the fifty-sixth year after Captain America's initial copyright registration, making it eligible for renewal under the new Copyright Act. In December of that year, two years after Jack Kirby's passing, Simon again began legal action to reclaim Captain America. Kirby's heirs contacted him about joining the suit but dropped out because of expense, according to Simon.[12] (Another possible reason was Kirby's 1966 agreement that Captain America belonged to Timely.)

Marvel argued that Simon's termination notices were invalid—*they* owned Captain America's copyright. Marvel sought a declaratory judgment in its favor from the US District Court for the Southern District in New York; Simon filed a counter claim for his own declaratory judgment asserting he was the author, the termination notices were valid, and copyright must revert to him because he had been "neither an employee for hire nor a creator of a work for hire."[13]

Marvel moved for summary judgment, arguing "fundamental principles of contract law," and *res judicata* and *equitable estoppel* (the latter defined by *Webster's* as preventing "a person from making an affirmation or denial because it is contrary to a previous affirmation or denial" by that person). Marvel argued Section 304 did not apply because the earlier settlement agreement stated Captain America was a work for hire, which the 1976 Act excluded from its termination provision.

The district court found Marvel's *equitable estoppel* argument without merit and rejected Marvel's contention that Simon could not raise the issue of authorship. But it ruled *res judicata* did apply—Marvel was entitled to summary judgment on its claims as sole owner. "Simon's unambiguous acknowledgment in the Settlement Agreement that he created the Works 'for hire' prevented Simon from exercising the termination rights under 304 (c)."[14]

Simon found success in the US Court of Appeals, 2nd Circuit, before district judge Haight and circuit judges Kearse and McLaughlin. The court, in its decision on November 7, 2002, agreed that Simon was not "precluded from asserting that he is the author of the Works for purposes of exercising his statutory termination right." The ruling addressed the Copyright Act's provision that authors *could* terminate copyright grants "notwithstanding any agreement to the contrary." Simon's counsel argued that the previous court's failure to take this aspect of the new act into account "contravenes the legislative intent and purpose." The ruling added:

> Marvel's only response to Simon's contentions is that if Simon's reading of the statute is upheld, no litigation concerning a claim to authorship could ever be resolved by settlement. We find Simon's arguments persuasive and Marvel's prediction unfounded.
>
> Contrary to Marvel's dire prediction about an expansive interpretation of 304 (c), we believe that parties will still be able to resolve their authorship disputes by settlement. . . . We hold that an agreement made subsequent to a work's creation which *retroactively* [author's emphasis] deems it a "work for hire" constitutes an "agreement to the contrary"

under 304 (c) (5) of the 1976 Act. Therefore, Simon is not bound by the statement in the Settlement Agreement that he created the Works as an employee for hire. Because Simon has proffered admissible evidence that he did not create the Works as an employee for hire, the district court's grant of summary judgment to Marvel was erroneous. It will be up to a jury to determine whether Simon was the author of the Works and, therefore, whether he can exercise 304 (c)'s termination right.[15]

In 2001, in the midst of the proceedings, Simon suffered a stroke. As he recovered in the hospital, he sketched Captain America for nurses and patients. By September Joe happily returned to his Manhattan apartment and his drawing board.[16] On the eleventh of that month, New York was the epicenter of a foreign terrorist plot that hijacked commercial airplanes and turned them into weapons that, among the targets, flew into and brought crashing down the twin towers of the World Trade Center in lower Manhattan. In the aftermath, Captain America became a symbol of national mourning and resolve.

Simon did not pursue litigation after the appeals court decision of 2002. The appeals court was right—parties *could* come to equitable settlements. Joe settled with Marvel, and the agreement would honor his late pal and partner: Captain America credits in comics and movies would read: "Created by Joe Simon and Jack Kirby."

"I don't think Joe ever forgot how Martin Goodman began to charge all of Timely Comics' expenses to *Captain America* to make sure there was very little left over to become those royalties Joe had fought for," reflects editor Steve Saffel. "But as throughout his entire life, he found a way to move on to the next thing. If comics weren't working, he did advertising art. He did work for Nelson Rockefeller's political committees. He created *Sick* magazine, which at the time was the most successful challenger to *Mad* magazine."

In the aftermath of terrorist attacks on United States soil in in 2001, Captain America embraced his roots as a patriotic icon. The story by John Ney Rieber opens with Cap frantically searching for survivors in the ruins of New York's World Trade Center. The cover pays homage to a World War II poster featuring a fighting Uncle Sam.

"BUY WAR BONDS," BY N. C. WYETH, US GOVERNMENT PRINTING OFFICE, 1942.

CAPTAIN AMERICA, VOL. 4, #1 (JUNE 2002), COVER ART BY JOHN CASSADAY.

Saffel adds: "Joe always respected the court's request not to make the Marvel settlement public. The other thing he tended to say about the case was that if you wanted to waste five years of your life, depositions were a great way to do it. But they arrived at a decision he seemed to find comfortable."[17]

THE FIRST AVENGER

A building block for *The Avengers* movie was the theatrical release of director Joe Johnston's *Captain America: The First Avenger* on July 22, 2011.[18] *Captain America*, starring Chris Evans as Steve Rogers/Captain America (the actor played Johnny Storm/Human Torch in a 2005 *Fantastic Four* film), faithfully retold the Simon and Kirby origin. The movie departed from the Golden Age story in presenting Cap as a costumed showpiece at USO stage shows and War Bonds drives before he finally gets to prove himself on the battlefield.

Joe Simon arranged for his grandchildren to fly to the Los Angeles premiere, where they walked the red carpet, while Joe attended a preview screening in New York. *Captain America* was a box-office hit—Box Office Mojo calculated domestic earnings at $176,654,505 (47.7 percent). America's patriotic superhero did even better in foreign markets, with $193,915,269 (52.3 percent).

In November 2011 Simon held a *Captain America* DVD party at his apartment for a few friends and family. "That's when Joe really got to sit back and sort of revel in it," recounts Saffel, who enjoyed watching Joe watch the movie.

> There's this point in the film where Steve Rogers, before he's transformed, gets in a fight and picks up a trash can lid and uses it like a shield. And Joe goes, "Hmmm. That was good." There's another moment where Captain America is in these snow-covered woods where he spots a Nazi in a tree and uses his shield to knock the Nazi out of the tree. Joe really loved

that! I think he felt as if that was really *his* Captain America. And the whole origin scene is straight out of Simon and Kirby. His vision was showing up in a major motion picture that was done *really* well. But the fact is here he was, at his age and point in his lifetime, looking at the dynamics of this film, its execution, and appreciating and enjoying all the subtleties.[19]

In 2012 *The Avengers* assembled: Captain America (Chris Evans), Iron Man (Robert Downey Jr.), Thor (Chris Hemsworth), Dr. Bruce Banner/Hulk (Mark Ruffalo), Hawkeye (Jeremy Renner), and Black Widow (Scarlett Johansson). The release, directed by Joss Whedon, reflected expanding international box office—before opening in the United States, the film played in thirty-nine foreign markets, including Great Britain, France, Australia, and Mexico, grossing over $185 million. The US opening weekend was massive—a record $200.3 million. *The Avengers* eventually grossed more than $1.5 billion in global box office.[20]

The theme of different characters—including a Norse god, a super soldier resurrected from World War II, and a narcissistic billionaire weapons manufacturer—working as a team resonated internationally, with $888 million in foreign box office. "The narrative arc transcends borders," media researcher Kristen Simmons notes. "You have these flawed characters coming together for the common good and that is culturally appealing across the world."[21]

Superhero movies were no longer "tent-pole" franchises—they had become "universes." The question was what of the comics creators? Did they have a stake in *this* billion-dollar action, given that the 1976 Act favored artists?

Entertainment attorney John Mason notes the rules of work for hire were "locked into stone" not only by the 1976 Act's statute but by Supreme Court precedent. In many areas of the entertainment industry, issues of ownership had become normalized and accepted. Cast and crew coming onto a film or television project routinely signed a work-for-hire agreement and got to work. If not, a movie producer or director might discover they did not hold the rights they thought they had. "For example," Mason explains, "independent movie producers working on smaller budget film sometimes forget, or neglect, or don't know they have to have their contractors execute the proper work made for hire agreements."

Precedent included a 1989 Supreme Court ruling in *Community for Creative Non-Violence (CCNV) v. Reid*, in which the CCNV, a charity organization, paid sculptor James Earl Reid to create a statue on the plight of the homeless. Reid was paid but claimed copyright, and the charity made a competing claim. The district court held the charity owned the copyright; the Court of Appeals, DC Circuit, held that Reid was an independent contractor. In the Supreme Court, Justice Thurgood Marshall affirmed Reid was an independent contractor and the copyright at least partly belonged to him. The takeaway was that a freelancer creating a commissioned work retained copyright unless otherwise contractually stipulated.

The 1976 Act also made illegal "restrictive endorsement," the old practice of stamping a check with a notice stating all rights for a work were assigned to the entity issuing the check, often used to retroactively designate an independent contractor's work as "for hire."

"It's okay to retroactively deal with lack of clarity in copyright status," Mason notes, "but the copyright status is what it is at the time of creation. Say, Stan Lee tells an artist, 'Let's do a character that has wings on his feet.' If the artist draws the character, the artist *owns* it, unless the artist is an employee of Marvel or signed a work-for-hire contract. You can't copyright an idea! This is what the law *is*!"[22]

CHAPTER 21

THE KING AND THE MAN

From its beginnings in the 1930s through the 1960s, the comic book business was very much a fly-by-night industry. Jack Kirby's career is emblematic of its haphazard, un-businesslike nature during this period. . . . Given the chaotic and depressed nature of the comic book industry during the late 1950s, Atlas/Marvel and others also rarely, if ever, wrote contracts with free-lancers. Kirby did not have a written contract regarding the freelance artwork he sold to Marvel from 1958 through 1970, and certainly not in the 1958–1963 period at issue in this case.

MARK EVANIER, JOHN MORROW, AND PEN CENTER USA
brief for the Supreme Court, *Kirby v. Marvel, et al.*, June 13, 2014

The petition of the day is: Kirby v. Marvel Characters, Inc. 13–1178 issue:

"Whether a court can constitutionally take copyrights to works originally owned and authored by an independent contractor [Kirby] and hand them to a private party by judicially re-designating them "works for hire" . . . whether "employer" under the Copyright Act of 1909 can be judicially extended beyond conventional employment to independent contractors . . . whether "work for hire" can be determined based on post-creation contingencies . . . when authorship and ownership of a copyrightable work, including "work for hire," vests at inception.

MAUREEN JOHNSTON
blog, SCOTUS, July 21, 2014

In 2009, pursuant to the 1976 Copyright Act, Kirby's children—Neal, Susan, Barbara, and Lisa—began the legal process with attorney Marc Toberoff to reclaim Marvel characters they argued their father created. And while *Kirby v. Marvel Characters, Inc.*, made its way through the courts, the stakes kept rising, given the release of Marvel films grossing billions in box-office dollars.

District courts follow the legal procedure established in circuit court cases, and as the case would be heard in the 2nd Circuit Court of New York, that meant the instance and expense test was mandatory, a disadvantage for the Kirby side given that the test favored publishers. "It's almost impossible for works *not* to be for hire unless you can prove it was created independently," Toberoff notes. "So we took on the Kirby case knowing how difficult it would be. On the instance and expense test, we'd have a negative ruling in the district court and maybe a chance of swaying the 2nd Circuit, but that was highly unlikely. [One of the reasons I took the case] was because I wanted to change this highly criticized test under the 1909 Act."

Toberoff felt that the application of the instance and expense test in determining the copyright holder essentially constituted a "taking" of the work. "In the Kirby case this meant a transfer of wealth worth hundreds of millions of dollars from the family of Jack Kirby to Marvel/Disney." For almost sixty years the work-for-hire definition of "employer" had been construed by the courts to mean traditional full-time employment and did not apply to independent contractors like Kirby. Toberoff notes there was no dispute that Kirby was not under contract with Marvel and thus met the *Nimmer on Copyright* definition of an independent creator that automatically owned copyright upon creation.

On September 16, 2009, on behalf of the Kirby heirs, Toberoff served plaintiff Marvel and others with forty-five notices to terminate Kirby's assignment of copyright for 262 works published between 1958 and 1963, based on Section 304(c) of the 1976

Copyright Act. The "Kirby Works" included runs of *Strange Tales*, *Tales of Suspense*, *Tales to Astonish*, and *Journey into Mystery*, as well as *The Fantastic Four*, vol. 1, #1–21, *The Fantastic Four Annual* #1, the first seven issues of *Spider-Man*, the first two issues of *The Avengers*, *The Incredible Hulk*, vol. 1, #1–6 (the entire first-volume run), and *Sgt. Fury and His Howling Commandos*, vol. 1, #1–41.

Negotiations went nowhere. Marvel sued for a declaratory judgment that Kirby produced works for hire and had no termination rights to exercise. Kirby's heirs counterclaimed for a declaration that termination notices *were* valid and they controlled the copyright.[1] US District Judge Colleen McMahon would hear the Kirby case in the US District Court for the Southern District of New York.

STAN "THE MAN" LEE

In a 1990 interview with Gary Groth for the *Comics Journal*, Kirby was adamant: "Stan Lee and I never collaborated on anything! I've never seen Stan Lee write anything. I used to write the stories just like I always did. . . . Stan Lee is essentially an office worker, O.K.? I'm essentially something else: I'm a storyteller. My job is to sell my stories."

Roz Kirby added during the interview: "It's just his word against Stan's."

But Steve Saffel observes:

> The problems with Jack's claim—that Stan did nothing—would be John Romita, Don Heck, Gene Colan, Gil Kane, Joe Maneely, and all of the other artists with whom Stan worked. My view is that Kirby and Ditko had a tremendous impact on the creation of many characters and concepts. Even if they provided the fire that led to the Marvel Universe, it seemed as if Stan provided the spark that lit the fire. He also seemed to have

the unique long view, weaving it all together. I don't think Stan did it all, and I don't think he believed it either. However, without him, I don't believe a lot of the concepts would have been created, and without him I don't believe the Marvel Universe would have emerged. Because it did happen, we'll never know. But the Stan I knew, albeit in snippets, was warmer and more generous than the public persona. Even the public persona was generous in making his fans feel important, remotely and in person.

"The creation of the Marvel universe was a collaborative process, pure and simple," concludes Andrew Farago, curator at the Cartoon Art Museum in San Francisco. "Kirby and Ditko deserve full credit for the visual design of those characters, absolutely, but their personalities and their stories were the product of the artists and Stan Lee, whose editorial guidance, storytelling, and ear for dialogue were an indispensable part of the creative process. Together, Lee, Kirby, and Ditko made magic."

A blurb above the title to *Stan Lee's How to Write Comics*, published in 2001, is perhaps the most reasonable conclusion: "From the Legendary *Co-creator* [author's emphasis] of Spider-Man, The Incredible Hulk, Fantastic Four, X-Men, and Iron Man."[2]

In *Kirby v. Marvel et al.*, the Marvel side included testimony from Marvel editor Roy Thomas, artist John Romita, and Stan's brother, writer/artist Larry Lieber. But the "most percipient of witnesses . . . and a legendary figure in his own right," Judge McMahon observed, was eighty-seven-year-old Stan Lee. A videographer had recorded Lee's two-day deposition at US District Court, Central District of California, at 515 Flower Street in Los Angeles, on May 13, 2010. Attorneys present included Kirby counsel Toberoff, with Jim Quinn of Weil, Gotshal & Manges representing the "Marvel entities."

One Kirby argument held that freelancers shouldered the expenses of creating work and were always at risk of it being rejected; in his deposition Lee said it was company policy to pay the artist, regardless of whether work was accepted: "If an artist drew a ten-page story, and the artist rate was $20 a page, I would put in a voucher for $200 for that artist. . . . If we decided not to use the story, the artist would still keep the money because he had done the work."

Of the Marvel Method, Lee explained:

I was writing so many stories that I couldn't keep up with the artists. . . . If Jack was working on a story, and Steve was waiting for me to give him a story . . . he wasn't making money. He was a freelancer. He wasn't on salary. So I would say: "Look, Steve, I don't have time to write your script for you, but this is the idea for the story. . . . You go ahead and draw it any way you want to, as long as you keep to that main theme. And I will keep finishing Jack's story. And when you finish drawing this one, I will put in all the dialogue and the captions."

Lee's testimony established there was never a written contract between Marvel and Kirby, but Jack got the highest page rate. "I considered him our best artist. . . . I wanted to use Jack for everything, but I couldn't because he was just one guy." As an example, Lee testified to giving Iron Man to artist Don Heck

after I came up with the idea. . . . I don't know why I thought it—somebody in a suit of armor. And what if it was iron armor. . . . I thought I would get a hero like Howard Hughes. He's an inventor. He's a multimillionaire. He's good looking. He likes the women. And I got to make something tragic about him. And then it occurred to me . . . his heart gets injured and he has to wear this little thing [on his chest] that runs the iron armor. . . . It also keeps his heart beating. And that would make him a tragic figure as well as the most powerful guy. So I thought the readers would like him even more with that little bit added to it.

Wealthy scientist Tony Stark seems to have it all—but he's "the most tragic figure on earth," Larry Lieber writes in Iron Man's first appearance. During Stark's tour of Vietnam (his inventions are vital to America's undeclared war there), a booby-trap mortally wounds Stark, and he must create an electronic iron suit to survive. The origin story was plotted by Stan Lee and written by Larry Lieber.

"IRON MAN IS BORN!," *TALES OF SUSPENSE* #39 (MARCH 1963), P. 4, ART BY DON HECK.

Jack Kirby might have cocreated Captain America, but Stan Lee claimed he was
the one who brought him back from superhero limbo, having Cap frozen in ice and
time-defying suspended animation and brought back in *Avengers* #4 (1964). The
premise had staying power, with Cap on ice when the Avengers was updated in *The
Ultimates* by Mark Miller and Bryan Hitch, a continuity carried over in the Marvel
Cinematic Universe.

THE ULTIMATES, VOL. 1, #2 (APRIL 2002), P. 32, PENCIL ART BY BRYAN HITCH, INKS BY
ANDREW CURRIE.

The one star superhero he did not create, Lee testified, was Captain America, but he *had* figured out how to bring the Timely star into the Marvel Age.

> We weren't publishing [Captain America] because Martin Goodman thought it was just a World War II character and people wouldn't be interested in it anymore. I always loved the character so I decided to bring him back. And I tried to write a story where he had been frozen in a glacier for years, and they found him and he came back to life. . . . He was an anachronism. . . . He had the values of thirty years ago. . . . And Jack just drew him so beautifully, and the stories worked out so well.

During the deposition, the attorney read from an affidavit that stated the practice for the comics industry during the years 1958–1963, was work for hire. "And that was your understanding—"
"Yes," Lee replied.
"So that would include the time period of the 1950s and 60s?"
"Yes."[3]

TRIAL AND RULING

US District Judge Colleen McMahon was aware of fandom interest in the Kirby lawsuit: Would the trial reveal the true architect of the Marvel Age, or would unfair treatment of comics creators be exposed? The trial would be *none* of those things, McMahon declared: "It is about whether Kirby's work qualifies as work-for-hire under the Copyright Act of 1909, as interpreted by the courts, notably the United State Court of Appeals for the Second Circuit. If it does, then Marvel owns the copyright in the Kirby Works, whether that is 'fair' or not. If it does not, then the Kirby Heirs have a statutory right to take back those copyrights, no matter the impact on a recent corporate acquisition or on earnings from blockbuster movies made and yet to be made."

On the Kirby side, Mark Evanier and publisher John Morrow provided expert testimony, bolstered by declarations from James Steranko and Kirby inkers Joe Sinnott and Dick Ayers. Evanier disputed some of Lee's assertions: "I have great respect and affection for Stan Lee, but I disagree with the accounts he has sometimes given of the creation of the Fantastic Four in which he solely created the concept and characters and Kirby's role was limited to simply drawing up Lee's creation."

Toberoff supported his argument that Kirby was not a work for hire, offering into evidence Marvel paychecks from the period stamped with the restrictive endorsement stating Marvel forever owned the copyright for the particular work. "Why would you need this language if it was a work for hire?" Toberoff argued. "The publisher would already own it the moment the author's pen hit paper."

Another example of the fast-and-loose definition of work for hire was an incident where Kirby emerged from Stan Lee's office in an angry mood with *Hulk* pages in his hands, ripped them in two, and tossed them in the garbage. Lee's brother Larry, who thought Kirby a genius, fished out the pages and later taped them together. In his deposition, Larry Lieber assumed that Kirby was upset that his art had been rejected. "We showed [Marvel] did not, in fact, pay for rejected material," Toberoff explained.

Toberoff further argued the agreement Marvel demanded that Kirby sign on May 30, 1972—assigning "any and all right, title and interest [Kirby] may have or control" in all his works—meant Kirby had rights to assign. The judge disagreed:

The agreement contained explicit language that was obviously intended to negate any suggestion that Kirby actually owned any federally-protected copyright in his work. . . . The assignment also describes all of Kirby's work for Marvel (which includes the Kirby Works) as work done by Kirby as "an employee for hire of the Goodmans," the owners of Timely/ Marvel. . . . The fact that the assignment was executed when it was—in 1972—actually suggests that the parties intended to memorialize an understanding that the Kirby Works were works for hire.

The judge observed that 1972 was shortly before Congress passed the 1976 Act clarifying the vague work-for-hire issues, rather than leaving it to the courts to interpret. The first drafts of the new copyright law produced in 1963 clearly showed an altering of "the court-created presumption" that works commissioned from independent contractors were likely works for hire. The judge noted that a 1965 draft of the work-for-hire statute limited it to works prepared by an employee within their scope of employment and set categories of commissioned works from a nonemployee that required a contractual agreement as "a contribution to a collective work," such as a motion picture. The establishment of the 1976 Act confirmed the statute in subsequent precedents, such as the Supreme Court's ruling in *CCNV v. Reid*.

The judge was essentially arguing in favor of Marvel's retroactive application of ownership by way of works made for hire over works Kirby delivered as an independent contractor. "With a definition of work for hire on the horizon that would severely restrict the ability of a party in Marvel's position to claim copyright in works created by independent contractors—it is easy to see why the company and Kirby entered into the 1972 Agreement—even though the Act did not apply to works created before January 1, 1978," Judge McMahon concluded.[4]

As the Copyright Act of 1909 was the "controlling law" in *Kirby v. Marvel et al.*, the question of whether Kirby Works were "for hire," had to be applied from that act, the judge summarized. "This is important, because the 1976 Act, which is far more artist-friendly than the 1909 Act as interpreted by the courts, substantially narrows the scope of works for hire when the work is commissioned from a person who is not an 'employee' of the commissioning party," the judge added.

The ruling by Judge McMahon on July 28, 2011, opened by acknowledging Kirby's stature:

> Jack Kirby is a legend in the comic book industry. During his long association with Marvel Comics, Kirby, working as a freelance artist, played a key role in the creation of a number of iconic characters, including "The Fantastic Four," "The Incredible Hulk," and "The X-Men."

"Under the 1909 Act, the term 'author' includes 'an employer in the case of works made for hire,'" the judge noted. This included commissioned works, with court precedent presuming the "commissioned party had impliedly agreed" to convey copyright and work to the employer who induced the work's creation. Thus, Stan Lee and Marvel induced the creation of the "Kirby Works" because Kirby was not working on "spec" but on assignment from Lee.[5]

The Kirby position was that the artist worked out of his own studio, set his own hours, purchased his supplies, paid bills, provided his own benefits—he incurred the expenses. McMahon ruled that those issues were of concern only if deciding whether the artist was an employee or independent contractor. Circuit rulings established the "expense" concern was borne by the employer simply by paying the artist for assigned work. It was the argument Liebowitz once gave Siegel—DC took the risk and bore all expense in publishing *Superman*.

On every front the Kirby heirs' arguments were blocked. Toberoff argued that Marvel never had a written contract with Kirby, so the publisher did not own the work; the judge ruled that the lack of a written contract did not mean there was no contractual obligation as long as the hiring party exercised control and direction over an assignment.

> Lee supervised the creation and publication of Marvel's comic books from beginning to end. . . . It was Lee who generated

the plot or synopsis from which an artist created the pencil drawings for each assignment . . . , [Lee] who created the plot and dialogue for the characters after the pencil drawing was completed, often times ignored any "margin notes" submitted by the artist with suggestions as to the plot or dialogue in the story. . . . [Lee] gave artists assignments, reviewed their work, and made changes when necessary. Marvel *did* control and supervise all work that it published between 1958 and 1963.

It was a broad interpretation, given the Marvel Method and Kirby's freedom in plotting stories and creating characters outside of Lee's direction.

McMahon concluded, "Thus, none of the evidence submitted by Defendants makes so much as a dent in the 'almost irrebutable' presumption that the Kirby Works were works for hire. Therefore the Section 304 (c) Termination Notices [from the 1976 Act] did not operate to convey any federally-protected copyrights in the Kirby Works to the Kirby Heirs. Marvel's motion for summary judgment is granted; the Kirby Heirs' cross motion is denied."[6]

The Kirby heirs appealed to the 2nd Circuit Court of Appeals in New York, but the court's August 2013 ruling favored Marvel, applying the instance and expense test in concluding Marvel provided the impetus for creation of the work and incurred the expense.

ONWARD TO SCOTUS

After two negative rulings, the Kirby children were surprised when their lawyer announced, "We're going to the Supreme Court." Court watchers were obsessed as to the statistical chances of getting a case before the high court—zero without counsel, one in a hundred with counsel. Toberoff could live with those odds.

The Kirby heirs had to petition the Supreme Court of the United States (SCOTUS)—in legalese a "writ of certiorari"—for a hearing on their case for issuing copyright termination notices on 262 works created by Jack Kirby between 1958 and 1963. The cert was filed with the Supreme Court on March 21, 2014, case number 13-1178. If a majority of justices voted in favor, *Kirby v. Marvel Characters, Inc.*, would be on the docket. If the court decided not to hear it, or did hear it and ruled in Marvel's favor, then the lower court decision would stand.

Unlike in normal court proceedings, in which attorneys respond to everything, the counsel for Marvel remained silent. But if a minimum of four justices favored the cert petition, SCOTUS would ask Marvel for a response, and a date would be set for the court to convene and decide whether they would take the case.

Four weeks out from the deadline, there was no call from SCOTUS for a response from Marvel. Three weeks out, two weeks out, no call. Going into the last week, SCOTUS remained silent. "As the end ticks away," Toberoff recalls, "I'm thinking this is over. We'd get a letter saying 'cert denied,' and that would be the end of the Kirby case. Then, on the final day, an email pops up on my computer—the Supreme Court is demanding a response from Marvel! That was very exciting."

The Kirby side had a thirty-day deadline to gather amicus ("friend of the court") briefs. As Toberoff contacted guilds, experts in copyright law, and groups supporting creator rights, a momentum of support began to build. There was interest among the press and in legal circles about the historic potential of the case. One law blog observed:

> The implications would be significant and far-reaching. . . . Kirby's heirs could license several current Marvel properties, valued in the billions of dollars, to other entities. Even if the Kirbys licensed those properties back to Marvel, its plans to commercialize those properties through films, comics, and elsewhere may be profoundly altered. You would be remiss to think these ramifications would only affect Marvel's multi-billion-dollar properties. Several amici have noted the potentially

massive impact this case would also have on the music industry as well.[7]

Also at issue was the chance to change the instance and expense
test for pre-1978 copyright cases. Toberoff had noted that in Joe
Simon's final fight to reclaim Captain America, the 2nd Circuit
correctly considered Simon's claims as an independent contractor and applied the legislative intent and "primary purpose" of
Section 304 of the 1976 Act, *not* the instance and expense test—
another example of the "consistently inconsistent" application of
the test. Legal observer Thomas Deahl echoed Toberoff in claiming that the work-for-hire standard under the old act was "overbroad, vague" and that it "does not advance the policies behind the
Copyright Act."

Deahl noted: "If the Supreme Court grants certiorari, the Court
has the opportunity to make the equitable decision and rule in
favor of Kirby's heirs. However, if there is an inequitable result,
Congress must adapt the Copyright Act to further the equitable
needs of the writers, authors, and artists as is consistent with what
Congress has on multiple occasions expressed to be their intent.

He concluded: "Joe Simon once said that they 'always felt [like
they] wuz robbed' and to correct this injustice there needs to
be change."[8]

FRIENDS OF THE COURT

On June 13, 2014, three briefs of amicus curiae, by which persons or organizations not party to an action can present a brief on
behalf of the legal questions at stake, were submitted in support
of the Kirby petition for a writ of certiorari.

One brief came from Bruce Lehman, former assistant secre-
tary of commerce and director of the US Patent and Trademark
Office; Ralph Oman, former US registrar of copyrights; the Artists
Rights Society; the International Intellectual Property Institute;

twelve professional organizations; and dozens of illustrators and cartoonists. The amici represented freelance artists with a stake in the outcome: "The ability to make effective use of the termination rights at issue in this case is essential if these artists are to retain meaningful benefit from the use of their copyrights, as Congress intended, in the face of the disproportionately greater negotiating power of their clients."

The brief "vehemently" disagreed with the court of appeals' "retroactive re-characterization of Kirby's freelance work as 'made-for-hire' under the 1909 Act. The Second Court's controversial 'instance and expense' test unfairly imposes an 'almost irrebuttable presumption' that commissioned works were 'for hire' under the 1909 Act, effectively gutting the termination rights provided by the curative 1976 Copyright Act."

Congressional research that formed the 1976 Act "shows that certainly no one in 1958–63 construed work for hire to include the copyrighted material of freelancers like Kirby." The brief contended the Kirby Works fell under "commissioned works," with Kirby conveying copyright to Marvel, not Marvel owning Kirby's work at its creation.

"Marvel's relationship with Kirby is symptomatic of the predatory practices of publishers, and the very imbalance Congress sought to remedy by the 1976 Act's termination provision." The brief concluded that the 2nd Circuit disregarded the definition of "employer" as commonly understood in 1958–1963 and thus "renders meaningless the termination rights established for the benefit of freelance authors and artists under the 1976 Act and should be rejected by this court [consistent with earlier decisions]."[9]

The amicus curiae of the California Society of Entertainment Lawyers (CSEL), a recently formed nonprofit group of attorneys representing writers in every phase of the entertainment industry, also characterized the 2nd Circuit's instance and expense ruling as a controversial way of *redefining* copyrightable works produced by independent contractors, retroactively, as works for hire:

Despite the clear legal doctrines laid out by Congress and this Court pertaining to the adjudication of copyright claims, district and appellate courts frequently subvert those doctrines . . . destabilizing the copyright ecosystem in the process. . . . [This Court] should abolish the Second Circuit's overbroad and unprincipled "instance and expense" test. . . . Modern copyright litigation has become unjustifiably unpredictable, with the determination of each case resting almost entirely on the unfettered discretion of the judiciary.[10]

A third brief came from Kirby friend and biographer Mark Evanier and from John Morrow (whose TwoMorrows company published books and magazines related to the comics industry, including works on Kirby), and Pen Center USA, an organization of over seven hundred novelists, journalists, editors, playwrights, screenwriters, and other creators. The brief's opening noted the consequences of a precedent-setting Supreme Court judgment: "Petitioner's position in this case as the determination of the important issue presented—whether 'work for hire' is applicable to an independent content creator under the 1909 Copyright Act—will have a broad and profound impact on nearly all artists, writers, and creators of comic books and other works, and their families."

They objected to Justice McMahon's ruling that Stan Lee supervised creation and publication of Marvel's comic books from beginning to end. The brief explained how comics writers typically prepared detailed, panel-by-panel scripts for artists to "fill in" according to the writer's instructions, whereas the whole point of the vaunted Marvel Method was "to relieve Lee of his heavy workload and to take advantage of the artists' skills as storytellers." In story conferences Lee might come up with the basic story idea, other times it was the artist, and sometimes it was collaborative. Kirby often took the lead, developing plots and new characters at the drawing stage and adding margin notes directing what the writers should put in word balloons and captions.

The brief dismissed Marvel's work-for-hire premise, particularly given that most of the work in the contested years of 1958–1963 came from freelancers.

> None of the relevant players involved in the comic book industry during this time period—not Goodman, Lee, or freelance artists such as Jack Kirby—would have considered [Kirby Works] to be "work made for hire," owned by Marvel from the moment the work was created on the freelancer's drawing table. . . . In fact, Kirby amassed a sizeable collection of pages while working on Marvel projects at home in the 1960s, keeping them for possible future use. Kirby developed a new version of *Captain America* that Marvel rejected, and Kirby later used this artwork to create *Captain Glory*, published by Topps. Marvel never objected, even though under Marvel's new theory the company would have owned this Kirby creation as "work for hire."

The brief observed that prior to Kirby, Marvel had not created "any significant original creations." *Captain America, The Fantastic Four, The Incredible Hulk, The Mighty Thor, Ant-Man, Sgt. Fury and His Howling Commandos, The Avengers,* and *X-Men*

> were all created or co-created by Kirby or jointly created by Kirby and Lee. . . . All contain the markings of [Kirby's] fertile creative mind and fascination with science, science fiction, astronomy, mythology and religion. Kirby created the iconic "look" of these characters, which have largely remained unchanged to this day, and would often work on his own to *both* plot and draw the original storylines of these comics.
>
> Marvel is in many ways "the house that Jack built." With little or no financial security, the prolific Kirby created a wealth of material featuring novel storylines and characters, while Marvel alone has reaped the benefits of Jack Kirby's most valuable creations. . . . He did not receive any of the benefits,

security or guarantees of employment in producing what are considered to be seminal characters and stories. . . . For the foregoing reasons . . . the petition for writ of certiorari should be granted.[11]

SETTLEMENTS

The Supreme Court was set to take the case into conference on September 29. But on September 26 came this announcement: "Marvel and the family of Jack Kirby have amicably resolved their legal disputes, and are looking forward to advancing their shared goal of honoring Mr. Kirby's significant role in Marvel's history."

During the countdown to the SCOTUS decision, Marvel/Disney had contacted Toberoff about a settlement. They went through twenty arduous rounds of negotiations, Toberoff explains. It was a risk, he adds, but the global entertainment giant clearly felt the risk most keenly.

Although no details were released, the settlement was no surprise to many observers. The potential damage to Marvel/Disney of airing allegedly predatory practices in the Supreme Court would have been bad, but a high court ruling favoring Kirby's heirs "would have thrown Marvel/Disney into turmoil," as Dominic Patten writes in a *Deadline* article. The Kirby children would have controlled "all the characters in the notices if they wanted to keep the franchises going at Disney and other studios." Copyright claims would be in play throughout the entertainment industry—including the music industry, Warner Bros., and DC Comics—"as the work of writers, composers and others designated under a freelancer or the work for hire status could suddenly gain a piece of what they created."

Toberoff was happy with the settlement but conflicted by the failure to achieve his other goal. "At the end of the day, you have to do what's best for your client. But my goal was to change copyright law and they knew it. I still intend to do that. All the copyright authorities have said the instance and expense test makes no sense, that it has nothing to do with work for hire, that it's elastic, vague, problematic. But there will be another case. There will be."[12]

Meanwhile, less than two weeks after the Kirby settlement, SCOTUS declined to hear the Superman petition of the Shuster heirs. The Supreme Court had been the last chance, after the US Court of Appeals for the 9th Circuit affirmed the earlier ruling by Judge Otis D. Wright that the 1992 agreement invalidated the copyright-termination notice filed by Joe Shuster's nephew, Mark Peary. "The case regarding the Shuster termination notice *ended* with their wrongly decided decision by a split 9th Circuit panel which left the Shusters out in the cold regarding their clear termination rights under the US Copyright Act," Toberoff summarized.

The Shuster's 9th Circuit appeal had been heard before circuit judges Reinhardt and Thomas and district judge Sedwick, with a strong dissent by Thomas. The majority agreed that the 1992 agreement superseded Shuster's 1938 assignment of copyrights to DC, revoking and regranting Superman's copyright back to DC. The earlier district court ruled the estate itself was bound to the agreement, and the circuit agreed.

Judge Thomas's dissent argued that in 1992, when Joe's brother and sister signed the agreement, Congress had not yet extended termination rights to include an author's executors, meaning Frank Shuster and Jean Peavy had no rights to terminate. The question was whether the 1992 agreement was a "novation" (a mutual agreement between parties to substitute a new contract in place of an existing agreement), that "validly revoked and re-granted Joe Shuster's 1938 copyright grant. If not, then the agreement is either (1) simply a pension agreement that had no effect on the heirs' later-created statutory termination rights; or (2) an 'agreement to the contrary' . . . because it waives the heirs' termination rights [which an author cannot, in Congress' intent, agree to waive]."

Thomas's dissent concluded that neither Frank Shuster nor

Jean Peavy had any authority to enter into a novation, and therefore the 1992 agreement was not a valid novation under the New York law cited by the majority.

> Given that the 1992 Agreement had no effect on the statutory right of termination and did not effect a novation, the statutory right of termination became part of Joe Shuster's estate. The record is not developed fully enough for me to determine what consequences actually flow from that conclusion. It may well be, under California probate law, that the ultimate outcome is unchanged. But on the record before us, and the narrow question presented in this appeal, I must respectfully dissent.

A law blogger commenting on the Shuster case reduced it to the biblical metaphor of Esau selling his birthright to Jacob for a serving of lentil soup. It was, of course, bigger than a pension-type agreement. And the Shuster side was left out in the cold.

Laura Siegel Larson had her own prior "agreement" setback in Judge Otis D. Wright's court when he ruled that under the October 19, 2001, letter, "Larson and her family transferred to DC, worldwide and in perpetuity, any and all rights, title, and interest, including all copyright interests, that they may have in Superman, Superboy, and Spectre."

On Larson's behalf, Toberoff appealed to the 9th Circuit in 2015. In the process Larson, for the first time, argued that her mother had *rescinded* the 2001 settlement agreement in 2002 "and that DC had acquiesced in the recision." Since Joanne had since died, this new argument would "prejudice" DC, which would have to rework its defense strategy and "the litigation would effectively have to begin all over. The recision and acquiescence affirmative defenses are therefore waived." The circuit court also ruled against DC's request to "revisit" Judge Larson's 2008 ruling that the early Superman works were not for hire: "We find no error in Judge Larson's finding that these works were not made at DC's 'instance and expense.'"

"In the Siegel case, their statutory termination was upheld," Toberoff concludes. Ultimately, the Siegel settlement included the credit on DC comics, movies, and other media: "By special arrangement with the Jerry Siegel family."[13]

"It's big business now," attorney John Mason muses. The major companies "have very sophisticated lawyers, and if they ever hire freelancers they're going to lock them down with work made for hire and assignments of copyright built in. They'll never have these questions again. Maybe an independent company will, but not the big boys."

In an echo of Toberoff, Mason envisions a future ruling for comic book creators that will have industry-wide impact. "Taking a case to the US Supreme Court is immensely expensive, unless there are major interests involved as amicus. But significant issues always bubble their way up, no matter how many settlements you have. Sooner or later there has to be a decision."

Paul Levitz is philosophical about industry-wide rules.

There is no universal rule for anything—why should there be? It's a big field now. When I first got into it, there were about two hundred people doing comic books in America. I don't know what the number is now, but it's [at least] in the many thousands. There are about fifty to a hundred different comics publishers now, and every deal imaginable in the field. Some company may pay more in order to [keep] the art, because they want it for some reason. There have always been [contractual] variations in the field from publisher to publisher. I'm really happy that there have been contracts modeled on the contracts we put in place at DC in the late seventies, early eighties, that included provisions for things like the artist getting their art back.

In the final analysis, and despite Congress's best intentions in copyright law, the courts remain a formidable, alien realm for comics creators. As Frank Miller, writing on behalf of Kirby's fight for his Marvel art, lamented in 1986:

> Anybody who's plunged into the maelstrom of creator's rights can testify that the laws surrounding copyright and trademark, though created specifically to protect the artist, are maddeningly complex, constantly subject to redefinition and reinterpretation and occasionally rewritten altogether. Attorneys and legislators devote entire careers of their own to understanding and manipulating them. So do businessmen. . . . It is unreasonable, even unconscionable, to suggest that the cartoonists of past generations, underpaid and overworked as they were, should have been experts at anything but writing and drawing comics.[14]

CINEMATIC UNIVERSES

The impact of what comics creators had created was illustrated in big box-office numbers. Over in the "DC Extended Universe," five recent offerings—*Man of Steel* (2013), *Batman v. Superman: Dawn of Justice* (2016), *Wonder Woman* (2017), *Justice League* (2017), and *Aquaman* (2018)—grossed over $4 billion worldwide.

In April 2019, heading into the opening weekend for *Avengers: Endgame* (the fourth film in the Avengers series and the twenty-second MCU release), the *New York Times* declared the conventional wisdom that audiences had become splintered. Why head for a communal theatrical experience when you could stream a movie from a device that fits in your pocket? "Yet almost every multiplex on the planet was gridlocked this weekend," Brooks Barnes reported.[15]

Endgame was the number-one movie in at least fifty-four countries, including a record-breaking $350 million opening in the United States and Canada, while the global weekend box office rang up an astonishing $1.2 billion.[16] By its second weekend *Endgame* passed $2 billion on its way to becoming the highest-grossing film ever (passing *Avatar*, thanks to a theatrical rerelease).

At opening weekend screenings, there had been hushed expectation as final credits rolled, anticipating the teaser as to what was next in the Marvel Cinematic Universe. To the surprise of audiences, the credits rolled to the end, the screen went black, and the house lights came up. *Endgame* marked the closing of a chapter, perhaps the end of an era.

Stan Lee's MCU cameos had become as much a tradition as the end-credit teasers, and *Endgame* was his last, posthumous appearance—Lee died in 2018 at Cedars-Sinai Medical Center in Los Angeles. A memorial column by *San Francisco Chronicle* critic Peter Hartlaub lauds Lee for reengineering superheroes, in tandem with superstars like Kirby and Ditko:

> But the writer, publisher and editor in chief who died at age 95 on Monday, Nov. 12, may have had an even more impressive second act. When comic book culture went mainstream beginning in the 1990s, and the geeks inherited the Earth, Lee reinvented himself as a suave cultural elder statesman... sharing the stage with the biggest stars at comic book conventions, never letting the world forget that the nerd had become alpha in the entertainment world. . . . Often wearing an ascot with oversize sunglasses and his wild hair slicked back, Lee the comic book king was the coolest guy in the room.[17]

Michael Uslan recalls having a meal with Stan at Nate and Al's in Beverly Hills when the subject came up of the only superhero Lee couldn't make a success—Ant-Man. The amusing story was testament to the power of the MCU to lift all characters, even one that began in the tale, "The Man in the Ant Hill" in *Tales to Astonish* #27 (January 1962). The story of Henry Pym, a scientist who develops a serum that shrinks him to ant size, garnered a few fan letters. "So we put him in a superhero costume and Ant-Man didn't sell," Lee told Uslan. "We gave him a girlfriend, the Wasp,

Marvel built an enduring comics and cinematic empire on an astonishing run of success in the early to mid-sixties. Beginning with the Fantastic Four, every character was golden: Hulk, Thor, Iron Man, Spider-Man, and so on—all except for one character. It began when scientist Henry Pym created a serum that shrank him to ant-size in a little thriller published at the twilight of Marvel's monster stories, "The Man in the Ant Hill!"

"THE MAN IN THE ANT HILL!," *TALES TO ASTONISH* #27 (JANUARY 1962), COVER ART PENCILS BY JACK KIRBY, INKS BY DICK AYERS.

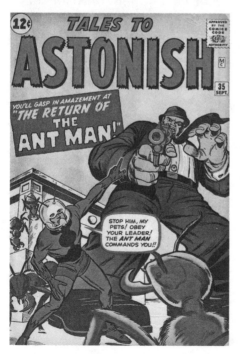

Pym's appearance won some favorable fan letters, giving stan lee an idea. Marvel superheroes were going gangbusters—so he brought back Pym as the Ant-man, complete with superhero costume (including a "cybernetic helmet" that allows him to communicate with insects).

"THE RETURN OF THE ANT MAN!," *TALES TO ASTONISH* #35 (SEPTEMBER 1962), COVER ART PENCILS BY JACK KIRBY, INKS BY DICK AYERS.

Ant-man was a *Tales to Astonish* cover feature and member of the avengers, along with girlfriend Janet van Dyne, who could similarly shrink to become the wasp. But something about an ant-sized hero wasn't grabbing fans, so stan went in the opposite direction— and made him giant-sized!

"THE BIRTH OF GIANT-MAN!," *TALES TO ASTONISH* #49 (NOVEMBER 1963), COVER ART PENCILS BY DON HECK, INKS BY STAN GOLDBERG.

Making Pym gigantic didn't seem to work either, so stan introduced the "new" giant-man, and so on. Stan was determined to make Henry Pym a star, which finally came with the MCU's *Ant-Man* movie (2015), and sequel, *Ant-Man and the Wasp* (2018), which together grossed over a billion dollars.

"PRESENTING THE NEW GIANT-MAN!," *TALES TO ASTONISH* #65 (MARCH 1965), COVER ART BY JACK KIR.

and it didn't sell. I then thought, 'I'll make him Giant Man.' It didn't sell. Then the New Giantman, and it didn't sell. And then Goliath. Then I thought it was the wrong insect and I made him into Yellowjacket. And then Disney spends $200 million to make an *Ant-Man* movie." MCU's *Ant-Man* did global box office of half a billion, with an *Ant-Man and the Wasp* sequel bringing in over $600 million.

"I really think Stan Lee is integral to making this whole thing happen the way it has," says comics shop owner Shelton Drum. "He brought so many people of my generation into comics and kept us engaged and excited through a very important time in our lives. And we stayed with it. A lot of people who were fans then are the creative people now."

Drum, founder and owner of the Heroes Aren't Hard to Find comics store in Charlotte, North Carolina, was bitten by the comic book bug in the form of *The Amazing Spider-Man* #7 when he was nine-years old and growing up in Newton, a small town outside Charlotte. The Heroes shop is in a building built in 1934 that originally housed Stanley's Drug Store.

Charlotte was a sleepy little town in 1938, but I believe *Action* #1 was on sale in the very building I am now.

Obviously, the technology of filmmaking has caught up to the imagination of comics creators. The things we vicariously lived through on the page, and imagined in our minds, we can now see on the screen. . . . The big movies coming out are superheroes, and that was from the rebirth in 1956, when Julie Schwartz and Carmine Infantino were doing *The Flash*. After that, everybody was revamping and bringing back [Golden Age heroes] and creating new superhero characters. By the early sixties, Stan knew how to market it right. And we're still riding that wave. It's still all about the superheroes. I guess we all wish we could *be* them, you know? I remember daydreaming, "Man, instead of sitting here in the back row, if I were Spider-Man I'd be up in the rafters watching this concert." If you had a super power, what would you do with it? You wouldn't have to be one of the masses. But, "With great power comes great responsibility." That's what I hear. Who wrote that? [laughter][18]

The question of who created the new gods of the Marvel Universe is debate material for hardcore fans and historians. Regardless, the names of Stan "The Man" Lee and Jack "King" Kirby will always be linked. Lee and Kirby were among honorees of the Disney Legends Award held at the Anaheim Convention Center on July 14, 2017. Kirby's posthumous award was weeks shy of what would have been his hundredth birthday. The unpleasantness of the lawsuit behind them, a Marvel statement honoring Kirby's Legends Award hailed his "defining work helping to create the foundations of the Marvel universe."

The year before Marvel had celebrated "Kirby Week"; activities included charitable promotions like Kirby4Heroes, begun in 2002 by Kirby's granddaughter, Jillian, to benefit The Hero Initiative: Helping Comics Creators in Need, a nonprofit created by publishers. "All of which makes Marvel's celebration of 'Kirby Week' so bittersweet," writes Asher Elbein. "Kirby's vast legacy marches on. So, unfortunately, does its shadow: the long history of the industry using up artists and tossing them aside like so much crumpled paper."

Graphic novelist and fine artist James Romberger recalls attending a comic book convention sometime in the eighties, and showing Jack Kirby his portfolio of art. Kirby said to him, "Kid, you're one of the best. Don't do comics. Comics will break your heart."[19]

CHAPTER 22

LEGACY

Artists sat lumped in crowded rooms, knocking it out for the page rate. Penciling, inking, lettering in the balloons for $10.00 a page, sometimes less; working from yellow type scripts which on the left described the action; on the right gave the dialogue. A decaying old radio, wallpapered with dirty humor, talked race results by the hour. Half-finished coffee containers turned old and petrified. . . . We'd talk nothing but shop. A new world; new super-heroes; new arch villains. We'd compare swipes—and then, as our work improved, we'd disdain swipes. . . . Eighteen hours a day of work. Sandwiches for breakfast, lunch, and dinner. An occasional beer, but not too often. And nothing any stronger. One dare not slow up.

JULES FEIFFER
Great Comic Book Heroes

We're comic book people.

JOE SIMON
My Life in Comics

ACTION #1

At the dawn of the new millennium there was a celebrated heist worthy of fictional private eye Sam Spade. The stolen item wasn't the jewel-encrusted statuette of *Maltese Falcon* fame but the world's most valuable comic book—*Action Comics* #1. The 130,000-print run of the comic book that launched America's superhero

402

mythology had dwindled to a hundred known copies, making it the Holy Grail of comics collecting.

The stolen *Action* #1 first surfaced at a 1992 Sotheby's auction when it was offered by an anonymous seller and sold to an anonymous bidder for $86,000, a price that set a world record for a comic book. In 1997 Metropolis Collectibles of New York acquired it for $138,000 and sold it for $150,000 to a mysterious "West Coast collector." Metropolis protects its clients' privacy, but media reports deduced the buyer was Oscar-winning actor Nicolas Cage, a renowned comic book collector who had been up for the role of Superman in a proposed Tim Burton film that was never made.

On January 21, 2000, Cage filed a report with the Los Angeles Police Department: his *Action* #1, among other rare comics, had been taken out of a security frame mounted to a wall in his home. Detective Donald Hrycyk of LAPD's art theft detail was on the case. Metropolis Collectibles provided information on the *Action* #1, including its condition and appearance and possible venues where it might be fenced. "For years we tried to find it," explains Metropolis Collectibles COO Vincent Zurzolo. "Not a month went by that we didn't think about it."

"It's such an important book and it meant a lot to me," recalls Stephen Fishler, CEO of Metropolis Collectibles and ComicConnect.com. "How could a book of this magnitude just disappear?" Fishler contacted Los Angeles comics shops, tracked Internet auction sites, alerted the collector's market—every avenue hit a dead end.

Eleven years later, in April 2011, a Southern California collector bought a storage locker, a common gambit for collectors hoping to strike it big. And this one did—inside was an *Action* #1. The collector, known as "Sylvester," bought the locker through American Auctioneers and asked company co-owner, Don Dotson, about the book's value. Dotson brought in collector Mark Balelo, who contacted Metropolis Collectibles. "We were offered the book, and, within seconds of receiving a scan, we recognized that it was the copy stolen from our client," says Zurzolo.

Fishler flew to California to meet the seller with Detective Hrycyk, who warned him to hit the floor if the seller pulled a weapon. But when the detective identified himself and declared the *Action* #1 stolen, the world's most valuable comic book was quietly handed over. Balelo began talking to the media about his role in recovering the lost comic book. "I don't want to prejudge anybody," Hrycyk replied when asked if there was a suspect. "It's just too bad that Balelo with his big mouth thought it was necessary to contact the media."

Balelo, a star of the reality TV show *Storage Wars*, once hosted a Halloween auction dressed as Superman. In 2013 he was arrested for drug possession and soon after was found in his garage with his car's motor running, dead from carbon monoxide poisoning. It was a tragic end to a case full of unanswered questions. "No one was arrested; we were shocked," Zurzolo said in 2017.[1]

Despite its lost decade, the recovered *Action* #1 was graded 9.0, "very fine/near mint," the highest known grade of any unrestored *Action* #1 as ranked by Certified Guaranty Company (CGC), the first independent comics grading service (founded in 2000, the year Cage's comics were stolen). It was the centerpiece of ComicConnect's November/December 2011 Event Auction, promoted by Zurzolo as the "Ultimate Superman Auction." *The Overstreet Comic Book Price Guide*, the bible of comics collecting, estimated its value at $1.4 million. The *Action* #1 went for $2.16 million, a Guinness World Record for "most expensive comic ever sold."[2]

The auction included items from Jerry Siegel's personal collection, notably the Royal Portable Quiet DeLuxe typewriter he purchased in 1938 to celebrate the Superman sale. "The very foundation of the Superman mythos . . . came to life from these typewriter keys," the auction catalogue declared. "It is the equivalent of having Da Vinci's paint brushes, Edison's wrench or Steve Jobs' first motherboard."

One item, not then up for bid, was a slip of paper thought lost: check number 649 from Detective Comics, Inc., dated March 1, 1938, totaling $412, including $130 for that first Superman story. The check was last seen in the autumn of 1973 when it was used as evidence in court during the copyright renewal battle for Superman. After the trial DC's victorious lawyers returned a box of court documents to the publisher. An employee, ordered to trash it all, noticed the check and plucked it from the ash heap of pop culture history. In addition to the incorrect spellings of the creators' names on the "Pay to the Order of" line, it bore a stamp: "EXHIBIT U.S. Dist. Court S.D. of N.Y. APR 6 1939," with a penciled-in "25" marking its exhibit number in the Superman versus Wonder Man trial. In April 2012 it was auctioned for $160,000, a Guinness World Record for most expensive check ever sold.[3]

THE ESCAPISTS

On December 11, 2000, the year Cage's *Action* #1 was stolen, the man who'd negotiated for and bought Superman died in Great Neck, New York, aged one hundred. Jack Liebowitz had remained active on the Warner Communications board before stepping down in 1991. He took pride in the explosive growth of comics and ancillary merchandising, pinpointing 1961, when DC went public, as a turning point. "In 1967 we grossed $64,000,000; we merged with Warner Communications the following year," he recalled. "It was gratifying to see DC become a vital, expanding company, one that has continued to be successful. That is the satisfaction one gets in business."[4]

Another seminal event in 2000 came when Random House published Michael Chabon's novel of the Golden Age of Comics, *The Amazing Adventures of Kavalier & Clay*, which won the Pulitzer Prize for fiction. Chabon's research included talking to Golden Age creators: his author's note first acknowledges Will

Eisner. Appropriately, in 2005 the sixth issue of *The Amazing Adventures of the Escapist*, a Dark Horse comic book series based on the hero of Chabon's novel, featured a meeting between the Escapist and the Spirit, written and illustrated by Eisner. In the story nefarious forces capture both characters but with teamwork they escape.

"Tell me, Escapist," the Spirit asks as they race across a rooftop, "have you ever wondered what heroes do for society?"

"Don't have much time to dwell on 'why'! But I guess what we give are instant solutions and happy endings!"

As they part, the Spirit hands his colleague a book rescued from a deadly ambush. "Here, give this to Kavalier and Clay," the Spirit says.

"Whew," exclaims the Escapist. "The first edition of their book. . . . Now that is a happy ending!"

It was Will Eisner's last story. "The day after Will sent me these finished pages, he went into the hospital," editor Diana Schutz writes. "He died there two and a half weeks later, and my heart broke." Schutz notes the irony that Will's last work was not a serious piece from the graphic novel storyteller. "Yet it is absolutely fitting that Will should come full circle and leave us with this one last Spirit story," she concludes, "a final gift to all his readers and fans who clamored for half a century for just this."[5]

Into the new millennium, Joe Simon was pushing the century mark, but he was working with editor Steve Saffel on a seven-book deal for Titan Books that included Simon and Kirby hardcover reprint collections and his autobiography, *Joe Simon: My Life in Comics*. Simon made an appearance at the 2010 New York Comic-Con to sign his Titan collections, with fellow living legends Jerry Robinson and Joe Kubert stopping by for a visit.

"What really blew me away was Titan's seven-book publishing program with Joe happened *after* he had a stroke," Saffel recalls. "And he was so good, so sharp—he could still do it, even after having suffered this debilitating illness."[6]

When young Joe Simon lost his newspaper job in upstate New York, he made a fresh start in New York City, his personal Mecca. "I wasn't going to give up until they *carried* me out," he vowed. Simon kept that promise for seventy-four years, until his death on December 14, 2011.

Saffel visited Joe in his apartment the night before he died. "We were talking politics a little bit. He was under the weather, so we also talked about how to deal with that. But he seemed to be okay. I think, the next day, he realized, 'I have a ninety-eight-year-old body.' He mostly passed away of being ninety-eight."[7]

With the support of the 2012 New York Comic-Con, held at the Jacob Javits Convention Center, Saffel organized a Joe Simon Memorial featuring a panel discussion. Paul Levitz was the first enthusiastic "yes," alongside Angelo Torres, who worked with Simon in the fifties, and artist Mark Waid, who had a long run on *Captain America*. Saffel approached featured guest Dave Gibbons about participating, and he joined the tribute.

The "Joe Simon Memorial Celebration" was held in one of the large convention rooms on Friday, October 12. A big screen, when not playing interview clips, showed the photo from the cover of Simon's autobiography—the young artist drawing at his easel, smoking a cigar, talking on a phone he held to his ear. "Sometimes these panels relating to Golden Age folks, even the Silver Age folks, don't tend to have much of an attendance," Saffel reflects, but

> this one had a lot of attendance, along with a lot of Joe's family. And we had a great time. We wanted it to be a memorial, but in the celebratory sense. I felt that Joe was there. It was Joe's last Comic-Con. Whenever I would go to a convention, I would try to find a Captain America thing for Joe. He was always surprised by these presents and took a childlike glee in them. And I say "childlike" in the right way, in that many people lose that sense of fun, and he never did. That's how I remember him.[8]

Dave Gibbons explains:

As I said at the panel, Joe Simon was there at the beginning when nobody knew how to do comics, and they were based on what happened in the newspaper. Somebody said, "Get a newspaper, we'll fold it, we'll trim it, we'll staple it." They put a ten-cent price sticker on it, and it sold out! They couldn't believe it! And people came along like Will Eisner, Joe Simon, Jack Kirby, and they perfected the storytelling and made it into a new medium with its own strengths and weaknesses. There was a whole generation of people who came up with a new art form! It was refreshing to go back to the primal days of Joe Simon.

In a way [the comic book] was a marriage of content and medium. Something like Superman actually lends itself to the printing of comic books, the fact that it's all in primary colors— bright red, bright blue, bright yellow—so, you can see every- thing is in full color. And as a kid growing up in black-and-white England, that aspect of color was important. I think a comic book is also a handy item for a kid. You roll it up and stick it in your back pocket. There's something very accessible about that. They used to be what we called in England "pocket money prices," or "allowance prices." Ten cents for something that's going to keep you occupied for an hour, or something like that, isn't a bad bargain. [Comic books] could have died out in the early or mid-sixties, but you kind of got the lunatics taking over the asylum. You got people like me.[9]

Even as the ten-cent superhero pulp fantasies evolved into global, multi-billion-dollar entertainment empires, the first gen- eration that created the superheroes was passing on.

Captain Marvel cocreator C. C. Beck had died on November 23, 1990.

Bob Kane passed on November 3, 1998, a decade after finally seeing Batman properly brought to the movie screen.

Julius "Julie" Schwartz departed on February 8, 2004.

Jerry Robinson died on December 7, 2011, a week before Joe Simon. On August 12, 2012, Joe Kubert followed them.

BILL FINGER

Many Golden Age creators left behind enduring creations, their bylines now attached to comics and movies. A few not properly recognized in life received posthumous justice—one so blessed was Bill Finger.

Athena Finger never knew her grandfather, who died two years before she was born. His legacy was kept secret to all except family and a few friends. "Unfortunately, I just got tired of being called a [liar]," she recalled of the times she tried to share her grandfather's achievements.

But a critical mass of industry pros, fans, and public documentation was building for recognition of Finger's unsung role in comic book history. In 2005, to honor his old friend, Jerry Robinson instituted the "Bill Finger Award for Excellence in Comic Book Writing," with first honors fittingly including Jerry Siegel. In 2012 Marc Tyler Nobleman told Finger's story in *Bill the Boy Wonder: The Secret Co-Creator of Batman.*[10]

In a 2018 interview, Athena Finger noted the precedent of Siegel and Shuster's shared byline on Superman but allowed that Bob Kane's solo credit was "standard for the time, so I don't think he was being intentionally malicious." But as decades went by, Kane had the opportunity to correct the record and never did. Rather than be embittered, she felt empowered to see her grandfather honored.

"It was when it got to be the 75th anniversary [of Batman] that the momentum finally shifted," she noted. "I really saw the public push for it, the industry push for it, my family was supportive [including an attorney sister, whose focus was copyright law]—so the timing was crucial. Plus, over at the DC offices a lot

of the old-timers had moved on and a lot of the younger generation who knew what was going on really wanted Bill to finally get
his credit."[11]

Batman's seventy-fifth anniversary was celebrated at the 2014
WonderCon in Anaheim, California, where Batman buzz included
Warner's upcoming *Gotham*, a television series set in the aftermath
of the murders of Thomas and Martha Wayne. During a Batman
panel, an audience member asked why Bill Finger—cocreator and
writer of Batman, author of the origin story, creator of numerous
characters—did not have a cocredit. The awkward moment passed
with the panel moderator concluding DC was "all good" with the
Finger family.

Athena disagreed, sharing her thoughts in a press release:

> 75 years of Batman! No one could have predicted the longev-
> ity and the continued relevance of this comic book hero that
> has become a cultural icon when my grandfather, Bill Finger,
> collaborated with Bob Kane back in 1939. My grandfather
> has never been properly credited as the co-creator of Batman
> although it was an open secret in the comic book industry
> and is widely known now. It is now my time to come out of the
> shadows and speak up and end 75 years of exploitation of
> my grandfather, whose biggest flaw was his inability to defend
> his extraordinary talent. Due to what I feel is continued mis-
> treatment of a true artist, I am currently exploring our rights
> and considering how best to establish the recognition that my
> grandfather deserves.[12]

This time there was no legal wrangling. In 2015 DC announced
the Gotham crime fighter would get a cocreator credit—"Batman
created by BOB KANE with BILL FINGER"—in the comics, on
Gotham, and in the upcoming feature film, *Batman v. Superman:
Dawn of Justice* (a milestone movie leading to a Justice League
team-up). "Bill Finger was instrumental in developing many of
the key creative elements that enrich the Batman universe, and

we look forward to building on our acknowledgement of his significant role in DC Comics' history," DC Entertainment president Diane Nelson announced.

Paul Levitz was not involved in the Finger cocredit but recalls meeting Athena Finger when she first emerged from her silence. "I had the great fun of giving her one of her grandfather's scripts that I had collected," he says. "She had nothing that had survived of her grandfather, so it was a great moment to be able to give that to her." Levitz adds the ultimate compliment to Bill Finger: "I don't know if I can define the difference between Bill Finger's work and that of Otto Binder or Gardner Fox or John Broome, what made Finger's work unique. He was just a great storyteller."

Michael Uslan notes Finger's origin story is a key reason for Batman's longevity. "The origin story is so primal; it doesn't matter your religion, where you came from, your politics—it hit you in the gut! This little kid seeing his parents murdered in front of his eyes, and he makes this vow to sacrifice his childhood to get all the bad guys who did this, even if he has to walk through hell for the rest of his life to do it—that is the stuff of *myth*."

Uslan first met Finger at a DC "bullpen" tour; the second time was with his pal Bobby Klein at the Broadway Central Comics Con. Their friend Otto Binder was there, with an irresistible offer: "How would you like to meet the creator of Batman? Boys, meet Bill Finger!" "We were totally confused," Uslan confesses.

> We'd spent the better part of our lives looking at that little box that said, "Bob Kane." So in talking to him, Bill began to explain how artists and writers worked. From Otto and the DC tours we already understood there was this thing called original art that had pencilers and inkers and colorists and editors. But how much *he* had contributed to the creation that we knew as Batman was jaw dropping. I can't remember if we were asking questions. We were spellbound. Otto gave him a little elbow to push him. He was a little reticent. It was this big secret the pros were in on, but we were in the dark. Otto

clearly knew the whole story. I remember [Finger] saying you can't just sit down and write stories. Things in life influenced him. He said to be a good writer you have to be a good reader. I left [realizing] I had to read as much as I can.

I have been regaled about any number of things that [Bob Kane] claimed credit for that Bill and Jerry [Robinson] created. That's the way it was. Bill suffered the most, . . . but he got his credit. It's great to see some of these things rectified.[13]

MARVELS

Artist Alex Ross grew up in the era of "the big DC super-hero epics" like *Crisis on Infinite Earths, The Dark Knight Returns,* and *Watchmen.* Next-generation artists like Ross weren't deconstructing superhero myth—they were glorifying it.

Ross followed the tradition of casting models, usually friends or family with a physical semblance to the characters he wished to portray, and photographing them for artistic reference. "Alex paints what the camera sees," a *Wizard* publication noted. "By shooting each character and scene, I ensure I get the lighting exactly right and catch the nuances of expression," Ross explained.

By this technique he and writer Kurt Busiek created *Marvels,* a four-part 1994 series spanning the history of Timely/Marvel Comics as seen through the camera lens of Phil Sheldon, introduced as a young photojournalist at New York's *Daily Bugle* in 1939. Sheldon's camera captures the moment a scientist unveils a man who bursts into flame. Then Sheldon's sweetheart gives a firsthand account of her lunch break on the waterfront and seeing a "big, eerie-looking naked man" being fired on by the police. The bullets don't hurt him; then he picks up and tosses the police car at the officers and disappears back into the sea. Sheldon tells "Mr. Goodman," his publisher, to withdraw his request to cover the war in Europe. Something was going on here at home—the emergence of beings that were more than human.

"[No other graphic novel has] brought the reader into the story the way *Marvels* does.... [Ross and Busiek] have made the reader feel as though he or she is on the scene, witnessing the history in the way *Marvels* does," marveled Stan Lee.

While working on *Marvels*, Ross was planning an exploration of the DC universe, a work with writer Mark Waid that would become *Kingdom Come*, a graphic novel that included a faceoff between Superman and Captain Marvel, yet another inspiration from Wally Wood's "Superduperman."

Ross also turned his painterly technique to an exclusive Captain Marvel story in a series of one-shots celebrating DC's classic characters (Superman, Batman, Wonder Woman). Captain Marvel's effervescent combination of innocence and strength had often eluded DC creators, but instead of trying to update him, Ross and writer Paul Dini distilled Billy Batson's wide-eyed innocence and magical superhero duality in the one-shot *Shazam!* Captain Marvel represented "Power of Hope."[14]

In 2012, as part of "The New 52" reimagining of the DC universe, writer Geoff Johns and artist Gary Frank presented a serialized Justice League Captain Marvel story that opens: "For centuries science has ruled the world. Now magic is returning." Batson is back, but not the wide-eyed, go-getter Fawcett kid. Set in present-day Philadelphia, Billy is a cynical and world-weary orphan when he is adopted by the Vasquezes, a young couple whose happy home includes five other teen and preteen orphans—all destined to be changed by Billy's marvelous encounter with the last of the ancient Council of Wizards.

The series, collected into a *Shazam!* graphic novel in 2013, informed the April 5, 2019, Warner's release, *Shazam!*, directed by David F. Sandberg, with Asher Angel as young Billy and Zachary Levi as Captain Marvel. The movie credits included "created by Bill Parker and C. C. Beck."

In early May there was another *Captain Marvel* movie in theatres. Attorney Mark Zaid took his kids to see it, but they were expecting the Big Red superhero pictured on the two original

Adventures of Captain Marvel Republic movie posters on their family-room wall. "They asked me why Captain Marvel was now a woman!" Zaid laughs, recalling the very long answer about how DC returned Captain Marvel from twenty years of limbo, but not before Marvel bought the name rights for its space-born hero who died in the 1982 graphic novel *The Death of Captain Marvel.* The mantle eventually fell to Carol Danvers (introduced in 1967 in *Marvel Superheroes* #13), who evolved into super-powered Ms. Marvel before becoming Captain Marvel—"Earth's Mightiest Hero"—in 2012. *Captain Marvel* was the Marvel Cinematic Universe's first film starring a female superhero, with actress Brie Larson playing the strong character of the comics: "Danvers got a new military look, shorter hair, and the sort of narcissistic swagger that has long been carried by men like Robert Downey Jr. [Tony Stark/Iron Man] but women are rarely allowed to own," observes Eliana Dockterman in *Time.*[15]

The empowerment of female superheroes goes back to Wonder Woman, who is still going strong—the mighty Amazon was #1 on the 2016 *Entertainment Weekly* "50 Most Powerful Superheroes" list. Although comics historian Les Daniels first revealed the unconventional lifestyle and philosophy of Wonder Woman creator William Moulton Marston, it was writer Jill Lepore who fleshed out the details of Marson's unconventional life and posited Wonder Woman as a "missing link" between early suffrage campaigns and the modern feminist movement in her aptly titled book, *The Secret History of Wonder Woman* (2014).

In 2016 Lee and Kirby's Silver Age cocreation, T'Challa, the Black Panther, ruler and protector of the African nation of Wakanda, got a "comic book reboot" with writer and National Book Award–winner Ta-Nehisi Coates, along with artist Brian Stelfreeze and others. *Black Panther* became another billion-dollar grossing MCU release in 2018, starring Chadwick Boseman as T'Challa. Director Ryan Coogler observed that *Black Panther* was a rare but emerging genre: "Superhero films that deal with issues of being of African descent."[16]

Not all characters were inspiring figures of diversity. The Joker seemed to draw evil forces from the flipside of the American Dream. In 2012 a gunman killed twelve and wounded seventy at an Aurora, Colorado, movie theater showing *The Dark Knight Rises*, a film featuring Heath Ledger's psychopathic turn as the Joker. In 2019 Warner's *Joker*, with Joaquin Phoenix in the title role, got off to a distinguished start before its theatrical release, winning the Golden Lion for Best Film at the Venice International Film Festival. But FBI intelligence monitoring dark-web extremist groups picked up "disturbing and very specific" chatter about a "credible potential mass shooting" at a *Joker* screening at an unspecified movie theater somewhere in the United States, reported military officials at Fort Sill Army base in Oklahoma. The news prompted families of Aurora victims to send a letter to Warner Bros. demanding it support the cause of gun control. The studio responded with a statement extending sympathy to victims of gun violence, adding: "Make no mistake: Neither the fictional character Joker, nor the film, is an endorsement of real world violence of any kind."

Other than reports of a disturbed moviegoer at a New York theater clapping and cheering as Joker goes on a murderous rampage—the police ushered the man out without incident—the opening in the first week of October 2019 was all about the money. The *New York Times* reported, "Hollywood's latest comic book movie, 'Joker,' laughed its way to the bank . . . opening to robust ticket sales and signaling to Warner Bros. that a risky movie had paid off." The domestic box office was an estimated $93.5 million, with foreign markets totaling $140.5 million. Slightly over a month later, *Joker* was on its way to a billion dollars in box-office receipts, with over $300 million taken domestically and a huge $637.7 million in international gross, or 68 percent of the total.[17]

That September, in a relatively feel-good contrast to *Joker* controversies, Marvel Studios and Sony settled an impasse that had threatened Spider-Man's presence in the Marvel Cinematic Universe. Sony, which had owned the Spider-Man film rights since the 1990s, had partnered with Marvel Studios on two *Spider-Man* movies, and, reportedly, Marvel wanted a bigger gross from Sony. Not only had the studios brokered a deal, it was announced that Marvel Studios president Kevin Feige would produce the third *Spider-Man* movie, featuring Spidey star Tom Holland.

IMMIGRANT FROM KRYPTON

Harry A. Manhoff is no ordinary Superman fan. As rabbi of Temple Beth Sholom in San Leandro, California, he often wears a Superman "S" yarmulke. He and his son, Eitan, began an interest in comics in 1992, when it was announced Superman would die. "I tried to explain to Eitan, who was then almost nine years old, why an icon cannot die. I suggested we buy the issue where Superman dies and then pick up the next issue when he was brought to life. As we all know now, the 'next issue' was a year later. But we were sucked in." Father and son eventually amassed tens of thousands of comics, Eitan opened Cape and Cowl Comics in downtown Oakland, and Manhoff's studies of superhero history inform his occasional lecture subject: "If there were no Jews there would be no superheroes."

"It is possible that Siegel and Shuster were influenced by their Jewish upbringings," muses Rabbi Manhoff. "But in my opinion, the 'Jewish' Superman came from Mort Weisinger and my dear friend, Julie Schwartz, of blessed memory."

Rabbi Manhoff's superhero studies began in earnest when he and his son attended their first Comic-Con, a year or two after becoming comics fans.

> I was constantly embarrassing my son by introducing myself to the Jewish writers, artists, and editors. I met Julie, and at a number of Comic-Cons he would nod to me, call me "Rabbi," and invite me to sit and talk with him about the early days of superheroes.

Julie Schwartz shared with me that Mort Weisinger referred to the escape from Krypton as a "Moses in the basket story." And it was Julie's Jewish upbringing that he said made him insist that Superman always win by out-thinking the villain instead of using brute force. Julie pointed out that Clark Kent was every klutzy Jewish boy who secretly wished he were Superman. Like Superman, we were aliens trying to blend in and trying to disguise our real strengths.[18]

Superman was the ultimate orphan immigrant, the native of a doomed world shot into space to land on a backwater planet in a remote corner of the Milky Way. In the immigrant tradition he wanted to blend in and contribute to the greater good. A son of America's rural heartland, Kal-El sought his fortune in Metropolis as Clark Kent, becoming a paragon of American values and iconic embodiment of endless possibility—when Kent pulled open his suit shirt, revealing his Superman costume, it was a metaphor for unleashing the hero within.

In the beginning Superman was brash and cocky, wisecracking and exulting in his physical prowess as he humbled a bully or criminal. Soon his physique began changing, the dangling forelock moved to the right, and the "S" chest emblem became bigger, more defined. There were "scientific" rationales for his powers. Kryptonians represented the apex of mortal evolution. One version accounted gravitational differences between Krypton and Earth. Another theory deduced it was the energy of Earth's yellow sun.

From that seminal *Action* image of a costumed man lifting a car overhead, everything about the Man of Tomorrow was an evolution. Superman lost his youthful brashness. Grace and nobility grew as his powers expanded: the strength to lift a car became the power to move mountains; the ability to leap tall buildings became the power of flight; skin impervious to bullets would withstand nuclear explosions, the freezing depths of outer space, and the blazing heart of the sun.

Superman and the superheroes, and the comic book medium, survived by adapting and evolving but never losing their unique qualities. It has been remarked that musical scores and motion pictures go together perfectly—exactly *why* is a mystery—and the same could be said for the happy blending of text and imagery.

American comic book superheroes, born of a Machine Age, four-color pulp medium in the years just prior to World War II, represented the summit of American power—a *super* power that helped a devastated postwar world rebuild, unlocked secrets of atomic energy, won the Space Race to land a man on the Moon. Superman and his progeny were heralds of an advanced technological civilization—a possible future—but they were also modern incarnations of dreams humankind has been dreaming since the epic of Gilgamesh was etched on clay tablets.

And behind the new gods of pulp fiction were the creators: former ghosts in the shadows finally were remembered and honored, and their lives and careers set precedents for respect and just treatment for the creators of the future.

In 2019 both Marvel Comics and Batman celebrated their eightieth birthdays. The progenitor celebrated his eightieth the previous year, with former DC president and publisher Paul Levitz and Superman artist and writer Dan Jurgens discussing the anniversary at an event cosponsored by DC and the Library of Congress in Washington, DC, at the Coolidge Auditorium in the Thomas Jefferson Building. Superman's anniversary included the ultimate milestone—the April 2018 release of *Action Comics* #1000 (counting for *Action* reboots). One of the issue's variant covers, by artist Michael Cho, pictured German soldiers in awe as Superman takes the full force of a tank blast. In the cover's upper left corner was the icon of Superman busting those binding chains. Inside was the notice: "Dedicated to Jerry and Joe."

Alex Ross, speaking for himself and *Kingdom Come* writer Mark Waid, adds his own homage: "I'm just satisfied that we got the opportunity to work in the same playground as the creators who preceded us. There is a long, long list of people to pay homage to, and so it may be best to simply give my appreciation to the two men to whom we owe everything: Jerry Siegel and Joe Shuster, who created the super-hero in the first place."[19]

The Siegel and Shuster Society of Cleveland made sure the creators were not forgotten. The apartment building where Joe and his family lived, long ago demolished, was marked off with a fence hung with blow-up panels from the *Action* #1 story and a placard reading: "On this site once stood the home where Superman was turned from words into pictures. . . . With his best friend Jerry Siegel, [Joe Shuster] turned amazing stories about a Man of Steel into four-colored reality."

Nine blocks from Joe's place, Jerry's house still stands at 10622 Kimberley Avenue. The Siegel and Shuster Society and other supporters raised $150,000 to restore it, attaching a metal casting of the red chest emblem with the classic "S" in front and raising a sign: "This is the house where Superman was born."

Siegel's compelling account of creating Superman within these walls is its own great story, full of elemental touches: a summer's night so hot it banishes sleep, creativity boiling over in a fever dream between wakefulness and Slumber Land, the promise of dawn seeing young Jerry running through the sleepy, silent streets to Joe's house to begin the first day of creation.

The story shines with the joy of youth and pure creativity— before the Golden Age publishing boom unleashed the super progeny, before the lawsuits and comic book burnings and censorship, the cyclical rebirths and myths manifesting as spectacle on movie screens around the planet, before the rise of the Empire of the Superheroes . . .

ACKNOWLEDGMENTS

Jim Burr, senior editor
Sarah McGavick, assistant editor
Lynne Ferguson, senior manuscript editor
Leslie Tingle, freelance copyeditor
Cassandra Cisneros, designer and production coordinator
Derek George, freelance art director
Alex Camlin, cover designer
Cameron Ludwick, publicist

The above are among the talented team that made this book come together. For the writer's part, there are others who helped in the journey of research and writing. A special appreciation to Mark Zaid, super attorney, with whom this project was conceived and research begun; Zaid could not continue with the writing phase—he had to fight the good fight in Washington—but his support and contacts were invaluable. My thanks to Steve Saffel for sharing his memories of Joe Simon and for other acts of support, including putting me in contact with Michael Uslan, Paul Levitz, and others. And a tip of the hat to Breck Kadaba, for the Marc Toberoff connection, and to Marc Neuman of House of Comics, for the Zaid connection.

My gratitude to editor Jim Burr at the University of Texas Press, who believed in this book, and a grand huzzah to my agent, John Silbersack of the Bent Agency, for his dedication and relentless spirit. Thanks also to Indiegogo campaign supporters Jim and Susan Bacchi, Jean Rolf, Bettylu and Teresa Vaz, the family of Brock and Kate Weaver, and Mary Williams.

And high-fives all around to my tech-savvy nephew, the *great* Daniel "Dano" Duarte, to Josetta Bull and her son John Bull; to Joe Labat; to Ricky Borba for leading the Indiegogo campaign and for scanning the images for this book; and to Josh Hunter at Crush Comics in the East Bay for doing most of the scanning, with thanks to shop folk Andrea Hunter, Billy Moeller, Tyler Fredendall, Cole Sanders, et al., for their support.

NATIONAL ARCHIVES AND
RECORDS ADMINISTRATION (NARA)
Regional Archives: Northeast Region, New York City

NARA provided invaluable support and assistance during several research trips delving into the Superman and Captain Marvel lawsuit and related material. Special appreciation to archives technicians Sara Lyons Pasquerello and Angela Tudico, archivists Gregory J. Plunges and Patrick Connelly, and senior records analyst Chris Gushman.

NOTES

INTRODUCTION

1. For the Broadway Central Hotel and the shooting of James Fisk, Wikipedia, s.v. "Grand Central Hotel" and "James Fisk (financier)"; Uslan originally recalled the date of the convention as 1964, while other sources put that seminal fan gathering at 1965; Vaz, *The Spirit*, 40, 42.

2. Vaz, "Martial Art," 93; Uslan, Vaz telephone interview, July 5, 2019.

3. Vaz, *Tales of the Dark Knight*, 29.

4. Kobler, "Up, Up And Awa-a-y!," 71; Liebowitz cosigned under "Accepted: DETECTIVE COMICS, INC." The document was dated with a "3/1/38" pencil notation; "The Check That Bought Superman," ComicConnect November/December 2011 Event Auction Catalogue, 7.

5. Siegel and Shuster undated payment contracts from National Archives and Records Administration, Regional Archives, Northeast Region, New York City (hereafter cited as NARA, RA, NR, NYC); Kronenberg, "Auteur Theory," 39; ComicConnect 2011 Catalogue, 6.

6. Uslan, Vaz telephone interview, July 5, 2019.

7. Canwell, "Stage Dressing," 17, 19; Marschall, *America's Great Comic Strip Artists*, 227, 229.

8. Caniff, sidebar essay, *Milton Caniff's Steve Canyon* #19 (December 1987), 40th Anniversary Special (Princeton, WI: Kitchen Sink Press, Inc.), 2, 10.

9. Canwell, "Stage Dressing," 12, 14.

10. Taraba, *Masters of American Illustration*, 30–31.

11. Vaz and Zaid interview, New York, October 19, 2010.

12. Evanier, "The King and I," 54.

13. Solomon, *Enchanted Drawings*, 75.

14. Mason, Vaz telephone interview, June 7, 2019.

15. US Court of Appeals, 2nd Circuit, Marvel Characters, Inc., Plaintiff-Counter-Defendant-Appellee, v. Joseph H. Simon, Defendant-Counter-Claimant-Appellant, Docket No. 02-7221, Decided, November 7, 2002; "II. The Copyright Act of 1909."

16. Zaid, Vaz telephone interview, May 24, 2019.

CHAPTER 1: IN THE BEGINNING

1. Kobler, "Up, Up And Awa-a-y!," 70.

2. Jones, *Men of Tomorrow*, 111.

3. *Siegel and Shuster: Dateline 1930's* #1 (November 1984): "Previously unpublished

work from the creators of Superman," Eclipse Comics; Andrae, "Of Supermen and Kids with Dreams," 8–9.

4. Andrae, "Of Supermen and Kids with Dreams," 9.

5. The rescinding of publishing offer is from *Joanne Siegel and Laura Siegel Larson, plaintiffs, v. Warner Bros. Entertainment, Inc., Time Warner, Inc., and DC Comics, defendants*, 542 F. Su 2d 1098, US District Court, CD California, March 26, 2008 (F. Su 2d 1103); the *Superman* cover can be seen in Daniels, *Superman: Complete History*, 16.

6. Andrae, "Of Supermen and Kids with Dreams," 9.

7. Watson, "Tarzan the Eternal," 72.

8. Ibid., 64, 69; Tarzan.org, "about erb inc.," http://www.tarzan.org/about_erb_inc .html, accessed March 16, 2020.

9. Young, "Serious Funnies," 80–81.

10. Andrae, "Of Supermen and Kids with Dreams," 15.

11. Ibid., 15.

12. Dr. Zarkov hopes his rocket will deflect a comet from colliding with Earth, but the "comet" is actually the planet Mongo. Doug Murray, "Flash Gordon Conquers the World," essay from Raymond, *Flash Gordon*, 7–8.

13. Alex Ross, "The Flash Gordon Legacy," essay from ibid., 7–8.

14. Andrae, "Of Superman and Kids with Dreams," 14.

15. Steranko, *Steranko History of Comics*, 35, 37.

16. Wylie, *Gladiator*, 51.

17. Barshay, *Philip Wylie*, 53–55; Edwin Balmer and Philip Wylie, *When Worlds Collide* (copyright 1932, 1933), and *After Worlds Collide* (1933, 1934), published together by J. B. Lippincott in 1961; plot elements cited from foreword to *After Worlds Collide*.

18. Daniels, *Superman: Complete History*, 28–29.

19. Writer and translator Frederik L. Schodt makes the case that one of the early American comic books, and one of the first autobiographical works, was Henry (Yoshitaka) Kiyama's *The Four Immigrants*, self-published in San Francisco in 1931. See Kiyama, *The Four Immigrants Manga: A Japanese Experience in San Francisco 1904-1924*, trans. with introduction and notes by Frederik L. Schodt (Berkeley, CA: Stone Bridge Press, 1998).

20. Goulart, *Great History of Comic Books*, 4–7.

21. Goulart, *Comic Book Culture*, 35; Zaid, Vaz telephone interview, May 24, 2019.

22. Goulart, *Great History of Comic Books*, 55.

23. Creig Flessel, "Batcave" letters section, *Detective Comics* #512 (March 1982).

24. Pasko, *DC Vault*, 13.

25. Ibid., 13, 18; Daniels, *Superman: Complete History*, 23, 25.

26. Saunders, "Harry Donenfeld," *Field Guide to Wild American Pulp Artists*, online.

27. Saunders, "Joseph Szokoli," *Field Guide to Wild American Pulp Artists*, online.

28. "New Incorporations, New York Charters," *New York Times*, September 6, 1924; Saunders, "Moses Annenberg,"

29. *Field Guide to Wild American Pulp Artists*, online. "New Incorporations, New York Charters," *New York Times*, June 5, 1931; Saunders, "Harry Donenfeld."

30. News articles are linked in Saunders's informative website, *Field Guide to Wild American Pulp Artists*, "Harry Donenfeld" entry: Judge Coxe, "Business Records:

Bankruptcy Proceedings," *New York Times*, September 13, 1932; Elmo Press, "Business Records: Bankruptcy Proceedings," *New York Herald Tribune*, September 16, 1932.

31. Saunders, "Joseph Szokoli," *Field Guide to Wild American Pulp Artists*, online; "The Press: Barber's Bible," *Time*, July 31, 1933.

32. "Obscenity Decision Awaits a Reading," *New York Times*, March 8, 1934; Tye, *Superman: High-Flying*, 25.

33. Saunders, "Joseph Szokoli," 16, 20.

34. Jack Liebowitz on incorporation date taken from his sworn statement in *Detective Comics, Inc., plaintiff, against Bruns Publications, Inc., et al., defendants,* March 16, 1939, 1, NARA, RA, NYC (hereafter cited as *DC v. Bruns*). Liebowitz's trial testimony also fixed DC's incorporation date as December 30, 1936, before US Circuit Court of Appeals for the 2nd Circuit, Transcript of Record, 25, NARA, RA, NR, NYC.

35. Siegel and Shuster letters to Dick Giordano, editor, DC Comics, printed in *Detective Comics* #512 (March 1982). Siegel's letter includes the Major's "Slam Bradley" quote.

36. Contractual history recounted in *Joanne Siegel and Laura Siegel Larson, plaintiffs, v. Time Warner, Inc., Warner Communications, Inc., DC Comics, et al., defendants,* US District Court, CD California, 496 F. Su 2d 111; 2007 US.Dist. LEXIS 56910, 3 (hereafter cited as *Siegel and Larson v. Warner Bros./DC*).

37. Pasko, *DC Vault*, 9, 18. Pasko writes that Liebowitz claimed the historic comic book was his idea.

38. Siegel, letter to Liebowitz, December 6, 1937, NARA, RA, NR, NYC; *Siegel and Larson v. Warner Bros./DC*, 542 F. Su 2d 1098, March 26, 2008 (section 1106, 4).

39. Goulart, *Great History of Comic Books*, 60.

40. Uslan, Vaz telephone interview, July 5, 2019.

CHAPTER 2: WORLD OF TOMORROW

1. Jerome Siegel testimony, *DC v. Bruns*, 64–65, Transcript of Record, November 10, 1939, NARA; Saunders, "Harry Donenfeld."

2. *DC v. Bruns*, M. C. Gaines testimony, 131–133, and Sheldon Mayer testimony, 140, NARA, RA, NR, NYC.

3. *Siegel and Larson v. Warner Bros./DC*, 542 F. Su 2d 1098 (2008), US District Court, CD California, March 26, 2008, 4–5.

4. Andrae, "Of Supermen and Kids with Dreams," 15.

5. *Siegel and Larson v. Warner Bros./DC*, 542 F. Su 2d 1098 (2008), US District Court, CD California, March 26, 2008, 5.

6. Ibid.

7. Goulart, *Great History of Comic Books*, 86–87.

8. Jerry Siegel, letter to Jack Liebowitz, March 8, 1942, NARA, RA, NR, NYC; Pasko, *DC Vault*, 20.

9. Distribution explained by Liebowitz in testimony at trial, *National Comics Publications, Inc., v. Fawcett Publications, Inc., et al.* (hereafter cited as *National Comics/DC v. Fawcett*), March 15, 1948, before Hon. Alfred C. Coxe, district judge, US District Court, SDNY, 606–607, NARA, RA, NR, NYC.

10. Mikulovsky, "Before Superman!," 73–74.

11. "Futurama," New York World's Fair exhibition brochure for 1939–1940, Mark Cotta Vaz collection.

12. *Siegel and Larson v. Warner Bros./DC*, 542 F. Supp 2d 1098 (2008), 6; Jerome Siegel letter to Mr. J. S. Liebowitz, DC Comics, April 18, 1938, NARA, RA, NR, NYC.

CHAPTER 3: MORE SUPER THAN TARZAN

1. Kobler, "Up, Up And Awa-a-y!," 71.

2. Richard Waldo, McClure Newspaper Syndicate, letter to Detective Comics, Inc., and Jerome Siegel and Joseph Shuster (in care of American Artists League of Cleveland), September 22, 1938, 1, Box 838, NARA, RA, NR, NYC.

3. Ibid., 2.

4. Ibid., 2–3.

5. Detective Comics, Inc., contract letter to Jerome Siegel and Joseph Shuster, September 22, 1938, reproduced in "'A Curse on the Superman Movie!': A Look Back at Jerry Siegel's 1975 Press Release," 20th Century Danny Boy, https://ohdannyboy .blogspot.com/2012/07/curse-on-superman-movie-look-back-at.html, accessed March 17, 2020; *Siegel and Larson v. Warner Bros./DC*, 542 F. Su 2d 1098, March 26, 2008 (section 1107), 6.

6. Jerry Siegel, letter to Jack Liebowitz, September 26, 1938, NARA, RA, NR, NYC; Liebowitz, letter to Siegel, September 28, 1938, as reprinted on 20th Century Danny Boy website.

7. Ibid., Siegel, letter to Liebowitz, September 30, 1938, as reproduced on 20th Century Danny Boy website.

8. *Joanne Siegel and Laura Siegel Larson v. Time Warner, Inc., Warner Communications, Inc., DC Comics, et al.*, 496 F. Su 2d 1111, 2007 US Dist. LEXIS 56910, 4 (hereafter cited as *Siegel and Larson v. Time Warner/DC*).

9. *DC v. Bruns*, Jacob S. Liebowitz deposition, March 16, 1939, 2, NARA, RA, NR, NYC.

10. *Superman: Dailies 1939–1942*.

11. Levitz, *75 Years of DC Comics*, 51.

12. Pasko, *DC Vault*, 31, 33.

13. Ibid., 33, 35.

CHAPTER 4: SHADOW REALM

1. Vaz, *Tales of the Dark Knight*, 66.

2. Feiffer, *Great Comic Book Heroes*, 29.

3. Pasko, *DC Vault*, 35.

4. Daniels, *DC Comics*, 33.

5. Murray, "Shadow Origins of Batman," 70.

6. Tollin, "The Invisible Shadow," 75, 78.

7. Steranko, *Steranko History of Comics*, 1:16.

8. Gibson, "Million Words a Year," 4.

9. Saunders, "Walter M. Baumhofer," 24, 26.

10. Tollin, "The Invisible Shadow," 79.

11. Robinson, foreword in *The Shadow* #9, 4.

12. Robinson, foreword in *The Shadow* #9, 4; Murray, "Shadow Origins of Batman," and Tollin, "Spotlight on the Shadow," 70–71, 75, 132–133; Daniels, *Batman: Complete History*, 65.

13. Kane and Andrae, *Batman and Me*, 43.

14. Murray, "Pulp Roots of Batman," 53.

15. Vaz, *Tales of the Dark Knight*, 27.

16. Uslan, Vaz telephone interview, July 5, 2019.

17. Eisner, *Eisner/Miller*, 232.

18. Vaz, *Tales of the Dark Knight*, 29–30.

19. Heintjes, "Setting Up Shop," 8.

20. Jones, *Men of Tomorrow*, 148.

21. *DC v. Bruns*, Liebowitz testimony, April 6, 1939, 40, 48–49, Transcript of Record, NARA, RA, NR, NYC.

CHAPTER 5: SUPERMAN VERSUS WONDER MAN

1. Ibid., 2–3, 9.

2. Ibid., 1–3, 5.

3. At trial Warren Angel, vice president and general manager of Kable News, estimated 230,000 copies distributed; Victor Fox testified to 300,000, with production expenses of $67,000. *DC v. Bruns*, April 6, 1939, Angel testimony, 71, Victor Fox testimony, 121, Transcript of Record, NARA, RA, NR, NYC.

4. Andelman, *Will Eisner*, 44–45.

5. *DC v. Bruns*, April 6, 1939, Mr. Manges statement, 36, Mr. Blum statement, 80, 82, Transcript of Record, NARA, RA, NR, NYC.

6. Ibid., Siegel testimony, 54, 59–60.

7. Ibid., Liebowitz testimony, 51.

8. Ibid., Fox testimony, 124–126; Donenfeld testimony, 143–144; Iger testimony, 114.

9. *DC v. Bruns*, trial, April 6, 1939, Eisner testimony, 87–88, 93, Transcript of Record, NARA, RA, NR, NYC.

10. Judge Woolsey, USDJ, Opinion, *DC v. Bruns*, 157, 160–161, NARA, RA, NR, NYC.

11. Goulart, *Comic Book Culture*, 48; Quattro, "Superman vs. Wonder Man," 58.

12. Eisner, foreword to *The Dreamer*.

13. Jerry Siegel, letter to Jack Liebowitz, July 1, 1941, NARA, RA, NR, NYC.

14. Quattro, "Superman vs. Wonderman," 55.

15. Groth, "Interview: Jack Kirby," 66–67.

16. *DC v. Bruns*, Justice Hand ruling, No. 203, Circuit Court of Appeals, 2nd Circuit, April 29, 1940, Federal Reporter, Second Series, vol. 111 F 2d., 433.

17. *National Comics/DC v. Fawcett*, Jack Liebowitz testimony at trial, March 25, 1948, 1137, Box 834, Vol. 3 Book, NARA, RA, NR, NYC.

18. Feiffer, "Great Comic-Book Heroes," 77.

CHAPTER 6: THE FIRST GENERATION

1. Schwartz, *Broadcast Hysteria*, 104–105.
2. Simon, *Joe Simon*, 51–53.
3. Ibid., 55–57.
4. Ibid., 57, 61.
5. Ibid., 57, 61.
6. Ibid., 64, 66.
7. Steve Saffel, Vaz telephone interview, New York, January 18, 2013.
8. Price of painting in "pay copy," *Marvel Comics* #1, auctioned by Heritage Auction Galleries, "Heritage: Comics and Comic Art Auction" catalogue, February 25–27, 2010, Dallas, Texas, 59.
9. Daniels, *Marvel*, 26.
10. Thomas interview, "Everett on Everett," 13.
11. Ibid., 13, 15–16.
12. Benton, *Comic Book in America*, 26–27.
13. Skelly, *Comics Journal Library*, Jack Kirby interview 2, 1:15.
14. *Woodwork: Wallace Wood (1927–1981)*, IDW exhibition catalogue (2012), 21.
15. Feiffer, "Great Comic-Book Heroes," 81.
16. Nowak, "Ace of Cartoons," 36.
17. Don Rico, interview with Mark Cotta Vaz, Bay Con I Comic Convention, Berkeley, CA, October 1975.
18. Evanier, "The King and I," 54.
19. Feiffer, *Great Comic Book Heroes*, 51–52.
20. Andelman, *Will Eisner: A Spirited Life*, 47.
21. Dick Sprang, Q&A letter exchange with Vaz, June 30, 1988.
22. Kronenberg, "Auteur Theory," 41.
23. Schumacher, *Will Eisner*, 36.
24. Kronenberg, "Auteur Theory," 40.
25. Schumacher, *Will Eisner*, 56–57.
26. Ibid., 57.
27. Ibid., 59.
28. Vaz, *The Spirit*, 244; Andelman, *Will Eisner*, 54–55.
29. Levitz, *75 Years of DC Comics*, 135.
30. Compare strip from *Superman: Dailies*, 93, to the *Superman* #3 sequence as reprinted in DC's *Superman: Golden Age Omnibus Vol. 1*, 374–375.
31. Sales figures provided by Liebowitz in trial testimony, *Detective Comics and Superman, Inc., v. Fawcett and Republic, et al.*, US District Court, SDNY, March 25, 1948, Box 834, Vol. 3, 1282, 1318, NARA, RA, NR, NYC. Hereafter, this case reference will be cited as *DC/Superman v. Fawcett et al.* (or "National Comics" where applicable).
32. *Siegel and Shuster v. National Periodical Publications, Inc.*, NO 69 Civ. 1429, 364 F. 1032, US District Court, SDNY, October 18, 1973 (section 1034), 2.
33. Jack Liebowitz, letter to Jerry Siegel, March 1, 1940, found at 20th Century Danny Boy website; *DC/Superman, v. Fawcett et. al.*, March 18, 1948, 648, Box 835, NARA, RA, NR, NYC.

34. *DC/Superman v. Fawcett et al.*, Capt. William Parker deposition, direct examination by Wallace Martin, 1944, pp. 12–13, NARA, RA, NR, NYC. Parker was nine years old when his father gave him *Stories of the King* by James Baldwin, an account of King Arthur and his Knights, with the inscription: "Billy from Daddy, April 5, 1921."

35. *DC/Superman v. Fawcett et al.*, Parker, cross-examination at trial by Louis Nizer, March 20, 1948, Box 835, transcripts, p. 844, NARA, RA, NR, NYC.

36. Murray, "Rise of Captain Marvel," 28.

37. *DC/Superman v. Fawcett et al.*, Parker direct examination at trial, March 18, 1948, Box 835, p. 707, NARA, RA, NR, NYC.

38. Murray, "Rise of Captain Marvel," 28.

39. Steranko, *Steranko History of Comics*, 2:11.

40. *DC/Superman v. Fawcett et al.*, Bill Parker, Fawcett interoffice memo, November 22, 1939, cited in court transcripts; Nizer cross-examination of Parker, Big Book, vol. 2 (stamped April 10, 1950), p. 848, NARA, RA, NR, NYC.

41. Groth, interview with C. C. Beck, "With One Magic Word," 58.

42. Murray, "Rise of Captain Marvel," 28.

43. Zaid, Vaz interview, May 24, 2019; Steranko, *Steranko History of Comics*, 2:11. Steranko suggests Timely's *Marvel Mystery Comics* might also have influenced the new name.

CHAPTER 7: SUPERMAN, INC.

1. Daniels, *Wonder Woman: Complete History*, 20–24, 28, 31, 61, 63.

2. *DC/Superman v. Fawcett et al.*, Robert Maxwell cross-examination, March 4, 1948, 264, NARA, RA, NR, NYC.

3. *DC/Superman v. Fawcett et al.*, Jack Liebowitz testimony at trial, March 1948, Box 835, "Big Book," vol. 2, p. 609, NARA, RA, NR, NYC.

4. Ibid., March 15, 1948, Box 835, pp. 632, 635.

5. Robert J. Maxwell, deposition by Fawcett at the New York office of Phillips, Nizer, Benjamin & Krim, September 18, 1946, p. 5, NARA, RA, NR, NYC; Maxwell deposition, November 12, 1946, p. 101, ibid. A court document places the radio show's debut "on or about the 12th day of February, 1940." *DC/Superman v. Fawcett et al.*, "As and for a First, Separate and Distinct Cause of Action," presented by plaintiff attorneys, c. 1941, clauses 52–53, p. 20, Box 825, ibid.

6. Douglas Martin, "Jason Beck Dies at 92, Radio Voice on 'Superman,'" *New York Times*, July 30, 2004: A-12. Beck reportedly worked about 1,600 *Superman* broadcasts.

7. Cowsill et al., *DC Comics: Year by Year*, 33.

8. Morrison, *Supergods*, 13.

9. Jack Liebowitz, letter to Jerry Siegel, January 25, 1940, p. 2, on 20th Century Danny Boy website.

10. Jerry Siegel, letter to Jack Liebowitz, June 25, 1940, NARA, RA, NR, NYC; Kobler, "Up, Up And Awa-a-y!," 76.

11. Jerry Siegel and Joe Shuster, letter to Harry Donenfeld and J. S. Liebowitz, May 8, 1940, NARA, RA, NR, NYC.

12. Jerry Siegel, letter to Jack Liebowitz, February 13, 1942, p. 2, ibid.

13. Whit Ellsworth, letter to Jerry Siegel, November 4, 1940, ibid.

14. Couch, *Jerry Robinson*, 38; Kane and Andrae, *Batman and Me*, 46.

15. Couch, *Jerry Robinson*, 41.

16. Ibid., 44.

17. Daniels, *Batman: Complete History,* 39, 41.

18. Kane and Andrae, *Batman and Me*, 105, 107.

19. This author was the interviewer.

20. Pasko, *DC Vault*, 26–28; Levitz, *75 Years of DC Comics*, 139.

21. Letter excerpted, *DC/Superman v. Fawcett et al.*, Jack Liebowitz testimony at trial, March 18, 1948, Box 835, "Big Book" (stamped April 10, 1950), p. 659, NARA, RA, NR, NYC.

22. Hill, "Who Was H. J. Ward?," 37–38.

23. Wikipedia, s.v. "Master Man (Fawcett Comics)," for origin background.

CHAPTER 8: PATENTS AND PATRIOTS

1. *Look* strips from February 27, 1940, reprinted in *Superman: Sunday Classics.*

2. Bowers, *Superman versus the Ku Klux Klan*, 100–101.

3. Nowak, "Ace of Cartoons," 36.

4. Couch, *Jerry Robinson*, 73–74, 76.

5. *Marvel Mystery Comics* #20 (June 1941), reprint from Marvel Masterworks, *Golden Age Marvel Comics, Vol. 5* (New York: Marvel Entertainment, 2010), 203, 218.

6. Simon, *Comic Book Makers*, 49–50.

7. Simon, *My Life in Comics*, 85–87.

8. Jones, *Men of Tomorrow*, 200.

9. Simon, *Comic Book Makers*, 52.

10. Simon, *My Life in Comics*, 99–100.

11. House ad for *U.S.A. Comics* #1 (August 1941), reprinted in Marvel Masterworks, *Golden Age U.S.A. Comics, Vol. 1* (New York: Marvel Publishing, 2007), back page.

12. Simon, *My Life in Comics*, 112; Simon, *Comic Book Makers*, 63; *Kirby vs. Marvel et al.*, Stan Lee deposition in Los Angeles, May 13, 2010, p. 5.

13. Kidd, *Shazam*, 30.

14. *DC/Superman v. Fawcett et al.*, C. C. Beck trial testimony, March 22, 1948, Box 835, p. 202, NARA, RA, NR, NYC; Origin of "Sivana" name discussed by attorneys Nizer and Martin, March 19, 1948, Box 835, p. 815, ibid.

15. Kidd, *Shazam*, 141.

16. DC Archives Editions, *The Shazam! Archives: Volume One*, foreword by Richard A. Lupoff, 6–7.

17. Feiffer, *Great Comic Book Heroes*, 24.

18. "The Marvel Family Fights the Sivana Family's Newspaper," *The Marvel Family* #23 (May 1948).

19. Feiffer, "Great Comic-Book Heroes," 77–78.

CHAPTER 9: UP, UP AND AWA-A-Y!

1. Wikipedia, s.v. "Republic Pictures," for background.

2. Brown testified, "We had continuities on about 13 episodes, I recall." *DC/Superman v. Fawcett et al.*, Hiram S. Brown deposition taken in Los Angeles County, April 9, 1945, pp. 66, 76, 80, 118–119, NARA, RA, NR, NYC.

3. *DC/Superman v. Fawcett et al.*, Robert Maxwell direct examination, March 4, 1948, p. 265, ibid.

4. Hiram S, Brown, pretrial deposition taken in Los Angeles County, April 9, 1945, Box 836, pp. 66–67, ibid.

5. Ibid., 19, 75–76.

6. Ibid., 16–17.

7. Wikipedia, s.v. "*Adventures of Captain Marvel.*"

8. Wikipedia, s.v. "Tom Tyler."

9. *DC/Superman v. Fawcett et al.*, Hiram S. Brown Jr., pretrial deposition taken in Los Angeles County, May 21, 1945, Box 836, p. 50, NARA, RA, NR, NYC.

10. Solomon, *Enchanted Drawings*, 30–31.

11. Liebowitz cross-examination, March 25, 1948, Box 835, p. 634, NARA, RA, NR, NYC; Solomon, *Enchanted Drawings*, 80, 82–84. The follow-up Fleischer feature, *Mr. Bug Goes to Town*, was another box-office disappointment. Fleischer Studios had produced nine *Superman* shorts when Paramount fired the brothers and changed the studio name to Famous Studios, which produced eight more *Superman* short cartoons.

12. Kane and Andrae, *Batman and Me*, 125, 127.

13. Jack Burnley, foreword to *Superman Archives: Vol. 3* (New York: DC Comics, Inc., 1991).

14. Whit Ellsworth, letter to Jerry Siegel, February 19, 1941, NARA, RA, NR, NYC.

15. *DC/Superman v. Fawcett et al.*, Robert Maxwell, direct examination, March 4, 1948, Box 832, p. 114, NARA, RA, NR, NYC.

16. Kobler, "Up, Up And Awa-a-y!," 14–15, 74, 76, 78. The article included Siegel's description of how Superman "sprung practically full-blown" in 1932, but it wasn't until 1933 that Siegel wrote "The Reign of the Super-Man." In the 1985 *Nemo* interview, Siegel placed the date as the summer of 1934. The *Post* seemingly conflates, or Siegel mistakenly describes, a full-blown legend when it was still bare-bones myth.

17. Jack Liebowitz, letter to Jerry Siegel, June 27, 1941, NARA, RA, NR, NYC.

18. Jones, *Men of Tomorrow*, 185–186.

19. Jerry Siegel, letter to Jack Liebowitz, July 1, 1941, NARA, RA, NR, NYC.

20. Whit Ellsworth, letter to Jerry Siegel, October 2, 1941, NARA, RA, NR, NYC.

21. Jerry Siegel, letter to Jack Liebowitz, October 15, 1942, p. 1, NARA, RA, NR, NYC.

22. Levitz, *Golden Age of DC Comics*, 301; "Superman a Money Maker," *Kansas City Star*, May 22, 1941.

23. Pasko, *DC Vault*, 38, 45–46.

24. Superman, Inc., formation summarized in *National Comics Publications, Inc., v. Fawcett Publications et al.*, US District Court, SDNY, 93 F. Su 349 (April 10, 1950), US Dist. LEXIS 2324; 87 U.S. P.Q. (BNA) 12, 2–3; *DC/Superman v. Fawcett et al.*, Liebowitz trial testimony, March 9, 1948, p. 609, and Whitney Ellsworth trial testimony, March 11, 1948, pp. 47, 293, NARA, RA, NR, NYC.

25. Saunders, "Joseph Szokoli," 23–25.

CHAPTER 10: BATTLE OF THE CENTURY

1. Ibid., 4, 17, 29–30.

2. *DC/Superman v. Fawcett et al.*, statement from Meyer H. Lavenstein, for defendants Republic Pictures Corporation and Republic Productions, Inc., October 28, 1941, Box 825, NARA, RA, NR, NYC.

3. Cowsill et al., *DC Comics: Year by Year*, 36–37.

4. Hamerlinck, foreword to *The Shazam! Family Archives*, 5–6.

5. Simon, *My Life in Comics*, 124; Evanier, "War and Adventure," in Simon and Kirby, *Best of Simon and Kirby*, 99.

6. House ad, *U.S.A. Comics* #4, reprint, Marvel Masterworks *Golden Age U.S.A. Comics, Vol. 1*, 220.

7. Tye, *Superman: High-Flying*, 107. The novel gave Joe Shuster first billing.

8. Richard H. Waldo, letter, McClure Syndicate to Detective Comics, Inc., September 2, 1944, Box 838, NARA, RA, NR, NYC.

9. Jerry Siegel, letter to Whit Ellsworth, February 12, 1942, NARA, RA, NR, NYC.

10. Whit Ellsworth, letter on Superman, Inc. letterhead, to Jerry Siegel, Saturday, February 21, 1942, NARA, RA, NR, NYC.

11. Jerry Siegel, letter to Jack Liebowitz, March 8, 1942, NARA, RA, NR, NYC.

12. Jerry Siegel, letter to Jack Liebowitz, October 15, 1942, NARA, RA, NR, NYC.

13. Jerry Siegel, letter to Jack Liebowitz, October 16, 1942, NARA, RA, NR, NYC.

14. Levitz, *Golden Age of DC Comics*, 132.

15. Evanier, "War and Adventure," in Simon and Kirby, *Best of Simon and Kirby*; Simon, *My Life in Comics*, 124.

16. Couch, *Jerry Robinson*, 79–80.

17. Evanier, *Kirby: King of Comics*, 57, 67, 69.

18. Essay by Eddie Campbell, "A PS Briefing," from Will Eisner, *PS Magazine: The Best of The Preventive Maintenance Monthly* (New York: Abrams ComicArts, 2011), 11–12; Schumacher, *Will Eisner*, 59.

19. *DC/Superman, Inc., plaintiff*, Bill of Particulars, signed by Louis Nizer, November 13, 1943, Box 825, p. 4, NARA, RA, NR, NYC.

20. Ibid., "Supplemental Schedules to Be Answered to Plaintiffs' Bill of Particulars to Defendant Fawcett Publications, Inc.," January 7, 1944, p. 55.

21. Honorable Judge Bright, US District Judge, SDNY, order dated October 17, 1945, pp. 3–5. NARA, RA, NR, NYC.

22. "With respect to the Bill of Costs of defendant, Fawcett Publications, Inc.,"

from Phillips, Nizer, Benjamin & Krim to Nims, Verdi & Martin, Esq., and Meyer H. Lavenstein, Esq., June 14, 1950, p. 2, NARA, RA, NR, NYC.

23. *DC/Superman v. Fawcett et al.*, Hiram S. Brown Jr., "Depositions of witnesses on behalf of defendants Republic [et al.], taken in Los Angeles County, commencing April 9, 1945," pp. 86–87, for Republic defendants, Los Angeles County, NARA, RA, NR, NYC.

24. Hiram Brown deposition, May 21, 1945, Box 836, p. 122, NARA, RA, NR, NYC.

25. Norman S. Hall deposition, p. 233, NARA, RA, NR, NYC.

26. Hiram Brown deposition, May 21, 1945, pp. 126, 129–130, NARA, RA, NR, NYC.

27. *DC/Superman v. Fawcett et al.*, deposition quotes as noted in Parker direct examination at trial, March 19, 1948, Box 835, p. 789, NARA, RA, NR, NYC.

28. *DC/Superman v. Fawcett et al.*, Capt. William Lee Parker deposition, 1944, p. 25, NARA, RA, NR, NYC.

29. Ibid., deposition quotes as noted in C. C. Beck's direct examination at trial (1948), Box 835, pp. 998, 1009.

30. Ibid., Jacob Liebowitz deposition, August 14, 1946, p. 47.

31. Ibid., direct examination of Jack Liebowitz, August 14, 1946, pp. 11–13, 16–18, 23, 42, 44, 47–48, 109–112, 119–120, 159; August 23, 1946, pp. 206–208.

32. *DC/Superman v. Fawcett et al.*, Jack Liebowitz deposition, February 20, 1948, Box 834, pp. 248–249, 255–256, 292; Wallace Martin sworn statement, January 23, 1948, witnessed by John J. Horan, notary public in the State of New York, NARA, RA, NR, NYC.

CHAPTER 11: THE ADVENTURES OF SUPERBOY

1. Joe Shuster, letter to Jerry Siegel, October 1, 1944, NARA, RA, NR, NYC.

2. "The Atomic Age," editorial, *Life* magazine, August 20, 1945, 32.

3. Daniels, *DC Comics*, 81.

4. *DC/Superman v. Fawcett et al.*, Jack Liebowitz deposition, February 20, 1948, Box 834, pp. 247–248, NARA, RA, NR, NYC; Merger date in Levitz, *75 Years of DC Comics*, gatefold timeline.

5. Paul Levitz interview with Joe Kubert, in Levitz, *Golden Age of DC Comics*, 7.

6. Infantino, *Amazing World of Carmine Infantino*, 24.

7. *DC/Superman v. Fawcett et al.*, Harry Donenfeld deposition, November 12, 1946, pp. 6, 10–13, 19, 27–30, NARA, RA, NR, NYC.

8. Jerry Siegel, letter to Jack Liebowitz, April 1, 1945, pp. 1–2, NARA, RA, NR, NYC. Siegel mistakenly refers to "a dropping plant."

9. *Siegel and Larson v. Time Warner/DC*, US District Court, CD California, 496 F. Su 2d 1111; 2007 US Dist. LEXIS 56910, item 183.

10. Ricca, *Super Boys*, 222.

11. *Siegel v. Warner Bros. Entertainment, Inc.*, 542 F. Su 2d 1098 (2008), p. 8; *Lois Lane* grievance noted by Siegel in his 1975 press release, "A Curse on the Superman Movie!"

12. *Siegel and Shuster v. National Periodical Publications, Inc., et al.*, No. 69 Civ. 1429, 364 F. Su 1032 (1973), section 1034, end of part II.

13. Murray, "Rediscovered Schwartz," 24.

14. Zaid, Vaz telephone interview, May 24, 2019; Levitz, Vaz telephone interview, June 18, 2019.

15. Daniels, *Superman: Complete History*, 70, 72.

16. Decker and Groth, "Interview with William M. Gaines," 55.

17. Reidelbach, *Completely Mad*, 10.

18. From summary, *Siegel and Larson v. Time Warner/DC*, US District Court, CD California, 496 F. Su 2d 1111; 2007 US Dist. LEXIS 56910, sections 1115-1116, pp. 4-5, 7-8.

19. *Siegel and Shuster v. National Periodical Publications, Inc., et al.*, No. 69 Civ. 1429, 364 F. Su 1032 (1973), section 1036, p. 4.

20. *Siegel and Larson v. Time Warner/DC*, US District Court, CD California, 496 F. Su 2d 1111; 2007 U.S. Dist. LEXIS 56910, p. 8.

21. Jones, *Men of Tomorrow*, 252.

22. Zaid, Vaz interview, May 24, 2019.

23. Ricca, *Super Boys*, 226-228.

CHAPTER 12: THE TRIAL

1. Simon, *My Life in Comics*, 145-146.

2. The *Captain Marvel* magazine was not a "one-shot" but rather the first issue of the popular series *Captain Marvel Adventures*.

3. Simon, *Comic Book Makers*, 64.

4. Eric Pace, "Louis Nizer, Lawyer to the Famous, Dies at 92," *New York Times*, November 11, 1994, late edition, final correction appended, LexisNexis website.

5. Nizer, *My Life in Court*, 34-35.

6. *National Comics/DC v. Fawcett*, Thomas Diskin, sworn statement, March 24, 1952, Box 826, pp. 2-3, NARA, RA, NR, NYC; US District Court, SDNY, "Stenographer's Minutes: Index to Witnesses and Exhibits, Stipulation," March 9, 1948, Hon. Alfred Coxe, Civ. 15-383, NARA, RA, NR, NYC.

7. *DC/Superman v. Fawcett et al.*, Louis Nizer, March 9, 1948, trial opening, Box 832, pp. 4-5, 8, 10, 17-19, NARA, RA, NR, NYC.

8. Ibid., Frederick Whitney Ellsworth, testimony at trial, March 9-11, 1948, pp. 76-77, 80, 266, 293-299.

9. Ibid., Joe Simon testimony at trial, March 9, 1948, pp. 394-397, and March 15, 1948, pp. 460-462, 476. Blue Bolt first appeared in 1940, in *Blue Bolt Comics*, published by Novelty Press.

10. *DC/Superman v. Fawcett et al.*, Manly Wade Wellman, testimony at trial, March 9, 1948, pp. 478-479, 483-485, 487-489, 493, 495-496, 500-501, NARA, RA, NR, NYC.

11. Ibid., Edward Herron, testimony at trial, March 11-12, 1948, Box 831, "Big Book," pp. 318-319, 331, 335, 362-363, 365-367, 376.

12. Ibid., Jacob Liebowitz, testimony at trial, March 15, 1948, Box 835, pp. 612, 642-643, 648-650, 666-668.

CHAPTER 13: PROGENITORS

1. Arnold's estimate was slightly off; by the time Donenfeld had control of DC he was publishing three magazines, with *Action* making a fourth.

2. *DC/Superman v. Fawcett et al.*, Everett M. Arnold, testimony at trial, pp. 403–415, NARA, RA, NR, NYC.

3. Steranko, *Steranko History of Comics*, 2:15.

4. *DC/Superman v. Fawcett et al.*, Arnold, testimony at trial, pp. 419–421, 423–426, 444–446, 448–449, NARA, RA, NR, NYC.

5. Ibid., William Lee Parker, testimony at trial, Box 835, pp. 681, 697, 728, 749, 751, 755–757, 771, 786, 789–790, 798–799, 807–808, 829–832, 844–845, 848.

6. Ibid., C. C. Beck, testimony at trial, March 22, 1948, Box 835, pp. 914–915, 944–946, 948, 955, 992–994, 997–998, 1009–1010, 1015–1017.

7. *DC/Superman v. Fawcett et al.*, Harrison Steeves, testimony at trial, Box 833, p. 1147, NARA, RA, NR, NYC. The "magnificent boy" comment was in response to testimony by Whit Ellsworth, who felt Batson was a "helpless" character.

8. Ibid., March 24, 1948, Box 833, pp. 1133–1139, 1145, 1147, 1149, 1184–1185.

9. Keefer, *Philip Wylie*, 48.

10. *DC/Superman v. Fawcett et al.*, Dean Cornwell, testimony at trial, March 23, 1948, Box 833, pp. 1066–1067, 1074, NARA, RA, NR, NYC.

11. Ibid., Otto Binder, testimony at trial, pp. 1052–1053.

CHAPTER 14: JUDGMENT DAY

1. The judge defined "joint venture" as "an association of two or more persons to carry out a single business enterprise for profit, for which purpose they combined their property, money, effects, skill, and knowledge."

2. *National Comics/DC v. Fawcett*, District Judge Coxe, judgment, 93 F. Su 349; US Dist., April 10, 1950, p. 7.

3. Wikipedia, s.v. "Learned Hand."

4. These and subsequent quotes are cited from *National Comics/DC v. Fawcett*, Opinion, Circuit Judge L. Hand, No. 197, Docket 21832, US Court of Appeals, 2nd Circuit, May 4, 1951, Argued; August 30, 1951, Decided, 1867–1882, Box 826, NARA, RA, NR, NYC. Justice Hand's statement uses excessive quotation marks regarding "strips," "Superman," and so on. Unless necessary, quotation marks have been removed for ease of reading.

5. *National Comics/DC v. Fawcett*, Thomas Diskin, sworn statement, March 24, 1952, NARA, RA, NR, NYC.

6. Ibid., Nizer before Hon. Vincent L. Leibell, May 19, 1952, pp. 121–122.

7. *National Comics/DC v. Fawcett*, Docket 21832, US Court of Appeals, 2nd Circuit; 198 F 2d 927; 1952 US A LEXIS 4363; 94 U.S. P.Q. (BNA) 289; Sept. 5, 1952, Decided, June 10, 1952, Filed.

8. Ibid., Jacob Liebowitz, affidavit, state and county of New York, November 14, 1952, Box 826.

9. Ibid., Thomas A. Diskin, affidavit before the US District Court, SDNY, notarized on December 17, 1952, pp. 1–4.

10. Jim Amash, "Fawcett Knew How to Do It," 4–5, 9.

11. *National Comics/DC v. Fawcett et al.*, Judgment, paragraphs two and three, August 18, 1953, Box 826, pp. 3–5, NARA, RA, NR, NYC.

12. "Supplemental Stipulation and Settlement Agreement," August 14, 1953, Box 826, NARA, RA, NR, NYC; "Amendment of Republic Defendants' Cross-Claim against Defendant Fawcett," signed by Meyer H. Lavenstein, attorney for the defendants, New York, May 5, 1953, ibid.; see Wikipedia, s.v. *"National Comics Publications, Inc., v. Fawcett Publications, Inc.,"* re: $400,000 settlement figure.

13. Reidelbach, *Completely Mad*, 23.

14. Dooley and Engle, *Superman at Fifty*, 42, 44.

15. *Kirby Heirs v. Marvel Characters, Inc., et al.*, Mark Evanier, John Morrow, Pen Center USA Brief of Amici Curiae on Petition for a Writ of Certiorari, July 13, 2014, p. 7.

CHAPTER 15: CRACKDOWN AND CRASH

1. Menand, "The Horror," 127.

2. Christensen and Seifert, "Dark Legend," 93–94; Crist, "Horror in the Nursery," 1948.

3. Wertham, *Seduction of the Innocent*, 33–34, 190–191.

4. Gilbert, "Total Control," 5.

5. Reidelbach, *Completely Mad*, 26.

6. Geissman, *Foul Play!*, 60–61; Simon quotes are from *My Life in Comics*, 185, and Groth, "Joe Simon: Interview," 106.

7. Thomas, *75 Years of Marvel*, 124, 165.

8. Christensen and Seifert, "Dark Legend," 97.

9. Hajdu, *Ten-Cent Plague*, 287, 291.

10. Cowsill et al., *DC Comics Year by Year*, 74; "What Do *You* Know About This Comics Seal of Approval?," sample pages reprinted in Levitz, *Golden Age of DC Comics*, 405.

11. Daniels, *Wonder Woman: Complete History*, 44, 76, 94.

12. Mark Evanier, "The Great Western," in Simon and Kirby, *Best of Simon and Kirby*, 180.

13. Hajdu, *Ten-Cent Plague*, 321–323.

14. Starger and Spurlock, *Wally's World*, 181.

15. Ibid., 191.

16. Stewart, "Pebbles in a Landscape," 99, 101; Alan Moore, writer, Dave Gibbons, artist, "For the Man Who Has Everything," *Superman Annual* #11 (1985).

17. "A Zap Oral History by Patrick Rosenkranz," *Complete Zap Comix: Vol. 5, The Zap Story*, 882.

18. Crumb, *R. Crumb Coffee Table Art Book*, 35.

19. Hajdu, *Ten-Cent Plague*, 228, 326.

20. Benton, *Comic Book in America*, 120–121, 124–125, 128, 149–150.

21. Pasko, *DC Vault*, 97.

22. Kitchen, "Biro and Wood," 20–21; Spiegelman, "Ballbuster," 73–74.

23. Uslan, Vaz telephone interview, June 6, 2019; Benton, *Comic Book in America*, 143.

24. Murray, "The Retrospective Stan Lee," 3.

25. Thomas and Sanderson, *Marvel Vault*, 45, 49–50, 56, 58.

26. The curious tradition of pulp publishing front companies held true. The covers of *Amazing Fantasy*, *Amazing Adventures*, and *Journey into Mystery* bore "mc," for Marvel Comics, and the books were published by Atlas Magazines; *Tales to Astonish* carried "Ind." and was published by Zenith Publishing Corp; *Tales of Suspense* carried "Ind." but was published by Male Publishing Corp, which became Vista Publications; *Strange Tales* bore the "Ind." and was also published by Vista. All had the same offices as Goodman's Magazine Management Company: 655 Madison Avenue, New York City.

27. Yoe, *Secret Identity*, 35.

28. Pasko, *DC Vault*, 104, 107.

29. Ricca, *Super Boys*, 244.

30. Jones, *Men of Tomorrow*, 291–293.

31. Pasko, *DC Vault*, 98.

32. Levitz, *Silver Age of DC Comics*, 17–18.

33. Murray, "Three Easy Pieces," 11.

34. Ibid.

CHAPTER 16: RESURRECTION AND RENEWAL

1. George, "Make Mine Magazine Management!," 58–59, 62–63.

2. Evanier, *Kirby: King of Comics*, 109.

3. Lee, *Origins of Marvel Comics*, 16–17; Evanier, *Kirby: King of Comics*, 112.

4. *Kirby v. Marvel Characters et al.*, Evanier, Morrow, Pen Center, Brief of Amici Curiae, on Petition for a Writ of Certiorari, June 13, 2014, pp. 9–11.

5. "Stan Lee's original typewritten synopsis for *The Fantastic Four* #1," in *The Fantastic Four Omnibus: Vol. 1* (New York: Marvel Entertainment, 2013); *Kirby v. Marvel Characters et al.*, Lee deposition, Los Angeles, May 13, 2010, p. 24.

6. Evanier, *Kirby: King of Comics*, 122.

7. Uslan, Vaz telephone interviews, June 6, July 5, 2019.

8. Lee, *Origins of Marvel Comics*, 132–134.

9. *Kirby v. Marvel Characters et al.*, Lee deposition, May 13, 2010, pp. 29–30.

10. *Kirby v. Marvel Characters et al.*, Evanier, Morrow, Pen Center, Brief of Amici Curiae, on Petition for a Writ of Certiorari, June 13, 2014.

11. *Kirby v. Marvel Characters et al.*, Lee deposition, Los Angeles, May 13, 2010, pp. 36–37.

12. Thomas, "Conversation with Larry Lieber"; Larry Lieber, deposition for *Lisa R. Kirby, Barbara J. Kirby, Neal L. Kirby, and Susan M. Kirby v. Marvel Worldwide, Inc., Marvel Characters, Inc., and MVL Rights, LLC* (hereafter cited as *Kirby Heirs v. Marvel*), posted by Rich Johnston on March 9, 2011, Bleeding Cool website,

https://www.bleedingcool.com; Lee, *Origins of Marvel Comics*, 182; *Kirby v. Marvel Characters et al.*, Lee deposition, p. 36.

13. Levitz, *Silver Age of DC Comics*, 26, 29, 45.

14. Uslan, Vaz telephone interview, June 6, July 5, 2019; Christensen and Seifert, "Dark Legend," 98.

15. *The Super Catalogue* #10, Passaic Book Center, circa 1974, Mark Cotta Vaz collection.

16. Bruning, "Guilty Pleasures Revealed!"

17. Irving and Kushner, *Leaping Tall Buildings*, 47.

18. Ibid.

19. "28 People Who Count," *Esquire*, September 1965, 97. Hulk and Spider-Man were listed 27 and 28, respectively.

20. Paste-ups were similar to the "cut-ups" by Beat writer William Burroughs and others that juxtaposed random montages of text, from news magazines to classic literature, creating fragmented and nonlinear narratives, a technique Burroughs also explored in audio recording "cut-ins."

21. Varnedoe and Gopnik, *High and Low*, 194, 200–201.

22. Russ Heath, text and art, "Hero in Action: Bottle of Wine," *The Overstreet Comic Book Price Guide*, 46th ed. (Gemstone Publishing, 2016), 1169.

23. Levitz, *75 Years of DC Comics*, 433.

24. Julius Schwartz essay, "Once Upon a Time in New York" [copy missing publishing history].

25. Joel Eisner, *The Official Batman Batbook*, 167–171.

26. Prideaux, "Whole Country Goes Supermad," 23.

27. In this wild story, a scientist discovers Alfred barely alive in his crypt and takes him to his lab, where a "cell regeneration machine" brings him to life as the crazed, deformed Outsider. At the conclusion, Alfred is back to normal, unaware of his brief career as a deranged criminal.

28. Uslan, Vaz telephone interview, June 6, 2019; Levitz, *75 Years of DC Comics*, 268.

29. *Kirby v. Marvel Characters et al.*, Lee deposition, Los Angeles, May 13, 2010, p. 23.

30. *Woodwork: Wallace Wood* (IDW exhibition catalogue, 2012), 196, 200–201.

31. Lente and Dunlavey, *Comic Book History of Comics*, 107, 110; Wells, "Once and for All," 76.

32. Bode, "Comic Book Artist KO'D," 36.

CHAPTER 17: COPYRIGHT WARS

1. Pasko, *DC Vault*, 107.

2. Jones, *Men of Tomorrow*, 290; Ricca, *Super Boys*, 261.

3. Jones, *Men of Tomorrow*, 308.

4. *Marvel v. Simon*, US Court of Appeals, 2nd Circuit, Docket No. 02–7221, decided November 7, 2002, I. Publication of Captain America Comics.

5. Simon, *My Life in Comics*, 226–227.

6. Howe, *Marvel Comics*, 77.

7. *Marvel v. Simon*, US Court of Appeals, 2nd Circuit, Docket No. 02-7221, decided November 7, 2002, III. The Prior Actions.

8. Simon, *My Life in Comics*, 227–228.

9. *Marvel v. Simon*, US Court of Appeals, 2nd Circuit, Docket No. 02-7221, decided November 7, 2002, III. The Prior Actions.

10. Simon, *My Life in Comics*, 228.

11. Mason, Vaz telephone interview, June 7, 2019.

12. Deahl, "Consistently Inconsistent 'Instance and Expense' Test," 100–101, 104–105.

13. Cooke, "Kirby's Kingdom," 49.

14. Howe, *Marvel Comics*, 75–76.

15. Siegel and Shuster were represented by the Coudert Brothers, with other counsel; National Periodical Publications by Weil, Gotshal & Manges, with additional counsel.

16. *Siegel and Shuster v. National Periodical Publications, Inc.*, 364 F. Su 1032, US District Court, SDNY, No. 69 Civ. 1429, October 18, 1973, pp. 1, 4, 6–7.

17. The plaintiffs were again represented by Coudert Brothers, as was National by Weil, Gotshal & Manges.

18. *Siegel and Shuster v. National Periodical Publications, Inc.*, 508 F2d 909, No. 36, Docket 73-2844, US Court of Appeals, 2nd Circuit, November 7, 1974, Argued; December 5, 1974, Decided.

19. Dennis O'Neil, "The Man of Steel and Me," in Dooley and Engle, *Superman at Fifty*, 49.

20. Levitz, Vaz telephone interview, June 18, 2019.

21. Infantino, *Amazing World*, 102–103.

22. Infantino, *Amazing World*, 116–117; Mike Conroy, "Kimota! The Secret Origin of Mick Anglo's Marvelman," *Marvelman Classic Primer* #1 (August 2010).

23. Pasko, *DC Vault*, 139; Howe, *Marvel Comics*, 75, 87.

24. Beck, "Are We Living in A Golden Age?," 118.

25. John Wells, "The Batman Family Way," *Back Issue* #50 (August 2011), 29.

26. Groth, "With One Magic Word," 75.

27. Pierce and Hamerlinck, "Shazam!," 4; Beck, "Are We Living in A Golden Age?," 118.

28. Keller and Willson, "Don Newton and Captain Marvel," and companion essay by Don Newton, "The 'New' Captain Marvel," both in *Alter Ego* #11, pp. 41, 43.

29. Infantino, *Amazing World*, 117.

30. Bishoff, "Siegel and Shuster Deal," 36–37.

31. Siegel, "Curse on The Superman Movie!" The full letter can be found on the 20th Century Danny Boy website.

32. Mary Breasted, "Superman's Parents Need Him Now," *New York Times*, as printed in *San Francisco Chronicle*, November 25, 1975; "'Superman' Creators Want Share," *Daily Review*, Hayward, CA, December 10, 1975.

33. Couch, *Jerry Robinson*, 185.

34. Ibid., 184–185.

35. Ibid., 186–187.

36. *Superman: The Movie* promotional program, 1975; box-office number from Box Office Mojo website.

37. Vaz, *Behind the Mask of Spider-Man*, 29–30.

38. As explained in *Marvel Characters, Inc., v. Joseph H. Simon*, case decided November 7, 2002, p. 3.

39. Work-for-hire definition as quoted in "copyright culture: a law blog," posted under category archives *Kirby v. Marvel*: "'Nuff Said? A Look at *Kirby v. Marvel Characters, Inc.*, and Works Made for Hire under the Copyright Act of 1909," posted on September 15, 2014; Terry Hart, "Copyhype" post, "*Marvel v. Kirby*: Work for Hire and Copyright Termination," August 3, 2011.

40. Mason, Vaz telephone interview, June 7, 2019.

41. Toberoff, Vaz telephone interview, July 4, 2019. As regards the Siegel ruling that overruled earlier work-for-hire judgments on Superman, attorney John Mason adds, "Cases are fact-specific. But the holdings can create legal precedent for similar fact situations." Vaz telephone interview, June 7, 2019.

CHAPTER 18: MASTERS OF INVENTION

1. Regarding conceding rights in 1975 agreement: Baker and Hostetler, LLP, "Pocket Full of Kryptonite: California Court Rules that Superman Heirs Forfeited Termination Rights," Lexology website, October 30, 2012, p. 2; Andrae, "Of Superman and Kids with Dreams," 19.

2. *Kirby v. Marvel et al.*, Lee deposition, Los Angeles, May 13, 2010, pp. 27–28.

3. Evanier, *Kirby: King of Comics*, 141, 161, 163.

4. Glen David Gold, "Lo, from the Demon Shall Come—the Public Dreamer," *Masters of American Comics*, catalogue for exhibition jointly organized by the Hammer Museum and the Museum of Contemporary Art, Los Angeles, in association with Yale University Press (2005), 263–264, 267.

5. Evanier, *Kirby: King of Comics*, 141, 161, 163.

6. *Kirby v. Marvel, et al.*, Evanier, Morrow, Pen Center, Brief of Amici Curiae on Petition for a Writ of Certiorari, July 13, 2014, p. 13.

7. *Woodwork: Wallace Wood* (IDW exhibition catalogue, 2012), 202.

8. Gilbert, "Total Control," 15.

9. Levitz, Vaz telephone interview, June 18, 2019.

10. Kane and Andrae, *Batman and Me*, 43–44.

11. Dick Sprang, Q&A letter exchange with Vaz, June 30, 1988.

12. Scholl, "Double Identity," 44–45.

13. DiFruscio, "Dark Rebirth," 13–14; Levitz, Vaz telephone interview, June 18, 2019; Uslan, Vaz telephone interview, June 6, 2019; *Siegel and Larson v. Warner Bros. Entertainment, Inc.*, US District Court, CD California, March 26, 2008, 542 F. Su 2d 1122.

14. Gibbons, Vaz interview, October 13, 2012.

15. Wikipedia, s.v. "Gary Arlington."

16. Patrick Rosenkranz, "A Zap Oral History," in *The Complete Zap Comics: Vol. 5: The Zap Story*, 876, 881.

17. Steve Gerber statement, "Friends of Old Gerber," in *Destroyer Duck*, Special Lawsuit Benefit Edition #1 (1982), inside back cover.

18. "Colouring the Akira Comics: Steve Oliff and Olyoptics Colour Katuhiro Otomo's Black and White Artwork for the Western Release of Akira," "Unofficial" *Akira* website, 1–2. The Harvey Awards, named after Harvey Kurtzman and started in 1988 by Gary Groth, honor excellence in comics based on voting by comics professionals.

19. Mike Gold, introduction, *Shatter* #1 (June 1985), First Comics, Inc.

20. Mike Gold, introduction to Pepe Moreno, *Batman: Digital Justice*, 1990, DC Comics, Inc., 2–3.

21. Gibbons, Vaz interview, October 13, 2012.

22. Pasko, *DC Vault*, 146.

23. Letter to the *Comics Journal*, signed by Jenette Kahn, Dick Giordano, and Paul Levitz, November 19, 1985, *Comics Journal* #105 (February 1986), 52; Uslan, Vaz telephone interview, June 6, 2019; Levitz, Vaz telephone interview, June 18, 2019.

24. Jenette Kahn, introduction to Frank Miller's *Absolute Ronin* (New York: DC Comics, 2008); Levitz, Vaz telephone interview, June 18, 2019.

25. Mike W. Barr, "Return to Camelot: An Introduction to the 2008 Edition," *Camelot 3000: The Deluxe Edition* (New York: DC Comics, Inc., 2008), 2.

26. Kahn, introduction to Miller's *Absolute Ronin*.

27. Ibid.

28. Marx, "Frank Miller: Experiment in Creative Autonomy," 50.

29. Mike W. Barr blurb, *Rōnin, Book Five* (DC Comics/A Warner Communications Company), 1984.

30. Dean, "Kirby and Goliath," 91–95; Bode, "Comic Book Artist KO'D," 38; *Kirby v. Marvel et al.*, Brief of Amici Curiae, Evanier, Morrow, Pen Center, in support of petitioners, On Petition for a Writ of Certiorari, June 13, 2014, pp. 21–22.

CHAPTER 19: EVOLUTIONARY IMPERATIVE

1. Michael Chabon, "Introduction: Chaykin and *Flagg!*," in *American Flagg! Definitive Collection Vol. 1* (Berkeley, CA: Image Comics and Dynamic Forces, 2008); "A Portal to Another Dimension," *Comics Journal* #116 (July 1987), 80, 85; Gibbons, Kidd, and Essl, *Watching the Watchmen*, 28.

2. Stewart, "Alan Moore: Synchronicity," 89; "A Man on Fifteen Dead Men's Chests," essay in *Watchmen* #5 (New York: DC Comics, 1986).

3. Alan Moore, "Harvey Kurtzman Tribute," *Comics Journal* #157 (March 1993), 11; House ad, *Batman* #395 (May 1986); Elbein, "Marvel, Jack Kirby."

4. Gibbons, Vaz interview, October 13, 2012.

5. Sprang, Q&A letter exchange with Vaz, June 30, 1988.

6. Paul Kupperberg, introduction "The Time Has Come!," in *Superman: "Whatever Happened to the Man of Tomorrow?,"* deluxe ed. (New York: DC Comics, 2009).

7. E. Nelson Bridwell, "Superman in Action," in *Action Comics* #583 (September 1986); *DC Comics: A Visual Chronicle*, 220–221.

8. George Pérez, introduction, "The Wonder of It all," *Wonder Woman* #1 (February 1987); Daniels, *DC Comics*, 194; Daniels, *Wonder Woman*, 100.

9. Kahn, "Deer Freelancer" letter, December 4, 1986.

10. Kim Thompson, "Howard Chaykin Puts It All Back Together,"in *Amazing Heroes* #132 (January 1, 1988), 30, 36–37; Levitz, Vaz telephone interview, June 18, 2019; Vaz, "Rocket Blast," 45; Jon J. Muth, afterword to *M: A Graphic Novel Based on the Film by Fritz Lang* (New York: Abrams, 2008).

11. Ray Orrock, "Panel Chairman," *Daily Review*, Hayward, CA, April 18, 1988.

12. Denny O'Neil, "Postscript," *Batman: A Death in the Family*.

13. Daniels, *DC Comics*, 201.

14. Vaz, *The Spirit*, 42, 44; IMDb, s.v. "Benjamin Melniker"; Uslan, Vaz telephone interview, July 4, 2019.

15. Jenette Kahn, six-page letter to Mark Canton, October 18, 1982.

16. Sam Hamm, *Batman* screenplay for Warner Bros., Inc., 3rd draft, February 29, 1988, p. 1.

17. Shannon, "Dark and Stormy Knight," 9.

18. Connie Bruck, "Deal of the Year," *New Yorker*, January 8, 1990, 66, 68; Bill Barol, "Batmania," *Newsweek*, June 26, 1989, 72–74.

19. *Batman* box-office data from Box Office Mojo website; Uslan, Vaz telephone interview, June 6, 2019; Rodman, "They Shoot Comic Books," 39.

20. *Leonard Maltin's 2010 Movie Guide*, "Captain America" entry (New York: Penguin), 212.

21. Vaz, *Behind the Mask of Spider-Man*, 31–33.

22. N'Gai Croal, "Marvelous Makeover," *Newsweek*, February 17, 2003, 50.

23. Mike Cotton, "The New Deal," *Wizard*, December 2005, 57.

24. Wikipedia, s.v. "Marvel Studios," section 3, "Character rights."

25. Wikipedia, s.v. "Marvel Studios," summation; *Iron Man* budget and box-office data from Box Office Mojo.

26. Brooks Barnes and Michael Cieply, "The Hulk and 4,999 Other Characters for $4 Billion," *New York Times*, September 1, 2009. The estimated number of Marvel characters varies. This *Times* article claims 4,999, but "Marvelous Makeover," *Newsweek*, February 17, 2003, counts 4,700.

27. Ray Subers, "Forecast: 'The Avengers' Takes Aim at Opening Weekend Record," Box Office Mojo, May 3, 2012.

28. Nicole J. S. Sudhindra, "Marvel's Superhero Licensing," *Wipo* magazine [World Intellectual Property Organization], June 2012, https://wipo.int/wipo_magazine/en/.

CHAPTER 20: SUPERMAN AND
CAPTAIN AMERICA ON TRIAL

1. Friedrich, "Up, Up and Awaaay!!!," 66, 69.

2. "Superman as Cyberman," *New York Times*, Tuesday, January 14, 1997.

3. "*Superman* #75 . . . The Death of a Hero," *DC: Direct Currents* #58 (January 1993).

4. Daniels, *DC Comics*, 228; "Superman's Death Is a Sign of the Times: Gallup Poll Finds Most in U.S. Want Superman Brought Back to Life," *San Francisco Chronicle*, Thursday, November 26, 1992. Reprinted from *Los Angeles Times*.

5. "Dear Superman Fans Everywhere," Laura Siegel Larson open letter, October 11, 2012, comicbook.com, https://comicbook.com/blog/2012/10/15/superman-co-creator-s-daughter-blasts-dc-defends-her-lawyer/.

6. Toberoff, Vaz telephone interview, July 4, 2019; *Siegel and Larson v. Warner Bros. Entertainment, Inc.*, 542 F. Su 2d 1098 (2008), 9–11 [542 F. Supp.2d 1138–1139, 1145]; Michael Cieply, "Ruling Gives Heirs a Share of Superman Copyright," *New York Times*, Saturday, March 29, 2008.

7. "Superman's WB Future at Stake as Appeals Court Battle begins," *Hollywood Reporter*, March 26, 2012.

8. Baker and Hostetler, "Pocket Full of Kryptonite," *Lexology*, October 30, 2012, pp. 2–3; DC 1992 agreement letter, Paul Levitz to Frank Shuster and Jean Shuster Peavy, August 1, 1992.

9. Eriq Gardner, "Hollywood Heist: How a Burglary May Impact the Future of 'Superman,'" *Hollywood Reporter*, May 27, 2011.

10. DC Comics, *The New 52!*, promotional guide, 2011.

11. Brooks Barnes, "Warner Brothers Wins Legal Case over Rights to Superman," *New York Times*, October 17, 2012; Joanne Siegel, letter to Jeffrey L. Bewkes, Chairman and Chief Creative Officer, Time Warner, Inc., December 10, 2010, various sources; "Dear Superman Fans Everywhere," Laura Siegel Larson letter, October 11, 2012.

12. Simon, *Joe Simon*, 241.

13. *Marvel Characters, Inc., v. Joseph Simon*, Docket No. 02–7221, Decided, November 7, 2002, V. The Proceedings Below, 3.

14. Ibid., 3–4.

15. Ibid., III. Application of Section 304 of the 1976 Act, 6–8.

16. Simon, *Joe Simon*, 243.

17. Saffel, Vaz telephone interview, January 18, 2013.

18. Director Joe Johnston's career began with visual effects design and storyboard work on *Star Wars*. His subsequent directorial projects include *The Rocketeer* (1991), a Disney adaption of Dave Stevens's fan-favorite comics series.

19. Saffel, Vaz telephone interview, January 18, 2013.

20. Yahoo News, "'Avengers' Shoots Higher Overseas with $185.1 M," AP report; Ray Subers, "Weekend Report: 'Avengers' Smashes Records," May 6, 2012, Box Office Mojo.

21. Brent Lang, "From 'Skyfall' to 'The Avengers,' How the Foreign Box Office Is Trouncing Domestic," *The Wrap*, 2013, Yahoo! Inc.

22. Mason, Vaz telephone interview, June 7, 2019; Wikipedia, s.v. "*Community for Creative Non-Violence v. Reid*," and other sources.

CHAPTER 21: THE KING AND THE MAN

1. Toberoff, Vaz telephone interview, July 4, 2019; *Kirby Heirs v. Marvel*, US District Court, SDNY, District Judge Colleen McMahon, "Memorandum opinion and order granting plaintiffs' motion for summary judgment and denying defendants' cross motion for summary judgment," July 28, 2011, p. 2.

2. Groth, "Interview: Jack Kirby," 80–82; Saffel, email comments to Vaz, May 22, 2019; Farago, email comments to Vaz, May 28, 2019; Lee, *How to Write Comics*.

3. *Kirby Heirs v. Marvel*, Judge McMahon, memorandum opinion, July 28, 2011, pp. 4–5; ibid., Lee deposition, Los Angeles, May 13, 2010, pp. 7, 8–12, 14, 22, 29, 32–33.

4. *Kirby Heirs v. Marvel*, Judge McMahon, memorandum opinion, July 28, 2011, pp. 3–4, 12 (Evanier comment), 21, 25, 40–41; Toberoff, Vaz telephone interview, July 4, 2019.

5. *Kirby Heirs v. Marvel*, Judge McMahon, memorandum opinion, July 28, 2011, pp. 1–2, 25–26.

6. Ibid., 4, 30–33, 48.

7. SCOTUSblog.com, see "Supreme Court Procedure"; Toberoff, Vaz telephone interview, July 4, 2019; "'Nuff Said?': A Look at Kirby v. Marvel Characters, Inc. and Works Made for Hire under the Copyright Act of 1909," copyright culture: a law blog, posted September 15, 2014, p. 12, https://copyrightculture.wordpress.com/category/copyright/.

8. Deahl, "Consistently Inconsistent 'Instance and Expense' Test," 95–97, 100, 111.

9. *Kirby Heirs v. Marvel*, Brief of Amici Curiae, Bruce Lehman, former Asst. Secretary of Commerce and Director of the US Patent Office; Ralph Oman, former US Register of Copyrights; the Artists Rights Society, the International Intellectual Property Institute, and various professional associations, illustrators and cartoonists, Brief of Amici Curiae, On Petition for a Writ of Certiorari, June 13, 2014, pp. 3–5, 14, 16–17, 22.

10. *Kirby Heirs v. Marvel*, the California Society of Entertainment Lawyers, Brief of Amici Curiae, On Petition for a Writ of Certiorari, June 13, 2014, pp. 1–3, 13.

11. *Kirby Heirs v. Marvel*, Evanier, Morrow, Pen Center, Brief of Amici Curiae, On Petition for a Writ of Certiorari, June 13, 2014, pp. 1, 3–5, 10–11, 14–20, 22–23.

12. Kevin Melrose, "Supreme Court Won't Intervene in Shuster-DC Fight over Superman," CBR.com, October 6, 2014; Dominic Patten, "Marvel & Jack Kirby Heirs Settle Legal Battle ahead of Supreme Court Showdown," *Deadline*, September 26, 2014; Toberoff, Vaz telephone interview, July 4, 2019.

13. US Court of Appeals for the 9th Circuit, *DC Comics, plaintiff, v. Pacific Pictures Corporation; Marc Toberoff; Mark Warren Peary, Laura Siegel Larson; Jean Adele Peavy, defendants*, appeal from the US District Court CD California, District Judge Otis D. Wright, Argued and Submitted May 23, 2013, Pasadena, California (ruling and dissent); "End of the Road for Siegel and Shuster Heirs' 'Superman' Battle? A Cautionary Tale," Authors Guild, November 26, 2013, https://www.authorsguild.org; Toberoff, Vaz telephone interview, July 4, 2019.

14. Mason, Vaz telephone interview, June 7, 2019; Levitz, Vaz telephone interview, June 18, 2019; Frank Miller, "God Save the King," in Skelly, *Comics Journal Library: Vol. 1*, 96.

15. Brooks Barnes, "'Avengers: Endgame' Shows Movie Houses Can Still Draw Crowds," *New York Times*, reprinted in *East Bay Times*, Monday, April 29, 2019.

16. Ibid.

17. Peter Hartlaub, "Lee Brought Superhero Stories into Mainstream," *San Francisco Chronicle*, November 11, 2018.

18. Uslan, Vaz telephone interview, June 6, 2019; Drum, Vaz interview, 2012.

19. Elbein, "Marvel, Jack Kirby."

CHAPTER 22: LEGACY

1. "'Storage Wars': Mark Balelo Commits Suicide," *Hollywood Reporter*, February 11, 2013 (and other on-line articles); Zurzolo, Vaz face-to-face interview, October 11, 2012, and phone interview, 2017.

2. "Prices: 1970 vs. Today," *Overstreet Comic Book Price Guide*, 41st ed. (Gemstone Publishing, 2011–2012), 68.

3. ComicConnect 2011 Event Auction Catalogue, 6–7.

4. Wikipedia, s.v. "Jack Liebowitz"; "Jack Liebowitz: Making Comics a Business," in Marx, *Fifty Who Made DC Great*, 7.

5. Diana Schutz tribute, "Will Eisner[:] March 6, 1917–January 3, 2005," in *The Amazing Adventures of The Escapist* #6 (Dark Horse Comics, 2005).

6. Saffel, Vaz telephone interview, January 18, 2013.

7. Ibid.

8. Ibid.

9. Gibbons, Vaz interview, October 13, 2012.

10. "Exclusive—Interview with Athena Finger (Granddaughter of Batman Co-Creator Bill Finger)," Comicbookmovie.com, January 15, 2015. The first Finger Award honorees included Arnold Drake, whose creations included *Doom Patrol* and *Guardians of the Galaxy*. Nobleman's book was illustrated by Ty Templeton and published by Charlesbridge.

11. "The Legacy of Bill Finger, Co-Creator of Batman," Salutemag.com, March 1, 2018.

12. Press release, "DC Comics 'All Good with Finger and His Family'? HIS FAMILY RESPONDS," 2014, Internet posting, Comics Arts Council.

13. "Batman Co-Creator Bill Finger Finally Gets Credit on Gotham and Batman v. Superman," Internet posting by Blair Marnell, September 18, 2015; Levitz, Vaz telephone interview, June 18, 2019; Uslan, Vaz telephone interviews, June 6, July 5, 2019.

14. *Wizard: Alex Ross, Millennium Edition* (Wizard Special Publication, 1999), 39; Stan Lee, foreword to *Marvels* graphic novel collection (Marvel Comics, 1994); Alex Ross, "Icons of Virtue" (essay), 222, and "Captain Marvel" (notes), 268, in *Absolute Kingdom Come* (DC Comics, 2006).

15. Zaid, Vaz telephone interview, May 24, 2019; Eliana Dockterman, "Marvel Not at the Superhero's Gender," *Time*, March 18, 2019, 49.

16. Jamil Smith, "Super Powered: Black Panther Marks a Major Milestone for Culture," *Time*, February 19, 2018, 40.

17. "'Joker' Movie Prompts Mass Shooting Threat at US Movie Theaters," MyCentralOregon.com, September 27, 2019; wire services, "'Joker' Film Showings Has Some Concerned," Bay Area News Group, October 6, 2019; Gabe Cohn, *New York Times*, in "Box Office" section, Bay Area News Group, October 7, 2019; Box Office Mojo.

18. Manhoff, email comments to Vaz, November 22, 2017.

19. Ross, "Icons of Virtue," in *Absolute Kingdom Come*.

BIBLIOGRAPHY

BOOKS

Andelman, Bob. *Will Eisner: A Spirited Life*. Milwaukie, OR: M Press, 2005.

Barrier, Michael, and Martin Williams, eds. *A Smithsonian Book of Comic-Book Comics*. New York: Smithsonian University Press and Harry N. Abrams, Inc., 1981.

Barshay, Robert Howard. *Philip Wylie: The Man and His Work*. Washington, DC: University Press of America, 1979.

Benton, Mike. *The Comic Book in America: An Illustrated History*. Dallas: Taylor Publishing, 1989.

Bowers, Rick. *Superman versus the Ku Klux Klan: The True Story of How the Iconic Superhero Battled the Men of Hate*. Washington, DC: National Geographic, 2012.

Canwell, Bruce. "Stage Dressing: Rembrandt Raises His Brush." In *The Complete Terry and the Pirates: 1934–1936*, by Milton Caniff. San Diego: IDW Publishing, 2009.

———. "Stage Dressing: Rembrandt Begins His Masterpiece." Introduction to *The Complete Steve Canyon*. Vol. 1, 1947–1948. By Milton Canfiff. San Diego: IDW Publishing, 2012.

Carlin, John, Stanley Crouch, Paul Karasik, Brian Walker, et al. *Masters of American Comics*. Exhibition catalogue, Hammer Museum and the Museum of Contemporary Art, Los Angeles. New Haven, CT: Yale University Press, 2005.

The Complete Zap Comix. 5 vols. Seattle: Fantagraphics Books, 2014.

Couch, N. C. Christopher. *Jerry Robinson: Ambassador of Comics*. New York: Abrams ComicArts, 2010.

Cowsill, Alan, Alex Irvine, Matthew K. Manning, Michael McAvennic, Daniel Wallace, and Alastair Dougal. *DC Comics: Year by Year: A Visual Chronicle*. New York: DK Publishing, 2010.

Crumb, Robert. *The R. Crumb Coffee Table Art Book*. Edited and designed by Peter Poplaski. Northampton, MA: Kitchen Sink Press, 1998.

Daniels, Les. *Batman: The Complete History*. San Francisco: Chronicle Books, 1999.

———. *DC Comics: Sixty Years of the World's Favorite Comic Book Heroes*. London: Virgin Books, 1995.

———. *Marvel: Five Fabulous Decades of the World's Greatest Comics*. New York: Harry N. Abrams, 1991.

———. *Superman: The Complete History*. San Francisco: Chronicle Books, 1998.

———. *Wonder Woman: The Complete History*. San Francisco: Chronicle Books. 2000.

Dean, Michael. "Kirby and Goliath: The Fight for Jack Kirby's Marvel Artwork." In *The Comics Journal Library*. Vol. 1, *Jack Kirby*. Seattle: Fantagraphics Books, 2002.

Dooley, Dennis, and Gary Engle, eds. *Superman at Fifty: The Persistence of a Legend*. New York: Collier Books, 1988.

Eisner, Joel. *The Official Batman Batbook*. Chicago: Contemporary Books, 1986.

Eisner, Will. *The Dreamer: A Graphic Novella Set During the Dawn of Comic Books*. Princeton, WI: Kitchen Sink Press, 1986.

—— (copyright holder). *Eisner/Miller: A One-on-One Interview Conducted by Charles Brownstein*. Milwaukie, OR: Dark Horse Books, 2005.

Evanier, Mark. *Kirby: King of Comics*. New York: Abrams, 2008.

Feiffer, Jules. *The Great Comic-Book Heroes*. New York: Dial Press, 1965.

Geissman, Grant. *Foul Play! The Art and Artists of the Notorious 1950s E.C. Comics!* New York: Harper Design, 2005.

Gibbons, Dave, with Chipp Kidd and Mike Essl. *Watching the Watchmen*. London: Titan Books, 2008.

Goulart, Ron. *Comic Book Culture: An Illustrated History*. Portland, OR: Collector's Press, 2000.

——. *Ron Goulart's Great History of Comics Books*. Chicago: Contemporary Books, 1986.

Hajdu, David. *The Ten-Cent Plague: The Great Comic-Book Scare and How It Changed America*. New York: Farrar, Straus and Giroux, 2008.

Heintjes, Tom. "Setting Up Shop." In *The Spirit #2: The Origin Years*. Princeton, WI: Kitchen Sink Press, 1992.

Howe, Sean. *Marvel Comics: The Untold Story*. New York: Harper Perennial, 2012.

Huebel, Harry Russell. *Things in the Driver's Seat: Readings in Popular Culture*. Chicago: Rand McNally, 1972.

Infantino, Carmine, with J. David Spurlock. *The Amazing World of Carmine Infantino: An Autobiography*. Lebanon, NJ: Vanguard Productions, 2001.

Irving, Christopher (text), Seth Kushner (pictures). *Leaping Tall Buildings: The Origins of American Comics*. Brooklyn: PowerHouse Books, 2012.

Jones, Gerard. *Men of Tomorrow: Geeks, Gangsters, and the Birth of the Comic Book*. New York: Basic Books, 2004.

Kane, Bob, with Tom Andrae. *Batman and Me*. Forestville, CA: Eclipse Books, 1989.

Keefer, Truman Frederick. *Philip Wylie*. Boston: Twayne Publishers, 1977.

Kidd, Chip. *Shazam: The Golden Age of the World's Mightiest Mortal*. New York: Abrams ComicArts, 2010.

Kitchen, Dennis. "Biro and Wood: Partners in Crime." In *Crime Does Not Pay: Blackjacked and Pistol-Whipped*. Milwaukie, OR: Dark Horse Books, 2011.

Lee, Stan. *How to Write Comics*. New York: Watson-Guptill Publications, 2011.

——. *Origins of Marvel Comics*. New York: Simon and Schuster, 1974.

Lente, Fred Van, and Ryan Dunlavey. *The Comic Book History of Comics*. San Diego: IDW Publishing, 2012.

Levitz, Paul. *The Golden Age of DC Comics: 1935–1956*. Köln, Germany: Taschen, 2013.

——. *75 Years of DC Comics: The Art of Modern Mythmaking*. Köln, Germany: Taschen, 2010.

——. *The Silver Age of DC Comics*: Köln, Germany: Taschen, 2015.

Marschall, Richard. *America's Great Comic Strip Artists*. New York: Abbeville Press, 1989.

Morrison, Grant. *Supergods: What Masked Vigilantes, Miraculous Mutants, and a Sun God from Smallville Can Teach Us about Being Human*. New York: Spiegel & Grau, 2011.

Pasko, Martin. *The DC Vault*. New York: Running Press, 2008.

Reidelbach, Maria. *Completely Mad: A History of the Comic Book and Magazine*. Boston: Little, Brown, 1991.

Ricca, Brad. *Super Boys: The Amazing Adventures of Jerry Siegel and Joe Shuster—The Creators of Superman*. New York: St. Martin's Press, 2013.

Sabin, Roger. *Comics, Comix, and Graphic Novels: A History of Comic Art*. London: Phaidon Press, 1996.

Schumacher, Michael. *Will Eisner: A Dreamer's Life in Comics*. New York: Bloomsbury, 2010.

Schwartz, A. Brad. *Broadcast Hysteria: Orson Welles's* War of the Worlds *and the Art of Fake News*. New York: Hill and Wang, 2015.

Simon, Joe, with Jim Simon. *The Comic Book Makers*. New York: Crestwood/II Publications, 1990.

———. *My Life in Comics*. London: Titan Books, 2011.

Skelly, Tim. *The Comics Journal Library*. Vol. 1, *Jack Kirby*. Seattle: Fantagraphics Books, 2002.

Solomon, Charles. *Enchanted Drawings: The History of Animation*. New York: Alfred A. Knopf, 1989.

Starger, Steve, and J. David Spurlock. *Wally's World: The Brilliant Life and Tragic Death of Wally Wood, the World's Second-Best Comic Book Artist*. Somerset, NJ: Vanguard Productions, 2006.

Steranko, James. *The Steranko History of Comics*. 2 vols. Reading, PA: Supergraphics, 1970, 1972.

Taraba, Fred. *Masters of American Illustration: Forty-One Illustrators and How They Worked*. St. Louis: Illustrated Press, 2011.

Thomas, Roy, and Peter Sanderson. *The Marvel Vault*. Philadelphia: Running Press, 2007.

Tollin, Anthony. "The Invisible Shadow." In *The Shadow Scrapbook*, by Walter B. Gibson, with Anthony Tollin (contributing ed.). New York: Harcourt Brace Jovanovich, 1979.

Tye, Larry. *Superman: The High-Flying History of America's Most Enduring Hero*. New York: Random House, 2012.

Varnedoe, Kirk, and Adam Gopnik. *High and Low: Modern Art and Popular Culture*. New York: Museum of Modern Art, 1990.

Vaz, Mark Cotta. *Behind the Mask of Spider-Man: The Secrets of the Movie*. New York: Del Rey, 2002.

———. *The Spirit: The Movie Visual Companion*. London: Titan Books, 2008.

———. *Tales of the Dark Knight: Batman's First Fifty Years: 1939–1989*. New York: Ballantine Books, 1989.

Wells, Earl. "Once and for All, Who was the Author of Marvel?" In *Comics Journal Library*, vol. 1, *Jack Kirby*, by Tim Skelly. Seattle: Fantagraphics Books, 2002.

Wertham, Fredric. *Seduction of the Innocent: The Influence of Comic Books on Today's Youth*. New York: Rinehart & Co., 1954.

Wylie, Philip. *Gladiator*. 1930. Reprint, Lincoln: University of Nebraska Press, 2004.

Yoe, Craig. *Secret Identity: The Fetish Art of Superman's Co-Creator Joe Shuster*. New York: Abrams ComicArts, 2009.

Young, William H., Jr. "The Serious Funnies: Adventure Comics during the Depression, 1929–1938." In *Things in the Driver's Seat: Readings in Popular Culture*, edited by Harry Russell Huebel. Chicago: Rand McNally, 1972.

SELECT PERIODICALS

Amash, Jim. "'Fawcett Knew How to Do It Better Than Anyone Else!' A Talk with Artist/Production Man Emilio Squeglio." *Alter Ego* #41, October 2004.

Andrae, Tom, with Geoffrey Blum and Gary Coddington. "Of Superman and Kids with Dreams: A Rare Interview with the Creators of Superman: Jerry Siegel and Joe Shuster." *Nemo: The Classics Comics Library* #2, August 1983.

Barnes, Brooks. "With Fan at the Helm, Marvel Safely Steers Its Heroes to the Screen." *New York Times*, July 25, 2011.

Barol, Bill. "Batmania: A Summer Struggle for the Dark Soul of a Mythic American Hero—and a Boom in Bat-Products." *Newsweek*, June 26, 1989.

Beck, C. C. "Are We Living in A Golden Age and Don't Know It?" *Comics Journal* #135, April 1990.

Bishoff, Murray. "The Siegel and Shuster Deal at Thirty." *Alter Ego* #65, February 2007.

Bode, Janet. "A Comic Book Artist KO'D: Jack Kirby's Six-Year Slugfest with Marvel." *Voice*, December 8, 1987.

Bruning, Richard. "Guilty Pleasures Revealed!" *Secret Origins*, replica edition. DC Comics, 1998.

Christensen, William, and Mark Seifert. "Dark Legend." *Wizard* #40, December 1994.

Cooke, Jon B. "Kirby's Kingdom: The Commerce of Dreams." *Comic Book Creator* #1, Spring 2013.

Crist, Judith. "Horror in the Nursery." *Collier's*, March 27, 1948.

Croal, N'Gai. "Marvelous Makeover." *Newsweek*, February 17, 2003.

Deahl, Thomas M., II. "The Consistently Inconsistent 'Instance and Expense' Test: An Injustice to Comic Books." *John Marshall Review of Intellectual Property Law*, 2014.

Decker, Dwight R., and Gary Groth, "An Interview with William M. Gaines." *Comics Journal* #81, May 1983.

DiFruscio, Mark. "Dark Rebirth." *Back Issue* #50, August 2011.

Elbein, Asher. "Marvel, Jack Kirby, and the Comic-Book Artist's Plight." *Atlantic*, September 1, 2016.

Evanier, Mark. "The King and I." *Amazing Heroes* #100, August 1, 1986.

Feiffer, Jules. "The Great Comic-Book Heroes." *Playboy*, October 1965.

Friedrich, Otto. "Up, Up and Awaaay!!! America's Favorite Hero Turns Fifty, Ever Changing but Indestructible." *Time*, March 14, 1988.

George, David. "Make Mine Magazine Management! The Good Ol' Days at Martin Goodman's Colorful Magazine Empire." *Alter Ego* #66, March 2007.

Gibson, Walter. "A Million Words a Year for Ten Straight Years." *The Shadow* #110, Sanctum Books reprint, 2016.

Gilbert, Michael T. "Total Control: A Brief Biography of Wally Wood." *Alter Ego* #8, Spring 2001.

Groth, Gary. "'With One Magic Word': An Interview with C. C. Beck." *Comics Journal* #95, February 1985.

———. "Interview: Jack Kirby." *Comics Journal* #134, February 1990.

———. "Joe Simon: An Interview with the Other Half of the Simon and Kirby Team, *Comics Journal* #134, February 1990.

Hamerlinck, P. C. Foreword to *The Shazam! Family Archives: Vol. 1.* DC Archives ed., DC Comics, 2006.

Hill, Roger. "Who Was H. J. Ward? The Spicy/Superman Artist." *Comic Book Marketplace* #100, March 2003.

Itzkoff, Dave. "Modern Marvel." *New York Times*, March 27, 2011.

Keller, Barry, with Jay Willson. "Don Newton and Captain Marvel: A Match Made at the Rock of Eternity." *Alter Ego* #11, November 2001.

Kobler, John. "Up, Up And Awa-a-y! The Rise of Superman, Inc." *Saturday Evening Post*, June 21, 1941.

Kronenberg, Michael. "Auteur Theory: CBM Interview: Will Eisner." *Comic Book Marketplace* #115, September 2004.

Marx, Barry, ed. "Frank Miller: Experiment in Creative Autonomy." In *Fifty Who Made DC Great*. New York: DC Comics, 1985.

Menand, Louis. "The Horror: Congress Investigates the Comics." *New Yorker*, March 31, 2008.

———. "Crooner in Rights Spat." *New Yorker*, October 20, 2014.

Mikulovsky, Michael. "Before Superman! Before Doc Savage! There Was Man-God." *Back Issue* #47, April 2001.

Murray, Will. "The Pulp Roots of Batman." *Comic Book Marketplace* #100, March 2003.

———. "The Rediscovered Schwartz." *Comic Book Marketplace* #104, July 2003.

———. "The Retrospective Stan Lee: A 1988 Interview with the Man behind 'The Marvel Age of Comics.'" *Alter Ego* #150, January 2018.

———. "The Rise of Captain Marvel." *Comic Book Marketplace* #120, March 2005.

———. "The Shadowy Origins of Batman." *The Shadow* #9, 2007.

———. "Three Easy Pieces Starring Julius Schwartz." *Alter Ego* #38, July 2004.

Nowak, Donna. "Ace of Cartoons Jerry Robinson: The Joker Was Just the Beginning." *Amazing Heroes* #167, June 15, 1989.

Patten, Dominic. "Marvel and Jack Kirby Heirs Settle Legal Battle Ahead of Supreme Court Showdown." *Deadline*, September 26, 2014.

Pierce, John G., with P. C. Hamerlinck. "Shazam! In the Bronze Age: The Original Captain Marvel's '70s and '80s Comebacks." *Back Issue* #93, December 2016.

Prideaux, Tom. "The Whole Country Goes Supermad." *Life* magazine, March 11, 1966.

Quattro, Ken. "Superman vs. the Wonder Man 1939." *Alter Ego* #101, May 2011.

Richard, Olive. "Don't Laugh at the Comics." *Family Circle*, October 1940.

Robinson, Jerry. Foreword to *The Shadow* #9. Sanctum Books reprint, 2007.

Rodman, Howard A. "They Shoot Comic Books, Don't They?" *American Film*, May 1989.

Saunders, David. "Harry Donenfeld" and "Moses Annenberg." *Field Guide to Wild American Pulp Artists*. http://www.pulpartists.com/. Accessed March 16, 2020.

——. "Joseph Szokoli." *Illustration* #35, Fall 2011.

——. "Walter M. Baumhofer." *Illustration* #44, April 2014.

Scholl, Barry. "Double Identity: The Two Lives of Dick Sprang." *Salt Lake City*, May/June 1996.

Shannon, Jody Duncan. "A Dark and Stormy Knight." *Cinefex* #41, February 1990.

Siegel, Jerry. "A Curse on the Superman Movie!" [Press release.] 20th Century Danny Boy. https://ohdannyboy.blogspot.com/2012/07/curse-on-superman-movie-look-back-at.html#.T_Ybb-kbZa0.twitter. Accessed March 18, 2020.

Spiegelman, Art. "Ballbuster: Bernard Krigstein's Life between the Panels." *New Yorker*, July 22, 2002.

Stewart, Bhob. "Alan Moore: Synchronicity and Symmetry." *Comics Journal* #116, July 1987.

——. "Pebbles in a Landscape (Interview with Dave Gibbons)." *Comics Journal* #116, July 1987.

Thomas, Roy. "A Conversation with Artist-Writer Larry Lieber." *Alter Ego* 3:2, Fall 1999.

——. Interview: "Everett on Everett." *Alter Ego* #11, June 1978.

Tollin, Anthony. "Spotlight on the Shadow: Foreshadowing the Batman." In *The Shadow* #9. Sanctum Books reprint, 2007.

Vaz, Mark Cotta. "A Knight at the Zoo. *Cinefex* #51, August 1992.

——. "Martial Art." *Cinefex* #68, December 1996.

——. "Rocket Blast." *Cinefex* #48, November 1991.

Watson, Bruce. "Tarzan the Eternal." *Smithsonian*, March 1, 2001.

SELECT GRAPHIC NOVEL COLLECTIONS

DC Comics. *Absolute Ronin*, 2008.

——. Batman: *The Golden Age Omnibus, Vol. 1*. 2015.

——. Superman: *The Golden Age Omnibus, Vol. 1*. 2013.

——. *Superman: "Whatever Happened to the Man of Tomorrow?"* Deluxe edition, 2009.

——. *Wonder Woman: The Golden Age Omnibus, Vol. 1*. 2016.

Gerber, Ernst, and Mary Gerber. *The Photo-Journal Guide to Comic Books*. 2 vols. Minden, NV: Gerber Publishing, 1989.

Marvel Comics. *Marvels: 10th Anniversary Edition*. 2004.

Marvel Masterworks. *Golden Age Marvel Comics, Vol. 1*. 2004.

——. *Golden Age Marvel Comics, Vol. 3*. 2008.

Raymond, Alex. *Flash Gordon: On the Planet Mongo* (Sunday Strips 1934–1937). London: Titan Books, 2012.

Simon, Joe, and Jack Kirby. *The Best of Simon and Kirby*. London: Titan Books, 2009.

Superman: Sunday Classics: 1939–1943. New York: Sterling Publishing, 2006.

Superman: The Dailies 1939–1942. New York: Sterling Publishing, 2006.

SELECT INTERVIEWS AND CORRESPONDENCE

Drum, Shelton. Interview by Mark Cotta Vaz. New York Comic Con, 2012.

Ellsworth, Whitney. Letters to Jerry Siegel: Saturday, February 21, [1940]; November 4, 1940; October 2, 1941. National Archives and Records Administration, Regional Archives, Northeast Region, New York City.

Farago, Andrew. Email comments to Mark Cotta Vaz, May 28, 2019.

Gibbons, Dave. Interview by Mark Cotta Vaz. New York Comic Con, October 13, 2012.

Kahn, Jenette. Letter to Mark Canton, October 18, 1982; "Dear Freelancer" letter, December 4, 1986.

Levitz, Paul. Telephone interview by Mark Cotta Vaz, June 18, 2019.

Liebowitz, Jack. Letters to Jerry Siegel: September 28, 1938; January 25, 1940; June 27, 1941. National Archives and Records Administration, Regional Archives, Northeast Region, New York City.

Manhoff, Rabbi Harry. Email comments to Mark Cotta Vaz, November 22, 2017.

Mason, John. Telephone interview by Mark Cotta Vaz, June 7, 2019.

Sattel, Steve. Telephone interview by Mark Cotta Vaz, January 18, 2013.

———. Email comments to Mark Cotta Vaz, May 22, 2019.

Siegel, Jerry. Letters to Jack Liebowitz: December 6, 1937; April 18, 1938; September 26, 1938; May 8, 1940 (to Donenfeld and Liebowitz); June 25, 1940; July 1, 1941; March 8, 1942; October 15, 1942; October 16, 1942; April 1, 1943. National Archives and Records Administration, Regional Archives, Northeast Region, New York City.

———. Letter to Whitney Ellsworth, February 12, 1942. National Archives and Records Administration, Regional Archives, Northeast Region, New York City.

Shuster, Joe. Letter to Jerry Siegel, October 1, 1944. National Archives and Records Administration, Regional Archives, Northeast Region, New York City.

Simon, Joe. Interview by Mark Cotta Vaz and Mark Zaid. Manhattan, October 19, 2010.

Sprang, Dick. Q&A letter exchange with Mark Cotta Vaz, June 30, 1988.

Toberoff, Marc. Telephone interview by Mark Cotta Vaz, July 4, 2019.

Uslan, Michael. Telephone interview by Mark Cotta Vaz, June 6, July 5, 2019.

Zaid, Mark. Telephone interview by Mark Cotta Vaz, May 24, 2019.

Zurzolo, Vincent. Interview by Mark Cotta Vaz, New York Comic Con, October 11, 2012; phone interview, 2017.

SELECT DEPOSITIONS, TRIAL TRANSCRIPTS, AND COURT RULINGS

Detective Comics, Inc., v. Bruns Publications, Inc. (*DC v. Bruns*)

Kirby v. Marvel Characters, Inc. (*Kirby v. Marvel et al.*)

Lisa R. Kirby, Barbara J. Kirby, Neal L. Kirby, and Susan M. Kirby v. Marvel Worldwide, Inc., Marvel Characters, Inc., and MVL Rights, LLC (*Kirby Heirs v. Marvel*)

Joanne Siegel and Laura Siegel Larson v. Time Warner, Inc., Warner Communications, Inc., DC Comics, et al. (*Siegel and Larson v. Time Warner/DC*)

Joanne Siegel and Laura Siegel Larson v. Warner Bros. Entertainment, Inc., et al.
    (*Siegel and Larson v. Warner Bros.*)
Marvel Characters, Inc., v. Joseph H. Simon (*Marvel v. Simon*)
National Comics Publications, Inc., v. Fawcett Publications, Inc., et al. (*National
    Comics/DC v. Fawcett*)
Siegel and Shuster v. National Periodical Publications, Inc., et al.

INDEX

Jason Todd (character), 345–346. *See also* Batman

Jay Garrick (character), 99, 253, 266. *See also* The Flash (Golden Age character)

Johnny Thunder (character; also known as John L. Thunder), 98

Johnston, Joe, 372, 442n18

The Joker, 112–114, 415, 429n19

Jones, Gerard, 15, 66, 138, 251

Justice League of America, 253–254, 266

Justice Society of America, 99, 253

Kable News Company, Inc., 26, 68–69, 72, 247

Kahn, Jenette: and Batman movie meeting with Warner Bros., 348–350; and *Camelot 3000* as direct market title, 322–323; changing the industry, 320–324; and Comics Code and rating system, 341; as DC publisher, 319–320; and Kirby letter of support, 326; and Wonder Woman, post-*Crisis*, 340

Kahn, Robert. *See* Kane, Bob

Kane, Bob, 53; and *Batman* contract rumors, 63; and *Batman* serial, 133–134; and "Birdman" idea, 54; credit for Batman given to, 12, 54; Bill Finger, collaboration with, 53–54; and the Joker, 112, 114; reflections on, 308–309; and Siegel and Shuster, alleged betrayal of, 172; signature of, 54

Keaton, Michael, 350, 352

Keefer, Frederick, 213–214

Kirby, Jack: and the battle for original art, 325–327; and business, reflections on, 9; and Cadence/Marvel, 1972 agreement with, 276; and Captain America, cheated out of royalties, 121–122; comes to DC, 304; creates *The Fantastic Four*, 256–257, 259–260; DC work of, 145–146; death threats received by, 120–121; and "Fourth World" saga, 304; at Fox Comics, 76–77; at Harvey Comics and Crestwood Publications, 179; influence of Raymond and Caniff on, 87; kinetic style of, 88; and Lee and Kirby team (Marvel), Disney Legends Award, 401; and Mainline Publications, 238–239; marries Rosalind "Roz" Goldstein, 151; and Marvel, returns to Goodman, 249, 256; and pioneering romance titles, 216; *Sgt. Fury* strip idea of, 263; Silver Surfer and estrangement from Lee, 304–307; Simon and Kirby team, 81–82, 119; and World War II, 151

Kirby v. Marvel Characters, Inc.: and blogger on work-for-hire issue, 375; and "Kirby Works," 377; and the legal process to reclaim characters, 376–377; and "Marvel entities," 378; and 1909 Act as "controlling law," 384–385; and Judge Colleen McMahon, trial question, 382; ruling in, 386; and the Supreme Court, 375, 386–392; and Toberoff, work for hire dispute, 383

Klein, Bobby, 2, 246, 260–261, 269, 411

Krigstein, Bernie, 235, 239, 245

Krypton, 18–19, 22, 52, 92–93, 106, 164–165, 416–417

Kryptonian names, 52, 165

kryptonite, 166, 281, 319, 339, 364

Kubert, Joe, 167, 320, 406

Kurtzberg, Jacob. *See* Kirby, Jack

Kurtzman, Harvey, 230, 235, 244, 331, 334

Larson, Laura Siegel: and failed settlement with Warner Bros., 373; and father's dying wish, 362; and ruling in Judge Wright's court, and appeal, 394–395; on settlement, 363–364; and Siegel settlement and credit, 395; Michael Siegel warns about attorney's motives, 366; *Superboy* rights recaptured by, 363; Superman fans, open letter to, 367–368; and termination rights, 362–363

Lavenstein, Meyer H., 141, 144, 214

Lee, Stan: and creative conflicts at Marvel, 12, 277–279; Disney Legends Award given to, 401; as elder statesman, 397; and

and Superman offered to, 24; and *Funnyman* feature, 175, 177; and "The Reign of the Super-Man," 15; as science fiction fan, 15, 20; Shuster, partnership and tensions with, 36, 148, 194–195
—and DC: *Action Comics* #1, pitches features for, 30; and contract renewal, 110–111; copyright byline of, 76; and DC retribution against, 281; and *Detective Comics* #1, features, 28; as "Funny Face," 176–177; grievances with, 171, 296–297; and Liebowitz, affectionate letter to, 169–170; pay increase demand of, 109–110; and proposal, 50; returns to, 250, 280–281; and *Robotman*, 138–139; and *Spectre*, 94; and success, peak of, 135–137; and *Superboy*, 50, 170–171
—and Superman: belief of, that all superheroes are infringers of Superman, 94; and copyright renewal claim, 281; creation of and inspiration for, 14, 19–21, 430n16; fiftieth anniversary, reaction to, 358; and Lois Lane, on Clark revealing secret identity to, 139; sells to DC, 4; shopping *Superman* strip, 3, 33; Superman Corporation, lobbies for place in, 139, 147, 149–150; supervises reformatting of Superman *Action* #1 story, 34–35
Siegel, Joanne: gets DC to take Jerry back, 250; letter to Levitz from, 363; letters to Time Warner executives from, 363, 366; Lois Lane, as model for, 177; marries Jerry, 177; presses Siegel case, 362–363; Superboy, recaptures rights to, 363; Toberoff as counsel to, 363
Siegel, Michael (father of Jerry), 21
Siegel, Michael (son of Jerry and Bella), 171, 177, 366
The Siegel and Shuster Society of Cleveland, 419
Siegel and Shuster v. National Comics Publications, Inc. (1947) ("Westchester action"), 173–175
Siegel and Shuster v. National

Periodical Publications, Inc. et al. (1973), 286–287, 438n15; appeal, 287–288
Siegel v. Warner Bros. Entertainment, Inc. (2008), 358, 363–364
"Silver Age," of Comics, 253, 267
Silver Surfer (character), 304–307. *See also* Kirby, Jack
Simon, Joe: and first comic book assignment, 81; at Fox Comics (meets Jack Kirby), 81–82; on Golden Age publishers, 9; and Kirby, as team, 81–82, 119–122, 145–146, 179, 216, 238–239, 280, 282; marries Harriet Feldman, 179; and *National Comic/ DC v. Fawcett* copyright infringement trial, 179–180, 188–190; original art, treatment of, 320; pilgrimage of to Manhattan, 79–80; right of, to terminate prior agreements upheld, 369–370; on Senate Subcommittee investigating comics, 236; and settlement agreement with Marvel, 283; stroke of, 370; as Timely Comics' first editor, 81; and Titan Book deal, 406
—and Captain America: and *Captain America: The First Avenger*, DVD party, 372–373, 442n18; declares ownership of, 368–369; handshake deal over, 119; suit against Goodman et al., 282
Sivana (character), 123, 125, 291. *See also* Captain Marvel
Solomon, Charles, 10, 132, 133
Spider-Man (a.k.a. Peter Parker, character), 248, 261–262
Spider-Man (2002 movie), 353–354
Spiegelman, Art, 245–246
The Spirit (character), 91, 151, 243–244, 271, 321, 406
Sprang, Dick: in Arizona, 309–310; as *Batman* "ghost" artist, 88; classic Batman, reflects on, 336–337; Whit Ellsworth hires, 140; on Bill Finger, 337; meets Bob Kane, 309; on Miller's *Dark Knight*, 337; and "movies on paper," 88–89
Steeves, Harrison: and Captain Marvel's dual personality, 213; and Hugo